THE RELIGIOUS CULTURE OF THE HUGUENOTS, 1660–1750

The Religious Culture of the Huguenots, 1660–1750

ANNE DUNAN-PAGE
Université de Montpellier III, France

LONDON AND NEW YORK

First published 2006 by Ashgate Publishing

Reissued 2018 by Routledge
2 Park Square, Milton Park, Abingdon, Oxon OX14 4RN
605 Third Avenue, New York, NY 10017

First issued in paperback 2021

Routledge is an imprint of the Taylor & Francis Group, an informa business

© Anne Dunan-Page 2006

Anne Dunan-Page has asserted her moral right under the Copyright, Designs and Patents Act, 1988, to be identified as the author of this work.

All rights reserved. No part of this book may be reprinted or reproduced or utilised in any form or by any electronic, mechanical, or other means, now known or hereafter invented, including photocopying and recording, or in any information storage or retrieval system, without permission in writing from the publishers.

A Library of Congress record exists under LC control number: 2005037426

Notice:
Product or corporate names may be trademarks or registered trademarks, and are used only for identification and explanation without intent to infringe.

Publisher's Note
The publisher has gone to great lengths to ensure the quality of this reprint but points out that some imperfections in the original copies may be apparent.

Disclaimer
The publisher has made every effort to trace copyright holders and welcomes correspondence from those they have been unable to contact.

ISBN 13: 978-0-815-39814-1 (hbk)
ISBN 13: 978-1-351-14556-5 (ebk)
ISBN 13: 978-1-138-35593-4 (pbk)

DOI: 10.4324/9781351145565

Contents

List of Tables	*vii*
List of Contributors	*ix*
Acknowledgements	*xiii*
List of Abbreviations	*xv*

Introduction
Anne Dunan-Page   1

Part 1 The Issue of Conformity

1 Conformity, Non-conformity and Huguenot Settlement in England in the Later Seventeenth Century
   Robin Gwynn   23

2 Differing Perceptions of the Refuge? Huguenots in Ireland and Great Britain and their Attitudes towards the Governments' Religious Policy (1660–1710)
   Susanne Lachenicht   43

3 The *Oxford Dictionary of National Biography*, the du Moulin Connection and the Location of the Church of England in the Later Seventeenth Century
   Vivienne Larminie   55

Part 2 Church Organisation and Social Structure

4 *Dominus Providebit*: Huguenot Commitment to Poor Relief in England
   Randolph Vigne   69

5 Killing in Good Conscience: Marshal Schomberg and the Huguenot Soldiers of the Diaspora
   Matthew Glozier   87

6 The Huguenot Soul: The Calvinism of Reverend Louis Rou
   Paula Wheeler Carlo   109

Part 3 The Circulation of Ideas

7   The Influence of the Huguenots on Educated Ireland: Huguenot
    Books in Irish Church Libraries of the Eighteenth Century
    Jane McKee 121

8   The Role of Huguenot Tutors in John Locke's Programme of Social
    Reform
    S.J. Savonius 137

9   The Rainbow Coffee House and the Exchange of Ideas in Early
    Eighteenth-century London
    Simon Harvey and Elizabeth Grist 163

10 Huguenot Traces and Reminiscences in John Toland's Conception
    of Tolerance
    Myriam Yardeni 173

Bibliography *189*
Index *213*

List of Tables

Table 1.1	Arrivals of Huguenots at Amsterdam and Threadneedle Street, London, 1681–88	25
Table 1.2	New French congregations in England, 1680–1705 surviving into the eighteenth century	29
Table 1.3	Conformists and non-conformists in London and Westminster, 1681–1710	35
Table 7.1	Principal Church of Ireland and Presbyterian libraries	123
Table 7.2	Huguenot authors occurring in the libraries of Cashel and Armagh	126
Table 7.3	Huguenot authors in Cashel or Armagh who appear in other libraries	131
Table 7.4	Titles appearing in both Cashel and Armagh	134

List of Contributors

Paula Wheeler Carlo is Associate Professor of History at Nassau Community College. She received her Ph.D. from the City University of New York. She has presented numerous conference papers and published scholarly articles on the Huguenot diaspora. In 2004 she was awarded the State University of New York Chancellor's Award for Excellence in Teaching. Her monograph, *Huguenot Refugees in Colonial New York: Becoming American in the Hudson Valley*, was published by Sussex Academic Press in 2005.

Anne Dunan-Page is University Lecturer in English at the University of Montpellier (France). She is a member of the *Institut de Recherche sur la Renaissance, l'Age Classique et les Lumières* (UMR, CNRS 5186) and serves on the editorial board of *Cahiers Elisabéthains*. She has written extensively on dissenting literature and culture and is senior editor of a database on references to France in English drama from the Middle Ages to 1642. Her book, *Grace Overwhelming: John Bunyan and the Extremes of the Baptist Mind* will be published shortly.

Matthew Glozier (Ph.D., University of Western Sydney) is a researcher for the Official History of Australian Peacekeeping, Strategic and Defence Studies Centre, The Australian National University (Canberra). He has published widely on Scottish and Huguenot soldiers, society and culture, including *The Huguenot Soldiers of William of Orange and the Glorious Revolution of 1688* (Brighton and Portland, 2003) and *Scottish Soldiers in France in the Reign of the Sun King: Nursery for Men of Honour* (Leyden and Boston, 2004).

Elizabeth Grist received a Ph.D. from London University in 2001 entitled 'The Salon and the Stage: Women and Theatre in Seventeenth-Century France'. Her research interest is in the history of ideas and seventeenth-century French dramatic literature. She is currently working on the life and work of the Huguenot writer and translator Pierre-Antoine Motteux.

Robin Gwynn was Director of the British 1985 'Huguenot Heritage' tercentenary commemoration under the patronage of H.M. The Queen. While a History Professor at Massey University, New Zealand, he edited the letter books (1643–59) and consistory minutes (1679–92) of the French Church of London. Recent works include *The Huguenots of London* (Brighton, 1998) and an enlarged revised edition of *Huguenot Heritage* (Brighton and Portland, 2001).

Simon Harvey is Senior Lecturer at Queen Mary, University of London. He has published critical editions of Diderot's *Lettre sur les aveugles* (Paris, 2000) and of Voltaire's treatise on tolerance (Cambridge, 2000). He has also edited a volume entitled *Re-appraisals of Rousseau* (Manchester, 1980).

Susanne Lachenicht received an M.A. in Modern History from the Université de Paris I, Panthéon-Sorbonne and an M.A. and her Ph.D. in History and German literature and linguistics from the University of Heidelberg. In February 2004 she was awarded a Marie Curie EIF postdoctoral fellowship and is now a postdoctoral researcher at the Centre for the Study of Human Settlement and Historical Change at the National University of Ireland, Galway.

Vivienne Larminie following publication of *Wealth, Kinship and Culture: The Seventeenth Century Newdigates of Arbury and their World* (Woodbridge, 1995), worked on religion in Switzerland, contributing to F. Flouck *et al.* (eds), *De l'Ours à la cocarde: régime bernois et révolution en pays de Vaud (1536–1798)* (Lausanne, 1998). She has written almost one hundred articles for the *Oxford Dictionary of National Biography* (Oxford, 2004 and ongoing), of which she is research editor for the seventeenth century; she is also research development officer for the History Faculty, University of Oxford.

Jane McKee is a Senior Lecturer in French at the University of Ulster. Her research on the Huguenots focuses on the Drelincourt family, and recent publications deal with the correspondence of Charles Drelincourt, the poetry of Laurent and on the ecclesiastical career of Pierre. She has also published on French Enlightenment influences on Irish Church libraries, on Computer-assisted Language Learning and on the novelist Romain Gary.

S.J. Savonius is a Fellow of Clare Hall, Cambridge, and is currently working on the aspirations to reform the rhetorical culture of humanism in early-modern Europe. His research interests also include Locke's political thought, and in his publications he has discussed Locke's circle of Huguenot friends. He is now completing a monograph, *John Locke and the Science of Liberty in the Early Enlightenment*.

Randolph Vigne, M.A. (Oxon.), Fellow of the Society of Antiquaries of London, has served as Editor of Huguenot Society publications in Britain and Ireland since 1987. He has published widely on Huguenot themes, recently co-editing *From Strangers to Citizens: Integration of Immigrants in Britain, Ireland and the American Colonies, 1550–1750* (2001) and as co-author of *Britain's Huguenot War Leaders* (2003).

Myriam Yardeni is Emeritus Professor of Modern History at Haïfa University. A specialist in social history and *histoire des mentalités*, she has written extensively on the history of the Huguenot refuge and on anti-semitism in the early-modern period. Her work includes *La Conscience nationale en France pendant les Guerres de Religion, 1559–1598* (Paris and Louvain, 1971); *Utopie et révolte sous Louis XIV*

(Paris, 1980); *Le Refuge Protestant* (Paris, 1985) and, in Hebrew, *Huguenots et Juifs* (Jerusalem, 1998).

Acknowledgements

Some of the articles in this volume sprang from the colloquium on the Huguenots in the British Isles and the American Colonies (1550–1789) held at the University of Montpellier on 25–27 March 2004 under the auspices of the *Institut de Recherches sur la Renaissance, l'Age Classique et les Lumières* (UMR, CNRS 5186) and the *Institut Protestant de Théologie*. A selection from the conference proceedings will appear shortly in the collection 'La Vie des Huguenots' (Paris: Honoré Champion). I wish to thank the colleagues with whom I organised the event, Marie-Christine Munoz-Teulié and Bertrand van Ruymbeke, together with Luc Borot, Hubert Bost and Charles Whitworth, for the financial support granted by the Institutes and a donation from the *Institut Universitaire de France*. Contributions were also received from the *CNRS*, the *Région Languedoc-Roussillon*, the *Pôle Universitaire Européen* and the *Conseil Scientifique de l'Université de Montpellier III*. I am especially grateful to Patricia Dorval, Jean-Christophe Mayer and Nick Myers for editorial help and to Emilie Devogelaere for assistance in preparing the manuscript. My husband Christopher has contributed to the conception of this volume more than I can possibly express. I also owe a special debt of gratitude to Thomas Gray, Anne Keirby and Liz Pearce at Ashgate and to the President and Fellows of Clare Hall, Cambridge for electing me to a Visiting Fellowship during which the introduction to this volume was written.

Anne Dunan-Page,
University of Montpellier

List of Abbreviations

BSHPF	*Bulletin de la Société de l'Histoire du Protestantisme Français.*
Caldicott *et al.*, *Huguenots in Ireland*	C.E.J. Caldicott, H. Gough and Jean-Paul Pittion (eds), *The Huguenots in Ireland: Anatomy of an Emigration*, Dublin Colloquium of the Huguenot Refuge in Ireland, 1685–1985, 9–12 April 1985, Trinity College, Dublin (Dun Laoghaire, 1987).
Cottret, *Terre d'exil*	Bernard Cottret, *Terre d'exil. L'Angleterre et ses réfugiés français et wallons de la Réforme à la Révocation de L'Edit de Nantes, 1550–1700* (Paris, 1985).
Cottret, *Huguenots in England*	*The Huguenots in England: Immigration and Settlement*, c.*1550–1700*, trans. Peregrine and Adriana Stevenson (Cambridge, 1991).
Fontaine, *Memoirs*	*Memoirs of the Reverend Jaques Fontaine, 1658–1728*, ed. Dianne W. Ressinger, Publications of the Huguenot Society of Great Britain and Ireland, New Series 2 (London, 1992).
Gwynn, *Heritage*	Robin D. Gwynn, *Huguenot Heritage*, 2nd revised edn (Brighton and Portland, 2001).
Gwynn, *Minutes*	*Minutes of the Consistory of the French Church of London, Threadneedle Street, 1679–1692*, ed. Robin D. Gwynn, Huguenot Society Quarto Series, 58 (London, 1994).
Haag	Eugène and Emile Haag, *La France Protestante, ou vies des protestants français qui se sont fait un nom dans l'histoire* (Slatkine Reprints, 1966).
HSQS	Publications of the Huguenot Society, Quarto Series.

PHS	*Proceedings of the Huguenot Society of Great Britain and Ireland* (formerly *of London*).
Oxford DNB	H.C.G. Matthew and Brian Harrison (eds), *Oxford Dictionary of National Biography* (Oxford, 2004).
Scouloudi, *Huguenots in Britain*	*Huguenots in Britain and their French Background, 1550–1800*, Contributions to the Historical Conference of the Huguenot Society of London, 24–25 September 1985 (Basingstoke, 1987).
Vigne and Littleton, *Strangers*	Randolph Vigne and Charles Littleton (eds), *From Strangers to Citizens: The Integration of Immigrant Communities in Britain, Ireland and Colonial America, 1550–1750* (Brighton and Portland, 2001).

Introduction

Anne Dunan-Page
University of Montpellier, France

On 5 October 1885, the Reverend John de Soyres, the curate of St Martin-in-the-Fields, left his London flock unattended. He was answering an invitation to preach on Sunday morning in the University Church of Great St Mary's, Cambridge, on the occasion of the two-hundredth anniversary of the Revocation of the Edict of Nantes by Louis XIV (22 October 1685). He entitled his sermon 'The Huguenots and the Church of England', a fitting subject for an Anglican minister and scholar of French descent, indeed the son of a minister of the Bristol Huguenot Church.[1] In many ways, de Soyres was on home territory; the church of Great St Mary's, on one side of Market Hill, lay opposite his old college of Gonville and Caius, and as a lecturer in Modern History at Queen's College, London, he was used to addressing a university audience. The sermon was printed soon after its delivery with fairly copious endnotes explaining de Soyres's references, which suggests a readership not entirely familiar with some aspects of his subject matter. Some time before, the *Kentish Magazine* had reported the bemused reactions of Victorian tourists to the crypt of Canterbury Cathedral, home to the French church; among obvious signs of boredom and remarks about the chill and dampness of the place, 'not perhaps more than half had a very well defined idea of what French Protestantism is or was'.[2] It seems that the anniversary of the Revocation would serve as a timely reminder in England of the nature of French Protestantism and the contribution of the early-modern *réfugiés* to English culture. This is also the aim of the present volume, which offers a fresh study of the British refuge in the context of the European diaspora, from the Restoration of Charles II to the middle of the eighteenth century, thus

---

1   On de Soyres's sermon, see *Cambridge University Reporter, 1884–1885*, p. 970 and the following comment in *The Cambridge Chronicle and University Journal*, 9 October 1885, p. 4, 'This pulpit last Sunday was occupied by the Rev. J. De Soyres of Caius, who alluded to the fact that this year is the 200th anniversary of the Revocation of the Edict of Nantes. As the descendant of an old Huguenot family, he made an eloquent appeal to the members of the English Church to extend warmer sympathy towards French protestants in the present day'. Some letters from de Soyres to the chief librarian of Cambridge University Library are preserved in Cambridge University Library Additional MS. 6463, letters 9519 and 9525.

2   Quoted in Joseph August Martin, *Christian Firmness of the Huguenots and a Sketch of the History of the French Church at Canterbury* (London, 1881), pp. 33–4.

encompassing the major upheaval of the Revocation of the Edict of Nantes by Louis XIV.

John De Soyres, high in the pulpit before the students and fellows assembled for one of their first gatherings of Michaelmas Term, certainly took this educative mission to heart.[3] While praising leading figures such as Jean Daillé, Jean Durel, Pierre du Moulin and André Rivet (all the objects of bibliographical notes in the printed version and many of them, no doubt, a mystery to his audience), he lamented the severing of ties between the Victorian Church of England and the Protestant Church of France. Whereas both churches had once enjoyed an intimate relationship through a shared experience of persecution and martyrdom, little attention was nowadays paid, according to de Soyres, to the common heritage of French and English Protestants. He blamed this on the 'dualism' of the Church of England, half way between Catholicism and Protestantism, on the isolation of the French Church '*au Désert*' (in the wilderness) for the greater part of the eighteenth century, and on the gradual weakening of a 'combative' union against the arch enemy. The Church of Rome, like John Bunyan's Pope in *The Pilgrim's Progress* (a work that de Soyres could still assume his audience would know very well), was now simply 'grinning' at those he could no longer terrify.[4]

De Soyres sought to reestablish a union between European Protestants, in the midst of a deep moral crisis he perceived in nineteenth-century France, to be fostered and led by the Church of England. Even though he paid particular homage to the theological influence of Huguenots, he confidently asserted that the refugees were not only welcomed but were also nurtured by a more mature, established church, ready to open its arms and embrace them. Taking the example of the Huguenots who worshipped in the crypt of Canterbury cathedral, he expatiated on the French Protestants, 'nestling under the shadow and protection of the Church of England'.[5]

---

3   The involvement of John de Soyres in the commemoration of the bicentenary is not as straightforward as it might seem. De Soyres had probably been approached by Giraud Browning (the Honorary Secretary of the French Hospital) in his capacity as chaplain of the Hospital, to be a founder member of the Huguenot Society of London. At the inaugural meeting of the Society on 15 April 1885, de Soyres was proposed as the first Honorary Secretary, a post he resigned for no apparent reason at the first annual meeting, on 10 June. The Council, far from lamenting his departure, noted in the minutes that the post was unlikely to stay vacant for long, given the 'many' members who would be happy, and qualified, to serve in that role. At about the same time, de Soyres also resigned his chaplaincy. Although de Soyres was supposed to serve as Secretary, his name is not included in the list of 126 founder fellows. See *PHS*, 1 (1885): 10, 64, 69–95; for accounts of the celebrations, see *The Times*, 19 October 1885, p. 10, and 23 October 1885, pp. 9, 12; for the beginnings of the Huguenot Society of London, see Jean Tsushima, 'The Founding Fathers', *PHS*, 24/3 (1985): 178–88. Tsushima notes in a short bibliographical notice on de Soyres that he was 'founder fellow', but the printed minutes bear no trace of this.

4   John de Soyres, *The Huguenots and the Church of England* (London, 1885), pp. 7–8.

5   De Soyres, p. 13.

This 'claim of the Huguenot church to brotherhood and communion' was 'based upon the simple and irrefragable ground that her origin, evolution, and dogmatic articles are almost identical with those of the Reformed Church of England'.[6] The setting of French Huguenot worship, in the crypt, provided de Soyres with an opportunity to develop some potent themes. The image of the persecuted foreign church worshipping underground evoked the experience of the early Christian martyrs, referred to again in the persecution narratives of French Huguenots such as Jean Migault, whose children fled the *dragonnades* by hiding in a subterranean cave strewn with the bones of animals, as if buried alive.[7]

Yet the 1885 sermon epitomises much more than deep reverence for those who maintained their faith in the face of persecution and esteem for the foreign churches and nations who gave them sanctuary. De Soyres read his sources with a curious historical bias. In 1885, the year when the Huguenot Society of London began working on aspects of the Huguenot Refuge and promoting the printing of primary sources on which modern scholars still rely, de Soyres could have based his comments on a study of the French Church of Canterbury by Joseph Martin (cited in the endnotes to his sermon), a more general, albeit essentially descriptive, volume by John Burn, histories of the Huguenot diaspora by Reginald Poole and Charles Weiss and studies of the British Refuge by Samuel Smiles and David Agnew (by then running into a second edition) with whom he mixed at the meetings of the Society.[8] These studies present quite a different picture from de Soyre's perfect union between French and English Protestants. De Soyres preaches unity and

---

6 Ibid., p. 8.

7 *Journal de Jean Migault ou malheurs d'une famille protestante du Poitou victime de la Révocation de l'Edit de Nantes (1682–1689)*, ed. Yves Krumenacker (Paris, 1995), pp. 69–71, 123–4.

8 John S. Burn, *The History of the French, Walloon, Dutch, and other Foreign Protestant Refugees Settled in England, from the Reign of Henry VIII to the Revocation of the Edict of Nantes* (London, 1846); Charles Weiss, *Histoire des Réfugiés Protestants de France depuis la Révocation de l'Edit de Nantes jusqu'à nos jours* (2 vols, Paris, 1853); Samuel Smiles, *The Huguenots, their Settlements, Churches and Industries in England and Ireland* (London, 1867); R.L. Poole, *A History of the Huguenots of the Dispersion at the Recall of the Edict of Nantes* (London, 1880); David C.A. Agnew, *Protestant Exiles from France in the Reign of Louis XIV; or, The Huguenot Refugees and their Descendants in Great Britain and Ireland*, 2nd revised edition (3 vols, London 1871). Burn's title is slightly misleading, as numerous examples are taken from after the Revocation. For Canterbury, these are to be completed by Samuel Kershaw's *Refugee Inscriptions in the Cathedral of Canterbury* (London, 1886) and Francis W. Cross's more ambitious *History of the Walloon and Huguenot Church at Canterbury* (London, 1898). However, the most comprehensive nineteenth-century study of the English refuge is undoubtedly Fernand de Schickler, *Les Eglises du Refuge en Angleterre* (3 vols, Paris, 1892), still a mine of information. Poole, Kershaw and William Minet were founder-members of the Huguenot Society and were joined on the second meeting by Schickler, Agnew and Martin as Honorary Fellows. On their contribution to Huguenot historiography, see Robin Gwynn, 'Patterns in the Study of Huguenot Refugees in Britain: Past, Present and Future', in Scouloudi, *Huguenots in Britain*, pp. 217–35.

concord, but he does not expatiate on the fact that the French church meeting in the crypt was in fact a non-conforming church, which was taking advantage of the legal dispensations granted to the foreign churches to avoid adopting the liturgy of the Church of England. He chose to ignore the bitter quarrels among Canterbury Huguenots, especially at the time of the Restoration, when Le Keux, the minister of the crypt, was temporarily driven out of the Cathedral by a small faction of conformist Huguenots led by Jannon.[9] Canterbury's most distinguished historian would later pronounce the dispute 'a deplorable strife ... which the historian would gladly pass over in silence'.[10] This is precisely what de Soyres does, when choosing to emphasise instead the sound of the French psalms and hymns mounting from the crypt and mixing with that of the English service above in divine harmony.[11] Whereas Joseph Martin is passionately in favour of the independence of the French church which would otherwise risk committing 'moral suicide',[12] de Soyres delights in their supposedly harmonious reunion, creating the myth of a uniform Huguenot church, and an equally enthusiastic English clergy. His singling out of men such as du Moulin or Durel, leading exponents of the Huguenot 'communion' with the Church of England, reinforced his historical myth-making, necessarily centred on a marginalisation of the foreign churches.

It is somewhat surprising that a community with such a shifting or, at times, even inconsistent position within or without the Church of England does not feature more prominently, with a few notable exceptions, in the work of historians who have paid particular attention to religious dissidence or non-conformity in Britain and America.[13] In the case of the Huguenots, this is a particularly complex story

---

9   Martin, pp. 53–62. See also Cross pp. 119–42, Schickler, vol. 3, pp. 234–44 and Smiles, pp. 143–50 which incidentally compares the sobriety of the Victorian furnishing of the Huguenot chapel to that of a 'dissenting place of worship'.

10   Cross, p. 123.

11   'It may be that the worshipper in that cathedral hears, amid the pealing chords of the Anthem, the lowly echoes of the old Protestant psalmody. Surely this is not discord: for there is a diviner music than unison, and that is harmony' (de Soyres, p. 13). See also Smiles who mentions 'a noble and touching concurrence' (Smiles, p. 150). It seems that not everybody was as happy as Smiles or de Soyres with the divine concord of French and English voices during the Canterbury service. A '14-inch thick wall' was erected in the late nineteenth century 'for the purpose of preventing the sounds of the French service from penetrating to the Western transept' (Martin, p. 42).

12   Martin, p. 61.

13   On the issue on non-conformity in Restoration England, see Anne Whiteman, 'The Restoration Church of England', in Geoffrey Nuttall and Owen Chadwick (eds), *From Uniformity to Unity, 1662–1962* (London, 1962), pp. 19–88; Douglas R. Lacey, *Dissent and Parliamentary Politics in England, 1661–1689* (New Brunswick, 1969); Michael R. Watts, *The Dissenters: From the Reformation to the French Revolution* (1978; Oxford, 1985); Neil Keeble, *The Literary Culture of Nonconformity in Later Seventeenth-Century England* (Leicester, 1987) and *The Restoration: England in the 1660s* (Oxford and Malden 2002), pp.132–58; John Spurr, *The Restoration Church of England, 1646–1689* (New Haven and London, 1991); Mark Goldie, Tim Harris and Paul Seaward (eds), *The Politics of Religion*

of soul-searching prevarications, appeals to conscience and liberty and competing allegiances, influenced by the particular situation of each individual church.[14] On the one hand, the Huguenots were undeniably attached to France, the French language and the French Reformed liturgy, if not actually to the French King who could be said, after the Revocation, to have been misled by a fanatical clergy; on the other hand, the gratitude they felt towards a church and a Stuart prince who had protected them from the onslaught of the dragoons (and who was ready to offer economic incentives to those judged fit to receive state bounty) manifested itself in obedience to foreign civil and ecclesiastical laws, acceptance of a foreign form of worship and ordination, and, ultimately in complete assimilation into a foreign culture. It is their story which opens this volume, a story of competing, and at times irreconcilable, allegiances.

One hundred years after John de Soyres's pulpit apology for the Church of England, public and scholarly interest was once again directed to the Huguenot contribution, or 'heritage' (to borrow the title of Robin Gwynn's study), on the occasion of the tercentenary of the Revocation. England shared in the general mood of sympathy for those persecuted for their faith. Exhibitions and conferences were organised;[15] monographs, collaborative works and volumes of proceedings appeared, contributing greatly to our understanding of the Refuge in the British Isles.[16] In

---

in Restoration England (Oxford, 1990); and the trilogy of Richard Greaves on political and religious radicalism, *Deliver Us from Evil: The Radical Underground in Britain, 1660–63* (New York and Oxford, 1986); *Enemies under his Feet: Radicals and Nonconformists in Britain, 1664–77* (Stanford, 1990); *Secrets of the Kingdom: British Radicals from the Popish Plot to the Revolution of 1688–1689* (Stanford, 1992).

14   For patterns of religious immigration in London, see Andrew Pettegree, *Foreign Protestant Communities in Sixteenth-Century London* (Oxford, 1986) and for the later period, Robin Gwynn's ground-breaking articles, 'Arrival of Huguenot Refugees in England, 1680–1705', *PHS*, 21/4 (1969): 366–73; 'The Distribution of Huguenot Refugees in England', *PHS*, 21/5 (1970): 404–36 and 'The Distribution of Huguenot Refugees in England, II: London and Its Environs', *PHS*, 22/6 (1976): 509–68. See also *The Huguenots of London* (Brighton, 1998) and *Heritage*, pp. 130–31. Broadly speaking, after 1661, the community in East London worshipped under the auspices of Threadneedle Church while in the more fashionable West End, the main church was the Savoy (see chapter 3). It was created by Charles II in 1661, on condition that it should conform to the Church of England. Assimilation into English culture was quicker in the West than in the East of the capital, due to the proximity to the Court, religious conformity and commercial exchanges between the Huguenots and their English patrons.

15   See Tessa Murdoch (comp.), *The Quiet Conquest: The Huguenots, 1685 to 1985*, Catalogue of the Museum of London Exhibition, in association with the Huguenot Society of London, 15 May–21 October 1985 (London, 1985).

16   There were numerous contributions appearing between 1985 and 1987. On French protestantism, see Janine Garrisson, *L'Edit de Nantes et sa Révocation. Histoire d'une intolérance* (Paris, 1985); Elisabeth Labrousse, *'Une foi, une loi, un roi?' Essai sur la Révocation de l'Edit de Nantes* (Geneva and Paris, 1985); Roger Zuber and Laurent Theis (eds), *La Révocation de l'Edit de Nantes et le protestantisme français en 1685* (Paris,

addition to studies that concentrated on the Huguenots' position within Britain, there appeared timely re-appraisals of their influence on the European scene in the eighteenth century and their contribution to the European intellectual history and the Enlightenment.[17] At a time when the second and third generations of refugees were being assimilated in British culture, another kind of Huguenot weaving activity came into view: their unceasing work as teachers, printers, booksellers, translators and journalists that created a web of exchange stretching across Europe. And yet, as Robin Gwynn remarks (chapter 1), French scholars, with the very notable exception of Bernard Cottret who re-invigorated a tradition somewhat forgotten since Fernand de Schickler, have on the whole rarely directed their efforts solely to the British Refuge.[18]

This book is naturally indebted to these studies and the chapters which follow strike a balance between the analysis of the minutiae of the Huguenots' ecclesiastical positions and their wider influence in the European network of ideas, in the context of what Paul Hazard termed, sixty years ago, *'la crise de la conscience européenne'*.[19] This collection has its origin in the first colloquium in France specifically devoted to

---

1986); see also the special issue of *Dix-Huitième Siècle*, 17 (1985) entitled *Le Protestantisme français en France*. On the Refuge, see Michelle Magdelaine and R. von Thadden (eds), *Le Refuge Huguenot* (Paris, 1985); Mena Prestwich (ed.), *International Calvinism, 1541–1715* (1985; Oxford, 1986). On Britain and Ireland, see Robin Gwynn, *Heritage*; C.E.J. Caldicott, H. Gough and Jean-Paul Pittion (eds), *The Huguenots in Ireland: Anatomy of an Emigration*, Dublin Colloquium of the Huguenot Refuge in Ireland, 1685–1985, 9–12 April 1985, Trinity College, Dublin (Dun Laoghaire, 1987). The 1985 publications are reviewed in Mark Greengrass, 'Protestant Exiles and their Assimilation in early-modern Europe', *Immigrants and Minorities*, 4/3 (1985): 68–81.

17 Anne Goldgar, *Impolite Learning: Conduct and Community in the Republic of Letters, 1680–1750* (New Haven and London, 1995); Graham C. Gibbs, 'Huguenot Contributions to England's Intellectual Life, and England's Intellectual Commerce with Europe, c.1680–1720', in Scouloudi, *Huguenots in Britain*, pp. 20–41. See also the proceedings of the Münster round table of 1995, Jens Häseler and Antony McKenna (eds), *La Vie intellectuelle aux Refuges protestants*, 'La vie des Huguenots' 5 (2 vols, Paris, 1999).

18 See Cottret, *Terre d'exil*, translated as *The Huguenots in England: Immigration and Settlement, c.1550–1700*. Recent French publications focus on more general aspects of the diaspora. See for instance, Eckart Birnstiel and Chrystel Bernat (eds), *La Diaspora des Huguenots. Les réfugiés protestants de France et leur dispersion dans le monde (XVIe–XVIIIe siècles)*, 'La vie des Huguenots' 17 (Paris, 2001). The British Refuge is analysed by Fabienne Chamayou, pp. 43–62. Chamayou concludes that the desire to conform to the National Churches came from the Huguenots themselves, a position challenged by Robin Gwynn (below, chapter 1). Aspects of the Refuge are also referred to in more general works dealing with representations of French people in England, or conversely. In the wake of George Ascoli, *La Grande-Bretagne devant l'opinion française au XVIIe siècle* (Paris, 1930), see for instance René Ternois, 'Les Français, en Angleterre au temps de Charles II, 1660–1676', *Revue de littérature comparée*, 34 (1960): 196–211.

19 The title of Paul Hazard, *La Crise de la conscience européenne (1680–1715)* (2 vols, Paris, 1935) referred to in English as 'the crisis of European thought'.

the religious ideas of the Huguenots in the early-modern period and it is conceived as a companion volume to the forthcoming selection from the colloquium's proceedings.[20] In the absence of a book-length study of the Huguenots in Britain during the long eighteenth century, it concentrates on the period from the Restoration of Charles II in 1660 to the mid-eighteenth century[21] and deals essentially with the Huguenots' religious position or religious impact, from resistance to, or compliance with, the Church of England's imposed liturgy (chapters 1–3), to Locke's association with a group of anti-Trinitarians whom he enlisted as part of his educational programme for England, or John Toland's toleration of religious minorities (chapters 8 and 10).[22] The main focus is on the British Isles, with a necessary incursion into the reformulation of some debated issues in the American colonies (chapter 6).[23]

The volume spans various phases of the British Refuge from the late seventeenth century onwards. The story opens in the early 1660s, with the Restoration of Charles Stuart and the beginning of Louis XIV's personal rule following the death of Mazarin, and their respective treatment of religious minorities; in one instance, Protestant dissenters such as Quakers, Baptists, Congregationalists, and eventually Presbyterians; in the other, members of the *'Religion Prétendue Réformée'*, or *R.P.R.*, the acronym under which it came to be known. This coincided in England with a major division in the London Huguenot community, which led to the constitution of the Savoy Church, under the leadership of the conforming minister Jean Durel who oversaw a new translation of the Book of Common Prayer into French (chapter 3).[24]

---

20   *Les Huguenots dans les îles britanniques et les colonies américaines. Ecrits religieux et représentations*, 'La vie des Huguenots' (forthcoming).

21   The Revolution extended the privileges already granted to the Huguenots by the Edict of Toleration in 1787. This is the period covered in Part VI (for the American colonies), Part VII (for England) and Part VIII (for Ireland) of the invaluable collection of papers given in 2000 at the conference celebrating the 450th anniversary of the charter granted by Edward VI: Randolph Vigne and Charles Littleton (eds), *From Strangers to Citizens: The Integration of Immigrant Communities in Britain, Ireland and Colonial America, 1550–1750* (Brighton and Portland, 2001).

22   See for instance S. O'Cathasaigh, 'Bayle and Locke on Toleration' in Michelle Magdelaine, Maria-Christina Pitassi, Ruth Whelan and Antony McKenna (eds), *De l'Humanisme aux Lumières. Bayle et le protestantisme, Mélanges en l'honneur d'Elisabeth Labrousse* (Paris and Oxford, 1996), pp. 679–92 and John Marshall, *John Locke: Resistance, Religion and Responsibility*, Cambridge Studies in Early-Modern British History (Cambridge, 1994), especially pp. 3–154 and 'Huguenot Thought after the Revocation of the Edict of Nantes: Toleration, "Socinianism", Integration and Locke', in Vigne and Littleton, *Strangers*, pp. 383–96.

23   Jon Butler's study *The Huguenots in America: A Refugee People in New World Society* (Cambridge, Mass, 1983) is complemented by Bertrand van Ruymbeke and Randy J. Sparks (eds), *Memory and Identity. The Huguenots in France and the Atlantic Diaspora* (Columbia, 2003) and Bertrand van Ruymbeke, *From New Babylon to Eden: The Huguenots in Colonial South Carolina* (Columbia, 2005).

24   For many Huguenot pastors, see the corresponding entries in *Oxford DNB*. On the dictionary itself, see below chapter 3. On the French translations of the Book of

With the onslaught of the *dragonnades* in the summer of 1681, Charles facilitated the arrival of persecuted Huguenots by publishing a 'Brief for the Persecuted Protestants of France' (10 September 1681).[25] It opened the first major wave of immigration into Britain since the wars of religion, but this died down when the Huguenots took the full measure of the shambles of British domestic policies (chapter 1).[26] Persecutions in France peaked again with the Revocation of the Edict of Nantes in 1685, a few months after Charles was replaced on the throne by his openly Catholic brother James. Gruesome stories of those those who stayed in France have often been told: the solution was either to convert (failure to do so would entail prison sentences or the gallows and the forfeiture of one's property) or to flee to the 'wilderness' and attend clandestine meetings.[27] The Huguenots did not, however, immediately take refuge *en masse* in England, waiting instead for James's Edict of Toleration proclaimed in 1687.[28] In 1688, the Glorious Revolution gave the crown to Mary,

---

the Common Prayer, see D. N. Griffiths, 'The French Translation of the English Book of the Common Prayer', *PHS*, 22/2 (1972): 90–114 and 'The Early Translations of the Book of the Common Prayer', *The Library*, sixth series, 3/1 (1981): 1–16. On Durel's position on conformity, see John McDonnell Hintermaier, 'Rewriting the Church of England: Jean Durel, Foreign Protestants and the Polemics of Restoration Conformity', in Vigne and Littleton, *Strangers*, pp. 353–8.

25   The Brief is reprinted in George B. Beeman, 'Notes on the City of London Records Dealing with the French Protestant Refugees, Especially with Reference to the Collections Made under Various Briefs', *PHS*, 7 (1901–04): 164–6.

26   In the sixteenth and seventeenth centuries, there were many instances where the lack of understanding between the French and British Protestant Churches came to the fore. Elisabeth Labrousse, while studying to what extent the Church of England's ecclesiastical discipline was known to the French Protestants, concluded that 'the scantiness of their knowledge is staggering'. Blunders such as Pierre du Moulin's application for the Bishopric of Gloucester are, according to Labrousse, a case in point. See Labrousse, 'Great Britain as Envisaged by the Huguenots of the Seventeenth Century', in Scouloudi, *Huguenots in Britain*, pp. 143–57 and Cottret, *Terre d'exil*, pp. 142–50.

27   One might cite two of the best-known accounts, that of Jacques Fontaine and Jean Migault. For editions of their texts, see Jacques Fontaine, *Les Mémoires d'une famille huguenote victime de la révocation de l'Edit de Nantes*, ed. Bernard Cottret (Montpellier, 1992) and in English, *Memoirs of the Reverend Jaques Fontaine, 1658–1728*, ed. Dianne W. Ressinger, Publications of the Huguenot Society of Great Britain and Ireland, New Series 2 (London, 1992) and *Journal de Jean Migault*, ed. Yves Krumenacker. For the horrors of persecution, see Garrisson, pp. 226–37.

28   Philippe Joutard, 'The Revocation of the Edict of Nantes: End or Renewal of French Protestantism?', in Prestwich, *International Calvinism*, pp. 339–68; for the English point of view, see John Miller, 'The Immediate Impact of the Revocation in England', in Caldicott *et al.*, *Huguenots in Ireland*, pp. 161–203. Miller examines the reaction of James II to the Revocation as a combination of distate for religious persecution, fear of dissent and respect for international law. For another point of view, see Gwynn, *Huguenot Heritage*, pp. 166–82: 'While in public he posed as the protector of the refugees, James deliberately shut his eyes to the violence practised against them in France and did what he could to discourage them from coming to England and to unsettle those who had sought asylum in his kingdoms'

the daughter of James, and her husband William, kindling the Huguenots' hope that the European diplomatic ventures of the Protestant prince would soon put an end to their exile (chapter 5). These men belonged to the first generation of the Huguenot 'second' refuge in Britain, which until the Peace of Ryswick (1697) and the Treaty of Utrecht (1713) expected to return to France. From 1713, when the hope for such a return was abandoned, the Huguenot *mentalité* changed from that of '*émigrés*' to that of '*émigrants*', a transformation so aptly commented upon by Elisabeth Labrousse, Myriam Yardeni, Ruth Whelan and Carolyn Lougee Chappell.[29] From then on, eagerness to conform to British culture, which meant above all conforming to its Church, resulted in their virtual disappearance as a separate object of enquiry for the historian.[30] The studies gathered here reflect this diversity, from periods of chaos and urgency in the face of persecution, to organisation yet separation from British mainstream culture and finally to assimilation, when Huguenots become Englishmen of French origin.[31]

But this evolution is not specific to the British Refuge, and neither was it as linear or as gradual as one might suppose.[32] Religious and political events in Britain

---

(p. 174). For emigration to Britain after the Revocation, see Gwynn, 'The Distribution II'; *Heritage*, pp. 42–51.

29 See the collection of articles by Elisabeth Labrousse, *Conscience et Conviction. Etudes sur le XVIIe siècle* (Paris and Oxford, 1996) pp. 120, 156, 188; Myrian Yardeni, *Le Refuge protestant* (Paris, 1980), pp. 105–108 and *Le Refuge huguenot. Assimilation et Culture*, 'La vie des Huguenots' 22 (Paris, 2002), pp. 39–57; Ruth Whelan, 'Persecution and Toleration: Changing Identities of Ireland's Huguenot Refugees', *PHS*, 27/1 (1998): 20–35 and Carolyn Lougee Chappell, '"The Pains I took to Save My/His Family": Escape Accounts by a Huguenot Mother and Daughter after the Revocation of the Edict of Nantes', *French Historical Studies*, 22 (1999): 1–64. Carolyn Lougee revised Labrousse's and Yardeni's distinction between *émigrés* and *émigrants*, by proposing a third category, the 'exile'. Yardeni examines how in the last instance utopian projects, such as Henri Duquesne's, to found a new Protestant colony outside Europe corresponded to an impossible ideal of reconciliation between Protestantism and national feeling; an ideal that would circumvent incompatibilities between French refugees and the countries of the Refuge (pp. 53–7). On the same questions, see also Cottret, *Terre d'exil*, pp. 292–8 and Gwynn, *Heritage*, pp. 202–19.

30 On reasons for the widespread acceptance of conformity as the eighteenth century progressed, see Labrousse, 'Great Britain as envisaged by the Huguenots' and for America, Robert M. Kingdon, 'Pourquoi les réfugiés huguenots aux colonies américaines sont-ils devenus épiscopaliens?', *BSHPF*, 115 (1969): 487–509.

31 Yardeni, *Refuge Huguenot*, pp. 83–92. See also, Ronald Mayo, *The Huguenots in Bristol* (Bristol, 1985). Mayo dates the assimilation of the Huguenot in Bristol from the first decade of the eighteenth century, the first 'mixed' marriage having taken place in 1700 (p. 18).

32 See Eileen Barrett, 'Huguenot Integration in late 17th- and 18th-century London: Insights from Records of the French Church and some Relief Agencies', in Vigne and Littleton, *Strangers*, pp. 375–82 and Ruth Whelan's analysis of Isaac Dumont de Bostaquet's autobiography, 'Writing the Self: Huguenot Autobiography and the Process of Assimilation', ibid., pp. 463–77.

necessarily qualified this pattern.[33] From the beginning of the *dragonnades* to 1688, the Huguenots in Britain lived under more or less openly Catholic kings. Few were free to worship in exactly the same way as they had in France. In 1688, they were asked to choose between loyalty to the (Catholic) dynasty that had sheltered them, and allegiance to a new (Protestant) monarch on account of his faith, a dilemma touching upon matters of conscience with which they were only too familiar and had not left behind when setting foot on the British coast. Huguenots were used to a dual allegiance to God and king; they could become used to a dual allegiance to a persecuting king in France, and a more enlightened (albeit Catholic) monarch in England; but when the Glorious Revolution demanded once again that they choose sides between Jacobites and Orangistes, deeply-felt questions of loyalty resurfaced.[34]

In such circumstances, one might expect from a persecuted religious community, especially at the time of massive exodus from its motherland, a certain degree of cohesion. As Randolph Vigne shows in chapter 4, the Huguenot churches and the networks of state or private charitable institutions, of financial, familial and geographical ties, all necessarily contributed to such solidarity. However, any monolithic view of the Huguenot community does not stand the test of even the most cursory examination.[35] In the following pages, stories of national cohesion, mutual help and cultural uniformity are almost systematically shattered by stories of dissension, at times extremely moving: brother cuts himself off from brother; uncle from nephew; the church from its pastor; the pastor from his flock (as embodied, for instance, in the stories of the du Moulin and Rou families, and in the tensions within the church in Ireland, as examined below in chapters 2, 3, 6 and 7).[36] These internecine feuds, severing church and family ties within the exiled community, were sometimes healed by deathbed changes of heart, duly recorded and publicised,

---

33   For comparisons with other countries, see Joutard, 'The Revocation of the Edict of Nantes', pp. 352–7.

34   These questions are embodied in the well-documented quarrel between Pierre Bayle, a staunch advocate of toleration and absolutism, who thought the Huguenots' support for William would endanger their return to France, and Pierre Jurieu, the ardent supporter of the Glorious Revolution who was deeply suspicious of toleration. Among the vast literature dealing with their respective positions, see for instance, Guy H. Dodge, *The Political Theory of the Huguenot of the Dispersion, with Special Reference to the Thought and Influence of Pierre Jurieu* (New York, 1947), pp. 34–93; Labrousse, *Conscience*, pp. 135–237; and recently, Antony McKenna and Gianni Paganini (eds), *Pierre Bayle dans la République des Lettres. Philosophie, religion, critique*, 'La vie des Huguenots' 36 (Paris, 2004).

35   For the complicated motives presiding over the choice to conform or not to a national Church, see Ruth Whelan, 'Sanctified by the Word: The Huguenots and Anglican Liturgy', in Kevin Herlihy (ed.), *Propagating the Word of Irish Dissent, 1650–1800* (Dublin, 1998), pp. 74–84. See also her 'Persecution and Toleration'.

36   For an insight into the moral and social regulation provided by the French churches, see Cottret, *Terre d'exil*, pp. 271–92 and Eileen Barrett, 'Regulating Moral and Social Behaviour in the French Church of London, 1680–1689', *PHS*, 27/2 (1999): 232–45.

as in the case of Louis du Moulin; but just as often they were not, leaving dissenters the choice of either leaving their community or of waiting, in embittered silence, for better times to come (chapters 2 and 6). Britain seems to have witnessed, with particular sharpness, the ambiguity of French Protestantism in early-modern Europe, encapsulated in the apt definition of Raymond Mentzer and Andrew Spicer who view the Protestant as 'a complex and contradictory character: at times violent and driven to direct action, on other occasions prepared to work within the legal system; militant yet innately conservative and loyal to the crown; the persecuted victim of papacy and Roman Catholicism but a member of the Body of Christ'.[37]

Already ill-at-ease with religious settlements in exile which were hardly satisfying and the ambitions of the European monarchs, the Huguenots in Britain were also part of the wider community of Calvinists, the 'Calvinist International' whose tolerance of heterodoxy did not exactly allow dissenting systems to flourish (chapters 8 and 10). According to de Soyres, with whom I began, the best illustration of the Huguenot theological influence in England was Moïse Amyraut, hardly the least controversial figure in French Protestantism (chapter 7).[38] Universalism, Arminianism, Socianism, as heretical heirs of Calvinism, were hotly debated and as often as not, vehemently suppressed by more orthodox ministers. Obedience to Calvinist orthodoxy that transcended the limits of the national churches produced another layer of competing allegiance for Huguenot refugees.

The question of whether the Huguenot Church may be called non-conformist, and if so in what sense, provides one of the key issues addressed in this volume. This, again, came dramatically to the fore at the Restoration, both in England and in Ireland (chapters 3 and 7).[39] The body of legislative documents that came to be

---

37 'Introduction', in Raymond Mentzer and Andrew Spicer (eds), *Society and Culture in the Huguenot World, 1559–1685* (Cambridge, 2002), p. 8.

38 See Brian G. Amstrong, *Calvinism and the Amyraut Heresy: Protestant Scholasticism and Humanism in Seventeenth-Century France* (Madison, 1969). On Amyraut's influence in England, especially on Richard Baxter, see Neil H. Keeble, 'Richard Baxter', *Oxford DNB* and Matthew Kadane, 'Les bibliothèques de deux théologiens réformés du XVIIe siècle, l'un puritain anglais, l'autre pasteur huguenot', *BSHPF*, 147 (2001): 67–100. Baxter kept in his library six books by Amyraut, which he recommends to his readers in the *Christian Directory* to heal the disputes between the Protestants. On the controversies within the Huguenot community after 1685, see Marshall, 'Huguenot Thought after the Revocation of the Edict of Nantes', pp. 383–5, and below, chapter 8. For Marshall, the tolerationist impetus of the Republic of Letters 'in intellectual space' did not actually translate into toleration in England for anti-Trinitarians, some orthodox Huguenots viewing with suspicion the extended 'latitude' of members of the Anglican clergy towards the colleagues whom they charged with heresy: 'The story, so far, then, is a story of the maintenance by the majority of orthodox Huguenots of a distinct, essentially Calvinist Huguenot identity in England and in the Netherlands, with Huguenots attempting to maintain in exile the orthodox faith for which they had gone into exile and attempting to police the belief of their fellow ministers as a separate community in England and internationally' (p. 384).

39 See Cottret, *Terre d'exil*, pp. 199–256. Specifically on Ireland, see James McGuire, 'Government Attitude to Religious Non-Conformity', in Caldicott *et al.*, *The Huguenot in*

known as the 'Clarendon Code' silenced those ministers who felt they could not conform to the Act of Uniformity of 1662. For the French community, it meant that no new church could be established if it did not conform to the Anglican liturgy, in defiance of the liberty of worship that the foreign churches had enjoyed since Edward VI. And yet, the foreigners were never made subject to the legal penalties imposed upon the English non-conformists and a pre-Restoration non-conformist church, like Threadneedle in London, continued to worship without interference from the authorities.[40] Robin Gwynn, who has devoted many pages to this complex issue, has devised a typological distinction between the English 'Nonconformists' persecuted by the Restoration authorities, and the French 'non-conformists', standing freely outside the Church of England (chapter 1).[41] Seventeenth-century observers perceived the irony of the situation. At times, they even put it in print at the peril of their reputation and livelihood, if not of their lives. On 26 March 1682, Samuel Bold, the conforming vicar of Shapwick in Dorset, had planned to preach in his parish church on *Galatians* 4:29 ('But as then he that was born after the flesh persecuted him *that was born* after the Spirit, even so *it is* now'). However, this was also the day on which he was asked to read from his pulpit the 'Brief for the Persecuted Protestants of France', the generous conditions devised by Charles to welcome the Huguenots who fled the *dragonnades*. Bold therefore preached against any persecution, not just that perpetrated on the Huguenots, and that included the persecution of English non-conformists. The sermon printed a year later as *A Sermon Against Persecution* (1683) took him straight into jail. Bold's tone is extremely harsh when he rails against the persecutors threatened with exemplary divine punishment for inflicting pains upon '*men of great* Learning, *exemplary* Piety, *strict* Devotion, *and* extrordinary Loyalty ... *Persons that could not be justly blamed for any thing, but that they had* straiter Notions *concerning* humane Impositions *in the* Service of God, *than we* Conformists *have'*.[42] Those '*lay*[ing] *aside* all Bowels of Compassion' in their defence of conformity commit 'a sin that destroys common Humanity: It makes [them] much more fit to be banish'd from all Reasonable Society, to abide in the

---

Ireland, pp. 820–33; Jean-Paul Pittion, 'The Question of Religious Conformity and Non-Conformity in the Irish Refuge', ibid., pp. 285–95; Raymond Pierre Hylton, 'The Less-Favoured Refuge: Ireland's Nonconformist Huguenots at the Turn of the Eighteenth Century', in Herlihy, *Irish Dissent*, pp. 48–67; Michelle Magdelaine, 'L'Irlande huguenote: utopie ou réalité?', in Magdelaine *et al.*, *De l'Humanisme aux Lumières*, pp. 273–87; Ruth Whelan, 'Liberté de culte, liberté de Conscience? Les Huguenots en Irlande, 1662–1702', in Häseler and McKenna, *La Vie intellectuelle*, vol. 1, pp. 69–83. Whelan concludes that non-conforming Huguenots would become the 'Cinderella' of the Irish Refuge and debunks the myth of a perfect harmony between the Huguenots on questions of conformity.

40 Cottret, *Terre d'exil*, pp. 203–4.

41 On questions of conformity and non-conformity, see Robin Gwynn's introductions to *A Calendar of the Letter Books of the French Church of London from the Civil War to the Restoration, 1643–1659*, HSQS, 54 (London, 1979) and Gwynn, *Minutes*.

42 Samuel Bold, *A Sermon Against Persecution* (London, 1683), sig. A2v.

Wilderness and Desart, with the Ravenous Devouring Monsters [they] resemble'.[43] Bold's sense of outrage before measures actively protecting foreign Protestants, while imprisoning home-bred non-conformists under the pretext of civil dissensions, pinpoints the legal oddities of the Restoration religious settlement.

But notions of what constituted conformity or non-conformity were not as clearcut as Bold's sermon suggests. The Restoration authorities were well aware that even conforming churches such as the Savoy practised an entirely personal (and not altogether orthodox) version of Anglicanism, or 'French Anglicanism'. Robin Gwynn cites the telling (albeit post-Revolution and highly biased) commentary of Michael Malard describing the Savoy as an 'amphibious church', 'a monstruous composition of an Episcopal face and a Presbyterian heart'.[44] In doing so, Malard imitates the standard style of seventeenth-century heresiographers whose favourite image to describe the spread of sects in England was that of an unnatural assemblage of eclectic, unrelated but equally heretical religious models. Bernard Cottret reiterates this contemporary observation when discussing the 'hybrid' Savoy Church.[45] This is where *mentalité* historians such as Ruth Whelan or Bernard Cottret make an invaluable contribution to our understanding of the motives behind the decision to conform. After an analysis of the political and religious motives put forward by exponents of conformity such as Louis Hérault and Claude Groteste de la Mothe, Cottret turns towards the concept of *acculturation* and analyses, with the scant documents we possess, how the French conformists could twist the Anglican liturgy to serve their needs and avoid the most offensive elements for a French religious sensibility; in a word, how the conformity of the French is simply another version of the occasional conformity practised among English non-conformists, the foreigners appropriating only selected elements of the Anglican ritual.[46]

The historical debate is therefore far from closed on the question of resistance, acceptance or selective acceptance of the English religious model by the Huguenots, and the possible alliances and sympathies this could add to the Restoration religious scene. We can approach the French community from many different angles: accepting Anglicanism; resisting Anglicanism but distancing itself from English non-conformity on account of its legal right to worship; resisting Anglicanism

---

43   Bold sig. A2r and p. 23. For a detailed study of this text, contrasted with another sermon by George Hickes, see Mark Goldie, 'The Huguenot Experience and the Problem of Toleration in Restoration England', in Caldicott *et al.*, *The Huguenots in Ireland*, pp. 184–8 and Spurr, p. 83.

44   Quoted in Gwynn, *Heritage*, p. 126. For the reaction of James towards the Savoy's imperfect conformity (what Bernard Cottret has termed its 'syncretism') see pp. 172–3. James objected, among other things, to the weaknesses of the French translation of the Anglican liturgy. For the different reactions of Henry Compton, Bishop of London and William Sancroft, Archbishop of Canterbury, to the supposed liberties the Huguenots were taking with the Anglican liturgy, see Sugiko Nishikawa, 'Henry Compton, Bishop of London (1676–1713) and Foreign Protestants', in Vigne and Littleton, *Strangers*, pp. 359–65.

45   Cottret, *Terre d'exil*, p. 220.

46   Ibid., pp. 212–25.

because of affinities with a Presbyterian system; resisting Anglicanism with surface conformity. All these patterns correspond to circumstances that can be glimpsed at different times, in different communities and with different individuals, and the articles below seek to map out this diversity rather than to suggest a single model of explanation.

There are, for instance, many examples, albeit sometimes purely incidental, of *rapprochements* between the Huguenots and the English non-conformists, and these offer many directions for future research. Robin Gwynn has stories of Huguenots turning Quakers, but also Methodists and Independents, or even forming their own non-conformist sect, as with David Culy and the Culimites in the Fens. In Dublin, there was at least one instance of Huguenots being enticed to join English-speaking conventicles, and, conversely, on 12 November 1683, James Mellish, the Mayor of Southampton, complained to Bishop Morley that English non-conformists were in fact taking refuge in the French church.[47] Ruth Whelan, when analysing resistance to Anglicanism, has observed among the Irish Huguenots 'a theology and a religious culture which converged in significant ways with the religious sensibilities of the Presbyterians'.[48] In 1683, the minutes of Threadneedle revealed, however, that English Presbyterians could also prove to be liabilities for the Huguenots. When leaving a service, John Quick, the ejected Presbyterian Minister of Plymouth, who was obviously attending the French church, suggested reading the *Vindiciæ Contra Tyrannos*. Needless to say, this was not well received by members of the foreign church still extremely careful not to revive distant memories of Huguenot rebellion. Quick's transcription of the French synods, and his manuscript biographical account of French ministers, testify to his personal attachment to the French Reformed system, but the reactions to his involvement with Threadneedle must have been very mixed, at a time when the Huguenot's day-to-day survival largely depended on the *bon vouloir* of the Stuarts.[49]

In the same way, not all Presbyterians felt deep sympathy with the French Protestants. In 1714, the 'autobiography' of the Presbyterian minister George Trosse, completed in 1693, appeared in print.[50] Trosse, when a youth of 14, was sent to France to improve his French and lodged with the family of minister Ramet, on the

---

47   Quoted in Malcolm R. Thorp, 'The Anti-Huguenot Undercurrent in Late Seventeenth-Century England', *PHS*, 22/6 (1976): 579. See, Hylton, 'The Less-Favoured Refuge', p. 87; Gwynn, *Heritage*, pp. 110–11.

48   Whelan, 'Sanctified by the Word', pp. 90–91. This is not the view of Robin Gwynn, however, who maintains that one should be careful not to draw too many parallels between French non-conformists and English Presbyterians on account of the 'gulf' that existed between them (Gwynn, *Heritage*, p. 128).

49   Gwynn, *Minutes*, pp. 104–10; Schickler, vol. 3, pp. 320–21; 'John Quick', in *Calamy Revised: Being a Revision of Edmund Calamy's Account of the Ministers and Others Ejected and Silenced, 1660–1662*, ed. Arnold G. Matthews (1934; Oxford, 1988).

50   *The Life of the Reverend Mr. George Trosse. Written by Himself, and Published Posthumously According to his Order in 1714*, ed. A.W. Brink (Montreal and London, 1974).

grounds of the castle of the duchess of Rohan, in Pontivy, Côtes du Nord. Ramet also ministered to the English merchants at Morlaix, but Trosse was less than impressed by his performance. First of all, Ramet completely failed to examine his transient flock, giving communion to all merchants indiscriminately; Trosse was then shocked by the absence of daily family prayers, and only once, on a Sunday, 'the *Minister*'s son read a *Chapter* and a *Psalm*, and some part of their *Common-Prayer*'.[51] Worst of all, 'a *Young Woman* of the *Minister's* Family' was seen dancing with papists on a Sunday afternoon without the slightest reproof, another sure sign, for Trosse, that the French Protestants did not hold the Sabbath in proper sanctity. Trosse did acquire some French among the Protestants of Pontivy, but he also turned into a debauched scoundrel, lapsing into a physical and spiritual decadence that he just stops short of blaming on loose Huguenot morals. When Ramet died one Sunday while supervising work on the castle in preparation for a visit by the Duchess of Rohan, Trosse concluded that, 'many such Providences have fallen out with relation to such as have concern'd themselves about *Secular Affairs* on the *Christian Sabbath:* Tho' it was not so sinful in [Ramet], who was taught to believe it *Judaical* to hold *one Day more holy* than *another*'.[52] This episode took place in 1646. There is no indication that, by 1693, the persecutions of the Huguenots had in any sense mellowed Trosse's Presbyterian indignation at the shortcomings of French Protestantism.[53]

But controversies over worship or questions of discipline have to be treated alongside cultural, or more precisely, literary affinities. The Huguenots and the English non-conformists could sympathise with one another through material circumstances and a shared experience of persecution. From 1662, the ejected English ministers began quite naturally to refer to the day when they were forced to leave their pulpits on 24 August as 'Bartholomew's Day', which allowed them to liken their experience to a bloody French massacre that evoked images of martyrdom with deep, symbolic significance. The dragoons breaking up Protestant assemblies in France must have seemed not unlike their counterparts across the Channel interrupting conventicles in the English countryside; and there are obvious similarities in the legal apparatus preventing ministers from returning within a certain distance from the place of their original congregation (compare the so-called 'Five Mile Act' of 1665 with the *arrêt du conseil* of 1683).[54] The authorities in both France and England came to rely on networks of spies, informers and intermediaries with financial, and in some cases, purely human incentives to give away the location of forbidden meetings and the names of neighbours who attended them. The Huguenot refugees were left in no

---

51 Trosse, p. 52.
52 Ibid., pp. 53–4.
53 For more general commentaries on anti-Huguenot sentiments, see Thorp, pp. 569–80.
54 For details of the acts, see Keeble, *Restoration*, pp. 120–4. The vast majority of the 2,000 or so ejected ministers were Presbyterians since few Baptists and Independents had held positions in the Cromwellian Church. On the *arrêt*, see Labrousse, *Une Foi*, pp. 181–4.

doubt, by their contacts with those remaining in France, that their co-religionists were compelled to meet in clandestine circumstances.

Huguenots and persecuted non-conformists tended to couch this experience of persecution, clandestinity or exile in the same terms because fear of either physical or spiritual persecution and coercion remained one of the central themes of their writings. Beyond the Biblical motifs of the Exodus and the Church in the wilderness, the ministers, for instance, felt the need to communicate with their flock in the form of pastoral letters.[55] English non-conformists had their own at the Restoration, although of a different nature.[56] Within his prison cell at Bedford, the Baptist minister John Bunyan compensated for his lack of direct contact with his congregation by writing pastoral letters that were published in 1765, almost a century after his release.[57] A series of pastoral letters was also printed as a supplement to the biography of the dissenter Joseph Alleine, this time shortly after his death.[58] The imprisoned ministers adopted the voice of the Pauline epistles to counsel, appease and encourage those who found themselves without spiritual guidance, those who would be tempted to turn their back from true worship in dire circumstances which after all made little sense in their providential understanding of the history of the Church. The sense of guilt that could be felt if one eventually surrendered, either to the pressure of external circumstances or to some dark sin lurking in one's soul, was the same for a French Protestant who abjured or for an English non-conformist who despaired.[59]

The Huguenots' experience in Britain and America thus cannot be seen in isolation from the stupendous changes rocking the fragile assemblage of religious factions, and their modes of expression. Sermons, psalms, martyrologies, pastoral letters, narratives of escape and autobiographies composed a vast literature, echoing that of other religious minorities.[60] But the most pathetic aspects of the Huguenot

---

55 On Biblical motifs, see Hubert Bost, *Ces Messieurs de la R.P.R. Histoires et écritures de Huguenots, XVIIe–XVIIIe siècles*, 'La Vie des huguenots' 18 (Paris, 2001), pp. 237–65 and Whelan, 'Writing the Self', pp. 467–8.

56 On pastoral letters, see Elizabeth Labrousse, 'Les premières "lettres pastorales"', in Zuber and Theis, *La Révocation*, pp. 229–38.

57 *A Relation of the Imprisonment of Mr. John Bunyan*, in *Grace Abounding to the Chief of Sinners*, ed. Roger Sharrock (Oxford, 1962) 104-31.

58 *The Life and Death of That Excellent Minister of Christ, Mr Joseph Alleine* (n.pl., 1671).

59 It is perhaps with a sense of those literary affinities that, in 1985, the editors of a volume of essays in memory of Irene Scouloudi chose to couch the history of the Huguenot refuge in terms reminiscent of Bunyan's allegory, hence *The Strangers' Progress*, thus effecting a literary link between the Huguenot refugees and the English victims of Charles's and James's fluctuating religious policies. The Huguenots' assimilation in British culture was then not only a cultural, but also a spiritual phenomenon, a hard-won victory to get final admission to the promised City, if only an earthly one for the time being. See Randolph Vigne and Graham C. Gibbs (eds), *The Strangers' Progress: Integration and Disintegration of the Huguenot and Walloon Refugee Community, 1567–1889*, PHS, 26/2 (1995): 135–316.

60 See Ruth Whelan, 'Writing the Self', and '"The Foolishness of Preaching": Rhetoric and Truth in Huguenot Pulpit Oratory', in Magdelaine *et al.*, *De l'Humanisme aux Lumières*,

literature of tears, or *larmes* (as in the title of Pineton de Chambrun's celebrated work) is only one aspect of the variety of Huguenot discourse. Hubert Bost has shown in the most effective terms the emotional streak of the Huguenot literature in the worship of a French community with its 'cries', 'groans' and 'sighs' under the Cross.[61] Marianne Carbonnier-Burkard has studied the almost 'dolorist' aspects of the literature of the exile.[62] But in parallel, in 1689, a pastor like du Bosc could write from Rotterdam to Abraham Tessereau on the latter's history of the Huguenot persecution, on the pressing need for studies not 'forged according to the author's pleasure, on imagination and fantasy', but full of 'original pieces ... edicts and declarations'.[63] This is the voice of one wishing for the literary tears to transform, or at least exist alongside, an historical experience of the Refuge, expressed by a new and distinctive voice that would carry Huguenot identity across Europe.[64]

It was up to the men of the Refuge to make this voice heard, a task they passed on to the second and third generations. While seeking to secure, day after day, year after year, the survival of their faith in France and England, Ireland, or America, caught between the Reformed discipline and the Book of Common Prayer, the refugees always kept an eye on the United Provinces, the Huguenots' 'great ark' according to Pierre Bayle and *plaque tournante* of eighteenth-century intellectual thought. Holland, free from the most obvious constrictions on liberties imposed in England, if not actually such a providential 'ark' as Bayle would have it,[65] afforded

---

pp. 289–300; Lougee, 'Escape Accounts'.

61   Bost, *R.P.R.*, p. 320.

62   'Larmes réformées', in Magdelaine *et al.*, *De l'Humanisme aux Lumières*, pp. 193–206.

63   My translation. Quoted in French by Thomas P. Le Fanu, 'Mémoires Inédits d'Abraham Tessereau', *PHS*, 15/4 (1937): 571. On Tessereau and Elie Benoît, see Bost, *R.P.R.*, pp. 267–79 and Muriel McCarthy, 'Elie Bouhéreau, First Public Librarian in Ireland', *PHS*, 27/4 (2001): 543–60. Benoît pronounced Tessereau a man 'painstaking, precise, curious, and perfectly capable of amassing pieces that could serve for a Great work', *Histoire de l'Edit de Nantes* (5 vols, Delft, 1693–95), vol. 1, sig. E3r. My translation. I am grateful to Charles-Edouard Levillain for sharing information on du Bosc and Tessereau.

64   On the question of Huguenot historiography, and biographical dictionaries in particular, see Hubert Bost, 'L'Histoire des Eglises Réformées de France dans le *Dictionnaire* de Bayle', in Häseler and McKenna, *La Vie Intellectuelle*, vol.1, pp. 227–52. Ruth Whelan, through the example of Dumont de Bostaquet, discusses the personal and collective significance of memoirs, as another example of 'the impulse to collect and create documentary evidence of a way of life – and the destruction of that way of life' (Whelan, 'Writing the Self', p. 466).

65   On censorship, see S. Groenveld, 'The Mecca of Authors? State Assemblies and Censorship in the Seventeenth-Century Dutch Republic', in A.C. Duke and C.A. Tamse (eds), *Too Mighty to be Free: Censorship and the Press in Britain and the Netherlands*, Britain and the Netherlands 9 (Zutphen, 1987), pp. 63–86 and 'The Dutch Republic, an Island of Liberty in the Press in Seventeenth-Century Europe?', in Hans Bots and Françoise Waquet (eds), *Commercium Litterarium: Forms of Communication in the Republic of Letters, 1600–1750*, Lectures held at the colloquia of Paris (1992) and Nijmegen (1993), Studies of the Pierre Bayle Institute 25 (Amsterdam and Maarsen, 1994), pp. 218–300. On the effects of the Revocation,

the Huguenot a remarkably powerful tribune.[66] In Holland, Huguenots intermingled with Englishmen as much as in London. It was a temporary refuge for men as different as John Locke and the Stuarts' licenser-in-chief, Roger L'Estrange. One wonders about the mood of L'Estrange, who had built a career on suppressing clandestine non-conformist presses, when he arrived in an Amsterdam teeming with booksellers and printers. The 'devil's bloodhound', as he was nicknamed by his opponents, the paranoid journalist who tracked down and sought to imprison anybody daring to sound a dissenting note, must have cut a singular figure in Amsterdam's paradise of the press. That same year, he translated into English a pamphlet entitled *Apologie pour les Protestans*. In his address to the reader, L'Estrange enlists the help of Etienne Le Moyne, Jean-Maximilien de L'Angle and Jean Claude in support of the Church of England's fight against the English dissenters.[67] His Huguenots were firmly on the side of the Stuarts' order. L'Estrange's *Apology* is an example of the complex journey of ephemeral literature throughout Europe, the way it was diffused, translated, appropriated, and sometimes greatly perverted, in the course of its printing history.[68] It also reminds us that Britain also saw the Huguenots both as potential allies and as enemies to be reckoned with on the British political scene, even before their involvement in pre-revolutionary propaganda against James.[69] In

---

see Hans Bots and G.H.M. Posthumus Meyjes (eds), *The Revocation of the Edict of Nantes and the Dutch Republic*, International Congress of the Tricentennial, Leyden, 1–3 April 1985 (Amsterdam and Maarsen, 1986).

66   On the Dutch Republic, see for instance, Graham C. Gibbs, 'The Role of the Dutch Republic as the Intellectual Entrepôt of Europe in the Seventeenth and Eighteenth Centuries', *Bijdragen en mededelingen betreffende de geschiedenis der nederlanden*, 86/3 (1971): 323–49 and 'Some Intellectual and Political Influences of the Huguenot Emigrés in the United Provinces, *c.*1680–1730', *Bijdragen en mededelingen betreffende de geschiedenis der nederlanden*, 90/2 (1975): 255–87; C. Berkvens-Stevelinck, Hans Bots *et al.* (eds), *Le Magasin de l'Univers. The Dutch Republic as the Centre of European Book Trade*, papers presented at the international colloquium held at Wassenaar, 5–7 July 1990, Brill's Studies in Intellectual History 31 (Leyden and New York, 1992), esp. Hans Bots, 'Le rôle des périodiques néerlandais pour la diffusion du livre (1684–1747)', pp. 49–70 and Françoise Weil, 'Le rôle des libraires hollandais dans la diffusion des livres interdits en France dans la première moitié du XVIIIe siècle', pp. 281–8.

67   Roger L'Estrange, *An Apology for the Protestants: Being a Full Justification of their Departure from the Church of Rome, with Fair and Practicable Proposals for a Re-Union* (London, 1681), sig. A3r–v.

68   The diffusion of clandestine literature is one important aspect of the history of the book. For examples, see Yardeni, 'Contrebande et circulation des livres religieux protestants en France au XVIIIe siècle', in Yardeni, *Le Refuge Huguenot*, pp. 177–86 and John Christian Laursen, 'Impostors and Liars: Clandestine Manuscripts and the Limits of Freedom of the Press in the Huguenot Netherlands', in John Christian Laursen (ed.), *New Essays on the Political Thought of the Huguenots of the* Refuge, Brill's Studies in Intellectual History 60 (Leyden, 1995), pp. 73–100.

69   W.A. Speck, 'The Orangist Conspiracy againt James II', *Historical Journal*, 30/2 (1987): 453–62.

the wake of L'Estrange's *Apology,* in the summer 1682, two Huguenots, Jean Dubois and Thomas Papillon, ran as the Whig candidates in the highly contested London sheriff elections. Both, at various times, had assumed important positions in the nonconformist Threadneedle Church and both witnessed the return of their 'Frenchness' in the course of the disputes, even though they were already well-established and integrated merchants whose interests differed widely from those of the newcomers of the 'second refuge'.[70]

In the 20 years since the last major commemoration of the Revocation, we have profited from invaluable studies on the circulation of men, texts and ideas leading up to the Enlightenment.[71] The Huguenots' involvement in the debate on toleration is now well charted (chapter 10).[72] Englishmen and Frenchmen conversed freely in

---

70 See, Gary S. De Grey, 'John Dubois', *Oxford DNB*. For Papillon, see A.W.F. Papillon, *Memoirs of Thomas Papillon* (London, 1887); Irene Scouloudi, 'Thomas Papillon, Merchant and Whig', *PHS*, 18/1 (1947): 49–72; Lacey, *Dissent* pp. 431–2; David Ormrod, 'Puritanism and Patriarchy: The Career and Spiritual Writings of Thomas Papillon, 1623–1702' in Alec Detsicas and Nigel Yates (eds), *Studies in Modern Kentish History. Presented to Felix Hull and Elizabeth Melling on the Occasion of the Fiftieth Anniversary of the Kent Archives Office* (Maidstone, 1983), pp. 124–37; Ole Peter Grell, *Calvinist Exiles in Tudor and Stuart England* (Aldershot, 1996), p. 139; Greaves, *Secret Kingdom*, pp. 96–7 and 'Thomas Papillon', *Oxford DNB*. For an analysis of the importance of foreigners in municipalities, see John Miller, 'Town Government and Protestant Strangers, 1560–1690', *PHS*, 26/5 (1997): 577–89. For the political thought of Huguenot refugees, most notably Paul de Rapin Thoyras, Emmanuel de Cizé, Jacques Abbadie and Armand Dubourdieu, see Myriam Yardeni, 'The Birth of Political Consciousness among the Huguenot Refugees and their Descendants in England (*c.*1685–1750)', in Vigne and Littleton, *Strangers*, pp. 404–11. Papillon served as deacon from July 1657 to June 1659 and Dubois from January 1657 to December 1660. Dubois also served as elder from 1670 to 1672. See Gwynn, *Calendar*, pp. 92–3 and *Minutes*, pp. 6–8. The consistory of Threadneedle was naturally anxious not to be seen in an unfavourable light by the Bishop of London, especially after his declaration that Threadneedle encouraged a 'religion which taught rebellious principles' (ibid., p. 101). See also Schickler, vol. 3, pp. 317–20; Beeman, 'Notes', pp. 111, 122, 155; Barrett, 'Regulating Moral and Social Behaviour', p. 239.

71 E.S. de Beer, 'The Huguenots and the Enlightenment', *PHS*, 21 (1965–70): 179–95; George Gusdorf, 'L'Europe protestante au siècle des Lumières', *Dix-Huitième Siècle*, 17 (1985): 13–40; Hans Bots, 'Le Plaidoyer des journalistes de Hollande pour la tolérance (1684–1750)', in Magdelaine *et al.*, *De L'Humanisme aux Lumières*, pp. 547–59; Myriam Yardeni, 'La présence des Lumières dans les sermons du Refuge Huguenot', in *Refuge Huguenot*, pp. 103–10; and *Commercium Litterarium*. More specifically on the Huguenots as journalists, see Elizabeth L. Eisenstein, *Grub Street Abroad: Aspects of the French Cosmopolitan Press from the Age of Louis XIV to the French Revolution*, Lyell Lectures, 1989–90 (Oxford, 1992) and below, chapter 9.

72 See Geoffrey Adams, *The Huguenots and French Opinion, 1685–1787. The Enlightenment Debate on Toleration* (Waterloo, 1991); Ole Peter Grell, Jonathan Israel and Nicholas Tyacke (eds), *From Persecution to Toleration: The Glorious Revolution and Religion in England* (Oxford, 1991); Martin Fitzpatrick, 'Toleration and the Enlightenment Movement', in Ole Peter Grell and Roy Porter (eds), *Toleration in Enlightenment Europe*

Holland, as exemplified for instance by the English Quaker, Benjamin Furly, and the group of men gravitating around his Dutch home (chapters 8 and 9). A rich merchant with wide-ranging interests, and an impressive library, Furly's house afforded sanctuary to such men as John Locke, Pierre Bayle, Jacques Basnage, Algernon Sidney, Anthony Ashley Cooper, Gilbert Burnet and Francis Mercury van Helmont.[73] The Huguenots contributed to the vital diffusion of English thought abroad (Pierre Coste translated John Locke's *Essay concerning Human Understanding* under the philosopher's supervision) and, conversely, to the advance of foreign literature in their host country (Des Maizeaux translated Bayle's *Dictionary* into English) in a 'cross fertilisation of ideas'.[74] The volume of essays presented here, having traced the Huguenots who took refuge in Britain from East London to the more fashionable West End, Dublin and New York, could not end without assessing their role in the republic of letters, a virtual space that gave them freedom from the constraints of geography, and allowed them to create networks of religious, intellectual and personal friendship.[75] The translations of Coste and Des Maizeaux, the latter's journalistic ventures, the Huguenot influence in the printing world, the intellectual milieu that helped John Toland shape his philosophical ideas, to cite only four of the examples developed in Part III below (chapters 7–10), are aspects of a religious culture which also gave birth to controversies such as Louis du Moulin's pamphlet denouncing the drift of the Church of England towards Rome, or the tract against the Dublin conforming pastor Jacques Abbadie (chapters 2 and 3).[76] In the last instance, the intellectual contribution of the men and women of the Refuge to the birth of the modern state, the formidable figures of the republic of letters, are the most vocal,

---

(Cambridge, 2000), pp. 23–68; Jonathan Israel, 'Spinoza, Locke and the Enlightenment Battle for Toleration', Ibid, pp. 102–13; Hans Bots, 'Le Plaidoyer des journalistes de Hollande pour la tolérance (1684–1750), in Magdelaine *et al.*, *De l'Humanisme aux Lumières*, pp. 547–59; Sean O'Cathasaigh, 'Bayle and Locke on Toleration', ibid., pp. 679–92; Ole Peter Grell and Bob Scribner (eds), *Tolerance and Intolerance in the European Reformation* (Cambridge, 1996) and more recently, Ruth Whelan and Carol Baxter (eds.), *Toleration and Religious Identity: The Edict of Nantes and Its Implications in France, Britain and Ireland* (Dublin, 2003).

73 See for instance, Gerald Cerny, 'Jacques Basnages and Pierre Bayle: An Intimate Collaboration in Refugee Literary Circles and in the Affairs of the Republic of Letters, 1685–1706', in Magdelaine *et al.*, *De l'Humanisme aux Lumières*, pp. 495–507 and W.H. Barber, 'Pierre Bayle, Benjamin Furly and Quakerism', ibid., pp. 623–33.

74 See Goldgar, 117–37; Gwynn, *Heritage*, p. 109.

75 For a general account of the 'wanderings' of the Protestant refugees whose sense of space cannot be defined by geographic boundaries but by spiritual ones, see Gusdorf, 'L'Europe protestante', pp. 21–4; Eisenstein, *Grub Street*, pp. 3–6 and Goldgar, 'Prologue', pp. 1–11.

76 For Des Maizeaux, see Joseph Almagor, *Pierre des Maizeaux (1673–1745): Journalist and English Correspondent for Franco-Dutch Periodicals, 1700–1720* (Amsterdam and Maarsen, 1989) and below, chapters 9 and 10. On Huguenot booksellers in England, see Catherine Swift, 'The French Booksellers in the Strand: Huguenots in the London Book-Trade, 1685–1730', *PHS*, 25/2 (1990): 123–39.

the most visible part of a culture that also became itself in the crypt of Canterbury Cathedral, St Mary's Chapel in St Patrick's Cathedral, the non-conformist churches of the 1690s, the weavers' workshops, and the charitable institutions such as 'La Soupe' or the 'Pest House' in Bunhill Fields, a place profoundly associated with the heyday of English dissent (chapter 4).

The following chapters reflect the diversity of the religious history, literature and culture of the British Refuge from the late seventeenth century. They move from resistance to obedience, from dissent to conformity, from social and cultural cohesion to disputes and schisms. They are also deeply concerned with the material conditions that gave birth to the Huguenots' experience of the Refuge, the places in which it was shaped: churches and libraries, coffee-houses and hospitals, the battlefields of Northern Europe and the muted studies of English country estates. They deal with pastors, tutors, journalists, translators and philosophers, as with the fourteen-year-old maiden who caused a scandal by marrying her minister, the simple soldier who charged the army of Louis XIV, or the refugee awaiting a free dinner from his local poor relief. With concerns, to borrow a last phrase from John de Soyres, not only 'sentimental and antiquarian',[77] but also scholarly and historical, we now bring out the fruits of a reflection on the religious culture of the Huguenots in what was, for them, a very long eighteenth century.

---

77 De Soyres, p. 11.

Chapter 1

Conformity, Non-conformity and Huguenot Settlement in England in the Later Seventeenth Century

Robin Gwynn

Working 12,000 miles away at the other end of the world, as a student of the refugees who left Louis XIV's France to make a new home in the British Isles, it has always puzzled me that there is so little writing in French on the British aspect of the Huguenot story. The foundations for such work were well and truly laid by Baron Fernand de Schickler, whose magisterial *Les Eglises du Refuge en Angleterre*[1] is infinitely superior to anything on the subject published in English in the nineteenth century. Schickler's *magnum opus* provides what should have been the perfect launch pad for further research, but somehow it has never eventuated. Perhaps the high standards he had set frightened off other workers in the field, or perhaps it was simply assumed that he had done such a thorough job that the last word on the subject had been said.

However, Schickler brought his massive three-volume effort to a close with the Revocation. True, he did write some substantial articles on the period that followed: 'Les Eglises Françaises de Londres après la Révocation';[2] '"Reconnoissances" et Abjurations dans les Eglises de la Savoie et de Hungerford à Londres (1684–1733)';[3] 'Un Chapitre de l'Histoire des Eglises du Refuge de Langue Française en Angleterre après la Révocation de l'Edit de Nantes: les Deux Patentes'.[4] But these articles lack the sure touch of his major work, and were never developed at book length. Nor has any subsequent French writer sought to fill the void. The main work on the refugees in England published in French in the twentieth century, Bernard Cottret's *Terre d'exil*,[5] also essentially draws to a close with the Revocation, with occasional glances beyond. The somewhat ironic result is that both the two main works published in French take as their primary focus not Huguenots, but Walloons, since it was not

---

1 Fernand de Schickler, *Les Eglises du Refuge* (3 vols, Paris, 1892).
2 *PHS*, 1 (1885–86): 95–115.
3 *BSHPF*, 39 (1890): 86–97.
4 *PHS*, 6 (1898–1901): 268–94.
5 Cottret, *Terre d'exil*, published in English as *The Huguenots in England: Immigration and Settlement c.1550–1700*.

The timing of arrivals from Louis XIV's France

The chronology of Huguenot migration to the British Isles from Louis's dominions has slight but significant differences compared with other parts of Europe. It began at the same time, perhaps slightly earlier. A logical starting date for studying migration caused by Louis's actions is 1673, the year in which the Calais representatives at the Synond of Charenton declared their church was overburdened by the number of refugees already heading to England.[7]

A large number of refugees crossed the Channel with the onset of the *dragonnades* in 1681, enough to introduce the very word 'refugee' – *refugié* – to the English language. Indeed so many came then as to cause William and Susan Minet to suggest that more refugees arrived before rather than after the Revocation.[8] That was not in reality the case. However while Huguenot migration to the Netherlands picked up sharply in 1685, peaked in 1686 and dropped off steadily thereafter,[9] migration to England was minimal in the year of the Revocation, began to pick up in 1686, and peaked – it is a particularly clear peak – only in mid-1687.[10] After 1689 the movement of Huguenots from France to Amsterdam 'more or less, came to an end', according to Hubert Nusteling, whereas England received a further influx in the years following the Peace of Ryswick.[11] The comparative popularity of London as a destination in 1681–82 and again in 1687, but *not* in 1685–86, becomes clear when the figures for new arrivals to the Walloon community at Amsterdam and the Threadneedle Street church in London are set side by side:

---

6   *A Calendar of the Letter Books of the French Church of London from the Civil War to the Restoration, 1643–1659*, ed. Robin D. Gwynn, HSQS, 54 (London, 1979), p. 7.

7   L. Rossier, *Histoire des Protestants de Picardie* (Paris, 1861), p. 206.

8   Susan and William Minet, *Livre des Tesmoignages de l'Eglise de Threadneedle Street, 1669–1789*, HSQS, 21 (London, 1909), pp. xxii–xxiii.

9   Hubert P.H. Nusteling, 'The Netherlands and the Huguenot émigrés', in J.A.H. Bots and G.H.M. Posthumus Meyjes (eds), *La Révocation de l'Edit de Nantes et les Provinces-Unies 1685* (Amsterdam, 1986), pp. 22–3.

10 Robin D. Gwynn, 'The Arrival of Huguenot Refugees in England 1680–1705', *PHS*, 21/4 (1969), 372–3, and Gwynn, *Minutes*.

11 Nusteling, p. 23; Gwynn, 'Arrival', p. 373.

Table 1.1 Arrivals of Huguenots at Amsterdam and Threadneedle Street, London, 1681–88

	Total 'settlements' ... for the Walloon community at Amsterdam'	Total arrivals at the French Church of London, Threadneedle Street
1681	475	1,182
1682	331	691
1683	195	339
1684	118	208
1685	675	283
1686	1,246	607
1687	1,067	2,497
1688	989	715

The lack of refugees coming to England in 1685 might seem strange at first sight, but at the time of the Revocation England was ruled by the avowedly Roman Catholic King James II, who had just come to the throne. The Huguenots were not willing to exchange the frying pan of persecution under one Catholic monarch for the possible fire of persecution under another. Moreover by 1685 it was known – as it had not been in 1681 – that refugees crossing the Channel would only be allowed to set up new congregations if they were prepared to worship according to Anglican forms, rather than in the way to which they were accustomed. This chapter will show that the abandonment of that policy, when James published his Declaration of Indulgence in the spring of 1687, was crucial in encouraging more Huguenots to pour across the Channel.

A significant influx of new refugees from France continued through 1688, while after the 'Glorious Revolution' the presence of William of Orange on the throne encouraged Huguenots who had previously moved to the Netherlands or elsewhere to consider removing to the British Isles. Such a chronology makes it impossible for Schickler and Cottret, in drawing their accounts to a close with the Revocation, to do justice to the main French Protestant influx into England.

There may also be a problem facing French scholars in accessing information about work appearing on the subject in English. Perhaps this is not really the case – it is impossible for a resident of New Zealand to be sure. I do know that in keeping my own work up to date, I rely heavily on reviews and information published in the *Proceedings of the Huguenot Society of Great Britain and Ireland* (formerly *of London*), and in the *Bulletin de la Société de l'Histoire du Protestantisme Français*. After all, these are reputable, regularly published journals with a very long history behind them, which specialise in the field. But I also know that after a lifetime's work on the subject not one of my own works has ever been reviewed in the *Bulletin*. Assuming that other works in English are likewise being ignored, then French scholars of the Huguenot refugees in England are necessarily being disadvantaged. That may explain why French writings on the refugees seem to pay more attention to the Netherlands, Germany, and Switzerland than to the British Isles.

Huguenot refugee congregations in England

These trends may also help explain why some of the information circulating in France about the Huguenot refuge in Britain – especially in England – is seriously misleading. This paper will concentrate particularly on the congregations, because if we cannot get the basic facts about the Huguenots' churches and communities right we are in no position to advance arguments about any other aspect of their settlement.

It was during the 'Huguenot Heritage' commemorations of 1985 that it first became apparent there might be a problem with comprehension of the real situation in later Stuart England. In that year Philippe Joutard published a piece which contrasted the 26 new churches he claimed were founded in England due to Louis XIV's persecution with 36 such foundations in Holland, remarking that the larger number in Holland 'logically presupposes a markedly smaller number of refugees' in England.[12] The problem with this argument is that while his figures for the United Provinces are reasonable,[13] those for England are not. By 1700, as we shall see, there existed over forty new Huguenot congregations in England formed across the previous twenty years. So the logic of the Joutard argument would in fact be that there were more refugees in England than in the United Provinces, a subject to which we will return.

In the same year of 1985 there appeared Bernard Cottret's major work, *Terre d'exil*. His map of refugee centres in England was not intended to be complete – it is a map only of principal locations mentioned in the text[14] – but for that very reason may perhaps confuse the casual reader. Professor Cottret showed a clearer idea of the scale of Huguenot settlement across the Channel, but there are still problems with his account. In the introduction to the enlarged English version of the book six years later, he refers to the Huguenot 'conquest of new sites, both in London and in the rest of the country, especially westwards, in expanding Bristol', but he never mentions the main western settlements which were at Plymouth and Exeter. Of London, he comments that 'the existence of thirty different locations' over the period 1680–1705 'does not imply thirty different communities: new sites and mergers were not uncommon'.[15] The point about there not being thirty different London communities is very valid; there was such a concentration of French churches and settlement in the western and the eastern suburbs that it is hard to see how one can talk of very

---

12   'The Revocation of the Edict of Nantes: End or Renewal of French Calvinism?', in Menna Prestwich (ed.), *International Calvinism, 1541–1715* (1986; Oxford, 1987), p. 354.
13   Nusteling, p. 24.
14   Cottret, *Terre d'exil*, p. 315; Cottret, *Huguenots in England*, p. 9.
15   Cottret, *Huguenots in England*, p. 11.

distinct 'communities'. But at their peak in the year 1700, there were between 28 and 30 separate groups of Huguenots worshipping simultaneously in the area that is now Greater London. If one is talking about the number of different sites occupied across a quarter of a century, the true figure for London would be about 40, with some of those sites being reoccupied by successive congregations.

It is however a very recent published work on French settlement in England that has elicited this present paper. Writing in *La Diaspora des Huguenots*, edited by Eckart Birnstiel and Chrystel Bernat and published by Honoré Champion in 2001,[16] Fabienne Chamayou seems to imply that the only new Huguenot churches in England formed outside London around the time of the Revocation were at Exeter (1685), Greenwich (1686), Bristol (1687) and Stonehouse (1692), and that it was only after 1685 that new creations were developed. By saying little about the London churches and by ignoring James II's reversal of policy in 1687, she leaves the impression that all the new congregations were conformist, that is, using the forms of worship of the Church of England translated into French.[17]

In the course of her essay, she develops an argument that would have been music to the ears of Charles II (1660–85) and James II (1685–88):

Le passage au conformisme des réfugiés huguenots peut être considéré comme une forme de loyalisme affiché envers le pouvoir monarchique qui les avait accueillis. En effet, le calvinisme français avait la réputation, de par l'esprit de ses institutions, d'avoir des tendances républicaines voire démocratiques. En se conformant à l'anglicanisme, les réfugiés essayèrent donc de se détacher de cette image de républicains, et témoignèrent aussi de leur volonté de s'intégrer dans la bonne société anglaise ou irlandaise. Faire preuve de loyalisme était alors devenu nécessaire pour rester en grâce auprès du roi, mais aussi pour se faire accepter par les élites des peuples indigènes.[18]

['The refugees' passage to conformity can be considered as a display of loyalty towards the monarchical power that had welcomed them. French Calvinism was reputed, from the spirit of its institutions, to have republican, even democratic tendencies. So in conforming to Anglicanism, the refugees would try to distance themselves from this republican image and to witness their wish to integrate into good English or Irish society. Giving proof of their loyalty had then become needful not only to stay in the king's favour, but to secure acceptance by the indigenous elites'].

The implication is that the initiative to conform came from the refugees. Charles, and initially James, would have been delighted if indeed it had been true that the great bulk of refugees in England enthusiastically embraced conformity. However, we will see that this was not the case. Many pre-Revocation refugees found they had little option but to accept conformity. Where conformist tendencies did exist,

---

16   Eckart Birnstiel and Chrystel Bernat (eds), *La Diaspora des Huguenots. Les réfugiés protestants de France et leur dispersion dans le monde (XVIe–XVIIIe siècles)*, 'La Vie des Huguenots' 17 (Paris, 2001).
17   'Le Refuge dans les Iles Britanniques', in Birnstiel and Bernat, pp. 55–6.
18   Ibid, p. 56.

they had more to do with practical and financial matters than any desire to shed a republican image. The growth of conformist congregations in the early 1680s owed much more to royal policy and the desires of the Anglican establishment than to any wish on the part of the refugees themselves.

The location of French congregations in England, and in most cases when they were established, has been clearly evidenced for many years, so this part of the paper is not reporting new work. Rather it draws attention to firmly established conclusions which seem to have escaped notice. These conclusions about when and where churches became established, and whether they were conformist or non-conformist, are not a matter of opinion or argument, but of simple fact. The evidence on which they are based is for the most part clear and uncontroversial. Substantial new sources would have to be brought to light for any major reappraisal to be needed.

Outside London, new Huguenot churches were indeed founded at Exeter, Greenwich, Bristol and Stonehouse, as Fabienne Chamayou suggests. (There were actually two at Exeter, one conformist and one non-conformist; some Huguenots had reached Exeter by 1683, but it is not clear when exactly the churches there and at Stonehouse were established.)[19] This is however a very incomplete list, for it ignores other new French congregations at Barnstaple (Devon), Bideford (Devon), Colchester (Essex), Dartmouth (Devon), Dover (Kent), Faversham and Preston (Kent), Ipswich (Suffolk), Plymouth (Devon – two congregations here, besides that at nearby Stonehouse), Rye (Sussex), Thorpe-le-Soken (Essex), and Wandsworth (now, like Greenwich, part of Greater London). All of these survived into the next century. There were also a further six short-lived congregations in Cambridgeshire, Cornwall, Essex, Kent, Somerset and Wiltshire, formed in the 1680s, which had disappeared by the mid-1690s.[20]

It is not true that all these churches came into existence after the Revocation. Ipswich and Rye were both founded in 1681, Wandsworth in 1682, one of those at Plymouth probably also in 1682, and Thorpe-le-Soken in 1683. Nor is it true that all the new congregations in late seventeenth-century England conformed to the Anglican liturgy. Far from it! Exeter and Plymouth each came to have both conformist and non-conformist congregations, while the majority of the new churches in London were non-conformist and worshipped according to the ways of the French Reformed Church. (French 'non-conformists', who had a legal existence in England, have to be differentiated from English Dissenters or Nonconformists who did not and who were being persecuted in the early 1680s even while Huguenot refugees were being welcomed.) The Chamayou argument is valid only for the brief

---

19   Minet, pp. 10, 195; Robin D. Gwynn, 'The Distribution of Huguenot Refugees in England', *PHS*, 21/5 (1970): 415, 426; Alison Grant and Robin D. Gwynn, 'The Huguenots of Devon', *Report and Transactions of the Devonshire Association for the Advancement of Science, Literature and the Arts*, 117 (1985): 166–7.

20   For this and the following paragraphs, see Gwynn, 'Distribution', pp. 404–36 (updated for Devon by Grant and Gwynn, 'Huguenots of Devon'), and 'The Distribution of Huguenot Refugees in England, II: London and its environs', *PHS*, 22 (1971–76): 509–68.

period before 1687 during which royal authority insisted that any new congregations must conform to Anglican ways. Once the monarchs abandoned constraint, the huge majority of new congregations were non-conformist. Five French churches existing in England before 1680 received Huguenot refugees. Four were non-conformist, at Canterbury, London (Threadneedle Street), Norwich and Southampton. One, the Savoy at Westminster, was conformist.

Table 1.2 shows, in chronological order, the new French congregations in England founded during the quarter century from 1680 to 1705. Only those which survived into the eighteenth century have been included. Even so, there are 43 in all. That there were 43 new French congregations does not mean there were 43 separate churches or communities. 'L'Eglise des Grecs' and Spring Gardens were annexes of the Savoy. 'L'Eglise de l'Hôpital' was an annexe of Threadneedle Street. Some of the London congregations jointly shared the same pastors while maintaining their own Consistories. However the sheer length of the table does suggest a scale and depth to Huguenot settlement in England which has rarely been reflected in French writings.

Table 1.2 New French congregations in England, 1680–1705 surviving into the eighteenth century

Church	Location [L=London]	Conformist [C] or non-conformist [NC]	Date founded
Ipswich	Suffolk	C	1681
Rye	Sussex	C	1681
'L'Eglise des Grecs'	L-Westminster/Soho	C	1682
Wandsworth	now Greater London	C	1682
Plymouth	Devon	C	1682?
Thorpe-le-Soken	Essex	C	1683
Stonehouse	Devon	C	1684? by 1692
Faversham and Preston	Kent	C	by 1685
Dover (4th foreign church)	Kent	C	1685
Barnstaple	Devon	C	1685/6
Bideford	Devon	C	1685/6?
Colchester	Essex	C	1686?
Exeter	Devon	C	c.1686
St Martin Orgars	L-Central	C	1686
Greenwich	now Greater London	C	1686/7
The Pest House	L-Central	C	by 1687
Bristol	Avon	C	1687

Dartmouth	Devon	C, then NC	1687?
Leicester Fields	L-Westminster/Soho	NC	1687?
St Jean, Spitalfields	L-Spitalfields	NC	1687
'L'Eglise de l'Hôpital'	L-Spitalfields	NC	1687/8
Castle Street	L-Westminster/Soho	C	1688
Le Carré	L-Westminster/Soho	C	1689?
Swallow Street	L-Westminster/Soho	C	1689
La Patente, Soho	L-Westminster/Soho	NC	1689
La Patente, Spitalfields	L-Spitalfields	NC	1689
Plymouth	Devon	NC	1689
Spring Gardens	L-Westminster/Soho	C	late 1680s?
West Street	L-Westminster/Soho	C	1689/90
Chapel Royal, St James	L-Westminster/Soho	NC	1689/90
Artillery (I/II)	L-Spitalfields	NC	1691/92
Exeter	Devon	NC	by 1692
Milk Alley (I/II)	L-Westminster/Soho	NC	1692
Crispin Street	L-Spitalfields	NC	1693/4
L'Ancienne Patente	L-Westminster/Soho	NC	1694
Pearl Street (I/II)	L-Spitalfields	NC	1697
Blackfriars	L-Central	NC	1698/9
Chelsea	now Greater London	?	by 1700?
Rider's Court	L-Westminster/Soho	NC	1700
Wheeler Street (I/II)	L-Spitalfields	NC	1700
Le Petit Charenton	L-Westminster/Soho	NC	1701
Hammersmith	now Greater London	C	by 1702
Wapping	now Greater London	NC, then C	1702

The role of the capital

By listing the congregations in chronological order, two aspects of the settlement become plain. One is the attempt made by the authorities, in the early years after the onset of the *dragonnades* in 1681, to deflect settlement away from London – an attempt that was doomed to failure. The other is the way Charles II, and James II until 1687, enforced a policy that new French congregations should be conformist. This policy was effective during those years, but then collapsed. If the 1680s was a decade of conformity, the 1690s was a decade of non-conformity.

The explanations most commonly offered for the magnetic attraction of London are economic. This is hardly surprising. Capital city and major deep-water port, manufacturing centre and hub of overseas trade, the one great English financial centre, the centre of fashion and specialised crafts, the London/Westminster conurbation offered unparalleled openings and employment opportunities. (Huguenot refugees, like English migrants to the capital, were to find it also offered in equal measure disappointments, overcrowded and unhygienic conditions and a high mortality rate: but that is another story.) London was, in addition, the fount of refugee relief. Equally important, it already housed by far the largest French-speaking community in England, and so was a centre offering advice, assistance, information, and the friendly voice of home. Thus when Huguenots landed at Weymouth in 1681, for example, a newsletter reported that they 'intend for London, to find out their ministers'.[21]

The English government had long been concerned about the mushrooming growth of the capital. By the end of the century it numbered some half a million inhabitants, was over twenty times the size of the next English city, and housed one in every nine or ten Englishmen. That was why, when the *dragonnades* began and the first wave of new refugees poured in, the authorities sought to house them in the countryside. This policy had the full support of the existing London churches of Threadneedle Street and the Savoy, which knew only too well that they could not cope with such a large influx. The earliest new refugee churches, at Ipswich and Rye, were organised from Threadneedle Street. The Savoy was behind a less successful colony of a hundred persons planted by the Marquis de Venours at Boughton Malherbe/Hollingbourne in Kent in 1682 (not included in table 1.2 because it did not survive to 1700).[22]

These and other colonies in the provinces often struggled, while the lure of London shone as brightly as ever. Consequently the attempts to found settlements away from the capital tailed off, and in the late 1680s and 1690s the historian's attention must be focused on London. One possible attraction of London not mentioned above is that its huge size made it easier to found congregations away from the watchful eyes of Anglican bishops and local officials. Certainly, while most of the provincial Huguenot churches were conformist, most of the London ones were not. This brings us, then, to the question of conformity, the use of the Anglican liturgy translated into French. Was this really a major issue, and if so, why? What motivated Huguenots arriving in England to conform or otherwise? Is there evidence to show they held any clear majority view on the subject?

---

21   *The Currant Intelligence*, no. 45, September 1681, pp. 24–7. A recent brief introduction to Huguenot settlement in the capital is Robin Gwynn, *The Huguenots of London* (Brighton and Portland, 1998).

22   For Boughton Malherbe see Bodleian Library, Oxford, Tanner MS cxxiv, f. 225; A.P. Hands and Irene Scouloudi (eds), *French Protestant Refugees relieved through the Threadneedle Street Church, London, 1681–1687*, HSQS, 49 (London, 1971), p. 16.

Pressures to conform and the elastic boundaries of 'conformity'

We can start with Fabienne Chamayou's description of conformity as a display of loyalty paraded by the refugees before the Restoration monarchy which had welcomed them. Charles II and James II did indeed feel the need for such a demonstration of loyalty. Their concern derived from the time of the English Civil War, when a large majority of members of the French churches in England had showed themselves firmly on the side not of the King, but of Parliament. Some had gone much further; one minister at Threadneedle Street had publicly called for the execution of Charles I at the remarkably early date of 1645 (Charles I was not actually executed until 1649), and another was a Cromwellian agent in Europe.[23] Such royalists as there were in London seem to have joined Jean d'Espagne's splinter congregation in Westminster, a congregation which was licensed as the Savoy church after the Restoration with the proviso it conformed to the Anglican liturgy translated into French. So from the very beginning, conformity could be perceived as a mark of loyalty to the Crown. As for the monarchs, Charles II determined that he would license no new non-conformist churches, a policy he bequeathed to his brother James II in 1685.

However, the true picture is more complex than Chamayou suggests. When the *dragonnades* began in 1681, most Protestants in France who decided to escape across the Channel did not have a full appreciation of the English situation. They had to act quickly in deciding whether to come. They knew that England was a Protestant country. They knew French Protestant churches had long existed in England. They would soon have heard about the remarkably speedy and favourable response King Charles II made to suggestions that he should welcome Huguenot refugees. What most of them did not comprehend were the finer details of current royal policy. Only with experience after arrival did they discover they had come to a country with deep religious and political tensions of its own, where the Anglican establishment of the day was persecuting English Dissenters in the aftermath of the Exclusion Crisis, and where they themselves were not to be allowed to form new congregations worshipping in the way they had in France.

They may have been reassured, though, to find the largest non-conformist and conformist French churches in the country, Threadneedle Street and the Savoy, co-operating in organising refugee relief, and to see that it was the non-conformist Threadneedle Street Consistory which arranged the first two new settlements at Ipswich and Rye even though the churches at both places were conformist. Besides, it was not at all clear what exactly 'conformity' entailed. At Wandsworth, now a London borough but then in the countryside and within the diocese of Winchester, the Bishop complained a year after the new congregation's formation that it was 'in some disorder for want of a due regulation', and ordered

> that henceforward there be no Consistory, but ... that they yearly chuse two Churchwardens, the one nominated by the Minister, the other by the heads of Familyes, who are to be

---

23 See the introduction to my *Calendar of the Letter Books of the French Church of London*.

regulated by the Canons and our Articles of Visitation in performance of theire duty; and that they call a Vestry consisting of the heads of Familyes soe oft as occasion shall require, according to the usage of the Church of England.[24]

Clearly the original arrangements, before the Bishop's intervention, had simply echoed those of the Reformed churches in France.

Huguenot resistance to conformity

Organisational structure may not have been a crucial matter, and many conformist congregations continued to refer to their 'Consistory' and 'elders' rather than their 'Vestry' and 'churchwardens'. When moves were made in more obvious ways towards Anglican worship, though, refugees were likely to resist them. At Rye, the minister Bertrand was by his own account too little Calvinist, too unwilling to preach what he satirically called 'happy deliverance from the ever-tyrannical yoke of the bishops' ['l'heureuse delivrance du joug toujours tyrannique des Eveques'], to please everyone in his congregation. His willingness to baptise infants at home and his use of fixed Anglican forms of prayer gave offence. Bertrand also noted signs of disturbance at Ipswich and Wandsworth.[25] There was no obvious trouble at Thorpe-le-Soken, but the opening of the Consistory register noted without enthusiasm the arrangements made to satisfy the Anglican regulations 'to which we are obliged to conform' ['à laquelle nous sommes obligez de nous conformer'].[26]

The early demise of the Boughton Malherbe colony is of special interest because it was the conformist church of the Savoy that had assisted with its foundation. Its members were spread through several small local Kentish settlements, and the church became centred on nearby Hollingbourne. There its minister Jacques Rondeau found himself obliged by local Anglican pressure to wear a surplice. Some of his flock preferred to travel twenty miles to Canterbury for worship rather than listen to him while he was so attired, even though it meant they had to leave on Saturday and return on Monday. The community had collapsed by 1690.[27]

Such examples show that new refugees did not expect, and did not want, to be constrained by Anglican ways. They also show that in smaller towns and the English countryside, Anglican authorities could apply more pressure than in the crowded conurbation of London and Westminster. There, the Savoy church continued to operate a Consistory after the French manner and its ministers did not wear surplices, while the remarkable later pastoral union between the conformist West Street and non-conformist Crispin Street churches shows there was much less effective supervision

---

24   Bodleian Library, Rawlinson MS C 984, f. 213r.
25   Ibid., ff. 51–2.
26   Huguenot Library, University College, London, Burn Donation MS 28, p. 2.
27   Bodleian Library, Tanner MSS xcii, ff. 134ff and cxxiv, f. 225; Gwynn, 'Distribution', p. 417.

of the affairs of the foreign congregations.[28] The two policies in place between 1681 and 1687 worked against one another. The royal policy of enforcing conformity placed added pressures and stress on the settlements formed away from London and so lessened the effectiveness of the other royal policy, to disperse refugees away from the capital. To the economic and social attractions of London has to be added, a greater degree of freedom of worship.[29]

There is other powerful evidence to confirm that, far from happily adopting Anglicanism as a demonstration of loyalty to the monarchs who had welcomed them to England, most first-generation Huguenot refugees were profoundly reluctant to follow the conformist path. First, there is the matter of the timing of refugee arrivals into England. By 1682, it had become plain that new refugee congregations would be permitted only if they conformed to the Anglican liturgy. Previously the policy had never been clearly enunciated and so was not widely understood. For the next five years, while that policy remained in place, Huguenot immigration was almost negligible, even though the period included the Revocation of the Edict of Nantes. Yet immediately James II abandoned the policy as part of his Declaration of Indulgence in the Spring of 1687, refugees poured across the Channel. James was still as Roman Catholic as ever, and the Huguenots distrusted him as much as they always had – but they seized the opportunity to come in large numbers once they could worship in the manner to which they were accustomed.

The second body of evidence is reflected in the table of new foundations above. Once the refugees had a free and unconstrained choice from 1687 onwards, there were very few new conformist foundations, even though these would certainly have received every encouragement from the Anglican episcopacy (and, until her death in 1694, from Queen Mary). Those that did come into existence all have unusual features. Spring Gardens was an annexe of the Savoy. The French at Hammersmith formed a favoured colony of wealthier refugees who had residences in Westminster and perhaps only used Hammersmith as a weekend retreat or summer resort.[30] We have already noted that West Street, while supposedly conformist, entered into a pastoral union with non-conformist Crispin Street (and later into another with non-conformist La Patente de Soho). The remaining three churches of Castle Street, Le Carré and Swallow Street were served by the same ministers as the congregation that became known as St Martin Orgars, and all four of these churches share perplexing statistics whose significance is not yet understood: in each case there are remarkably few baptisms for the number of marriages.[31]

---

28 Gwynn, *Heritage*, pp. 126–8; 'Distribution, II', pp. 521–2, 554–5.
29 This is further developed in Robin D. Gwynn, 'Disorder and Innovation: the reshaping of the French churches of London', in Ole Peter Grell, Jonathan I. Israel and Nicholas Tyacke (eds), *From Persecution to Toleration: The Glorious Revolution and Toleration in England* (Oxford, 1991), pp. 251–73.
30 J.H. Philpot, 'Annals of a Quiet Family', *PHS*, 7 (1901–04): 269–71.
31 Gwynn, 'Distribution II', pp. 518–19, 547, 551.

While there were few new conformist congregations after 1687, the number of non-conformist churches grew and grew. In other words, when they could exercise their own free choice, the Huguenots showed they had no wish to follow Anglican ways. Before the 1680s, there had been one conformist and four non-conformist churches in England. By 1685, the year of Charles II's death and of the Revocation, ten new conforming churches had been founded, as were a further eight in the first two years of James's reign before the King changed his policy and allowed free choice. After that almost all newly formed congregations were non-conformist, until by 1705 there were almost exactly equal numbers of the two kinds of churches. In terms of numbers of individuals, there were considerably more non-conformists than conformists. Moreover the percentage of non-conformists steadily increased, making the refugees' preference very plain. This becomes especially clear when the spotlight is shone on the capital, the choice of destination of the refugees themselves and the area where their freedom to worship in the way they preferred was most unconstrained.

During my doctoral studies, over 30 years ago, I made an attempt to estimate the size of every French congregation in London and Westminster from 1681 to 1710. Roughly two thirds of the total number of refugees could be estimated from extant baptism records. Where such records did not exist, estimates depended on whatever other indications could be found. For our present purposes, the accuracy of the individual figures matters less than the trend towards non-conformity which the analysis revealed. Excluding the distant suburban congregations, the breakdown showed:

Table 1.3 Conformists and non-conformists in London and Westminster, 1681–1710

Period	Non-conformists	%	Conformists	%
1681–85	6,131	62	3,800	38
1686–90	9,509	62	5,750	38
1691–95	14,457	67	7,200	33
1696–1700	15,166	70	6,600	30
1701–1705	18,448	76	5,925	24
1706–1710	16,002	76	5,175	24

In other words, in the 1680s there were approximately three refugees worshipping in French Calvinist churches in London for every two in French Anglican ones. However in the 1690s there were twice as many non-conformists as conformists. By the early eighteenth century, there were three times as many non-conformists.[32]

---

32   Robin D. Gwynn, 'The Ecclesiastical Organization of French Protestants in England in the Later Seventeenth Century, with Special Reference to London', Ph.D thesis (University

This trend towards non-conformity, once the Huguenots had freedom of choice, can be seen across different parts of the country in the 1690s. At Dartmouth in Devon, the re-ordained minister André Coyauld de Santé was forced to withdraw by his congregation, and was replaced by Jean Pentecoste who led Calvinist worship; thereafter the church remained non-conformist for the rest of its existence.[33] At Plymouth, the more recently formed non-conformist church rapidly proved more flourishing than the earlier conforming one.[34] In the West London suburbs, which in 1690 had seven conformist churches against only three non-conformist ones, the refugees used their new-found liberty to create four more non-conformist congregations, although this region continued to be predominantly conformist. Meanwhile every single one of the nine congregations that developed to serve the French community in the east London suburbs was non-conformist.

The strong inclination of most refugees not to worship according to the Anglican liturgy in French becomes all the more striking when one considers the very strong incentives that still existed for them to accept conformity. First, the aristocrats and leading gentry among the Huguenots tended to accept conformist worship, and members of their patronage chains likewise; thus the Marquis de Ruvigny was associated with Greenwich, the Marquis de Venours with Boughton Malherbe, the Marquis de Heucourt with Hammersmith. Second, for the refugee clergy it was much in their interest to accept re-ordination, which opened their way to preferment in the Church of England. Third, the briefs for public collections for refugees issued by James II benefited only those individuals conforming to the Church of England.[35] A non-conformist could circumvent this provision only by engaging in the practice of 'occasional conformity' – receiving communion in a conformist church and getting a certificate to that effect. Fourth, the French Committee administering charity to ministers tended to favour those who were re-ordained, to the fury of those who were not.[36] Finally, and perhaps most significantly, financial support for the ministry of refugee congregations was only available for those churches which accepted conformity. So the new non-conformist congregations got no help, the poorest among the conforming churches had no options, and Dartmouth was consciously shouldering a significant financial burden when it chose to replace its conformist minister by one leading non-conformist worship.

Early in the eighteenth century one non-conformist church agreed to accept conformity. The motive was not to show loyalty to the Crown, but simply financial. The congregation in question, Wapping, just recently founded in 1702, conformed in 1705. Alone among the 43 new French Protestant congregations of the quarter

---

of London, 1976), pp. 404–5.

33   Huguenot Library, University College, London, Bounty MS 6, 19 June 1690, 15 October 1690, 18 June 1691; Grant and Gwynn, 'Huguenots of Devon', 167–8.

34   Gwynn, 'Arrival Huguenot Refugees', p. 422.

35   British Library, 190.g.13 (394).

36   See for instance Bodleian Library, Rawlinson MS D 641, ff. 94–5.

century after 1680, it was not primarily a refugee church, being composed mainly of seamen from the Channel Islands. It was small and poor, and its founder Louis de Lescure de la Prade was unpaid and £50 in arrears by the time it was forced to petition Queen Anne for assistance.[37]

For another vantage point from which to ponder the failure of Anglican ways to impress most first generation refugees, consider the case of Dr Pierre Allix. Previously a minister at Charenton, he was perhaps the most eminent Huguenot pastor to come to England, and he was fully willing to embrace conformity. In June 1686 King James II issued a grant allowing him 'and such others as shall from time to time joine themselves to him' to meet at Jewin Street without Aldersgate or any other convenient place for worship 'in the French tongue, butt in all things else exactly according to the use of the Church of England'. The church was to be furnished and adorned as the Archbishop of Canterbury directed, and only Anglican priests and deacons were to officiate there. Interestingly, it was not the Bishop of London (Henry Compton, who was out of favour with James) but rather Archbishop Sancroft who was to license all appointments 'for to his care and inspection alone … wee do think fitt to recommend and committ the establishment and regulation of the said French congregation'. The petitioners, the grant said, have represented 'their firme resolution, to live in intire conformity and orderly submission to our government both in church and state'.[38]

Allix had royal support, archiepiscopal support, and the endorsement of the Anglican hierarchy (an attestation of 1699/1700 in support of his work on the early Church Councils is signed by the Archbishops of Canterbury and York, the Bishop of London and no fewer than 15 other bishops). He was a Doctor of Divinity of both Oxford and Cambridge, and published many theological works. His contacts were wide-ranging, from Sir William and Lady Trumbull to John Locke to the elder Marquis de Ruvigny. He had the patronage of the non-juring bishop of Ely Francis Turner in James's reign, and later of the Whig Bishop of Salisbury Gilbert Burnet, who appointed him diocesan treasurer. The implication of the wording of James's grant in 1686 is that Allix's church was chosen and licensed to set a new standard, closer than the Savoy church to what the authorities perceived as true Anglicanism. Yet though Allix had a high reputation and every conceivable advantage, and agreed and sought to 'help our people to comply more with the Church than with the dissenters',[39] his conformist congregation never really took off as he had hoped, and never challenged the prestige of the Savoy, let alone Threadneedle Street.

---

37   Gwynn, 'Distribution, II', p. 553.

38   The family papers, including the passport which permitted Allix, his wife Margaret and three children to leave France and go to England via Calais, survive in private hands in Cambridgeshire. For this paragraph see the folio volume amongst them, no. 46. The grant is also in the Public Record Office (SP/44/337, pp. 36–7), together with a progress draft which reveals some of the thinking behind it (SP/31/3, f. 336).

39   Allix family papers, quarto volume, no. 51; folio volume, nos. 49, 63, 194. See also the entries on Allix in Haag and *Oxford DNB*.

The fact is, most Huguenots of the first generation simply did not want to conform to the Church of England. This does not mean that the minority who did accept conformity were insignificant. Their number included many of the social elite and quite a few ministers (some of whom, if they needed pensions or employment, had little choice). Moreover it should be borne in mind that all the foreign churches in England – conformist and non-conformist alike – had always since Elizabeth I's reign, except during the Interregnum, acknowledged episcopal oversight to a greater or lesser extent. There was a wide range of opinion about bishops within the Huguenot camp. But many ministers were unhappy about having to be re-ordained in order to be accepted into the Church of England, especially since proselyte converts from Catholicism did not.[40]

Professor Cottret is well aware that 'in many cases ... the refugees resisted conformity', that 'undoubtedly, there were some obstinate critics of Anglicanism among the refugees'. Yet he also thinks that 'Huguenot episcopalianism has often been underplayed',[41] and that 'quite evidently, the adoption of Anglicanism was a clear choice on the part of all those who did not wish to maintain the 'Presbyterian' forms of French Calvinism, which were marred in their eyes by potential republicanism'.[42] From what we have seen in this paper, there were few who made such a clear determination. On the contrary, of the generality of refugees, only a minority wanted anything to do with Anglican worship. Conformity offered real, visible, practical and economic advantages. A combination of necessity and royal policy between 1681 and 1687 meant that many refugees were reluctantly bullied into Anglicanism. However what is shown by the evidence set out in this paper is the overwhelming rejection by most refugees of even the modified Anglicanism practised in the Savoy, which in the years after the Peace of Utrecht (1713) had to defend itself against charges that it was zealous for Presbyterianism and talked 'strangely of episcopacy' and disrespectfully of bishops.[43] Most first generation refugees wanted to use the form of worship they had practised in their homeland.

Fabienne Chamayou (whose argument here echoes that of Professor Cottret) asserts that the Huguenots were glad to emphasise their loyalty to the Restoration monarchy of Charles II and James II. It would be more to the point to underline that under the conditions of the early-mid 1680s, everyone in the French Protestant camp in England knew how vulnerable they were if they failed to emphasise their loyalty. As refugees, the Huguenots were dependent on royal favour, and it was ever in their interest to keep a low and respectful profile. The decade of the 1680s was a time of particular persecution of Englishmen who shared many of their religious views, a

---

40   John-Armand Dubourdieu, *An Appeal to the English Nation: or, the body of the French Protestants, and the honest proselytes, vindicated from the calumnies cast on them by one Malard and his associates ...* (London, 1718), pp. 81–2.

41   Cottret, *Huguenots in England*, pp. 171–2, 179; he reiterates the point about 'Huguenot episcopalianism' in *PHS*, 26/3 (1995): 369.

42   Cottret, *Huguenots in England*, p. 265.

43   Dubourdieu, *Appeal to the English Nation*, p. 85.

time of fear, tension, plots and rumours of plots, and draconian legal punishments.[44] No wonder refugee spokesmen, conformist and non-conformist alike, took pains to emphasise their loyalty.

Historians, though, should be on their guard against letting themselves be too carried away by such expressions of loyalty. Certainly there is no sign at all that refugees were loyal to the line of King James II during whose brief reign so many had entered the country. On the contrary, as Chamayou rightly says,[45] they clearly supported William and his successors.

Huguenot contacts were used as channels of communication between England and Holland in the months before William's invasion,[46] and the loyalty of the refugees remained committed to the Revolution of 1688 and its ousting of the line of James II. A memorial to the Pretender James III from his secretary of state in 1715 advised that 'the whole body of the French refugees ... more desperate and better disciplined than any other class of men in England' stood ready to oppose Jacobite invasion.[47] Huguenot descendants were again quick to volunteer their services against the younger Pretender, Bonnie Prince Charlie, in 1745.[48]

England and the Netherlands: the significance of England as a refugee centre

Scholarship regarding the two largest Huguenot refugee centres, England and the Netherlands, has been evolving in different directions in recent years. Estimates of the numbers of refugees in the Netherlands have declined. Traditionally the number supposed to have found refuge in the Netherlands was between 50,000 and 75,000. In the 1980s, Hubert P.H. Nusteling revised this downwards to some 35,000.[49] This new figure was accepted by Jonathan Israel,[50] and is accepted also – if perhaps with

---

44 See the forthcoming volume deriving from the conference under the auspices of the Roger Morrice 'Entring Book' project held in Cambridge in 2003, *Fear, Exclusion, and Revolution: Roger Morrice and his Worlds, 1675–1700*; also Gwynn, pp. 5–8.

45 Chamayou, 'Le Refuge', in Birnstiel and Bernat, *Diaspora*, pp. 59–60.

46 W.A. Speck, 'The Orangist Conspiracy against James II', *Historical Journal*, 30/2 (1987): 458.

47 Historical Manuscripts Commission 56: *Stuart I*, p. 527.

48 Tessa Murdoch (comp.), *The Quiet Conquest: The Huguenots, 1685 to 1985*, Catalogue of the Museum of London Exhibition, in association with the Huguenot Society of London, 15 May–21 October 1985 (London, 1985), p. 98.

49 Nusteling, 'The Netherlands and the Huguenot émigrés', pp. 17–34.

50 Jonathan Israel, *The Dutch Republic: Its Rise, Greatness, and Fall, 1477–1806* (Oxford, 1995), p. 628.

some reservations – in the most recent publications, for example by Hans Bots[51] and by Willem Frijhoff.[52]

In England, the number of Huguenots supposed to have found refuge has for some years been estimated as between 40,000 and 50,000. That estimate depends to a significant extent on calculations based on baptism records, just as does Nusteling's work. In editing registers for the Huguenot Society, William Minet made the assumption that 35 baptisms in one year might indicate a congregation of around 1,000.[53] Scholarly work in the 1950s and 1960s, when I began my own investigations into the subject, confirmed that was reasonable. Detailed research showed a birth rate of 36 per 1,000 in the parish of Crulai in Normandy, 1675–1749, and a birth (baptismal) rate of between 35 and 37 per 1,000 at Clayworth, Nottinghamshire, between 1676 and 1688. In large towns birth rates seemed to have been lower than in the countryside, but existing work suggested that overall they were between 30 and 40 per 1,000 in the late seventeenth century.[54] Consequently I continued to use the same basis for calculations as William Minet had done, using five-year averages to help even out any single aberrant years, while acknowledging that for a number of reasons the resultant estimates were likely to err on the side of caution.[55]

However the magisterial work of E.A. Wrigley and R.S. Schofield on English demography across the Early Modern period has subsequently suggested an average crude birth rate of 31.84 per 1,000 for this period,[56] and Professor John Miller has applied this figure to the French-speaking congregations at Canterbury and Norwich in a recent article.[57] Nusteling's work for Amsterdam is based on figures across the period 1666–1710 that average out to 34.6 per 1,000. Should either of these birth rates be accepted as a better base assumption than the 35 per 1,000 previously

---

51   In Birnstiel and Bernat, pp. 68–70; see also Hans Bots, 'La Migration Huguenote dans les Provinces–Unies, 1680–1715. Un nouveau bilan', in *In Dubiis Libertas. Mélanges d'Histoire offerts au Professeur Rémy Scheurer* (Hauterive, 1999), pp. 271–4.

52   Willem Frijhoff, 'Uncertain Brotherhood', in Bertrand van Ruymbeke and Randy J. Sparks (eds.), *Memory and Identity: the Huguenots in France and the Atlantic Diaspora* (Columbia, 2003), pp. 135–6.

53   'Notes on the Threadneedle Street Registers', unpublished typescript in the Huguenot Library (lodged by Susan Minet in 1954), pp. 93–5; and see the introductions to the various relevant volumes in HSQS.

54   E. Gautier and L. Henry, *La Population de Crulai, paroisse normande* (Paris, 1958), p. 232; H.E. Bell and R.L. Ollard (eds), *Historical Essays 1600–1750 presented to David Ogg* (London, 1963), pp. 173–74, 182; D.V. Glass and D.E.C. Eversley (eds), *Population in History* (London, 1965), pp. 444, 614; E.A. Wrigley (ed.), *An Introduction to English Historical Demography from the Sixteenth to the Nineteenth Century* (London, 1966), p. 264.

55   Robin Gwynn, 'The Number of Huguenot Immigrants in England in the Late Seventeenth Century', *Journal of Historical Geography*, 9/4 (1983): 384–95.

56   E.A. Wrigley and R.S. Schofield, *The Population History of England, 1541–1871: A Reconstruction* (1981; Cambridge, 1989), pp. 174, 311, 531–3.

57   'The Fortunes of the Strangers in Norwich and Canterbury, 1565–1700', in van Ruymbeke and Sparks, *Memory and Identity*, pp. 110–27.

used, then the effect would be to increase the overall estimate of the numbers of Huguenots in England. The difference would be only marginal in Nusteling's case, but the Wrigley/Schofield basis would yield estimates some 9 per cent higher for those congregations for which adequate baptismal records survive. However, for myself, I would rather stay with the basis of 35 per 1,000 and simply acknowledge that estimates based on it are likely to be conservative.[58]

In any event, the picture that emerges from current scholarship shows a declining estimate for the number of Huguenots in the later seventeenth-century Netherlands, but an estimate for England which continues to seem reasonable. The United Provinces were a vital transit point, and most Huguenot ministers – including the most vocal refugee leaders like Pierre Jurieu and Pierre Bayle – became based there. Unquestionably, the Netherlands were of greater importance than England at the time of the Revocation in 1685, since the post-Revocation flood only began crossing the Channel after James II issued his Declaration of Indulgence in 1687.

But after the Glorious Revolution of 1688 and William's accession to the British crown, the situation changed. The logical conclusion of modern scholarship is that by 1700 it was England that had emerged as the more significant centre for Huguenots than the Netherlands and become the 'great ark' – to use Bayle's phrase – for ordinary refugee families. This is not a contention previously proposed for serious consideration, but I put it forward now. Undoubtedly the conurbation of London and Westminster, with over 20,000 members of Huguenot churches throughout the 1690s and the opening decade of the eighteenth century, dwarfed any other European centre in its importance for the refuge; there were three or four times as many refugees there as in Amsterdam. Scholars should be reaching for their calculators. That they may need to do so confirms how important it is for more French scholars to start taking a serious interest in the fortunes of the Huguenot refugees in England, especially in its capital city.

---

58 So many difficulties stand in the way of certainty that any attempt at statistical precision becomes spurious. These difficulties include major gaps in the evidence, the impossibility of attempting family reconstitution on the requisite scale, the fluidity and peculiarity of the refugee situation, and the fact that so many Huguenots lived in the unparalleled situation of the London conurbation.

Chapter 2

Differing Perceptions of the Refuge?

Huguenots in Ireland and Great Britain and their Attitudes towards the Governments' Religious Policy (1660–1710)[1]

Susanne Lachenicht
National University of Ireland, Galway

Government and Church of Ireland policy towards Huguenot refugees

Due to the massive Protestant population loss resulting from the wars of the mid-seventeenth century, the Irish government needed to introduce more Protestants to Ireland to strengthen the Protestant interest. Thus, in 1662, the Duke of Ormond sent agents to France to attract Huguenots to come to Ireland granting them the preservation of their Calvinist form of ecclesiastical polity on condition that the congregations would formally conform to the Established Church. In the same year, the Irish Parliament enacted that for a period of seven years Protestant strangers should be enabled to become naturalised citizens and freemen of towns and guilds if they agreed to take the Oaths of Allegiance and Supremacy. The collective naturalisation made Ireland much more attractive as a place of refuge than Britain where collective naturalisation was not to be available until 1709.

In 1665 – about one hundred years after the first French Reformed Church had been established in England – sufficient numbers of French refugees had arrived in Dublin to justify the establishment of a separate place of worship. The Dean and the Chapter of St Patrick's granted the Huguenots the use of St Mary's Chapel within St Patrick's Cathedral, which was opened with pomp and ceremony in April 1666. Yet, what was expected by the Church of Ireland representatives was – similar to the situation in England at this time – official conformity. Already at this stage, the Church of Ireland was not satisfied with the fact that most of the newly arriving Protestants were Presbyterians. Only ten years later, the situation for the refugees in

---

[1] The results presented here are but preliminary findings gleaned from research conducted for a larger project located at the Centre of the Study of Human Settlement and Historical Change at the National University of Ireland, Galway (and funded by a Marie Curie European Individual Fellowship) treating of the integration and assimilation of Huguenot refugees in several European countries.

Ireland changed when, in 1687, the Catholic Richard Talbot, Earl of Tyrconnell, was appointed Viceroy in Ireland by the Catholic King James II. Then, the Act of 1662 was annulled and the vicar of the congregation attached to St Patrick's Cathedral was imprisoned.[2]

It was only after the successful military campaign in Ireland by William of Orange against the forces of his father-in-law King James that the British and Irish legislature both renewed their respective immigration policies. In 1692, a new act now even offered Irish naturalisation to foreign Protestants without obliging them to take the Oaths of Allegiance and Supremacy. Huguenots in Ireland thus enjoyed a degree of religious toleration greater than that which Huguenots in England could expect from any comparable act in that Kingdom or indeed elsewhere in Britain.

Three years later, in 1695, the Parliament in Dublin passed a statute stipulating that only French ministers willing to conform to the Anglican rites would be guaranteed livings within the state Church. This legislation thus tried to bring the situation of Huguenots in Ireland in line with the Toleration Act of 1689. This meant, in practice, that dissenting French reformed congregations would continue to exist only if they managed to sustain their own minister which was the case in Dublin (in Peter Street and Lucy Lane), in Portarlington (up to 1702) and in Cork where the Reverend Jacques Fontaine supported himself financially with his own business transactions.[3]

During the reign of Queen Anne, tendencies to bring dissenting churches into full conformity with the Episcopalian Church became more and more obvious. In 1704 an 'Act to prevent the further growth of popery' had been passed. It obliged all persons holding a civil or military pension under the Crown not only to take the oath of loyalty to the monarch and to subscribe to the declaration against transubstantiation before the customary courts but also under the terms of the Sacramental Test to produce a certificate of communion 'according to the usage of the Church of Ireland in some parish Church'.[4]

Further attempts by the Church of Ireland to make Huguenot dissenters conform were made. In 1710, William King, Archbishop of Dublin, complained to Bishop Vigors of Ferns that the French congregation at Carlow had received as their minister one who had been ordained by 'schismatical presbyters'. King expressed his fear that if they continued in this way 'they will place themselves on the same foot with the dissenters in relation to church communion, which would be of ill consequence both to them and us'. In his *Conduct of the Dissenters* (Dublin, 1712), King declared that 'the toleration extended to other Protestant dissenters had encouraged Huguenots who had conformed to the Established Church to break away'.[5] In 1711, the

---

2   William A. Maguire, *The Huguenots and Ulster, 1685–1985: Historical Introduction and Exhibition Catalogue, 1 October 1985–30 April 1986* (Lisburn, 1985).

3   Ruth Whelan, 'The Huguenots, the Crown and the Clergy, Ireland, 1704', *PHS*, 26/5 (1997): 604–5.

4   2 Anne c. 6 (1704), Irish statutes, IV 12–31. See Whelan, p. 601.

5   G.A. Forrest, 'Schism and reconciliation: the "Nouvelle Eglise" de Ste Marie, Dublin 1705–1716', *PHS*, 26/2 (1995), p. 208.

Convocation of the Church of Ireland thus enacted 'A representation of the present state of religion ... drawn up and agreed by both houses of Convocation' which condemned dissenters, including Huguenot non-conformists.

The government's policy towards Huguenots in Ireland makes it evident that, to attract French Protestants to come to that 'popish' country and to settle those who had helped William of Orange to the throne, in 1662 and in 1692 the legislature was willing to grant privileges that enabled French Calvinists to become naturalized citizens in Ireland. Both acts have to be considered to be direct responses to bellicose situations. In 1662, the Protestant interest in Ireland had to be strengthened due to the massive Protestant population loss in the 1640s and 1650s. The 1692 act came as a settlement after the Williamite Wars to permit Calvinist Protestants to be rewarded with confiscated lands in Ireland without engaging with issues of religious adherence. In both cases, the later governments tried to cut back these privileges. Attempts to make French Presbyterians in Ireland conform to the Established Church were vehemently supported by the Church of Ireland representatives, in particular from the early eighteenth century onwards.

The British government's immigration policy and the Church of England's attitudes towards French Huguenot refugees

After the Restoration in 1660, that is with the accession of Charles II, Huguenots in Britain found themselves in a much better situation than they had enjoyed during the reign of King Charles I and during the Interregnum. Now, French refugees no longer suffered from 'hostile scrutiny'.[6] Yet, from the 1660s onwards new congregations were only licensed if they accepted the Anglican liturgy translated into French. In 1661, Charles II took advantage of ongoing conflicts between pro- and anti-parliamentarian members of the French churches of London and established the first officially conforming French church in the chapel of the Savoy. This congregation was placed under the jurisdiction of the Bishop of London and had to use the Book of Common Prayer in a French translation. Jean Durel, a royalist pastor and friend of William Sancroft, was appointed minister of the Savoy Church.[7] This first attempt to make the French Protestant Church conform to the Church of England was followed in 1662 by the Act of Uniformity, which made it impossible for French reformed pastors to get benefices of the Church of England without being re-ordained.[8]

Throughout the 1680s, in spite of the Church's attempts to make the French churches conform, the French refugees found in Henry Compton, Bishop of London (1676–1713), a very welcoming benefactor who encouraged and supported French Huguenots whether they conformed to the Church of England or not.[9] This contrasted

---

6   Gwynn, *Heritage*, p. 54.
7   Ibid., pp. 122–3.
8   Ibid., p. 124.
9   Sugiko Nishikawa, 'Henry Compton, Bishop of London (1676–1713) and Foreign Protestants', in Vigne and Littleton, *Strangers*, p. 359.

with the outlook of other High Church clergy, such as William Sancroft, Archbishop of Canterbury who insisted on the French Protestants conforming to the Church of England and complained about the Savoy Church not being in sufficient conformity.[10] Yet, what the Crown guaranteed in spite of these attempts towards conformism and uniformity was denisation and financial support. Even though until 1709 no act of general naturalisation was passed in Parliament, the Crown took advantage of its right to grant denisation. These grants were made in abundance in particular with the beginning of the *dragonnades* in 1681.[11] In addition, under the reign of Charles II, collections were made to help the French churches sustain the increasing numbers of newly arriving refugees.

While in 1686 it had seemed that what King James had in mind when he pronounced a public collection for the relief of the refugees was to grant money only to those French Protestants taking the sacrament according to the Anglican ritual, his Declaration of Indulgence of 1687 led not only to the toleration of Dissenters in general, but also to the 'abandonment of the post-Restoration conformist policy and the creation of new non-conformist foreign churches'.[12] Even though James II did not particularly like the French Protestants in England he did not suppress the French Reformed Church in that kingdom.

With the accession of William and Mary and the Toleration Act of 1689 the non-conforming French churches hoped to gain even more ground. Dissenting Protestants were allowed to have their own teachers, preachers, services and churches, yet, without being sustained by the Church of England. Thus, by 1702, there were three times as many non-conforming as conforming French Calvinists in England.[13] Even though dissenting French reformed pastors were not sustained by the Church of England, the French reformed churches took advantage of a permanently established financial support. From 1689 to 1693 William and Mary allocated the refugees a sum of £39,000 from the Civil List, the so-called 'Royal Bounty'. This was supported by Parliament, which provided a precedent for further grants.[14]

Under the reign of Queen Anne, for three years, from 1709 to 1712, Huguenots achieved formal equality with Church of England Protestants. The Act of 1709 granted naturalisation under the condition that a Protestant stranger took both communion in an Anglican Church and the Oaths of Allegiance and Supremacy and, third, that he made some decreed declarations in open court.[15]

Restoration England seems to have had a deep interest in making the existing French congregations conform to the Church of England. Yet, with the *dragonnades* and the increasing influx of French reformed refugees at least Henry Compton,

---

10 Ibid., p. 359.
11 Gwynn, *Heritage*, p. 71.
12 Ibid., p. 130.
13 Ibid., p.132.
14 Ibid., p. 72.
15 See William O'Reilly, 'The Naturalisation Act of 1709 and the settlement of Germans in Britain, Ireland and the colonies', in Vigne and Littleton, *Strangers*, pp. 492–502.

Bishop of London, and in some respects also King Charles II supported newly arriving Huguenots whether they conformed to the Church of England or not. In the late 1680s, both King James II's Declaration of Indulgence and King William's Toleration Act of 1689 led to the establishment of more dissenting French reformed congregations. Yet, dissenting churches had to sustain their own ministers. Compared to the Act of Naturalisation in Ireland made in 1692 the first English Naturalisation Act of 1709 provided Huguenots in England with a less privileged legal status than the one Huguenots in Ireland had enjoyed. Still in 1709 Huguenots in England had to take both the Oaths of Allegiance and Supremacy and communion in an Anglican church to enjoy naturalisation. This had not been required of Huguenots in Ireland in 1692. Yet, the Irish government tried to correct the Huguenots' privileged situation. The 1695 act and then the Sacramental Test of 1704 were attempts to bring Irish policy in line with the English Act of Toleration of 1689. Now, Huguenots in Ireland, too, should only gain from naturalisation and state pensions on condition that they conformed to the Established Church. How did Huguenots in both England and Ireland react to this policy?

The Huguenots' reactions in Britain

Most Huguenots distrusted the government of King James II by virtue of his Catholicism and his known friendship with their persecutor, King Louis XIV of France. Thus, notwithstanding his Declaration of Indulgence of 1687, they persisted in suggesting that he aimed at the persecution of all Protestants and the re-introduction of Popery in England.[16] Therefore, in his *Défense de la nation Britannique ou les droits de Dieu, de la Nature & de la Societé clairement établis au sujet de la revolution d'Angleterre, contre l'auteur de L'Avis important aux Refugiés* Jaques Abbadie, minister of the French Church of the Savoy, described James II as a 'puissance tyrannique' [tyrannical power], a 'destructeur notoire de l'Etat' [notorious destroyer of the State] and an 'ennemi publiq' [public enemy].[17] Some of Abbadie's colleagues even preached for uniformity and against the maintenance of the original French reformed faith. One of these ardent defenders of Protestant conformity in Restoration England, as John Hintermaier has shown, was Jean Durel. In his sermon *The Liturgy of the Church of England asserted*, he opted for unity in the Church of England. Durel condemned all Presbyterians – including dissenting Huguenots – castigating 'them for breaking the requirements of both religion and morality'.[18] In Durel's view dissent was the very root of the Civil Wars. He believed that opposition

---

16   Gwynn, *Heritage*, pp. 158–65.
17   Jacques Abbadie, *Défense de la nation Britannique ou les droits de Dieu, de la Nature & de la Societé clairement établis au sujet de la revolution d'Angleterre, contre l' auteur de L'Avis important aux Refugiés* (London, 1692), pp. 52–3, 441.
18   John Macdonnell Hintermaier, 'Rewriting the Church of England: Jean Durel, foreign Protestant and the polemics of Restoration Conformity', in Vigne and Littleton, *Strangers*, p. 354.

to conformity had to be identified with sedition and regicide. What Durel seemed to have feared most was that dissent would again lead to struggles such as those of the 1640s and 1650s. And – considering fears as to the re-introduction of Popery under the reign of James II – conformity of all Protestant churches could have been the key to fight 'popery' in England. Reconciling Laudians and Conformists and integrating the French Reformed Church into the Church of England was for pastors such as Jean Durel necessary to guarantee the survival of Protestantism. Furthermore, this attitude showed loyalty towards the country of refuge. Obviously, this loyalty had been forged during the Civil War and the period of the Interregnum.

While the pastors of the newly established conformed French Church of the Savoy, such as Jean Durel and later Jacques Abbadie, approved Charles II's attempts to make more French congregations conform to the Church of England, not all French Calvinists in London were as happy as they were with the establishment of the conforming Church of the Savoy in 1661. Many French Calvinists in London wanted to maintain the Liturgy and Discipline of the French Reformed Church according to the 29 National Synods.[19]

One of these opposing voices was the Reverend Jacques Fontaine who in 1688 'had already taken communion in the manner of the Church of England'. Despite having done so, he refused to accept a pension as a reward for having taken communion because he regarded 'communion as one of the most sacred mysteries of our religion and thought it wrong to approach it with any other view than to receive the benefits that the death of Christ had gained for us'. He considered that compliance with a view to receiving a benefit was analogous to what the Papists had attempted in France: 'Come to mass and you shall be exempt from dragoons and taken care of like us'.[20]

What has also to be borne in mind is that even if the Savoy Church officially accepted the Liturgy and Discipline of the Church of England, French Protestant elements were kept alive – similar to what happened in the conforming church of St Patrick in Dublin. First, the Savoy Church had a Consistory. Second, even though the Savoy Church officially used the liturgy of the Anglican Church, Durel's translation differed from the English original. Third, despite being recognised by the Anglican Church, the pastor of the Savoy congregation wore no surplice as an Anglican pastor was supposed to do.[21] The liturgy and discipline of the French Church of the Savoy thus had a hybrid character meaning that French Calvinist elements endured even in the most conforming French church of London.

The question therefore becomes one of whether the officially conforming Church of the Savoy can really be considered to be a conformed church or whether Durel and others were only seeking to accommodate the French churches within a Church of England structure for the benefit of better conditions for future waves of refugees. That many French refugees in England, including the officially conforming Church

---

19   Gwynn, *Heritage*, p. 122–3.
20   Fontaine, *Memoirs*, p. 133.
21   Gwynn, *Heritage*, p. 126.

of the Savoy, were not fully satisfied with the support the Crown was willing to assure them, becomes evident from a petition presented in July 1681. Based on a memorial from the French Protestants of the Church of the Savoy the petitioners claimed at least 'free denisation' if not 'naturalisation', so equal rights with English Protestants.[22]

Robin Gwynn pointed out that due to the close relations established between the Savoy Church and the Church of England one could expect that many French Protestants would have been tempted to conform to take advantage of these relationships. Yet, the opposite was the case. Most French refugees in England turned towards the non-conforming churches as did their brethren in Ireland from the 1690s onwards. This was most certainly due to the fact that first, the dissenting Threadneedle congregation was able to guarantee relief and, second, that the eastern area of London offered better job opportunities.[23] Yet, it may be asked – it may be the case that Jacques Fontaine is typical of French refugees – if many Huguenots refused to conform because they considered the Anglican Church to be too close both to the Catholic Church and to the King who had persecuted them in France and thus refused conformism. In the 1680s – that is immediately after the *dragonnades* – this suspicion was probably keener because they were required to take Anglican communion to be able to enjoy the Crown's financial support.

With the accession of the Calvinist William of Orange – a 'true Protestant prince' – fears that the late Stuarts would turn England into a 'popish nation' vanished. Having vehemently helped William III in his campaign against the Jacobites, French refugees in England – and Ireland – trusted fundamentally in William's toleration policy.[24] Under William and Mary, conformism or dissent was no longer a question of loyalty towards the crown. Most Huguenots agreed with Jacques Abbadie who in 1692 defended William's policy as necessary for the survival of the Protestant church in England.[25] And some of them might even have agreed that not only the King but the entire British nation was a 'peuple liberateur duquel tous les autres attendent leur delivrance' [a liberating nation who is expected to liberate all other nations].[26] As such Britain was expected to establish the true Protestant faith all over the world.

The Huguenots' reactions in Ireland

In 1665, most of the French refugees arriving in Ireland officially conformed to the Church of Ireland. However, what was created was 'a paradoxical situation whereby the transplanted French Calvinist apparatus of an empowered consistory

---

22 Robin D. Gwynn, 'Government policy towards Huguenot Immigration and Settlement in England and Ireland', in Caldicott *et als*, *Huguenots in Ireland*, pp. 215–16.
23 Gwynn, *Heritage*, pp. 134–5.
24 Abbadie, *Défense de la nation Britannique*, pp. 64, 192, 209–10, 229, 290.
25 Ibid., pp. 14–15.
26 Ibid., pp. 505–6.

of pastors and elders, who exercised authority over the congregation's religious and social functions, existed under an Anglican canopy'.[27] Furthermore, the discipline and canons which should have been those of the Church of Ireland were replaced by the French refugees' own Calvinist discipline. Yet, Archbishop Marsh approved this very liberal interpretation of conformity, an interpretation which would remain the guiding principles of this so-called conforming church up to 1816. Psalm singing and the pastor's sermon remained central. Nevertheless, what the French refugees had to accept, if their pastors were to receive state stipends, was the Book of Common Prayer (in French translation), Episcopal ordination and the acknowledgement of the ultimate authority of the Archbishop of Dublin.[28]

Yet, the tolerance granted to the refugees who arrived in the aftermath of 1692 created a situation where large numbers of them – almost two-thirds of the newly arriving French Protestants – were unwilling to conform to the Church of Ireland. As with the group of immigrants who had arrived in Ireland following the *dragonnades* of 1681, these new immigrants came from the south of France where Protestantism was more entrenched, unlike the migrants of the Ormond years who had come mostly from northern France. Under the leadership of a self-confident reformed aristocracy they established an independent non-conforming congregation on Bride Street. Henri de Massue, Earl of Galway, tried to reconcile the dissenting and conforming parties as he feared that the Crown's support would not be guaranteed if the refugees created schism. However, as many of his 'brethren' were suspicious of his former 'quasi-sacrilegious loyalty to the French crown' his attempts to unify Ireland's *corps de refuge* and to make it assimilate to the wishes of the British crown were not supported. In particular the group of refugees arriving in Ireland directly from France, as opposed to passing through England, were less aware of the experience of the English civil war than were pastors such as Jean Durel of London. The searing memory of these new refugees was having been persecuted for their faith in France and they were therefore less willing than Huguenots coming from Britain to Ireland to give up the 'purity of their faith'.[29]

The Act of 1704 divided the *corps de refuge* in Ireland which had already consisted of conforming and dissenting churches. Ministers such as Jacques Abbadie, now Dean of Killaloe, who had conformed to the Church of Ireland, tried to convince their brethren to conform, too, to the Church of Ireland. He feared nothing more than schism which, in the end, could have separated refugees from the Crown's financial support.[30] This officially conformist party was supported by a number of conforming ministers such as Louis Saurin (Dean of Ardagh in 1726), Peter Drelincourt, Jean Jourdan and Louis Quartier and by the Precentor of St Patrick's, Elie Bouhéreau, and

---

27   Raymond Pierre Hylton, 'The Less-favoured Refuge: Ireland's Non-conformist Huguenots at the turn of the Eighteenth Century', in Kevin Herlihy (ed.), *The Religion of Irish Dissent, 1650–1800* (Blackrock, 1996), p. 85.
28   Ibid., p. 86.
29   All quotations from Hylton, pp. 86–91.
30   Whelan, p. 602.

others. They considered the act of conforming to the Church of Ireland as an 'act of civil obedience' to the Crown, a 'duty' – as Elie Bouhéreau put it in his last will – and as evidence of gratefulness towards the countries that had granted them refuge.[31] Nevertheless, this conviction did not prevent them from contributing money to one of Dublin's non-conformist congregations on Lucy Lane.[32]

Some French ministers, such as Jacques Fontaine of Cork, who in 1695 had moved from England to Ireland, remained throughout their lifetimes attached to the French Reformed Church established in Ireland. Fontaine, who would have had to accept ordination from the Bishop of Cork to maintain his ministry there, even requested that he be dismissed.[33] His refusal of the Anglican rite and hierarchy was too strong to accept any compromise. The counter argument – as expressed in the *Consideration sur le sermon de Monsieur Abbadie, pronouncé à Dublin, dans l'eglise parroissiale de St Patrick* (14 May 1704, Dublin) – was that the Act for encouragement of Protestant strangers in 1692 had granted the French refugees free exercise of their religion. Thus, the French Reformed Church had been officially allowed in Ireland and could not be considered schismatic or to be a threat to the peace of either Church or state.[34] Furthermore, the attempts by the Queen and by the Church of Ireland to suppress dissenters reminded many French Protestants of the 'papist' persecutions they had suffered in France.[35] Maintaining a French Reformed Church 'Suivant la discipline et la forme ancienne et ordinaire de nos eglises en France'[36] [according to the ancient and normal discipline of our churches in France] thus represented an important part of many refugees' identity. It was both a reaction to the British Crown's attempts to encourage them to conform to the Church of Ireland and an affirmation abroad that the French Reformed Church had survived the persecution in France and would one day return as such to France. 'The affirmation proclaims preservation of the old, unsullied faith, and keeping the torch of Coligny and Condé burning into the years of exile. Also in its deeper meaning, it was the affirmation that the exiles would presently return to the cleansed and godly France, suitable for the elect'.[37]

Conformed and dissenting churches clearly co-existed in Ireland's *corps de refuge*. Yet, what has to be borne in mind is that the conforming French Protestants – like their brethren in England – only officially conformed to the Anglican Church. Within the conforming French churches the French Protestant rites and discipline survived also up to the early nineteenth century. While the – in numbers larger[38]

---

31 Last will of Elie Bouhéreau translated and published in N.J.D. White, *Elias Bouhéreau of La Rochelle, First Public Librarian in Ireland* (Dublin, 1908), pp. 148–50.
32 Muriel McCarthy, 'Elie Bouhéreau, first public librarian in Ireland', *PHS*, 27/4 (2001): 555–6.
33 Fontaine, *Memoirs*, pp. 150–51.
34 Whelan, p. 603.
35 Ibid., p. 601.
36 Hylton, p. 83.
37 Ibid., p. 83.
38 Ibid., p. 90.

– dissenting group preferred dissent and open opposition to the 'popish Anglican Church' a smaller number of conforming refugees safeguarded parts of their Huguenot identity by officially compromising with the Church of Ireland.

There is evidence that Huguenots in Ireland, like their brethren in England, did not necessarily only react to the governments' policy towards French religious refugees but tried to directly influence the Crown's attitudes towards French Protestants. A document held by the Bodleian Library shows that under the reign of Charles II French Protestants sought to convince the English government to establish new colonies of French Protestants in Ireland. The effort already made by the Crown was – from the Huguenots' perspective – not enough to strengthen the Protestant interest in Ireland:

> La charité Chrétienne, Sire, l'exemple de vos ancestres, et le bien de vôtre état vous invitent a leur être propre et a les encourager dans leur dessein car outre les benedictions du ciel et l'amour de tous les protestants, que V.M. peut s'atirer par le nombre de vos sujets et de vos revenus peut s'acroitre notablement par l'accession d'un peuple dont l'industrie, et le travaill sera capable d'apporter dans peu de temps l'abondance, la richesse, et la sureté par la culture des terres que V.M. leur permettra de planter[,] par leur application au commerce et par leur vigilance, et leur fidelité.[39]

> [Christian charity, Sire, the example of your ancestors and the well-being of your state invite you to meet their expectations and to support them in their designs, because apart from the blessings of Heaven and the love of all Protestants, of which His Majesty disposes, the number of your subjects and of the amount of your income could increase with the accession of a nation whose industriousness and labour would produce in little time affluence, riches and safety by cultivating the soil which Your Majesty will allow them, by their application to the trade and their vigilance, and their fidelity].

Furthermore, French Calvinists' petitions to the Crown which concerned the 'promotion of the true Protestant faith' – and it could be doubted that the French refugees thought that this was the Anglican rite – can be found in the collections of the British Library. In 1712, the French Protestants of Kilkenny asked first the Lord Lieutenant, James, Duke of Ormonde, then Queen Anne herself to establish in Kilkenny a 'Minister of our own Nation', which meant that the officially conforming French refugees refused an English-speaking Anglican minister. The Crown was expected to support the French Protestant interest in Ireland and the maintenance of French services.[40]

---

39   'Address from Protestants in France to Charles II, praying for liberty to remove into Ireland, 17th c.', Bodleian Library, Rawlinson MS A 478.
40   British Library, Additional MS 21132.

Conclusion

It is evident that in both countries of refuge the Huguenot Diaspora was divided as to the questions of dissent or conformity. Voices preaching for conformity could be heard in both England and Ireland. Pastors such as Jean Durel and Jacques Abbadie of London and Peter Drelincourt and Elie Bouhéreau, not to speak of Henri de Massue in Ireland, tried to convince their brethren that it was the refugees' duty to conform to the Established Church of the respective kingdoms. Yet, it seems that these voices – even though somewhat stronger in England than in Ireland – were not representative for the majority of Huguenots in either of those kingdoms. In spite of differing government attitudes towards French reformed refugees, a larger percentage of French Reformed Protestants were unwilling to conform to the established rules of the official Protestant Churches of the respective kingdoms in the interest of safeguarding their French Protestant identity. Both the Church of England and the Church of Ireland were considered to be too close to 'popery' and even if opposition meant that government help might be withheld from the refugees loyalty to the Huguenot faith seems to have been more valuable to them than economic relief.

For both countries it has equally to be stated that French refugees were sufficiently self-confident to seek for more than what the governments were willing to give them. Thus, they attempted, especially in Ireland, to strengthen the French Protestant interest and they sought to better the legal status of Huguenots in both kingdoms. It seems that the aim was both naturalisation and the maintenance of their unsullied French reformed faith.

In Ireland, the Acts of 1662 and 1692 had provided French refugees with a much better legal basis than had been the case in England. Thus, Huguenots in Ireland were in a better position to defend their French Calvinist faith against the efforts of the Established Church to make them conform. The attempt in 1695 to economically 'blackmail' French ministers and that of 1704, to influence every refugee who held a state pension, failed abysmally. From the sources so far analysed, it thus seems that the Huguenots' resistance in Ireland against conformism seems to have been much stronger than those of their dissenting brethren in England.

Defining the questions of conformism and dissent in the British Isles as a relevant indicator as to the degree of assimilation of Protestant strangers, it has to be stated that in both kingdoms between 1660 and 1710 only a small number of Huguenots who mostly entertained close relationships with the King were willing to assimilate. Up to 1710, most Huguenots in England and Ireland were still not willing to conform and to give up their distinct Huguenot identity and faith. Furthermore, even those churches officially conforming to the established one conserved important Calvinist elements in liturgy and church government.

Chapter 3

The *Oxford Dictionary of National Biography*, the du Moulin Connection and the Location of the Church of England in the Later Seventeenth Century

Vivienne Larminie
University of Oxford, UK

The *Oxford Dictionary of National Biography*, as published in September 2004, contains nearly 9,500 mentions of the word France.[1] Even more than its late nineteenth century predecessor, the *Dictionary of National Biography*, it includes hundreds of people born there.[2] Among over 150 born between 1500 and 1700, we encounter queens consort like Madeleine de Valois, Marie de Guise and Henrietta Maria, as well as more humble subjects like Isaac Oliver the miniature painter, Pierre-Esprit Radisson the trader and explorer, and Marie Maillard, alleged beneficiary of miraculous healing. The old dictionary was generous in its inclusion of non-native people. The new, building on this liberal definition, has been even more imaginative: over the dictionary as a whole, there are more physicians, merchants, non-metropolitan figures and women, and in the early-modern period many of these are foreigners.[3]

---

1 H.C.G. Matthew and Brian Harrison (eds), *Oxford Dictionary of National Biography* (Oxford, 2004). Hereafter cited as *Oxford DNB*.
2 Leslie Stephen and Sidney Lee (eds), *Dictionary of National Biography* [hereafter *DNB*] (60 vols, London, 1885–1901). I wish to thank Professor Brian Harrison, Editor 2000–2004, and my present colleagues on the research staff of the dictionary for the many conversations which helped shape my thinking for this article. For an earlier discussion of 'foreigners' in the dictionary, see Vivienne Larminie, 'Immigrants in the *DNB* and British cultural horizons, 1550–1750', in Vigne and Littleton, *Strangers*, pp. 175–83.
3 On general differences between the old and new dictionaries, see for example: Brian Harrison, 'National Biography for a Computer Age', *History Today*, 51/8 (August 2001): 16–18, and Robert Faber and Brian Harrison, 'The *Dictionary of National Biography*: A Publishing History', in Robin Myers, Michael Harris and Giles Mandelbrote (eds), *Lives in Print: Biography and the Book Trade from the Middle Ages to the 21st Century* (London, 2002), pp. 171–92; 'Introduction', *Oxford DNB*, vol. 1, also accessible online at http://www.oxforddnb.com.

It is now easier to locate them, despite the fact that the text runs to 60 million words. The dictionary appeared simultaneously in 60 printed volumes and online. In the latter case, electronic tagging of key biographical information and a facility to search running text allows systematic interrogation of the dictionary. Thus between 1500 and 1700 we find seven subjects born in Rouen and 35 born in Paris; in the same two centuries there are 21 men educated at the University of Montpellier, and 19 at the Académie de Saumur.[4] References to Geneva, whether to the city, its students, its visitors or the version of the Bible in English, are legion. Huguenots (nearly 700 occurrences of the word) can be located not only in their own articles but in those of others; their links with each other and with their friends and patrons in Britain may be readily uncovered. We are reminded, for example, of the Huguenot chaplains of John Fell, bishop of Oxford, and the Huguenot clients of John Cosin, bishop of Durham.[5] We can trace some of the influence wielded by Huguenots who do not have their own article: there are 22 references to Pierre Bayle.

Statistics aside, compared to its predecessor the *Oxford DNB* also sees a qualitative increase in coverage, which in its turn illuminates Huguenot lives. The dictionary benefits from much greater precision with regard to foreign sources and foreign placenames; its 10,000 contributors have been drawn from around the world and some have appropriately international expertise.[6] People who in the old dictionary received a passing mention which left the reader puzzled as to why they had been included at all, now receive much longer entries, for instance Isaac Dubourdieu, Jean Despagne and Claude Groteste de la Mothe.[7] Whereas nineteenth-century

---

4   Of course, not everyone in the dictionary born in France was French, or born to French parents: among subjects recorded as born in France were children of royalist exiles of the 1640s and 1650s, like Charles Gerard, second earl of Macclesfield, James Stanhope, first earl Stanhope, and Jane Stuart, illegitimate daughter of the future James II. English and Scots account for a majority of dictionary subjects educated at Montpellier, but almost all subjects educated at Saumur were French-born.

5   Moïse Amyraut and Jean Daillé appear in Anthony Milton, 'John Cosin', *Oxford DNB*.

6   There has been a concerted attempt to ascribe towns and lands to the appropriate state or principality for the date, and an encouragement to contributors to pin down the political context of places like Sedan or Metz.

7   F.T. Marzials, 'Isaac Dubourdieu', *DNB*, in about 100 words notes a good pastor who took refuge in London and published a work on monarchical obedience; Vivienne Larminie, 'Isaac Dubourdieu', *Oxford DNB*, over 700 words, mentions his early career in France, the extended family which accompanied him to England, and the content of his work. F.T. Marzials, 'Jean Despagne', *DNB*, gives an intriguing but disjointed 280-word depiction of a critic of Calvin; Larminie, 'Jean Despagne', *Oxford DNB*, five times longer, reveals him as a respected authority on Calvin with many well-placed patrons, and as a liturgical conservative who still enjoyed favour under the protectorate. J.G. Alger, 'Claude Grostête de la Mothe' *DNB*, mentions two devotional works in a short article; Larminie, 'Claude Groteste de la Mothe', *Oxford DNB* reveals his far-flung and politically varied network of friends and correspondents, his arguments (in the tradition of John Durel, see below) for the *Correspondance fraternelle de l'église anglicane avec les autres églises réformées et*

entries may simply mention in passing the devotional or the literary publications of French Reformed ministers, or append lists of works at the end of the article, the new version also gives attention to the religious controversies in which they were engaged and, following the general policy of the dictionary, looks at their lives in the round. It integrates discussion of their family and public life with analysis of their writings at the chronological point at which they were composed. Thus we can more clearly view the works of Pierre du Moulin against the shifting context of Huguenot relations with Louis XIII, Richelieu and Mazarin, and of James VI and I's international ecumenical schemes, or of Peter Allix against the backdrop of later seventeenth-century theological disputes.[8]

Two men who in *DNB* suffered from attention so slight and glancing that their presence is hard to justify were Pierre du Moulin's sons Peter (1601–84) and Lewis (1605?–80).[9] In the interim, both have received some attention from historians, but neither, until the new dictionary, have been subjected to sustained and rounded analysis from an English perspective.[10] Peter makes several vivid but fleeting appearances in Bernard Cottret's *Terre d'exil*, translated as *The Huguenots in England*, as an indefatigable apologist for conformity to the Church of England.[11] So in most respects he was, but it is difficult to place him on the basis of these scattered references, and as a result his role in the canon of Anglo-French ecclesiological writing is obscured, and one or two disconcerting aspects of his career are overlooked. At the same time, the controversial nature of some of his later work is underplayed.[12] Peter's younger brother Lewis, on the other hand, was depicted by some contemporaries, including members of his own extended family, as a maverick figure, who in a final act of

---

étrangères (1705), and his role in advancing and publicising the work of the Society for Promoting Christian Knowledge (SPCK) and Society for the Propagation of the Gospel (SPG). In the text of this article I have used the form of names under which people are entered in the dictionary, usually that by which they were known in England by their contemporaries; in the notes I have given the form of name on the title page of the published work cited.

8   While the *DNB* article conveys neither the stature of Pierre du Moulin on the European stage nor the significance of his links with England, a much enlarged study by Brian G. Armstrong and Vivienne Larminie in *Oxford DNB* considers the importance of his writings and the nature of his collaboration with James VI and I, as well as exploring the character and motivation of this aristocratic leader of the Reformed church. At least half of W.G. Blaikie, 'Peter Allix', *DNB*, is devoted to listing his publications; Larminie, 'Peter Allix', *Oxford DNB*, analyses them in chronological context.

9   J.G. Alger, 'Peter du Moulin', *DNB*, is short and somewhat misleading on the chronology of Peter's activities in the 1640s and 1650s, following sources like Haag, vol. 4, pp. 430–31. J.G. Alger, 'Lewis du Moulin', *DNB* (1894) is dominated by a list of his publications, but fails to convey the scope and nature of his writings.

10 The most illuminating discussion of both is in Mark Goldie, 'The Huguenot Experience and the Problem of Toleration in Restoration England', Caldicott *et al.*, *Huguenots in Ireland*, pp. 188–96, but its focus on the toleration question and the constraints of space do not permit comprehensive biographical or contextual comment.

11 Bernard Cottret, *Huguenots in England*, pp. 87, 121, 128.

12 'Peter du Moulin', *Oxford DNB*.

deathbed repentance, saw the inescapable foolishness of his ways and apologised for his ungracious behaviour. Since then his political thought has received some serious scrutiny, but he has still been dismissed as a 'black sheep' who fitted no particular mould.[13] These perspectives also contain some truth, but Lewis's writings were at the same time more reasoned, and more subtle than has been recognised, and at the same time less unlike those of his conformist contemporaries.[14]

The lens through which we view seventeenth-century religion and politics has altered outside and inside the dictionary. The eminent historians Charles Firth and Samuel Rawson Gardiner, who wrote so many fine articles on figures from that period for the old version, saw early-modern Britain through the eyes of the late nineteenth century.[15] For all their respect for the 'Puritan revolution', and for the 'good old cause' of those who wanted to resist absolutist government and Arminianism in the church, their outlook was essentially secular. They saw the conflict through political rather than religious lenses, focusing on issues that presaged constitutional progress and legal toleration rather than on the nuances of opinion within the Church of England or the details of theological controversy which so exercised seventeenth-century writers. There was a tendency, replicated especially among some of the other historians who wrote about lesser figures, to apply retrospectively the party and denominational labels of the Victorian age: to their eyes, religious conformity was clear-cut; those who did not choose it were confidently labelled Roman Catholic, Presbyterian, Independent or fanatic.[16]

After a century of intense study of the period we now have a clearer grasp of the European dimension both of the sixteenth-century reformation and of seventeenth-century piety and ecclesiology, as well as a contemporary awareness of the combustible mixture of religion and politics.[17] Appreciation that episcopacy lingered in Scotland where once it had seemed that the Presbyterian triumph was instant and complete, and of the fact that episcopacy meant different things to different people all over Britain, has introduced greater subtlety into the positioning within the Protestant spectrum of the national Churches of England and Scotland.[18] As we

---

13   Cottret, *The Huguenots*, pp. 179–80.

14   'Lewis du Moulin', *Oxford DNB*.

15   They themselves have articles in *Oxford DNB*, as do many of their colleagues writing for *DNB*, freed from the relative anonymity of their initials.

16   Comments like this were made by several of the associate editors who reviewed seventeenth-century religious subjects in the old dictionary prior to making recommendations on commissioning for the new.

17   Among the most notable recent studies to view English religion in a European context are: Diarmaid MacCulloch, *Thomas Cranmer: A Life* (New Haven and London, 1996); Anthony Milton, *Catholic and Reformed: The Roman and Protestant Churches in English Protestant Thought, 1600–1640* (Cambridge, 1995); W.B. Patterson, *James VI and I and the Reunion of Christendom* (Cambridge, 1997).

18   For Scotland, see for example: Alan Macdonald, *The Jacobean Kirk, 1567–1625: Sovereignty, Polity and Liturgy* (Aldershot, 1998); David G. Mullan, *Scottish Puritanism, 1590–1638* (Oxford, 2000); Julia Buckroyd, *Church and State in Scotland, 1660–1681*

examine religious writers and their works in the round, a complex mesh of shifting viewpoints often becomes evident. People commonly took inconsistent stances on burning religious questions, changing their minds over time and with changing political circumstance. Equally, there seems to have been a substantial constituency of quiet moderates, perhaps a silent majority.[19] Party lines were fluid and labels often prove inadequate, yet we have learned that, for some, opinions were no less passionately held and no less inflammatory in their effects.

This has both resulted in reassessments in the dictionary, and emerged as a conclusion even more strongly from it. Space allows detailed discussion only of the du Moulin brothers and brief mention of a few of their circle. Nonetheless, I am conscious of the influence on my arguments both of the evidence of dozens of other English and French clergy I have contributed, but also of the hundreds I have been privileged to edit. Interconnections, common themes, shared preoccupations and parallel complexities have been revealed to a fascinating degree.

As became apparent when I came to write Jean Durel, the significance of *this* French-speaking minister on Anglican apologetics had been recognised both in Huguenot Society publications through the twentieth century, and more recently in the work of Cottret and of John Hintermaier.[20] This was the man who in 1661 claimed approbation of the English *Book of Common Prayer* by all continental Reformed churches and demanded adherence to it by all in England.[21] On the occasion of the inauguration of the French chapel at the Savoy Palace, licensed by Charles II to use only that liturgy, he pre-empted the result of the conference on the Church of England's future then taking place in the same building.[22] The text of his

---

(Edinburgh, c.1980), and *The Life of James Sharp, Archbishop of St Andrews, 1618–1679* (Edinburgh, c.1987). Among many distinguished studies on England, see: Patrick Collinson, *The Religion of Protestants: The Church in English Society, 1559–1625* (Oxford, 1982); Nicholas Tyacke, *Anti-Calvinists: The Rise of English Arminianism c.1590–1640* (Oxford, 1987); Kenneth Fincham, *Prelate as Pastor: The Episcopate of James I* (Oxford, 1990); Tom Webster, *Godly Clergy in Early Stuart England: The Caroline Puritan Movement, 1620–1643* (Cambridge, 1997); John Spurr, *English Puritanism, 1603–1689* (Basingstoke, 1998), and *The Restoration Church of England, 1646–1689* (New Haven, 1991).

19   See for example: Judith Maltby, *Prayer Book and People in Elizabethan and Early Stuart England* (Cambridge, 1998).

20   A.G. Browning, 'The influence asserted by the Huguenot Refugees of the seventeenth and eighteenth centuries upon the social and professional life of England', *PHS*, 7 (1901–04): 309–10; D.N. Griffiths, 'The translation of the English Prayer Book', *PHS*, 22/2 (1972): 95–6; Cottret, *The Huguenots*, p. 178; John McDonnell Hintermaier, 'Rewriting the Church of England: Jean Durel and the polemics of Restoration conformity' in Vigne and Littleton, *Strangers*, pp. 353–8, esp. p. 355. See also 'John Durel', *Oxford DNB*.

21   Jean Durel, *Sermon prononcé en l'eglise francoise* (London, 1661).

22   Mary Anne Everett Green (ed.), *Calendar of State Papers Domestic Series, of the Reign of Charles II, 1660–1661* (London, 1860), p. 529 (grant dated 10 March 1661). On the debate then taking place in the English Church, and the positions existing within it, see: Robert S. Bosher, *The Making of the Restoration Settlement: The Influence of the Laudians, 1649–1662*, revised edition (London, 1957); Spurr, *Restoration Church of England*.

sermon was 1 *Corinthians* 11: 6, 's'il y a quelqu'un qui pense estre contentieux, nous n'avons point une telle coustume, ni aussi les eglises de Dieu' ['if anyone wants to be contentious about this, we have no other practice, nor do the churches of God']. As the English translation of the sermon published in 1662 proclaimed, it was *The Liturgy of the Church of England Asserted*, and it received weighty social and political endorsement. In its previous manifestation at Durham House, Westminster (an evocative address), Durel's conservative French congregation had attracted to its services 'many of the Nobility, and the best of the Gentry, who rendered both to God and Caesar their due', or so Henry Brown noted in editing the work of its first pastor, Jean Despagne.[23] Philip Herbert, earl of Pembroke, John Egerton, earl of Bridgewater, and the countess of Annandale had been among its patrons.[24] The inaugural meeting at the Savoy attracted the premier Irish peer, Ormond (to whom Durel's published sermon was to be dedicated), leading English and Scottish nobles, and, in the person of the countess of Derby, a representative of the Huguenot super-élite, Charlotte de la Trémoïlle.[25]

Durel's base of support abroad was apparently equally impressive. In his next work, *A View of the Government and Publick Worship of God in the Reformed Churches beyond the Seas* (London, 1662), he printed letters of approval from the great and the good in Europe. For example, he quoted that from the eminent Rouen minister Jean-Maximilien de Baux de l'Angle (1590–1674), son-in-law of the equally eminent René Bochart, who had written in May 1661 to give his seal of approval, and by implication that of the Huguenots of Normandy, to 'the establishment of the Anglico-Gallicane church that the king your soveraigne hath made' ['l'establishment que le Roy vostre maistre a fait de l'Eglise Anglico-Gallicane'].[26] Although many avenues remain to be explored, it is clear that, while Durel may not have enjoyed quite the level of foreign endorsement he claimed, he was only one representative of a strong body of opinion. The role of John Cosin, Bishop of Durham, in the Anglico-Gallican cause and its advocates has been noticed, but de l'Angle's cousin Peter du Moulin, who in the summer of 1661 was working for Cosin, also played an important part.[27]

---

23   John Despagne, *An Essay of the Wonders of God* (London, 1662), sig. r2v. See also 'Jean Despagne', *Oxford DNB*.

24   Jean Despagne, *Abrege du sermon funebre sur la mort du tres-honorable Phillipe comte de Pembroke & Montgomery, advenue le 23 de Janvier l'an 1650* (London, [1651]), p. 17; C.L. Hamilton, 'Jean d'Espagne and the earl of Bridgewater (1622–1686)', *PHS*, 24/3 (1987): 232–9; *Journal of the House of Lords*, vol. 5 (1802), p. 566.

25   [White Kennett], *A Register and Chronicle, Ecclesiastical and Civil* (London, 1728), vol. 1, p. 494.

26   John Durel, *A View of the Government and Publick Worship of God in the Reformed Churches beyond the Seas* (London, 1662), p. 70. The work was dedicated to Charles II's chief minister, Edward Hyde, earl of Clarendon.

27   S. Doyle, '*La messe trouvée dans l'Escriture*: a new attribution', *PHS*, 24/5 (1987): 457–8.

In 1662 du Moulin published *The Novelty of Popery*, a translation of a work by his father. In the preface he revealed that Durel's *Vindication* owed much to collaborative effort by an international group of ministers. He also deployed similar arguments to Durel, but if possible more trenchantly. At the time of the Restoration, he asserted, 'a great cloud of French witnesses came over in favour of Episcopacie'.[28] Many letters from 'the prime Divines of France' were addressed to Durel's fellow Channel Islander, Daniel Brevint.[29] Brevint in turn 'commited them unto me', but when du Moulin left London for his prebend in Canterbury, he 'transmitted them to that deserving Master Durel, as one better able then I to make good use of them, among many other intelligences of the like nature. His excellent book about this matter, the substance whereof he was pleased to impart unto me, will ease me of that labour, and shorten my task'.

Du Moulin left it to Durel to defend the English liturgy, but set out even more starkly the English church's superiority. 'We have more of the Primitive and Apostolick Church-Government in England then any other Church in the rest of the world'.[30] Other Reformed churches, living under the cross, should be treated with 'compassion', 'not anger', however. 'The Anglican Church had Kings for her nursing Fathers, and Queens for her nursing Mothers: Whereas the French Churches were crusht from the Cradle with all the strength and indignation of their Kings and Queens'.[31]

The tone of patronising condescension toward those poor French unfortunates who were forced by political necessity to live without bishops, instead of under 'fatherly government and superintendancy', may or may not have been intentional.[32] But not content, like Durel, to invoke Calvin in support of episcopacy, with apparent deliberation he also turned the reformer and his city off their Protestant pedestal. 'I say it is utterly false ... that Calvin was one of the Planters of the Reformed Religion at Geneva': that accolade, he claimed, belonged to Guillaume Farel and Pierre Viret. 'My Lord Bishop of Durham, my most noble and constant friend,' he insisted, 'hath searcht into that business ... with great diligence'. In any case, the Reformation predated Calvin, the Geneva Bible was the work of English exiles, and 'howsoever matters were carried at Geneva, the Protestants of France were not answerable for their actions'.[33]

This was no mere Restoration opportunism. Unlike many who hailed the reintroduction of episcopacy, du Moulin had been rehearsing the same message for years. There are indications that another work in the same vein, *The History of the English and Scotch Presbytery*, sometimes ascribed to Isaac Basire, was actually by du Moulin. The British Library 1659 copy, endorsed 'Aprill', and Huntingdon

---

28   Pierre du Moulin, *The Novelty of Popery* (London, 1662), p. 9.
29   See Kenneth W. Stevenson, 'Daniel Brevint', *Oxford DNB*.
30   Du Moulin, *The Novelty of Popery*, p. 2.
31   Ibid., p. 11.
32   Ibid., p. 7.
33   Ibid., p. 6.

Library 1660 second edition, labelled on the title page in a similar hand 'Du Moulin P', is consistent with his other work.[34] Whatever the truth of that, however, du Moulin had expressed himself trenchantly on the subject as early as March 1640 in *A Letter of a French Protestant to a Scotishman of the Covenant*. Acknowledging the 'auld alliance' between Scotland and France, he nonetheless took the Scots to task for presuming on French Huguenot support in their rebellion against King Charles's attempts to introduce the Prayer Book.

His arguments in favour of Scottish episcopacy seem less ridiculous now historians are more aware that the triumph of Presbyterianism in Scotland was neither complete nor inevitable. Although it was said that the Scottish reformation began with the people, du Moulin claimed, it was not perfected until the king 'put the last hand to it, by reforming and restoring Bishops'. The French churches living under the cross were denied by their king the bishops they would otherwise have accepted, but they 'have no jurisdiction, and looke for none'. The Scots Presbyterians should 'contain themselves in the same modestie' and desist from 'fram[ing] another Ecclesiastical Discipline'; they should learn from Huguenot setbacks of the 1610s and 1620s and desist from challenging their king. Du Moulin himself was 'happily engrafted into the body of the Church of England ... And ... assured in my conscience, that when I was adopted by [that church] I was not removed to another Gospel'.[35]

Yet du Moulin did not always sit comfortably with the English episcopate, nor always express himself as an uncompromising episcopalian. Having arrived in England in the mid 1620s, by 1628 he had become chaplain to Lord Strange, husband of Charlotte de la Trémoïlle, and by 1630 he had migrated to the Church of England ministry.[36] Gilbert Primerose, minister of the French church in London, told du Moulin's uncle, André Rivet, that the motive was laziness, and indeed a reputation for idleness seems to have been widespread.[37] In 1635 du Moulin was summoned before the court of high commission, apparently for neglecting his parish in Leicestershire.[38] Although he participated in the vehement pamphleteering against

---

34 The editions are easily compared via *Early English Books Online*, by subscription or in major libraries.

35 Peter Du Moulin, *A Letter of a French Protestant to a Scotishman of the Covenant* (London, 1640), pp. 24, 27.

36 His verse celebration of James I, *Petri Molinaei filii carmen heroicum ad regem* (London, 1625), published the year that he presented his second thesis at Leyden, looks like an opening bid for patronage. On 3 February 1631 he wrote from London to secretary of state Dudley Carleton, Viscount Dorchester, to vindicate himself from accusations of idleness and immoral behaviour allegedly put before Charles I, stating that he had been chaplain to Lord Strange for the past three years, and that the bishop of Exeter had known of him even longer: *Calendar of State Papers Domestic Series, of the Reign of Charles I*, ed. John Bruce (23 vols, London, 1858–97), vol. 4 (*1629–31*), p. 497 [hereafter cited as *CSP Domestic + date*].

37 F.N.L. Poynter [and W. le Fanu], 'A seventeenth century London plague document in the Wellcome Historical Medical Library: Dr du Moulin's proposals to Parliament for a corps of salaried plague doctors', *Bulletin of the History of Medicine*, 34 (1960): 370.

38 *CSP Domestic 1635*, pp. 200, 208, 215; *CSP Domestic 1635–36*, p. 89.

the regicide in 1649–52, and had to retire to Ireland under the protection of the Boyle family, by the later 1650s he, like some of his patrons, had attained a surprisingly high profile within the Commonwealth.[39] With permission from the Council of State to hold office, between 1656 and 1658 he preached frequently in Oxford, whence he had accompanied Charles Boyle, viscount Dungarvan, and his younger brother, Richard Boyle; in 1657 and 1658 he accepted ministerial preferment.[40] He gained the approval of that uncategorisable Puritan stalwart Richard Baxter, and he returned the regard. Grateful to Baxter for defending mainstream royalist clergy against those who insisted 'the Episcopal are halfe Papists', he claimed that he was simply 'a French Protestant ... nothing engaged to the Episcopal party but an hereditary dislike of all violent ways of subjects to their soveraine'.[41]

This may sound disingenuous, but it may be revealing of a paradox at the heart of the thinking of many contemporary French and English Protestant conformists. Here du Moulin's political loyalty apparently trumped his episcopalianism, but it was insufficient to overcome his persistent anti-popery.[42] As the century progressed he found just as much of a potential clash between his royalism and his anti-catholicism as did notable Englishmen like Bishop John Fell of Oxford. When Du Moulin had first given notice of a Jesuit plot in *A Letter of a Frenchman*, accusing the order of masterminding Presbyterian rebellion in Scotland in the 1630s, it had been in a context where such comments might pass as unremarkable. But his 1664 work, *A Vindication of the Sincerity of the Protestant Religion in the Point of Obedience to the Sovereign*, and even more, his subsequent letter to Secretary of State Sir William Morrice, not only claimed that the martyrdom of Charles I was another Jesuit plot but also named the courtier Sir Kenelm Digby as its instigator. Out of tune with Restoration court politics, this provoked what du Moulin himself described as a

---

39   [Peter du Moulin], *Ecclesia gemitus sub anabaptistica tyrannide* (n.p., 1649) and *Regii sanguinis clamor ad coelum adversus paricidas Anglicanos* ([London], 1652). In June 1649 he was rector of Londesborough, Yorkshire, but he had left before 19 January 1652: A.G. Matthews, *Walker Revised, being a revision of John Walker's Sufferings of the Clergy during the Grand Rebellion 1642–60* (1948; Oxford, 1988), p. 392. According to the dedication to the third edition of his *A Week of Soliloquies and Prayers* (London, 1677), that work, which first appeared in 1657, was based on meditations presented to Elizabeth Boyle (née Clifford), countess of Cork, when he was living in her household about 1654.

40   Anthony Wood, 'Fasti Oxonienses' in *Athenae Oxonienses*, ed. Philip Bliss, 4 + 2 vols (Oxford, 1813–20), vol. 2, p. 195, says that he preached 'constantly for a considerable time in the church of St Peter in the East'. Du Moulin's DD from Leyden was incorporated at Oxford on 10 October 1656; the Boyle brothers matriculated as students of the university from Christ Church on 25 November: see also Joseph Foster, *Alumni Oxonienses 1500–1714* (4 vols, London, 1891–92), under 'Boyle'. Du Moulin was admitted to the vicarage of Bradwell, Buckinghamshire, on 20 October 1657 and instituted to the rectory of Adisham, Kent, on 8 October 1658 (*Walker Revised*, p. 392).

41   *Calendar of the Correspondence of Richard Baxter*, ed. Neil H. Keeble and Geoffrey F. Nuttall (2 vols, Oxford, 1991), vol. 1, pp. 412–13.

42   See also Goldie, 'The Huguenot Experience', p. 190.

storm.⁴³ 'We live in the worst of times', proclaimed du Moulin in a sermon of 1669.⁴⁴ As the duke of York's Catholicism became a more topical theme, du Moulin's pen never faltered, however ill his writings sat with his position as a royal chaplain. There appeared the ironically titled *The Great Loyalty of the Papists to K. Charles I ... Discovered* (1673), as well as *The Papal Tyranny* (1674) and *The Ruine of Papacy* (1678).

Unlike his brother, Lewis du Moulin was not a clergyman but a physician.⁴⁵ He had begun his career as a polemicist in 1637 with a Latin translation of one of his father's works, but departing from both father and brother, in 1639 he tells us that he 'wrote a piece ... against the corrupted part of the English hierarchy'.⁴⁶ He did not reject episcopacy per se, however, appearing instead to accept the 'primitive' version exemplified by the likes of Joseph Hall, bishop of Exeter. His anonymously published *Vox populi* (1641), a characteristically systematic and logical programme addressed to parliament, proposed an international convocation of clergy to reform the English Church. Delegates were to include Archbishop James Ussher of Armagh, Gilbert Primerose, his own father Pierre, and his uncle Rivet from Leyden. His programme – synods to work with bishops, carefully selected clergy, abolition of crucifixes and bowing at communion, and so on – would have been palatable to many in the early seventeenth-century mainstream; indeed, he specifically referred back to the standards set by James I and the Synod of Dort. But his solution to present ills went in a diametrically opposite direction to his brother's. He proposed that 'since our neighbour Churches have enjoyed more peace and safety under their discipline, our discipline bee framed upon the patron of theirs', though it should not be a slavish imitation: 'a sensible difference' was to be 'kept betweene theirs and ours'.⁴⁷ In his *Aytomaxia* (1643), reason, the foundation of his argument, dismissed the claim that God had 'expresly prescribe[d]' either episcopacy and presbytery; still less did he accept his brother's contention that episcopacy was unsuitable for a republic or presbytery unserviceable in a monarchy.⁴⁸ He was just as conscious of writing in a

---

43   British Library, Additional MS 8880, fol. 190, Peter du Moulin to William Sancroft from Canterbury, 12 January 1664.

44   Peter du Moulin, *A Sermon Preach'd at St Martin's Church ... Canterbury, Sept 14 1669* (London, 1709).

45   R.W. Innes Smith, *English-speaking Students of Medicine at the University of Leyden* (Edinburgh, 1932), p. 74; Poynter, pp. 370, 372. His MD was incorporated at Cambridge on 10 October 1634 and at Oxford on 14 July 1649, and he was admitted a licenciate of the College of Physicians on 7 February 1640. See John and J.A. Venn, *Alumni Cantabrigienses: from Earliest Times to 1751* (4 vols, Cambridge, 1922); William Munk, *The Roll of the Royal College of Physicians of London*, 2nd edition (3 vols, London, 1878), vol. 1, p. 227.

46   Lewis du Moulin, *Petri Molinaei SS. Theol. Doct & Profess. Anatome missae* (London, 1637), and *Of the Right of Churches* (1658), preface.

47   Irenaus Philadelphus [Lewis du Moulin], *Vox populi, expressed in xxxv motions to this present parliament* (London, 1641), p. 3.

48   Irenaeus Philanax [Lewis du Moulin], *Aytomaxia: or, the Selfe-Contradiction of some that contend about Church-Government* (London, 1643), p. 70.

European context, however, and just as concerned to mediate events in Britain to the wider world, as seen also in his *Declaratio regnorum Angliae et Scotiae* (1645).

Over the 1640s and 1650s Lewis's thoughts on the church changed little. Although political circumstances led him to conclude in *The Power of the Christian Magistrate* (1650) and *The Right of Churches* (1658) that private, Independent churches might be more expedient than one national church, he rejected neither episcopacy nor Presbyterianism, nor even some overarching ecclesiastical power. Indeed, he approved the royal supremacy of Elizabeth I, of James I and of Richard Hooker's *Laws of Ecclesiastical Polity*. He was a friend of prominent Puritans like John Owen and Richard Baxter, but also of Bishop Joseph Hall. Acknowledging a particular debt to the 'poor and mild' Hebraist Thomas Coleman, he rejected the inflammatory words of some Presbyterians like the Scots and the vituperative Thomas Edwards.

But he located his thought within a European, Erastian, Reformed mainstream, claiming much agreement with Zwingli, Bullinger, Bucer and John Jewel, and contemporaries like Rivet, moderate Puritans Edward Reynolds (later a Restoration bishop) and Jeremiah Burroughes, as well as ministers of Dieppe whom he had never met. Yet, he insisted, 'I honour the persons, learning and piety of those that I assent to, and dissent from' and 'I would make all churches and brethren friends without prejudice to the truth'.[49] He envisaged 'a National Church-way for Christians of all sizes and growth, particularly for the main body of the people of the land'.[50]

After the Restoration Lewis's moderation became obscured as he and others reacted to the changed political situation.[51] Baxter had found him 'more patient of confutation, contradiction and reproof than most men that I ever disputed with', but it is the judgement of the royalist anti-Puritan Anthony Wood which has thus far stuck: 'a fiery, violent and hot-headed independent, a cross and ill-natured man'.[52] Whatever the subtleties of his view of ecclesiastical settlement, the Hobbesian cast of his political arguments and the determination of a layman to engage in religious controversy had alarmed, and continued to alarm, conservative contemporaries,

---

49   Lewis du Moulin, *Of the Right of Churches and of the Magistrates Power over them* (London, 1658), pp. 6v–7r.

50   Lewis du Moulin, *Proposals and Reasons ... Humbly presented to the parliament* (London, 1659), p. 22.

51   In August 1646 du Moulin had been granted the Camden professorship of history at the University of Oxford, although he was not actually installed until 1648. In dedicating his inaugural oration to John Owen of Christ Church, he indicated that his tenure of the position was not without its difficulties, but like some others appointed during the late 1640s and 1650s, he was ejected in 1660. See Mordechai Feingold, 'The Humanities' and Blair Worden, 'Cromwellian Oxford' in Nicholas Tyacke (ed.), *The History of the University of Oxford*, vol. 4, *Seventeenth Century Oxford* (Oxford, 1996), esp. pp. 348–9 and pp. 754–60. Peter du Moulin petitioned unsuccessfully for the restoration to Lewis of both the professorship and the rectory of Llanrhaiadar, Denbighshire: *CSP Domestic 1660–1661*, p. 230.

52   Douglas Nobbs, 'New light on Louis du Moulin', *PHS*, 15 (1936): 491; 'Louis du Moulin', *DNB*.

both clerical and lay.[53] Even Richard Baxter, when he read the complimentary copy of Lewis's *Jugulum causae* (1671), a rejection of Voetius's claims for the political power of the church, responded to the gift by telling the author that he had taken insufficient account of ecclesiastical authority.[54] When in 1672 du Moulin published in Latin for an international audience his refutation of Jean Durel's *Vindication of the Church of England*, it was considered so offensive that he earned a spell in prison.[55] By this time Durel was the husband of the du Moulins's cousin Marie de l'Angle, and Peter, outraged by his brother's effrontery, had already withdrawn his financial support.[56]

In the dedication to the defiant *La tyrannie des prejugez* (1678), Lewis asserted the right of a physician, 'd'une profession plus désintéressée & dégagée de tout préjugé' ['a profession more disinterested and unencumbered by prejudice'], to engage in ecclesiastical controversy.[57] In this work he took on his sister Marie du Moulin, his nephew Pierre Jurieu and a swathe of leading French ministers, while in 1679 he had a bruising exchange with Jean-Maximilien de l'Angle as the latter took him to task for his disloyalty to church and family.[58] None the less, he was capable of appreciating his adversaries' viewpoints, even when they came from within his own family.[59] His evident hurt was grounded in a conviction that they had misunderstood him, and a close reading of his writings suggests that they probably had. Lewis's *A True Report* (1679) and *A Short and True Account of the Several Advances the Church of England hath made towards Rome* (1680) certainly made some of the stark criticisms of conformist clergy of which they accused him. He even attacked Jeremy Taylor's opinions, although tellingly he described Taylor as 'learned and exemplary in life'.[60] But in the shared fight against popery some of the villains, like Peter Heylyn, were also those of Peter du Moulin and Jean Durel. Lewis's English church was located not so far from theirs, even if the latter had only 'one-eyed Reformation' and needed the 'clear-sighted' religion of the Puritans. The heroes

---

53 Mark Goldie, 'The reception of Hobbes', in J.J. Burns and Mark Goldie (eds), *Cambridge History of Political Thought 1450–1700* (Cambridge, 1991), pp. 589–615, notes (p. 612, n. 13) his 'strikingly Hobbesian and Seldenian defences of Cromwell's church settlement' together with those of Joseph Hall.

54 Keeble and Nuttall, *Correspondence of Richard Baxter*, vol. 2, p. 111.

55 Nobbs, p. 493.

56 Ibid., p. 501.

57 [Lewis du Moulin], *La tyrannie des prejugez, ou reflexions sur le fragment d'une lettre de Mademoiselle Marie du Moulin... en forme d'Epitres sur la puissance ecclesiastique et l'excommunication, pour servir de response a Monsieur Jurieu* (London, 1678), esp. dedication, sig. [a4r].

58 'A true report of a discourse between Monsieur de l'Angle, Canon of Canterbury and minister of the French Church in the Savoy and Lewis du Moulin. The 10th of February 1678/9', printed in Lewis du Moulin, *A Short and True Account of the Several Advances the Church of England hath made towards Rome* (London, 1680), esp. 69–72.

59 A point made by Nobbs, p. 508.

60 Lewis du Moulin, *A Short and True Account*, p. 31.

of Lewis's church were bishops Joseph Hall, Ralph Brownrigg and James Ussher, those who 'did not bow the knee to Baal' but condemned popish ordination, the rigorous imposition of ceremonies and abuse of pluralism.[61] How, Lewis challenged de l'Angle, was this different from the aspirations of the Reformed at large?

Conclusion

According to the posthumous *The Last Words of Lewis du Moulin* (1680), on his deathbed Lewis repented of his bitterness and retracted criticism of Church of England clergy.[62] Whether the words came from his lips or not, their exhortation to Anglicans and dissenters to unite 'for the defence and preservation of the Holy Reformed Religion' does encapsulate much of both his own writings and his brother's. Both they and their circle conceived of the English church as an integral part of the European Reformed community; they addressed their polemic to its members, and they saw the common enemy as popery. Their disagreements had all the intensity of divisions between those who agree in many fundamentals but come at a problem from different perspectives and hence adopt subtly different solutions. Like other Reformed, English and French, they positioned themselves in minutely graded degrees of conformity and nonconformity, of principle and pragmatic compromise. Such nuances, such positioning, will be easier to plot for ministers of both nationalities against the multiple contemporary biographies in *Oxford DNB*. So will points of congruence and cross-fertilisation. The dictionary is an ongoing project, with thrice-yearly updates appearing online from January 2005: it is already stimulating further research and publishing both new information and new articles.[63] It is also a collaborative project, sustained by scholarship from around the world: it is hoped that those who use it will help to expand its coverage of foreigners who made an impact on life and thought in Britain.

---

61 Ibid., pp. 80, 74.
62 Taken ill at the end of September 1680, Lewis died on 20 October, and was buried on 22 October at St Paul's Church, Covent Garden, London: *The Last Words of Lewis du Moulin* (London, 1680); *The Registers of St Paul's Church, Covent Garden*, ed. W.H. Hunt, vol. 4, Harleian Society register series 36 (1903), p. 89.
63 Lawrence Goldman (ed.), *Oxford Dictionary of National Biography* (Oxford, http://www.oxforddnb.com).

Chapter 4

Dominus Providebit

Huguenot Commitment to Poor Relief in England

Randolph Vigne
Huguenot Society of Great Britain and Ireland, UK

This chapter is in three parts. It will look first at the development of poor relief and related social welfare systems in England, trying to assess the degree to which they were influenced by Huguenot immigrants. Second, there is the phenomenon of the relief made available to the mass of Huguenots in England which began with the *grand refuge* and continued into the nineteenth century. It has been said of the work of the French Committee, which distributed the Royal Bounty, that it was 'the first body ever set up in this country to distribute relief on a nationwide basis to persons of all social classes. Merely as an administrative experiment it is remarkable'.[1] A third development to be considered arises from the emergence of voluntary hospitals in the first quarter of the eighteenth century, and the outdoor relief that went with it. The Huguenots established, in the latter category, but only in London, the feeding scheme called 'La Soupe'. This was soon followed by residential care for the sick in the Pest House in the parish of St Giles Cripplegate, and (which was the apogee) the founding of 'The French Hospital for Poor French Protestants and their Descendants Residing in Great Britain' by the leaders of the Huguenot community in 1718. This 'monument of the piety of their ancestors' continues to offer sheltered homes to Huguenot descendants in need, a term more widely interpreted today than in former times.[2]

The Poor Law

The English have never been a people wedded to the theoretical discussion of practical matters, and despite the need to plan new approaches to poor relief in changing times, developments have occurred with little intellectual argument to support them. England did not have a steadily-progressing history of treatment for the poor, the old and the infirm in need. A great break had occurred during the Reformation, with

---

1　Raymond Smith, 'Financial Aid to French Protestant Refugees, 1681–1727: Briefs and the Royal Bounty', PHS, 22/3 (1973): 254.
2　*Statuts et Règlements* [of the French Hospital] (London, 1810).

the closure of ecclesiastical institutions that had performed these functions in earlier times. Some were taken over by laymen, who continued their work in different ways, among them St Bartholomew's and St Thomas's hospitals in London. There were new institutions established by the monarch, including Henry VII's great almshouse of the Savoy and the early form of workhouse and infirmary founded by Edward VI in Bridewell, his father's old palace. There was nevertheless a pressing necessity for poor relief throughout the country – as both a Christian duty, and as a response to acute social and economic need – but there was no central authority with the power, substance or will to provide it.

The great development as the Tudor dynasty came to an end was the passing of the Poor Law in stages from 1597 to 1601. It codified the powers and duties of local authorities entrusted with the care of the poor, taking a major and beneficial step away from the neglect and confusion of the past, but carrying ultimate responsibility even further away from the central authorities: King, Parliament and Established Church.

The Poor Law had categorised the poor into three groups: those who refused to work, those who could find no work and those unable to work. Workhouses often brought all three together, some of them treating these inmates with equal harshness. The object was almost always to reduce the burden that each inmate imposed on the rates by making life inside the workhouse even more unbearable than life outside. Outdoor relief was scant, usually covering the rent and, in some parishes, medical costs. Most workhouses strove to return the mentally ill to their homes rather than to provide them with permanent housing at the parish's expense.[3]

Medical treatment provided by infirmaries ('hospitals' is too general a term, for it also embraced almshouses), by dispensaries or by doctors in general practice was wholly inadequate until the early eighteenth century. 'For a period of 500 years neither the church nor the state chose to help the sick by founding hospitals [in the modern sense of the term]'. The essential of 'a well-developed local administration working under central supervision' was 'being allowed to lapse' to the extent that it had ever existed, by the end of the seventeenth century.[4] The lack of medical care for the poor and indeed (though less widespread) for those who could afford to pay for it, was widely perceived and lamented.

The inspiration for genuine improvement in this desperate situation came from writers and thinkers, and Sir Thomas More's *Utopia* has often been seen as the first great contribution.[5] Here we shall see a disproportionate role being played by new arrivals in England, who were perhaps able to see more clearly the country's needs and to pass on what they had learned in their homelands. Were they not also – some

---

3   Peter Wood, in *Poverty and the Workhouse in Victorian Britain* (Stroud, 1991) provides a useful summary of the rise and decline of the workhouses.

4   John Woodward, *To do the Sick no Harm: A Study of the British Voluntary System to 1875* (London and Boston, 1974), p. 8, and chapter 2.

5   *The Complete Works of Sir Thomas More*, ed. E. Surtz, S.J. and J.H. Hexter, vol. 4, pp. 139–41, quoted in Woodward, p. 6.

of them being fugitives from persecution, notably in France – more sympathetic to the misery and want around them because of their own sufferings?

Mayerne

A gigantic figure – physically, and in his impact on Jacobean and Caroline society – was Sir Theodore de Mayerne. He was physician to James I, who acquired his services from Henri IV in Paris, and later to Charles I and Cromwell. His stormy role in the College of Physicians, his foundation (in effect) of the Society of Apothecaries, his publication of Moffet's great work on insects and the circumstances of his life at court all made him an outstanding figure in his time and perhaps one of the most remarkable of French Protestants in England. His grandiose plan for London, more than a century after More, proposed 'a board of health, on foreign models, with "absolute power" over the whole metropolis, managing every aspect of social welfare, from vagrancy to food supplies'. Although three centuries ahead of its time, Mayerne's plan might have helped to set a standard for the aspirations of reformers, but the concept of 'absolute power' was out of tune with English national feelings on the conduct of public affairs, then as now.[6]

Hartlib

From James I's reign to the Restoration, another 'stranger', Samuel Hartlib, included among his many other activities new schemes for far-reaching systems of public welfare. He inspired many others, Huguenots among them, to promote the easing of the country's acute social problems. A native of Elbing in Prussia, who came to England in his twenties, he wrote prolifically on science, education, agriculture, the quest for Protestant unity, the development of weapons (during the English Civil War) and social welfare, while as an 'intelligencer' he also disseminated the ideas of others, many of them refugees from eastern Europe and France. Hartlib's closest associate, John Dury, also born in Elbing and the son of an exiled Scots minister – so another kind of stranger – was also close to the Huguenots as a result of his travels round Europe to promote Protestant unity. His links with Calvinist and Lutheran clergy in Europe, which put them in contact with their English counterparts, will be examined later.

Hartlib's social welfare projects were numerous, and so were the schemes of others that he circulated. Prominent in his circle was Sir Balthazar Gerbier, with whom he planned an Office of Public Address which would extend the structure of a merchants' exchange to embrace employment and 'the whole society of all men', particularly to serve the poor. Modelled on Théophraste Renaudot's institution in Paris, favoured by Richelieu, the Office would spread employment and training,

---

6   Paul Slack, *From Reformation to Improvement: Public Welfare in Early-Modern England* (Oxford, 1999), p. 72.

'the protection of public health and reformed hospitals, a clean environment and reformed cities [which] should all contribute to one end', that end being Hartlib's oft-stated concept of the 'public good'.[7] Renaudot, who had abjured his Calvinism to win favour, was indicted by Gerbier for gross usury and his Bureau d'Addresse was closed, though he later revived it. Born to noble Protestant parents from Normandy, exiled in Holland, Gerbier's picaresque career at court, in diplomacy, education, painting and architecture, included the publication of numerous pamphlets. They dealt with agriculture, where 'the publique good is much concerned', the development of South America ('manifesting how much the publique good is concerned'), while in *A New-Years Result in Favour of the Poore* he excoriated all who 'endeavour not to promote the publique good [as] no better than beasts with hornes and hoofs'. His short-lived academy at Bethnal Green catered for the young of both sexes and followed a French model. Education for the poor was of lesser concern to him, though Hartlib allowed for it in his workhouse schemes.[8]

The Chamberlens

Gerbier was one of the few who penetrated English public life, among many Huguenots in England who sought to conform in their social and religious lives. Others banded together as dissidents in English society, and none more so than the three generations of Chamberlens. They were the descendants of Guillaume, an exiled doctor in Amsterdam, who moved thence to England where he could practise the unorthodox medicine that was disallowed in the Netherlands. His son Peter the Elder spent some time in Newgate prison after a dispute with the College of Physicians; he was rescued by the Archbishop of Canterbury acting on behalf of James I's queen, Anne of Denmark. He proposed many public-health schemes, proposing also the employment and settling of poor families on land to be taken from the Church – feasible after the Civil War – where they would enjoy social welfare, including free hospitals. Peter the Younger invented the obstetric forceps which made the family rich, famous and deeply resented by the medical profession. Hugh Chamberlen the Elder, in the fourth generation, sold the secret that they had kept to themselves throughout the seventeenth century.[9]

---

7   Slack, p. 78.
8   Balthazar Gerbier, *A New-Years Result in Favour of the Poore* (1652), *Some Consideration of the two Great Staple Commodities of England* (1654), *A Summary Description Manifesting that rather Profits are to be made in the Hott than the Could Parts off the Coast of America*; Samuel Hartlib, *A Summarie of the Propositions to be tendered to the Parliament by the French Protestants mentioned by Mr Hartlib in the petition to the House of Commons* ... , quoted in Charles Webster, *The Great Instauration: Science, Medicine and Reform, 1642–1660* (London, 1975), p. 371.
9   Walter Randall, *The Secret Instrument: The History of the Midwifery Forceps* (London, 1947); Peter Chamberlen, *The Poore Man's Advocate, or, England's Samaritans,*

The Chamberlens made much of their charitable use of the forceps as male midwives to the poor, and as *accoucheurs* to the families of James I and Charles I they could withstand the blasts of the College of Physicians that descried their unorthodoxy and their ambition rather than their failing to share the secret of the forceps. The second Peter and Hugh Chamberlen of the third generation spanned the divide between the utopianism and near-millenarianism of the Hartlib circle and the more down-to-earth urge for reform, tempered with pity and compassion, of its post-Restoration successors. Peter Chamberlen proposed the creation of a public fund to subsidize employment and the building of 'collegiate habitations ... for workhouse, schools, hospitals etc'.[10] The scheme had won Charles I's approval and Chamberlen claimed that it had been recommended to Archbishop Laud. It was not until 1649 that he published the tract setting out the scheme, in the more favourable climate created by the Commonwealth. Hearing William Petty, the most influential economist in Hartlib's circle, discuss Peter Chamberlen's proposals, Hartlib wrote privately that he felt that the whole world might be made happy 'and at last come to live in plenty and peace &c and all wars cease'.[11] Hartlib was excited by Chamberlen's plans for the future, for which he expected support in Parliament: 'The City of Peace tending so much to community, he dares not yet divulge, lest people should be too much frightened'.[12] Petty's theorising survived the Restoration, which ended Hartlib's centrality, and his pension from Cromwell's council. He died in poverty in 1662.

The Chamberlens went on, eight of them well-known *accoucheurs* to the rich and poor, the most vociferous of the fourth generation being Hugh the Elder (1630–c.1720) who campaigned for free medical treatment for the sick of all classes and their exemption of the poor from rates.[13] He was a prolific pamphleteer, in the late seventeenth century, writing on obstetrical matters and promoting his public-health plan, land banks, plague prevention and other measures. Late in life he moved to the Netherlands to escape the consequences of the failure of his schemes and there sold the family secret of the obstetric forceps. Commissioned by the Duke of Buckingham, his magnificent monument in Westminster Abbey, by Scheemakers and Delvaux, attests to the capacity of the Chamberlens to maintain friendships in high places, while in conflict with their equals.

Hartlib's circle

Other Huguenot or Huguenot-related names appear among Hartlib's circle, or among those whom it inspired. After the Restoration, Samuel Fortrey, Gentleman of the King's Bedchamber and a descendant of sixteenth-century Walloon de La

---

Pouring Oile & Wine into the Wounds of the Nation. By making present Provision for the Souldier and the Poore (1649).

10   Slack, p. 78.
11   Ibid., p. 178; Chamberlen, *The Poore Man's Advocate*.
12   Slack, p. 83.
13   Hugh Chamberlen, *A Proposal for the Better Securing of Health* (London, 1689).

Forteries, sought to promote the 'public good' and the 'welfare and happiness' of the kingdom'. His pamphlet of 1668, *England's Interest and Improvement, Consisting in the Increase of the Store, and Trade of the Kingdom*, was an early example of the argument for the new concept of economic 'improvement'.[14] He argued strongly in favour of allowing foreign immigrants the rights and privileges of Englishmen, and was vehemently opposed to trade with France.[15]

The ideas put into circulation by Hartlib and his circle reflected more the zeal for universal reform generated by the 'second reformation' in the German states and eastern Europe. Reformers like Dury and the Slovak Comenius interacted fruitfully with their Calvinist counterparts in France and in exile. The du Moulins, Meric Casaubon and Isaac Basire were linked in various ways, as were such pastors as Peter Serrurier in Amsterdam; Charles Drelincourt, Edouard Aubertin and Jean Mestrezat in Paris; Prevost in Geneva; Daniel Toussain in Basle and du Bois in Hanau. Hartlib, Dury and Comenius also worked with the London physician Gourdain and Nicolas Oudart, a secretary at court and amanuensis to Charles I, Peter Le Pruvost and Hugh L'Amy. The latter two proposed plantations in the Indies and America, improved husbandry and agriculture and, like Gerbier, advocated a French-style academy for young gentlemen. Hartlib hailed Le Pruvost for having 'a truly public spirit, zealous for the Protestant cause [and in] no wayes covetously inclined'. The relief of poverty by the creation of employment was central to their plan for an American colony (originally for fellow Huguenots) which was put to Parliament in 1645 but not carried out. 'Multitudes of people ... desperat and wilde ... under noe Government' would achieve 'the attainment of Knowledge and the exercises of Temperance, Righteousnes & Godlinesse'.[16]

A positive development of their views on rehabilitation of the seemingly irreclaimable masses living in poverty was the Corporations of the Poor, established in Bristol, London and elsewhere to combine workhouse, almshouse and infirmary. The emphasis on the economic benefits of putting the poor to work was maintained. A greater concern for the miseries of poverty began to spread at the end of the seventeenth century and in the early 1700s, though the alleviation of poverty had always been recognised as a Christian duty.[17]

The London Corporation set up in 1702 by Sir Robert Clayton, the Quaker John Bellers and Thomas Firmin has been described as 'tending to the reformation, happiness and welfare of succeeding generations – a nicely Hartlibian trio of goals'.[18] Though Huguenots settled in England were not the protagonists, their ideas were

---

14   Slack, p. 88 and n. 51.

15   *A Select Collection of Early English Treatises*, Political Economy Club (London, 1858), pp. viii–ix.

16   G.H. Turnbull, *Hartlib, Dury and Comenius: Gleanings from Hartlib's Papers* (London, 1947); Mark Greengrass, Michael Leslie and Timothy Raylor (eds), *Samuel Hartlib and Universal Reformation: Studies in Intellectual Communication* (Cambridge, 1994), p. 213.

17   Slack, pp. 84–114.

18   Slack, p. 113.

current and influential as was knowledge of the institutions for the poor and sick in France, the Netherlands and Germany brought here by the 'strangers'.

Thomas Firmin

The old Huguenot churches of Threadneedle Street and the Savoy in London, and those in Canterbury, Norwich and Southampton, had long cared for their poor through specially assigned elders and deacons, but the numbers were manageable. A new generation committed to this duty was soon on hand to engage with the flood of Huguenots fleeing to England to escape persecution and forced conversion in France. The needs of the indigent refugees, whose plight was so strongly felt by those of their English co-religionists committed to the 'public good', became a special concern of the wealthy philanthropist and Unitarian, Thomas Firmin. Firmin provides a link between the contributors to the 'public good' centred round Samuel Hartlib, concerned with the English poor, and the new Huguenot poor, many of them with a far higher degree of skill, training and education than those whom Hartlib's circle tried to make economically productive, for their own and for the public's good. In the 1670s, when he was already a successful City merchant, Firmin contributed to the new purpose-built workhouses in London and elsewhere, training and employing young pauper children in the parish of St Botolph Aldersgate, helping to rebuild Christ's Hospital, following the lead of his patron and admirer, the Whig magnate Sir Robert Clayton, who erected a statue of Firmin in the garden of his house Marden Park at Woldingham, in Surrey. In 1681, with the Lord Mayor and Bishop of London, Firmin was among those who proposed that the Pest House in Finsbury Fields be given over to the Huguenot sick and needy, creating, as we shall see, the embryo of the great English Huguenot institution still thriving today.[19]

The title of his 1681 pamphlet puts his case clearly: *Proposals for the Employment of the Poor and the Prevention of Idleness and the Consequence thereof, Begging, a Practice so Dishonourable to this Nation and to the Christian Religion.* His case, to put the poor to work for their own profit, found support in Hugh Chamberlen's claim in *The Present State of England* that 'in the city of Norwich children from six to ten years have gained £12,000 a year more than they have spent, chiefly by knitting fine Jersey stockings'. He argues also for the appointment in every 'great parish' of 'men of the best reputation, both for honesty and estates', to visit the poor and 'inspect their wants'. As in the French and Dutch churches, they would be given the 'honourable title of Father for the Poor'. He urged his readers to 'show their charity to the poor by buying the cloth they make'.[20]

Firmin was able to put his proposals into practice, with adult labour, in his Royal Lustring Company, which became his closest contact with the Huguenot refugee

---

19   Charles Marmoy, 'The "Pest House", 1681–1717, Predecessor of the French Hospital', *PHS*, 25/4 (1992): 385–99.

20   Thomas Firmin, *Proposals for the Imployment of the Poor and for the Prevention of Idleness* ... (London, 1681), p. 46.

community. In London and Ipswich, his birthplace, the company employed Huguenot silk weavers on 718 looms, on lines similar to several enterprises elsewhere in England to give work to paupers for their own and for society's profit.[21] The company was also to make lustrings and alamodes, using a process to produce a glittering effect on the silk fabric which had been kept a close secret by the silk-weavers of Lyon. Firmin had the good sense to appreciate that men and women impoverished because of their flight from their motherland for adhering to strong religious principles, and who mostly came from skilled and materially successful home backgrounds, were likely to repeat and even to better that success in their new environment. He also had the acumen to meet a demand for a product unavailable from France in time of war.

Firmin obtained subscriptions from 70 'merchant adventurers', totalling £2,300. Among these subscribers can be found the names of ten Walloon and Huguenot refugee families: Carbonnel, Delmé, de Neu, de Père, du Bois, Frederick, Houblon, Papillon, Primrose and Reneu. Of these, Hilaire Reneu was the managing director of the company, founded in 1692. The brothers Hilaire and Pierre Reneu and the former's son, also Pierre, were exceptional as comparatively recent refugees, while their fellow French-speaking Protestant-descended investors were almost all products of earlier settlements.[22]

The Reneus

Pierre Reneu had come to England from Bordeaux before 1677, the date of his naturalisation, and Hilaire Reneu followed with his wife and son Pierre, in 1685.[23] They had clearly succeeded, unlike the vast majority of their fellow refugees, in bringing some capital with them. Hilaire, in his eloquent introduction to the English edition of Claude's celebrated *Plaintes des Protestants*, which he published in 1686, defends his fellow Huguenots in England from charges that they were, in today's terminology, 'economic migrants' rather than genuine 'asylum seekers', and he seeks to rebut the claim that all the refugees were poor.[24]

Hilaire and Pierre Reneu were directors of the Bank of England and held considerable bank stock as the members of a small financial elite among the late

---

21   W.H. Manchee, 'Some Huguenot Smugglers: The Impeachment of London Silk Merchants, 1698', *PHS*, 15 (1933–37): 406–27.

22   Ibid., pp. 406–14, 417, 422–7; Vincent B. Redstone, 'The Dutch and Huguenot Settlements of Ipswich', *PHS*, 12 (1917–23): 189–203, 201–4; G.B. Beeman, 'Notes on the City of London Records dealing with the French Protestant Refugees', *PHS*, 7 (1901–04): 145–8.

23   *Letters of Denization and Acts of Naturalization for Aliens in England and Ireland, 1603–1700*, ed. W.A. Shaw, HSQS, 11 (London, 1911), pp. 118, 120, 220, 255.

24   Jean Claude, *An Account of the Persecution and Oppression of the Protestants in France*, abridged and translated into English (1686). Edition with Hilaire Reneu's preface, 1707.

seventeenth-century refugees.²⁵ Hilaire's daughter married another member of this group, Sir Denis Dutry, of Protestant ancestry in Guienne and a worshipper at the Dutch Church Austin Friars. His executor was John Girardot de Tillieux, a city merchant and South Sea Company director. The Girardots had also succeeded in importing capital from France. Lady Dutry remarried another wealthy immigrant, of Flemish origin and Huguenot connexions, Gerard Van Neck.²⁶ Both she and John Girardot were directors of the feeding scheme for the Huguenot poor much helped by Hilaire Reneu and the Maison de Charité de Spittlefields, which we shall soon encounter.

This Huguenot elite was not uniformly a model of probity. Some among them sought to profit from the demand for lustrings and alamodes by a much more direct method than setting up their own factories. Etienne Seignoret, René Baudouin and others, known as the Combine, successfully smuggled into England vast quantities from Lyon and made huge fortunes. The Reneus, both to defend the honour of the Huguenots and to eliminate a major threat to their own business, exposed the Combine's illegal activities. Nine of the latter were impeached and paid enormous fines, which were credited to the funds of the Greenwich Hospital for seamen, a splendid project which benefited greatly from this enforced injection of Huguenot money. Of the £19,500 that was paid, £10,000 came from Seignoret alone. Another, unforced donation – £3,000 – came from one John de La Fontaine.²⁷

The Royal Bounty

From 1681, with the onset of the *dragonnades* in France, the numbers and needs of the destitute refugees became pressing. Funds were collected under a 'brief' issued to the churches by Charles II, as was his prerogative. Relief was then distributed by the Huguenot churches in London, Threadneedle Street (we have a detailed analysis of its work until 1687) and the Savoy, in Canterbury, in Ipswich and six smaller churches.²⁸ In 1696 and 1703 so-called French and English Committees were set up by the King's commissioners, charged with distributing the funds collected under further 'briefs' and later granted by William and Mary and their successors. Both Thomas Firmin and the Reneus served on the English Committee, whose task was

---

25 Alice C. Carter, 'The Huguenot Contribution to the Early Years of the Funded Debt, 1694–1714', *PHS*, 19/3 (1955): 26, 30, 37.
26 W.H. Manchee, 'The First and Last Chapter of the Church of "Les Grecs", Charing Cross Road', *PHS*, 13 (1937–41): 152.
27 Manchee, 'Some Huguenot Smugglers', p. 421; Randolph Vigne, 'In the Purlieus of St Alfege's: Huguenot Families in 17th- and 18th-century Greenwich', *PHS*, 27/2 (1999): 271.
28 *French Protestant Refugees Relieved through the French Protestant Church, London, 1681–1687*, ed. A.P. Hands and Irene Scouloudi, HSQS, 49 (London, 1971).

to audit the expenditures by the French Committee.²⁹ Hilaire had been an associate of Firmin's and of Sir Robert Clayton's in their charitable work towards the building of the Greenwich Hospital and the brothers appear to have moved away from the refugee community into the City of London 'establishment' of those days.³⁰

It was this French Committee which was described as 'the first ever set up in this country to distribute relief on a nationwide basis to persons of all classes'.³¹ It must be remembered that since the 1601 Poor Law (and indeed until 1834) there was no centralised system of poor relief, which was entirely the responsibility of parishes throughout the country. Furthermore, except for certain complicated exemptions, such relief was to be distributed only to residents of the parish concerned. The briefs of 1681, 1686, 1688 and 1694 all made possible assistance to the flood of Huguenots entering in the country in the years around the Revocation of the Edict of Nantes. The great defender of European Protestantism William III, and his wife Queen Mary who acted in his annual absences of six or eight months, greatly increased the funds available by royal gifts (from their Civil List grants from Parliament) and, in 1696 by the establishment of the Royal Bounty, maintained by their successors until George II's reign in 1727.³²

The French Committee, which was drawn from the nobility and gentry, the 'middling sort' and the clergy, both conformist and non-conformist, carried out its tasks most successfully. In 1710 at a meeting arranged by Hilaire Reneu with the Secretary of State, Lord Sunderland, to ask for increased funds, the Committee was represented by François Le Coq de Saint-Leger, described by John Evelyn 24 years earlier as 'a French refugie who left great Riches for Religion, a learned and civill person',³³ and Nicolas Rambouillet, sieur de La Sablière, a cousin of the illustrious Ruvigny, Earl of Galway. The Committee's work was greatly assisted by the Huguenot churches of Threadneedle Street and the Savoy in London and by the smaller *temples* in the provinces. Annual payments were made to Huguenot churches in the western and eight in the eastern counties, with larger grants to those with two ministers: Bristol, Norwich, Plymouth and Southampton. The lion's share went to the London churches in the City, Spitalfields and Westminster. The omission of the sixteenth-century Walloon and Huguenot church in the crypt of Canterbury Cathedral from the list may be due to its non-conformism, but this did not affect Threadneedle Street.³⁴

The funds were never enough, as the numbers of applicants grew and grew, and there were no precedents for the administration of such funds. There were also, it has

---

29   Roy A. Sundstrom, *Aid and Assimilation: a Study of the Economic Support given French Protestants in England, 1680–1727*, Ph.D. dissertation (Kent State University Graduate School, 1972) p. 39; Raymond Smith, *Records of the Royal Bounty and Connected Funds ... in the Huguenot Library*, HSQS, 51 (1974), pp. 16, 20, 31, 36.
30   Vigne, 'In the Purlieus of St Alfege's', pp. 270–71.
31   Smith, 'Financial Aid', p. 254.
32   Smith, *Records*; 'Financial Aid', pp. 1–10, 17–56; Sundstrom, pp. 56–131.
33   John Evelyn, Diary, *1621–1706*, ed. Austin Dobson (1908), p. 417.
34   Sundstrom, p. 94.

been said, 'continual accusations of incompetence, injustice, fraud and malversation' against the French Committee.[35] In our own time an American scholar has cross-checked 20 per cent of the 'acquittances' against the account-books entries and found 'very few errors'. Professor Sundstrom added: 'The fact that there is no record of the English Committee's auditors having rejected a statement by the French Committee speaks for itself'.[36]

The Royal Bounty was paid out, on average, to 3,000 recipients every quarter, many of them heads of families, and in its long history (the last payment was made in 1876, by then by parliamentary grant) many millions of pounds, at today's values, were distributed. The refugees left very few autobiographical accounts of their early struggle in exile and one might regret that the best known of these was by Jacques Fontaine, who complained of the way he was treated by the French Committee to whom he applied for relief. He wrote, 'They looked upon us as beggars, for our other good qualities were obliterated by poverty'.[37] By his account it was his refusal, as a pastor, to embrace episcopalianism that lost him the committee's favour. Professor Sundstrom, who is somewhat grudging in his judgement of the 'economic support given to French Protestants in England, 1680–1727', answers his own questions as to whether they found a happy home in England in this period – 'the answer is a qualified yes'.[38]

The Pest House

The pressing need of the multiplying thousands of destitute refugees was countered by the creation of two institutions, one that added a further dimension to the alms the French and English Committees were able to spread among the refugees, the other funded independently of it. The first development arose out of an approach by the Bishop of London – Henry Compton, a constant friend to the refugees – and by the Lord Mayor to the Common Council of the City of London, so that 'a large and commodious house at Bunhill Fields', one of a number of isolation hospitals erected for the plague victims in earlier years, be given over to the housing of the most infirm and helpless of the refugees.[39] The approach was supported by a number of others, who included Thomas Firmin. Known as the Pest House, it was soon brought into use and placed under the control of the French Committee, also set up in that year. For 36 years the Pest House gave a home to 30 to 40 'poor, infirm or ill' Huguenots at any one time. Funds were short – we find in 1709 the committee asking Hilaire Reneu for a loan of the considerable sum of £400 towards the maintenance of the inmates, to be repaid when the new grant was received. Space was limited and there

---

35 Smith, 'Financial Aid', p. 253.
36 Sundstrom, quoted by Smith, ibid., p. 253.
37 Fontaine, *Memoirs*, p. 134.
38 Sundstrom, p. 236.
39 Irvine E. Gray (comp.), *Huguenot Manuscripts: A Descriptive Catalogue of the Remaining Manuscripts in the Huguenot Library*, HSQS, 56 (London, 1983), pp. 1–2.

were some serious failings among the staff, although only three successive keepers were in charge in the 36-year existence of the Pest House, the third of whom was employed after the transformation that was to follow, to which we shall return.[40]

Before doing so, it should be realised that the Pest House, as a place of care for the sick, had few English precedents to follow. The ancient hospitals of St Thomas's and St Bartholomew's had come to care only for paying patients. It was 30 or more years before the idea of 'voluntary hospitals' was to gain hold. Though charitable trusts of all kinds had proliferated in the centuries following the dissolution of ecclesiastical foundations for the sick and poor, these had not made the sick their responsibility.[41] Such a trust, the Westminster Society, was set up in 1716, one of its chief initiators being the philanthropic banker, Henry Hoare, whose father Sir Richard had worked, through the SPCK, in support of continental Protestants under threat. It created the Westminster Infirmary in 1719, the first of the 'voluntary hospitals', which charged no fees.[42] Guy's, St George's, the London and Middlesex Hospitals followed between 1724 and 1745, as did others outside London.

The records do not show, nor does our knowledge of the French Committee members vouchsafe, that experience of the ancient infirmaries of Paris, Montpellier and elsewhere, and those in the Netherlands which some of them must surely have encountered, helped towards the creation of an institution that, like the Pest House under the French Committee, had no exact precedent in England. Perhaps there had been such experience, but in any event, the administration of the Pest House provided it in plenty, for the larger English Huguenot institution that was to succeed it.

'La Soupe'

A different kind of development came later, after the French Committee and the elders and deacons of the churches had gained much experience in the essential relief work. In 1689 the Maison de Charité de Spittlefields was set up. Known as 'La Soupe' it provided food for the refugees teeming in the liberties outside the City of London, in what had been the fields around the site of the ancient and long vanished Hospital (in the old sense) of St Mary's, known as Spitalfields.[43] Among a long list of donors we find Hilaire Reneu, who, from the beginning, gave frequently and generously, and was one of the directors for many years. In 1700, when 'La Soupe' was experiencing a severe financial crisis, he donated a further £100. In 1708 he made over £100 bequeathed by a member of the French Committee, an old soldier, Jacques de Gastigny, who had been Master of Buckhounds to the Stadhouder, William of Orange in the Netherlands, and had come to England in William's army

---

40   Marmoy, 'The Pest House', pp. 394, 398–9.
41   Woodward, pp. 8–11.
42   Woodward, pp. 11–12.
43   Charles Marmoy, '"La Soupe", La Maison de Charité de Spittlefields', *PHS*, 23/3 (1979): 134–47.

in 1688.⁴⁴ De Gastigny identified Reneu as 'father-in-law of Mr Dutry, who takes care thereof'. He made a like bequest to the Maison de Charité de Westminster, through 'Mrs Temple, who takes care of the kitchen'.⁴⁵ Perhaps she was the 'Mary Temple' naturalized in 1697.⁴⁶

'La Soupe' met an acute need among the Huguenot poor in London, as did its Westminster counterpart which served Soho but has left no surviving records. From 1689, based in a succession of houses in Spitalfields, 'La Soupe' provided 'a pan of good broth, mixed with six ounces of bread, half a pound of meat, and the same weight of good bread', three, four and even six times a week to refugee families most in need.⁴⁷ Its ledgers, dating from 1695, give details of the food supplied, its cost and the funding received, most of it from successful Huguenots and well-wishers like Henry Compton, Bishop of London and Sir Patience Ward, the Lord Mayor. A supporter from the start was the Reverend William Smythies of St Giles Cripplegate, remembered also for advertising in *The London Gazette* (2–5 January 1681) to refute the story that he had gone to visit some Huguenots unannounced and had found them saying the Mass. In 1728, Dutry, by then Sir Denis Dutry, Bart., left £200 to 'the house of charity called La Marmite ... for the soop of the poor French refugees situated in Spitalfields and also for the house of charity in Soho'.⁴⁸

The first ledger lists also 25 directors, 11 of them, surprisingly for those times, women. Among the men are both Hilaire Reneu and Etienne Seignoret, the latter to recover quickly from his impeachment, despite Reneu's enmity. Seignoret's fellow smuggler René Baudouin, fined £3,000, was memorialized at his death in 1728 with a splendid inscription extolling his virtues, in St Mary Aldermary Church in the City of London. He married two daughters into the English aristocracy, despite his earlier disgrace.⁴⁹ The active officers were the Secretary, Jacques Testard for many years, with Pierre Cabibel as Treasurer, later to succeed Testard as Secretary and to be succeeded in turn by Claude Desmarets, who served until his death in 1759. We shall meet Cabibel and Desmarets again.

The Maison de Charité de Westminster joined with 'La Soupe' in an appeal to the French Committee, but received only one small grant of £15 each. They benefited jointly, after some dispute, from the will of Pierre Daudé in 1733.⁵⁰ We may assume that the Wesminster charity was still active during the winter of 1739–40, the hardest of the century, when the price of coal soared, and 'La Soupe''s expenditure doubled. Perhaps the need for the Soho charity ceased thereafter.

---

44   A.G. Browning, 'On the Early History of the French Hospital (La Providence)', *PHS*, 6/1 (1897): 43–4; Huguenot Library Archives J4.

45   Huguenot Library Archives, Wagner Wills, De Gastigny; D.C.A. Agnew, *Protestant Exiles from France chiefly in the Reign of Louis XIV* (2 vols, 1886), vol. 2, pp. 523–4.

46   Shaw, p. 250.

47   William Maitland, *History of London* (1739), p. 665.

48   Wagner Wills, Dutry.

49   Randolph Vigne, 'René Baudouin: a Memorial Inscription', *Huguenot Families*, 3 (September 2000): 8.

50   Marmoy, 'La Soupe', pp. 41–2, 137.

That winter has left us the only detailed case-book among the records of 'La Soupe', providing a deeply interesting picture of the lives of 250 Huguenot underdog families, cared for by their fellow refugees. 'La Soupe' ceased to provide its 'good broth' in 1741 and became 'La Société du Pain autrefois La Soupe'.[51] It continued to feed the poor of Spitalfields and beyond, the need perpetuated by the precarious nature of the silk weaving trade, until it handed over its funds to the French Hospital in 1826. The last payment the latter made from its funds was in 1877.[52]

There was already in existence in 1824 a 'Spitalfields Benevolent Society for Visiting and Relieving the Sick and Distressed Poor at their own Habitations', with Thomas Fowell Buxton MP as its patron and Samuel Hoare Jr. as one of its two Vice-Patrons. Perhaps it too fed the hungry. It too had its Committee of Ladies whose 'sedulous and tender care [was] bestowed on poor women during the period of their confinement'.[53] This may explain the part played by the 'directrices' of 'La Soupe', which perhaps set an example the Benevolent Society followed when it took over some of the work of its Huguenot forerunner.

The French Hospital

A few kilometres away, again outside the boundaries of the City of London, was the Pest House. Regular supervisory visits were made by French Committee members, among them the old soldier Jacques de Gastigny. It is said that he so pitied the cramped and austere conditions in which the inmates were housed that he included in his will a handsome bequest of £500 to build apartments for at least 12 'poor, infirm and sick French Protestants above the age of 50 years', and a further £500 the interest on which was to provide linen, clothing and other essentials for them.[54] His executor, Philippe Ménard, was pastor at the Chapel Royal, St James, one of the most distinguished of the Huguenots in England, formerly chaplain to Queen Charlotte Amelia of Denmark, and before that at the great Paris *temple* of Charenton. Ménard spent the remaining 29 years of his life husbanding de Gastigny's legacy and more than fulfilling his wishes.

The French Committee asked the Reneu brothers to assist their member, the City merchant Jacques Baudouin, to approach the Lord Mayor and Court of Aldermen to allow space for extra accommodation at the Pest House, but the latter were reluctant to agree and Baudouin, Philippe Ménard and their colleagues tried for eight years to persuade the Corporation of the City of London to sell the required land adjacent to the Pest House.[55]

At last, in 1716 the Worshipful Company of Ironmongers agreed to lease, for 990 years, four acres of their land south of the Pest House, the so-called 'Golden

---

51   Ibid., p. 145; Wagner Wills, Dutry.
52   Marmoy, 'La Soupe', p. 147.
53   *Articles of the Society* (1824), p. 2.
54   Agnew, vol. 2, p. 524.
55   Marmoy, 'The Pest House', p. 394.

Acre' on the footway to the rural village of Islington. A premium of £400 was paid and a rent of one peppercorn agreed.[56] There was an immediate appeal for funds so that a suitable building could be erected to replace the increasingly decrepit Pest House. Here is evidence of the prosperity of many Huguenots in England 25 or more years after the refuge was at its height. Within three months of their first appeal, amongst themselves only, which raised £474 19s, a total of £2,272 could be added to De Gastigny's £1,000 plus eight years' interest.[57] Many large donations followed in the coming years – £1,000 from Henri de Ruvigny, Earl of Galway, the undisputed leader of the Huguenots in Britain if not of the diaspora as a whole, and £4,000 from Philibert d'Hervart, the sum being the portion that his deceased son would have received, as did the latter's two brothers and two sisters in their father's will.[58]

By November 1718 the building, the work of Pierre Le Grand, at a cost of £2,750, was ready for occupation by 70 inmates, a steward and his family, a surgeon, physician and indoor and outdoor servants. The life of the French Hospital, known almost from the beginning as 'La Providence', had begun. The French Committee had administered the Pest House, supervised by 'Messieurs les Commissaires Anglais' and it was the former who founded its successor. On 24 July 1718, however, after a petition by the 38 members of the French Committee, their signatures below that of the Earl of Galway, he and they were granted a royal charter creating them, their heirs and successors, 'for ever hereafter', 'One Body Corporate and Politick, in Deed and in Name, By the Name of the Governor and Directors of the Hospital for Poor French Protestants and their Descendants residing in Great Britain'.[59] There was continuity in this, Corporations having played an important part in social affairs in Britain since Tudor times, but the French Hospital, founded just before the term became accepted for what had been infirmaries, lacked the large endowments and, being entrusted to foreigners, the irreproachable status usually required of Corporations. The hospitals (in the modern sense) that followed were voluntary institutions, funded by subscription. It was, of course, often an advantage to foreign groups in Britain that the Sovereign himself and some of his confidents were of foreign birth. George I's charter refers at the start to 'our Right Trusty and Right Wellbeloved Cousin' Galway, whose heading of the petition must have given the King and his council full confidence in the project before them.[60]

There is continuity too among the 38 other petitioners, all but seven of them having been members of the French Committee, some for many years, among them Pierre Reneu, who died in 1729 and had served on the English Committee. Three did not become directors; one, Le Coq de Saint-Leger, was too old, another was bankrupt

---

56   Browning, p. 47.
57   Randolph Vigne, '"A Monument of the Piety of their Ancestors": Origin and Early History of the French Hospital, London, 1708–1740', *Huguenot Foundation Bulletin*, 39 (2002): 196.
58   Agnew, vol. 2, p. 192.
59   *The Charter and By-Laws of the Corporation [of the French Hospital]* (Rochester, 2000), p. 13.
60   Ibid., p. 12.

and the third, Jean Chaboussant, was appointed steward of the new institution a year after the Pest House steward and his wife had moved to the new French Hospital. Among the active directors the most distinguished was the pastor Louis Saurin, who chaired the first meeting of directors, at which Jacques Baudouin was elected Deputy-Governor. The list is representative of the church, the army, merchants and craftsmen, with nobility and the 'middling sort' side by side. Galway, the first Governor, died two years later, to be succeeded by Philibert d'Hervart, and in quick succession in 1721 by Jean de Robethon, who had come from Hanover with George I and was a Privy Councillor. The lack of rigid class observance is notable in that Pierre Cabibel, who became Governor in 1739, was a merchant and without noble lineage. He was one of the founding directors and succeeded Jacques Baudouin as Deputy-Governor in 1720. He died in 1745, when his grand-daughter Anne-Rose was living in Toulouse, married to the tragic Jean Calas.[61] Claude Desmarets, his colleague at 'La Soupe', became Deputy-Governor in 1759.

The French Hospital rapidly became an institution apart, despite these evidences of continuity – not least in the person of Pierre Reneu, brother of Hilaire, who had died in 1713, both protégés of Thomas Firmin, who had died in 1697, himself so admired by Sir Robert Clayton, MP and Lord Mayor of London, with links back to the Hartlib circle. It housed a French-speaking community with few links to the host society, other than through its adherence to the Church of England, established in the days of Ménard and Saurin (this did not in any way penalise non-conformist applicants or inmates). The history of the French Hospital has yet to be written and its survival to this day – in its fourth home, in Rochester, Kent, with a supplemental charter from Queen Elizabeth II granted in 1953, is one of the reasons why it overshadows in the public memory those other manifestations of Huguenot commitment to poor relief in England.

'La Providence' differed markedly in character from the workhouses and hospitals of its time. The former – despite the idealism of Hartlib, Thomas Firmin, the Quaker John Bellers and others, who saw workhouse inmates as families who would be enabled to support themselves by their labour, or be housed with tenderness if unable to labour[62] – became harsher places where, as an SPCK tract of 1725 put it, 'habits of sobriety, obedience and industry' would be instilled.[63] Such hospitals as those at Chelsea for soldiers and Greenwich for sailors, or Christ's Hospital for sons of deserving parents, were for reward rather than correction. Even there, however, those in authority were of the ruling class or slightly below it, and the inmates the humble recipients of their charity.

The French Hospital was always different. Within its walls, refugees cared for fellow refugees, as did their descendants, as directors or residents, in later generations. Every meeting of the Court, which meets quarterly, begins with a

---

61 Randolph Vigne, 'The Killing of Jean Calas: Voltaire's First Huguenot Cause', *PHS*, 23/5 (1981): 281–2.
62 Slack, pp. 106–25.
63 Ibid., p. 135.

prayer, beseeching Almighty God to 'look down ... with thine infinite mercy upon all those who are in any way afflicted or distressed, especially on those who suffer for the sake of thy Holy Gospel'. And adds later 'Since it is of thy favour, O Lord, that we are called to assist and comfort these our Brethren who are in want, grant that we may faithfully discharge our duty. Bless this habitation, which thy good providence has prepared for those among us who are in distress ... '.[64] The directors' duty was to their brethren, to those among them, the Huguenot refugee community, who were in distress. Discipline was maintained, punishments were inflicted, of a mild kind, serious offenders were expelled, but the spirit seems always to have been one whereby those not in distress cared for their less fortunate brethren.

There is no evidence of interaction between the French Hospital and such institutions as workhouses, hospitals old or new, or almshouses. The French Hospital cared for the mentally ill in its *petites maisons*, unlike other such institutions, but did occasionally send them to 'Bedlam' the Bethlehem Hospital, paid for by a sponsor. The sick, at least in the early years, were cared for 'in house', by the resident, paid physician or surgeon – those in voluntary hospitals were unpaid.[65] While most workhouses were believed to be grim, inhuman places – one of the most scandalous in the mid-eighteenth century was that of St Giles Cripplegate, a kilometre or two from 'La Providence'.[66] It seems not to have benefited in any way from the near-by example of 'La Providence'. In a very tentative judgement, however, John Woodward has written: 'Though the hospital served a small minority of the population it probably acted as an example to the rest of the country'.[67]

As with the directors, the inmates were from differing social classes, though the great majority were poor, working people. Among the early inmates was Marthe Aubrisset, daughter of the celebrated hornworker Jean Aubrisset (anglicised to Obrisset), sponsored by her sister Magdelaine Van Sommer, mother of one of the major Spitalfields silk designers. She left a nest egg of £65 to the hospital, which perhaps secured her better accommodation than that occupied by the poorest of the poor, such as the 17 who had been transferred from the Pest House and who had to be provided with all their clothing, down to stockings and shoes.[68] The 'gentleman private' Jacques du Plessis, retired from King William's First Troop of Guards, paid his own way and lived in the same quarters as the staff, albeit sharing a room. He paid for the education of a nephew who, in 1742, became chaplain to the Hospital and a person of consequence socially.[69]

In those early years all inmates had to be paid for and sponsors seem not to have been lacking. In 1739, by virtue of a splendid donation of £15,400 from Paul

---

64 *Charter and By-Laws*, p. 25.
65 Woodward, pp. 8–9.
66 Vigne, 'A Monument of the Piety of their Ancestors', p. 205.
67 Woodward, p. 9.
68 Charles Marmoy, *The French Protestant Hospital ... Inmates and Applicants, 1718–1957* (2 vols, 1977), vol. 1.
69 Charles Marmoy, 'The Chelsea Pensioner and the Chaplain: The Two Jacques du Plessis', *PHS*, 23/1 (1977): 36–48.

Dufour, treasurer since 1719, the provision of 'outgifts' to those outside the Hospital with specific and pressing needs, began. In the cruelly hard winter of 1739–40, £1,200 was distributed, in January, to Royal Bounty recipients in Westminster.[70] In Spitalfields a similar amount was spent by the directors of 'La Soupe'.

The numbers of inmates had grown to 250 by the 1760s, and the reputation of 'La Providence' seems to have been quite unlike that of the near-by workhouses, a sought-after place of reward rather than of correction. It kept alive the memory of those who had suffered 'for the sake of thy Holy Gospel', as it tries to do today for their descendants. In doing so it catered only for the Huguenots and their descendants, as did the distributors of the Royal Bounty, whose work went on until 1842. Their involvement in poor relief outside their own community, if it can be so called, doubtless continued, and the constant stream of visitors entertained by the directors in the first 'La Providence', and its later homes in Hackney, Horsham and Rochester, must have made its ways widely known. In 1853, Dickens's *Household Words* said of the inmates that they 'are more happy, have more confidence and comfort in a charitable establishment provided for their particular benefit under a body of Directors connected with them by common ties in a society in which they find the same habits and the same remembrances'.[71] In 1875, after the move to the green fields of Hackney, an inspector reported to the Charity Commission rather differently. The building was 'too handsome ... for the board and lodging of aged weavers and weaveresses, ordinary labourers and domestic servants' and better suited to 'aged and decayed French governesses', used to better living conditions 'than were ever dreamed of in the wretched hovels of Spitalfields'. The directors accepted this judgement as praise rather than blame.[72]

Perhaps the experiences of persecution and exile and a sense of duty to Almighty God who had preserved them inspired those Huguenots with a stronger sympathy for the poor and needy than was common among the native English or French at home. In England, individual Huguenots had contributed to the 'public good' before the *grand refuge* concentrated their minds on the needs of their fellow Huguenots 'who are in distress'. In both periods, while proclaiming, as on the seal of the French Hospital, that *Dominus Providebit*, they strove to assist the 'afflicted or distressed' in their own and their host community.

---

70 Charles Marmoy, *The Case Book of La Maison de Charité de Spittlefields*, HSQS, 51 (London, 1981), pp. iv–v.

71 *Household Words* 8 (1853).

72 Charles Marmoy, 'More Pages from the History of the French Hospital', *PHS*, 22/3 (1973): 246–7.

Chapter 5

Killing in Good Conscience
Marshal Schomberg and the Huguenot Soldiers of the Diaspora

Matthew Glozier
Australian National University, Canberra

The background

In 1559, at the onset of great persecution of the Protestants in France, Jean Calvin's lieutenant, Théodore de Bèze, wrote to Bullinger in Zürich:

> We are often asked whether it is permitted to take up arms against those who are the enemies not only of our religion, but also of the kingdom .... Up till now, our answer has always been that the tempest should be faced only with the arms of prayer and patience.[1]

This doctrine was soon altered. It took little account of the real difficulties facing Protestants 'under the cross' in France, Scotland or the Netherlands, and Calvin had difficulty in convincing hot-headed members of the nobility of its verity in those countries. In France, Jean de Berry de La Renaudie and his allies deviated clearly from the dictate, when planning the conspiracy of Amboise in March 1560, and even the heartland of Geneva faced growing willingness to resist so-called tyranny. Calvin and Bèze were cleared by a Geneva tribunal of complicity in the Amboise plot, but there remained much public support there for the endeavour. Their innocence was only convincing up to a point, and Bèze actually sent La Renaudie a small book authored by François Hotman, which denounced the Guise faction in France, along with his own translation of the appropriate Psalm 94: 'O Lord God, to whom vengeance belongeth, show thyself'.[2]

J.H. Elliott is one among a number of historians who has realised that, for Geneva to survive, its passive attitude towards authority had to change.[3] This was all the more so, in light of the emergence in France of the Protestant churches under the patronage of noblemen, thus securing their involvement in the struggles of high-politics and the court, one of whose weapons was revolt. It was the Amboise conspiracy that set the

---

1   Bèze quoted in Paul F. Geisendorf, *Théodore de Bèze* (Geneva, 1949), p. 116.
2   John H. Elliott, *Europe Divided: 1559–1598* (1968; London, 1990), p. 111.
3   Ibid., p. 111.

scene for later Huguenot resistance on a Europe-wide basis, as the Prince de Condé joined his royal brother, Antoine de Navarre, at Nérac. Bèze himself left Geneva for Nérac on 20 July 1560 and their discussions led to the resolution to contact Protestant leaders across Europe. Thus, when the colloquy at Poissy broke down in October 1561, Bèze and Calvin finally accepted (in Elliott's words) 'commitments which would lead inescapably to a recourse to arms'.[4] This set the scene for Reformed and *politique* noble resistance to the Valois monarchy as much as to the Guise-led Catholic League. The key feature of this whole scenario, from the point of view of later Huguenot belligerence, is the sublimation of Calvin's original theology to the worldly concerns of aristocratic violence and this theme would reappear in Europe in 1688 under the leadership of William of Orange.

The Revocation

The year 1685 was a momentous one for France's Protestant population. It marked the point at which Huguenots were forced to choose between their faith and their country, their conscience and their king. But the persecution of the Huguenots did not begin in 1685. In that year, the revocation of the Edict of Nantes, which had guaranteed freedom of worship to France's Protestants since 1598, was the last in a long line of attacks by the French Crown upon the rights and privileges of the small Protestant population in France. A general pressure upon Huguenot communities and their rights is evident from the beginning of Louis XIV's personal reign in 1661, when a series of protracted legal attacks took place upon the right of Huguenots to hold their religious services. However, the French king's persecution of his Protestant subjects only really gained its edge after the 1678 Peace of Nijmegen which brought to an end the Franco-Dutch war which had raged since 1672. The treaty ratified all the conquests made by Louis XIV as a result of his victories over the Dutch and the Spanish Army of Flanders during six years of war and the confirmation of these possessions to France, and the official peace which followed the treaty of 1678, allowed Louis XIV to concentrate on domestic issues with greater circumspection and force than he had hitherto been able to do. Ironically, the famous Marshal Schomberg, a Protestant, had done much to bring about this situation through his competent generalship.[5] From this point onwards, Louis XIV allowed the Huguenots those privileges that were in strictest accord with the stipulations of the Edict of Nantes, and he said this would allow them 'to consider from time to time by themselves, and without constraint, if they had any good reason for depriving themselves of the advantages that they could share with my other subjects [by remaining Protestant]'.[6]

---

4 Ibid., p. 111.
5 Matthew R. Glozier, *Marshal Schomberg, 1615–1690: 'The Ablest Soldier of his Age': International Soldiering and the Formation of State Armies in Seventeenth-Century Europe* (Brighton and Portland, 2005).
6 Louis XIV, *Memoires for the Instruction of the Dauphin*, ed. P. Sonnino (New York, 1970), p. 56.

Why King Louis revoked the Edict of Nantes is a question beyond the scope of this paper, which concentrates on the reaction of Huguenot soldiers to their betrayal by their king. Protestant soldiers were not expelled from the French army immediately after the Revocation. Whilst some did leave France along with droves of civilian refugees, sufficient remained to prompt Louvois, Minister of State for War, on 27 November 1685 to write to the provincial governors, *intendants* and inspectors of troops stating that whilst the continued employment of Protestants in the army was undesirable, a cautious approach should be adopted and they should be persuaded with financial inducements to convert to Catholicism.[7] However, when by 1686 these methods had proved ineffective, Louvois ordered that Huguenot officers should be imprisoned until they abjured. Most of the jailed officers did renounce their faith in order to obtain their freedom but then promptly departed to seek employment in foreign armies.[8] It is estimated that several thousand officers and at least 12,000 rank-and-file soldiers left France between 1685 and 1689, most going to Brandenburg-Prussia, Denmark, Great Britain, the Netherlands, and Savoy whose armies benefited from highly trained, veteran soldiers.[9]

The Protestant reaction to the Revocation was mixed, and many of the greatest Huguenot nobles in the land converted almost instantly. Yet their motivation is easily understood because they had been indoctrinated heavily into a cult of admiration of the king that left them few resources for countering his direct commands. Some never became truly Catholic at heart. Conversely, many of the lesser Huguenot nobility, and especially those in strongly Protestant regions of the north and south of the kingdom (Normandy and the Languedoc), vehemently opposed conversion, preferring flight to residence in a wholly Catholic country. At this time of enormous stress and uncertainty, leadership was not easily found, but two men who possessed the sway and confidence to petition the king on behalf of the Huguenots came to the fore, the Marquis de Ruvigny and Marshal Schomberg. Ruvigny's father had been Deputy-General for the Huguenots at the French court before retiring to England in 1686, now his son took on the role of protector. Schomberg, as a committed Protestant, and one who had long resented attempts by the French authorities to convert him, was naturally outraged that his religion should be outlawed in the kingdom of his

---

7   François-Michel Le Tellier, Marquis de Louvois, Secretary of State for War (1664–91). Cf. Camille Rousset, *Histoire de Louvois et de Son Administration Politique et Militaire*, 2nd edn (4 vols, Paris, 1862–1864) and Jean-Claude Devos and Marie-Anne Corvisier de Villèle (eds), *Service Historique de l'Armée de Terre. Guide des Archives et Sources Complémentaires, série A* (Vincennes, 1996), 'Le Tellier'.

8   V. Belhomme, *Histoire de l'infanterie en France* (4 vols, Paris, 1893–1902), vol. 2, p. 253 and *L'Armée française en 1690* (Paris, 1895).

9   Robin D. Gwynn, 'The Huguenots in Britain, the "Protestant International" and the defeat of Louis XIV' in Vigne and Littleton, *Strangers*, p. 421. I am indebted to Vivien Costello for this reference and to that of the work of Belhomme.

adoption.[10] Their petition was rapidly translated into English and copies made their way into that kingdom, despite the displeasure of James II.

The Revocation was accompanied by a general hope for the increased greatness of France based upon the systematising of religious worship within the country. Circumspect contemporary observers were in no doubt about the true 'reduction of France' that resulted from the act.[11] The Revocation forced out of France a significant minority of the population, including a large number of its most talented manufacturers, craftsmen and soldiers. It also hardened international Protestant opinion against Louis XIV, whose existing image as an aggressive war-monger, was now augmented as being a Catholic tyrant and a persecutor of his own subjects. As a result of the Revocation, an ultra-Protestant member of England's Verney family said of Louis XIV: 'I hear he stinks alive and his cankers will stink worse when he is dead, and so will his memory to all eternity'.[12]

After the revocation of the Edict of Nantes (22 October 1685), it was hoped (for what must have been a very short time) for the conversion to the Catholic faith of Frederick Herman von Schomberg, by birth German but now a naturalised Frenchman, a Calvinist and a marshal of the French army.[13] The fact that he was described as 'an amiable man to the highest degree, and his [Huguenot] wife even more agreeable', may have raised hopes for the compliance of this chief representative of French Protestantism.[14] At court, conversions were happening all around them, including members of his wife's family.[15] However, the marshal very soon made it clear that he would not take this course: 'My religion I cherish above all things: if I was forced to abandon it in favour of high office, there would be for me little consolation from the king as I would judge it poor recompense'.[16] Given this attitude, Schomberg was

---

10   *The Humble Petition of the Protestants of France Lately Presented to His Most Christian Majesty by the Marshal Schomberg and the Marquis of Ruvigny* (London, 1685).

11   Ezechiel Spanheim, *Relation de la cour de France, 1690*, ed. E. Bourgeois and M. Richard (Paris, 1973), p. 209; Alfred Rébelliau, *Bossuet historien du protestantisme* (Paris, 1899) 101–5.

12   *Memoires of the Verney Family*, ed. Margaret M. Verney (4 vols, London, 1899), vol. 4, chap. 8; Winston S. Churchill, *Marlborough his Life and Times* (2 vols, London, 1963), vol. 2, p. 231.

13   Letter to Prince de Condé, Paris, 9 January 1686 NS: 'Lettres adressées au Prince de Condé et conservées au Château de Chantilly (1685–86)', series P, 105, printed in F. Gonin and F. Delteil (eds), *La Révocation de l'Edit de Nantes vue par les informateurs du Grand Condé*, *BSHPF*, 118 (1972): 363.

14   Saint-Simon quoted in Philippe de Courcillon, Marquis de Dangeau, *Journal du Marquis de Dangeau*, ed. Soulie, Dussieux, de Channevières, Mantz, de Maintaiglou, with additions by the Duc de Saint-Simon (19 vols, Paris, 1854–60), vol. 3, p. 181 and vol. 4, p. 152.

15   Her niece, Mlle de Liembrune became a *nouvelle convertie* under the influence of the Duchesse de Ventadour: Letter to Prince de Condé, Paris, 5 February 1686 NS: 'Lettres adressées au Prince de Condé', series P, 105, printed in Gonin and Delteil, p. 112.

16   Haag, vol. 9, p. 230.

allowed to retire with his wife and family to Portugal, retaining, as a special mark of favour, his property and the pension conferred on him by Louis.[17]

Schomberg was one of the few leading military and naval figures who had decided to take up Louis's offer to absent themselves from the kingdom, rather than abjure their Protestant faith. While the marshal decided to reside on his estates in Portugal, other prominent Huguenots were said to be travelling in all directions. The great Abraham Duquesne, Marquis de Bouchet and Admiral of France, was understood to be heading to Switzerland, and the Marquis de Ruvigny to England.[18] They were the lucky few who could at least leave with permission and retain the revenues from their estates while in exile. In the circumstances it was no wonder that Madame de Maintenon received no goodbye from the Schombergs, but she had the temerity to chide the marshal's wife for this omission to their adieus. Maintenon said she desired to 'live in the same land as they', but was sorry to lose them to the 'very cruel fate that can be imagined' would be theirs. In a final outrage to the consciences of the Schombergs, she asked them to search for the light of God's Truth, meaning that they should convert and become good Catholics.[19] A more strongly worded letter followed a month later as the marshal's Huguenot wife, Susanne d'Aumale-Haucourt, had evidently sent a rather insulting letter to Maintenon in response to hers, and the lady threatened to take this to the king.[20] Others were much kinder, and the aged Prince de Condé spoke of the joy it would give him to see the marshal again in France and professed himself scandalised by their treatment.[21] The French king saw off Schomberg at the Louvre, according to the full honours of attendance that had a decade earlier been granted to him. However, on this occasion the favour was thought to be as a special favour designed to annoy the Spanish who still smarted over the marshal's role in the liberation of Portugal.[22] Schomberg took with him his Huguenot wife and his younger son, Charles.[23]

Samuel Mours concludes that no more than 19 per cent of France's Huguenots had actually fled the country by 1690.[24] The combination of large numbers of Protestant refugees escaping across France's borders and the international assistance lent to them, resulted in fears that international intervention would reach into the heart of France. Dauphiné was felt to be particularly prone to foreign influence, as it was a hotbed of Huguenot activity. Its proximity to Savoy, where a strong community of Vaudois Protestants lived, made it an even greater threat to France's domestic

---

17   *Journal du Marquis de Dangeau*, vol. 1, p. 294, 11 January 1686.
18   Newsletter, 18 February 1686: HMC, *Downshire* (London, 1924), vol. 1, pt 1, p. 122.
19   Johann F.A. Kazner, *Leben Friedrichs von Schomberg, oder Schönburg* (2 vols, Mannheim, 1789), vol. 2 (hereafter Kazner, *Sources*), no. 72, Maintenon to Susanne d'Aumale–Haucourt, Versailles, 2 April 1686.
20   Kazner, *Sources*, no. 73, Same to same, Versailles, 13 May 1686.
21   Kazner, *Sources*, no. 74. Condé to Schomberg, Chantilly, 25 October 1686.
22   Marquis de Sourches, *Mémoires*, vol. 1, p. 360.
23   *Journal du Marquis de Dangeau*, vol. 1, p. 294, 11 January 1686.
24   Quoted in Gwynn, *Heritage*, p. 23.

security, and Schomberg's son, Charles, would later (in 1692) plan an invasion here.[25] Furthermore, future events would bear out the sympathy that Schomberg felt for William of Orange's objectives, yet there is no evidence to suggest that he encouraged the marshal to accept employment from the Elector of Brandenburg as a mere cover to aiding the prince. However, neither Prince William nor the Elector doubted that Schomberg would attract experienced and very useful Huguenots to their service. When he arrived in the Electorate of Brandenburg, Schomberg was received with every mark of respect by the 'Great Elector', Frederick William. No time was wasted in creating him a Privy Councillor and *Stadholder* of the Duchy of Prussia, General-in-Chief of the armies of Brandenburg, and gifting him a regiment of dragoons to command.[26] He also purchased the Dohna Palace in the famous *Unter-den-Linden* in Berlin, to which Huguenot refugees flocked.

Something should be said about the situation in which Schomberg found himself in Berlin, for it is often claimed that he was a great patron of the Huguenots there. Indeed, the French refugees were strongly encouraged by many German princes to settle in their dominions and a number of them willingly opened their borders to the refugees, who were accepted into the Duchy of Brunswick-Lüneburg-Celle (largely due to the duke's Huguenot wife, Eleanor Desmier d'Olbreuse). They were also welcomed by Charles, Landgrave of Hesse-Cassel, whose aunt, Emilie, had married the Huguenot Prince de Tarente.[27] The Landgraves of Hessen-Homburg (who settled many of them at Friedrichsdorf-im-Taunus) welcomed them, as did the rulers of Hesse-Darmstadt and Württemberg.

The most enthusiastic host of the refugees, after William of Orange, was the Elector of Brandenburg.[28] But the establishment of Huguenot families in Brandenburg began before the Revocation, though it was only after 1685 that five Huguenot agents were

---

25   Rousset, *Louvois*, vol. 4, p. 15.

26   This later carried the name *Kürassier–Regiment groszer Kurfürst Nr. 1*. For his exact duties and responsibilities see Kazner, *Sources*, no. 75, 'Bestallungsbrief von Kurfürst Friedrich Wilhelm dem Grosen zu Brandenburg', 17 April 1687.

27   Emilie (1626–93), d. of Wilhelm V, Landgrave of Hesse-Cassel (1602–37), married Henri Charles, Duc de La Trémoïlle et Thouars, Prince de Tarente et Talmond (1620–72). She died a refugee at Frankfurt, having been granted permission to leave France in 1686.

28   On 29 October 1685, he issued the Edict of Potsdam, which allowed Huguenots to settle in his territories. Its terms promised, among other things, to cover the cost of establishing Huguenot communities in Hamburg and Frankfurt: Spanheim, *Relation*, p. 19; E.C. Privat, 'The Huguenots in Germany', *PHS*, 21/2 (1966): 115; Meta Kohnke, 'Das Edikt von Potsdam zu seiner Entetehung Verbreitung und Überlieferung', *Jahrbuch für Geschichte des Feudalismus*, 9 (1985): 241–75; Andreas Flick, 'Huguenot Research in the Hanover Area', *Huguenot Families*, 3 (September 2000): 9–14; W. Bielke, *Hugenotten in Niedersachsen (Quellen und Darstellung zur Geschichte Niedersachsens)* (Hilderhseim, 1960); A. Flick and S. Maehnert, 'Archivbestände der Französisch-reformierten Gemeinden Lüneburg und Celle sowie der Deutsch-reformierten Gemeinde Celle', *Geschichtesblätter des Deutschen Hugenotten-Vereins*, 24 (1997); K. von Düring, 'Auszüge aus dem Kirch enbücher der Französ. Reform. Kirchengemeinde zu Lüneburg', *Familiengeschichte Blätter Deutscher Herold, Monatsschrift für wissenschaftliche Genealogie*, 37/70 (1939).

charged with the mission of resettling French refugee families.²⁹ By 1700, about 13,200 Huguenots had settled in East Prussia, where they increased the population to such an extent that the Elector decided to convert the duchy into a kingdom: 'These people brought to the Kings of Prussia and to other German princes a reliable generation of army-leaders and officers.'³⁰ In fact, it seems that the reputation of Schomberg benefited from this general encouragement without him having to do very much. Yet, when he departed Berlin for the Netherlands in late 1688, the French diplomat, Jean-Antoine Mesmes, Comte d'Avaux, reported that the marshal took with him those Huguenot gentlemen who had not already been employed by the Elector.³¹ This implies that Schomberg was, indeed, involved in facilitating their employment in the Netherlands, though it was William who was most eager to take them into his service.

Such was the international nature of the Huguenots' flight, and such was their importance as a focus for international Protestant anti-Catholic action, that the Elector's motive in accepting both them and Schomberg was interpreted by many in Europe to be the result of political considerations rather than simple kindness. A pact for the preservation of the Protestant religion had been signed between the Elector and the Swedes on 10 February 1686, and a meeting also took place between the Prince of Orange and the Elector of Brandenburg at Cleves in August 1686.³² 'Some that pretend to see further into things' were prepared to interpret the meeting as the first step in a 'reuniting of the Lutheran and other princes' of Europe, against King Louis.³³ In England, James II's agents informed him that this supposed plan

---

29   Jean P. Erman, *Mémoires pour servir à l'histoire des réfugiés français dans les états du roi* (9 vols, Berlin, 1782), vol. 1, pp. 127–41; Uta Janssens, 'Jean Deschamps (1709–67) and the French Colony in Brandenburg', *PHS*, 23/4 (1980): 227; C. Friedrich Nicolai, *Beschreibung der Königlichen Residenzstädte Berlin und Potsdam* (3 vols, Berlin, 1779), vol. 1, p. 204.

30   Janssens, 'Jean Deschamps (1709–67)', p. 227; Nicolai, *Beschreibung der Königlichen Residenzstädte*, p. 204; T. Schmidt and H. Schnitter, 'Die Hugenotten in der Brandenburgisch-Preussischen armee', *Militärgeschichte*, 24/3 (1985): 233–9; H. Schnitter, 'Die Réfugiés in der brandenburgischen Armee', in G. Bregulla (ed.), *Hugenotten in Berlin* (Berlin, 1988), pp. 311–26; H. Schnitter, *Unter dem rotten Adler: Réfugiés im brandenburgischen Heer Ende des 17. Anfang des 18. Jahrhundert* (Berlin, 1996); D. Harms, 'Das Edikt von Potsdam vom 29 Oktober 1685: Die Integration und der soziale Aufstieg von Ausländern in der Preußischen Armee des 17. und 18. Jahrhunderts', in B.R. Kroener (ed.), *Potsdam: Staat, Armee, Residenz in der Preußisch-deutschen Militärgeschichte* (Frankfurt-am-Main, Berlin, 1993), pp. 159–71.

31   Archives du ministère des affaires Etrangères, Quai d'Orsay (Paris) (hereafter *Quai d'Orsay*), *Cahiers Politiques Hollande* 1656, September–December 1688, despatches D'Avaux, ff. 302–18, d'Avaux to Louis XIV, 28 October 1688. I am indebted to Dr David Onnekink, University of Utrecht, for this reference. Jean-Antoine Mesmes, Comte d'Avaux (1640–1709).

32   Louvois to Le Tellier, 17 September 1685, cited in Rousset, vol. 4, p. 2 n. 1.

33   7 August 1686, *CSP Domestic*, January 1686–May 1687, p. 229.

had already 'come to a very good issue', and Schomberg's transit towards the key players in such a scheme did nothing to ease fears on this point.[34]

The Huguenots were in fact the focus of extreme political negotiations between William of Orange, the Elector of Brandenburg and several lesser Protestant German rulers, and Schomberg seems to have been as interested as most in their salvation.[35] However, Schomberg was not actually present at the August meeting between William and the Great Elector, and the assertion (by some historians) that he was there is based on a misreading of Samuel Pufendorf's memoirs.[36]

This strong association between Brandenburg and the refugees did not effect Louis XIV's good will towards Schomberg, who was careful to avoid any open communication with the Prince of Orange. However, this evaporated upon the death of the Elector Frederick William (9 May 1688) whose successor, Frederick III, was strongly anti-French. His father's death left the new Elector free to pursue a strongly anti-French policy.[37] Furthermore, William sent to Schomberg in Berlin, an agent charged with the job of recruiting the marshal to the service of himself and the United Provinces. This man, Simon von Petticum, covered his mission by saying he was in Berlin to mediate in the bitter quarrel between the Great Elector and his eldest son.[38] On his way across Germany, Petticum acted as emissary to the ruler of Lüneburg and the Landgrave of Hesse-Cassel, and he resided in Berlin until 2 January 1688.[39] Even before Petticum's arrival, Schomberg was corresponding with his cousin, Henry Sidney, in England, suggesting that he was already deeply concerned about events in Britain, and that his relative was keen to keep him abreast of developments there.[40]

---

34   Ibid., p. 229.
35   Peter J.A.N. Rietbergen, 'William III of Orange (1650–1702) between European Politics and European Protestantism: The Case of the Huguenots', in Hans Bots and G.H.M. Posthumus Meyjes (eds), *La Révocation de l'Edit de Nantes et les Provinces-Unies, 1685.* Colloque International du Tricentaire (Amsterdam and Maarsen, 1987).
36   Samuel von Pufendorf, *De rebus gestis Friderici Wilhelmi Magni, Electoris Brandenburgici* (12 vols, Berlin, 1634; 1695 edition), vol. 2, p. 1509; Samuel von Pufendorf, *Friederich Wilhelm der Grosse Churfürsten zu Brandenburg, Leben und Thaten* (Berlin, 1710), p. 1222, cited in Lucille Pinkham, *William III and the Respectable Revolution: The Part Played by William of Orange in the Revolution of 1688* (Cambridge, Mass., 1969), p. 104.
37   Rousset, vol. 4, p. 115 n. 1.
38   *Correspondentie van Willem III en van Hand Willem Bentinck, eersteen Graaf van Portland*, ed. N. Japikse (The Hague, 1928), pp. 756–7, William III to Petticum, 28 November 1688 NS., cited in Pinkham, *William III and the Respectable Revolution*, p. 111.
39   *Correspondentie van Willem III*, ed. Japikse, p. 770.
40   *Diary of the Times of Charles the Second by the Honourable Henry Sidney, afterwards Earl of Romney; including his correspondence with the Countess of Sunderland and other distinguished persons at the English Court; to which are added letters illustrative of the times of James II and William III*, ed. R. W. Blencowe (London, 1843), pp. 265–7, Schomberg to Sidney, 25 September 1687 NS. Schomberg's maternal grandmother, Theodosia

From this point onwards, it was impossible for Schomberg to pretend that he was still France's friend, and he was now ready to participate in actions aimed at harming King Louis. In mid-July 1688, he was listed in a secret Dutch document as one of the generals who would lead William's invasion of Great Britain.[41] Significantly, he was not one of the 171 refugee officers who addressed a petition to William on 14 July, confirming that Schomberg had been recruited specifically for the operation.[42] He was named as general on the secret list of personnel for the invasion in June 1689, and Petticum undoubtedly used the Schomberg name to reaffirm the support of Celle and Wolfenbüttel while returning to The Hague.[43] The marshal joined with William when that prince concluded an agreement with the Elector Frederick in September 1688, freeing him to act directly against Louis's interests in Europe.[44] William's later, bitter, comments about his disappointment in Schomberg, and at having 'bought' him at too dear a rate, seem to confirm this interpretation.[45]

On 21 September 1688, 3,000 soldiers of the army of Brandenburg marched on Cologne. At this moment all Europe saw that Schomberg had allied himself with Louis's enemies to prevent the appointment of the French-sponsored prelate – Cardinal von Fürstenburg – to the bishopric of the strategically important see of Cologne.[46] The marshal took a prominent role in this campaign, a fact apparent to international observers such as John Evelyn: 'News of the French investing Philipsburg, and of the Marshal Schomberg's putting in 3,000 men into Cologne, upon the dispute of the Elector's interest against the Prince of Fürstenburg'.[47]

This was no token gesture of defiance by the marshal, as his activity in taking Cologne forestalled the French.[48] In October, Louis XIV's agent, d'Avaux, wrote to the French king with the news that Schomberg was to serve under William in the

---

Harington, was the daughter of Lucy Sidney, a child of Sir William Sidney, of Penshurst, Kent: G.E. Cokayne, *Complete Peerage* (14 vols, London, 1916), vol. 4, pp. 482–3.

41   *CSP Domestic*, June 1687–February 1689, vol. 3, pp. 244–5, 'Préventions necessaires pour le dessein de Juillet 1688'.

42   'Requête adressée aux États Généraux des Pays-Bas par cent soixante et onze officiers français, 14 July 1688', transcribed in *BSHPF*, 36 (1888): 196–203.

43   Pinkham, p. 111.

44   Henry L. King, *Brandenburg and the English Revolution of 1688* (London, 1914), pp. 17–24; James R. Jones, *The Revolution of 1688 in England* (London, 1972), p. 207; J. Childs, 'A Patriot for Whom? "For God and Honour": Marshal Schomberg', *History Today*, 38 (1988): 47.

45   *CSP Domestic*, 1689–90, pp. 381–2; HMC, *Downshire*, vol. 1, pt 1, p. 328; T. Bruce, Earl of Ailesbury, *Memoirs*, ed. W.E. Buckley, Roxburghe Club (2 vols, Edinburgh, 1890), vol. 1, p. 253.

46   Rousset, vol. 4, p. 116. For Schomberg's account of this vital period of his career see his letter to Pedro II, King of Portugal, London, 4 January 1689 (Kazner, no. 82).

47   *Diary of John Evelyn*, ed. E.S. de Beer (6 vols, Oxford, 1955), vol. 4, p. 598 (22 September 1688); *London Gazette*, 20 September 1688.

48   Jones, p. 207.

design on Britain.⁴⁹ By 29 October, the strength of Schomberg's forces on the right bank of the Rhine, north of Mainz, further checked the French advance.⁵⁰ Two months after Brandenburg forces marched against Cologne, the Prince of Orange's army departed for its invasion of Great Britain. William appointed Marshal Schomberg as his second-in-command for this November descent upon England, due in part to the fact that his friends assured him that he must have as his subordinate a man of sufficient standing to ensure the continuation of the plan should the prince be killed.⁵¹ Jonathan Scott has emphasised William's exploitation of existing, long-term religious divisions in England, suggesting that, at its most basic level, the employment of the rhetoric of religious struggle was probably an inevitable outcome of the events of 1688, regardless of the real strength of feeling behind it.⁵²

The association between the revolution and the international Protestant cause (exploited by William and typified by the presence of Schomberg), was overt. On 20 February 1689, Sir Edward Seymour said, referring to the assistance lent in the 1580s by Queen Elizabeth to the nascent Dutch Republic: 'England has done formerly for Holland, as Holland has now done for England'.⁵³ William also made heavy use of Schomberg, playing-up the marshal's status as an exile and patron of the Huguenots, in order to facilitate support from other German princes and the French Protestants themselves. Romeyn de Hooghe's engraving, *Allegory on William IIII crossing to England*, shows Schomberg standing at the Prince of Orange's right hand, while a figure, symbolising the unity of the United Provinces, stands at his left.⁵⁴ Schomberg can also be seen standing next to William in a political cartoon, entitled *The Protestant Grindstone*, depicting the prince and Queen Mary, holding the pope's nose to a grindstone driven by the Anglican clergy.⁵⁵ All such depictions of the marshal confirm his place in the propaganda wars fought by William and his supports against Catholic Europe and the forces of France.

---

49   Quai d'Orsay, *Cahiers Politiques Hollande* 1656, September–December 1688, despatches D'Avaux, ff. 286–7, d'Avaux to Louis XIV, October 1688.
50   Jones, p. 275.
51   Pinkham, pp. 148–9.
52   Jonathan Scott, *England's Troubles: Seventeenth-century English Political Instability in European Context* (Cambridge, 2000), p. 216.
53   Andrew Grey, *Debates of the House of Commons from the Year 1667 to the Year 1694* (10 vols, London, 1763), vol. 9, p. 97, cited in Scott, p. 214.
54   Franz Muller, *De Nederlandsche Geschiedenis in platen. Beredeneerde beschrijving van Nederlandsche historieplaten, zinneprenten en historische kaarten* (4 vols, Amsterdam, 1863), vol. 1, p. 414. Cited in Israel, *The Anglo-Dutch Moment*, p. 85.
55   See illustration published in B. Speck, 'Religion's Role in the Glorious Revolution', *History Today*, 38 (July 1988): 30.

The Soldiers

Soon after securing England, William III realised that, in order to secure the whole of the British Isles, he must fight against the exiled King James in Ireland. This duty he gave to Schomberg, and his role in the unfolding events that followed William's ascendancy in Britain and the necessary war that followed in Ireland is the best instance for observing the militant spirit of the French Calvinist refugees.

The culture and personality of the Huguenot soldiers has seldom attracted much scholarly comment. The general military competence and Protestant fervour shared by the majority of the soldiers is almost anecdotal. William of Orange certainly understood the usefulness of the Huguenot soldiers in the Irish campaign and the attitude of most of them towards their predominantly Catholic foe in Ireland offers strong evidence of their sentiments. Definite proof of the Huguenot soldiers' general attitudes can be found in a few firm comments by Huguenots about how they viewed their service under William of Orange, and some of these have been preserved in historical memoirs like those of Isaac Dumont de Bostaquet, Samuel de Pechels, Guillaume Chenu de Chalezac de Laujardière and Jean Martheile.[56] Just one example might suffice to demonstrate the militant Protestant spirit among William's forces. While marching through Ardee, in late 1690, a French soldier, who was very sick from drinking contaminated water and despaired for his life, fell to his knees and revealed himself as a Catholic by pulling out a rosary 'which one of the Danes seeing, shot the Frenchman dead, and took away his musket without any further ceremony'.[57]

Highly representative examples of the deeply pervading religiosity which underlay the decision of most refugees to flee from their homeland, are expressed by the Huguenot pastor, Jacques Fontaine, who characterised his former homeland as the 'Babylon' from which he had been released thanks to the grace of God.[58] Two themes emerge in Fontaine's autobiography, the first being the presence of divine favour in his family's lucky escape from their persecutors in France. The second theme is the perpetuation and celebration of their religion in their new land, and Fontaine saw Britain as a refuge for the re-growth of Huguenot faith. Fontaine may further have seen Ireland as a bastion for the refugees as he – like so many other Huguenots settled in Portarlington, the community established for retired and decommissioned French refugee officers, and the refugees in Dublin – became strong supporters of the Protestant ascendancy in Ireland during the closing years of the seventeenth century.

---

56   Isaac Dumont de Bostaquet, *Mémoires Inédites de Dumont de Bostaquet, Gentilhomme, Normand*, ed. F. Read and R. Waddington (Paris, 1864); Thomas P. Le Fanu, 'Dumont de Bostaquet at Portarlington', *PHS*, 14/2 (1931): 211–12; A.S. Pechels, *Mémoires de Samuel de Pechels* (Toulouse, 1878); Jean Martheile, *Mémoires d'un Protestant condamné aux Galères de France pour cause de Religion, écrits par lui-même* (Rotterdam, 1755).

57   G. Storey, *An Impartial History of the Wars of Ireland: With a Continuation Thereof* (London, 1693), pp. 151–3.

58   Fontaine, *Memoirs*, pp. 50–55.

Significantly for a pastor of the Reformed faith, Fontaine never drew back from violent action, and he was among the first of his region in France to advocate resistance to his persecutor. For example, he approved of the actions of his cousin, Jagault, who joined the English cavalry.[59] Similarly, his brother-in-law, the comfortably-born Rocmadou Borsiquot, also served as a common soldier in William's army in Ireland, revealing the quality of soldiery the prince possessed at all levels in his Huguenot regiments.[60]

While the Huguenot condition certainly involved persecution and struggle, it is clear that not all those refugee soldiers who fought under William of Orange were recent or traumatised escapees from France. Indeed, it is usually argued that militancy of any sort was alien to the Huguenots as a group. Generations of them had been subjected to sermons preaching obedience and loyalty to their king.[61] It is difficult to perceive any level of passivity in the actions of the Huguenot soldiers who served William of Orange, many of whom were country gentlemen, or belonged to the old military nobility. Robin Gwynn's insistence on the vehemence of Huguenot resentment towards the 'great persecutor', Louis XIV, is borne out by several examples of the spirit among the refugee soldiers. A short time before the invasion of 1688, some Huguenot soldiers in the Dutch Army were reported to be so violently opposed to the French interest, for example, that they were prepared to 'join with such English [exiles] as resolve to have at the king's person'.[62]

The memoirs of Jacques Fontaine mention two of his friends who similarly sought a violent vengeance against their persecutor. After the Irish campaign one of these friends, Jacques Fraineau, bought a shop in Dublin and settled down to trade, but his earlier years were far from calm. Fontaine tells how Rocmadou Boursiquot (whose sister Fontaine later married) had joined William of Orange's army and 'envisaged that they would conquer France and re-establish our religion there in spite of the great persecutor Louis XIV'.[63]

Fontaine also reported that William of Orange was accompanied, on his arrival in Britain, by a French refugee captain who craved the 'honneur de prendre les premiers ce jésuite français' ['honour of killing the first among the French Jesuits'].[64] Many of the Huguenot soldiers felt themselves to be on a similar mission from God. As a result, they trusted in 'une providence merveilleuse, et la bonté de Dieu' ['a marvellous providence and the Grace of God'].[65] This sentiment was ingrained in the Protestant faith itself. Bernard Cottret refers to 'Huguenot arrogance and disdain, their desacralisation of the world' which lent a powerful immediacy to their vehement struggle against persecution and any imposition on their consciences.[66] Rocmadou

59 Ibid., p. 35.
60 Ibid., pp. 111–12, 116–17, 120, 162.
61 John Stoye, *Europe Unfolding* (London, 1969), p. 372.
62 British Library, London, Additional MS 41816, ff. 242 *passim*, see f. 250.
63 Fontaine, *Memoirs*, p. 62.
64 Ibid., p. 62.
65 Ibid., p. 62.
66 Cottret, *Huguenots in England*, p. 251.

Boursiquot was killed at the Boyne in 1690, but Fraineau went on to live a long life.⁶⁷ The sentiment which underlay their decision to join William in Britain was in accord with the famous statement of Marshal Schomberg who said, when his regiment came face to face with James II's Catholic Frenchmen at the Boyne, 'Allons, mes amis! rappelez votre courage et vos resentiments: voila vos persecuteurs!' ['Forward my friends! Gather your courage and your resentment: there are your persecutors']. Fontaine's relation of his friends' feelings clearly adds credence to Schomberg's words. Some historians have chosen to believe that Schomberg's, admittedly florid, statement is apocryphal, but the words come straight from Paul Rapin de Thoyras's *History of England*.⁶⁸ Rapin de Thoyras was present at the battle of the Boyne in July 1690.⁶⁹

An informal network of friendship also promoted Jacques Fontaine into Ireland, where he met veterans of the Huguenot regiments, including Boursiquot 'et d'autres amis' ['and other friends'].⁷⁰ Fontaine and his friends would not have had the opportunity to participate in the Irish campaign without the serious advertising campaign carried out by William's senior Huguenot supporters immediately before the invasion of Ireland in 1689.⁷¹

Some of the refugees cherished the belief that their French assets were theirs to dispose of. One example of this can be found in the will of Colonel Pierre Chalant de Romaignac, the former commander of one of the two battalions of Schomberg's French Horse in 1689. He married Esther de Noguillon by whom he had several daughters, one of whom married Jean d'Arassus, minister of the Lucy Lane and Peter Street Churches in Dublin. The colonel's 1697 will bequeathed his French fief of Romaignac, in Burgundy, to his grandson by this marriage. The boy, Charles Pierre d'Arassus, was expected to take the designation of 'De Romaignac'.⁷² At the time (in 1697) it was perhaps thought to be a possibility that the colonel's grandson might secure the fief; after all, many Huguenots hoped that the terms of the 1697 Peace of Ryswick would favour their return to France. Ultimately, many of Colonel de Romaignac's grandsons joined the British Army. They could be found serving as officers in English regiments in the 1740s: Lieutenant Elias Darrassus was commissioned in Colonel Bragge's infantry regiment on 18 November 1721 (ensign,

---

67   Fontaine, *Memoirs*, p. 62.
68   For an assessment of Rapin's work see Hugh Trevor-Roper, 'A Huguenot Historian: Paul Rapin', in Scouloudi, *Huguenots in Britain*, pp. 3–19.
69   Samuel Smiles, *The Huguenots, their Settlements, Churches and Industries in England and Ireland* (London, 1867), p. 226.
70   Fontaine, *Memoirs*, p. 62.
71   Matthew R. Glozier, *The Huguenot Soldiers of William of Orange and the Glorious Revolution of 1688: The Lions of Judah* (Brighton and Portland, 2002), p. 70.
72   Will of Colonel de Romaignac, PCC 192, Whitefield; C.E. Lart, 'The Huguenot Regiments', *PHS*, 9/3 (1911): 484; H. Wagner, 'A List of Pensions to Huguenot Officers in 1692', *PHS*, 9 (1911): 585, n. 5; R.P. Hylton, 'Dublin's Huguenot Community: Trials, Developments and Triumph, 1662–1701', *PHS*, 24/3 (1985): 221–31; R. Whelan, 'Changing Identities of Ireland's Huguenots', *PHS*, 27/1 (1998): 20–35.

3 March 1718), and Captain John Darassus was commissioned in Major-General Hargarve's infantry regiment on 13 December 1739 (lieutenant, 17 November 1721).[73]

Colonel de Ramaignac was not alone in his desire to preserve his name, arms and seigneurial pretensions from far-off France. For many exile communities (the Huguenots included) the experience of uncertainty and disjointure induced by flight and expatriation represented a serious blow to personal and group identity. It is, therefore, somewhat surprising to find that one of the most obvious expressions of French noble group identity, the duel, features so little in the general story of the exiled Huguenot community in Britain, the Netherlands or Brandenburg. Of all of these kingdoms, it was only in Ireland that there appears to have been any notion of the concept of the duel as an acceptable expression among the refugees for the defence of a gentleman's honour. It is arguable whether Captain Claude Serment, a Portarlington retiree and veteran of Colonel de La Melonière's Huguenot infantry regiment, was aware of these precedents when he was killed in a duel at Portarlington in 1700. In every other way, Serment was a perfectly sound representative of the general Portarlington settlement.

Serment was a retired officer who had been wounded at Drogheda and later given a small plot on the Earl of Galway's estate. Like so many of his compatriots, he married a Frenchwoman, called Marianne Charrière.[74] Serment was therefore only exceptional in the general Portarlington community in the manner of his death. But it is in the exceptional nature of his demise that Serment proves the general rule that, while many Huguenot officers may have been French gentlemen, they were also restrained and generally highly disciplined Calvinists who attempted to observe the biblical dictate 'Woe to that man by whom the offence cometh!'[75] Huguenot communities placed great store on the regulation of the conduct of their members. Calvin himself suggested that 'each of us should watch himself closely ... lest we be carried away by violent feelings'.[76] Calvin hoped that the magistracy, or government, of Reformed communities by lay elders would inspire each disciple's personal government of their own soul. This would aid the purity of that person's relationship with God *via* the scriptures.[77]

---

73   *A List of the Colonels, Lieutenant Colonels, Majors, Captains, Lieutenants, and Ensigns of His Majesty's Forces, etc.* (London, 1740), pp. 20, 74.

74   *Dublin and Portarlington Veterans: King William III's Huguenot Army*, ed. Thomas P. Le Fanu and William H. Manchée (London, 1946), p. 66; Wagner, 'Huguenot Officers', p. 586, n. 23.

75   *Matthew* 18: 7.

76   Jean Calvin, *Institutions of the Christian Religion*, ed. John T. McNeill (2 vols, Philadelphia, 1960), vol. 1, p. 611, cited in Mack P. Holt, *The French Wars of Religion, 1562–1629* (1995; Cambridge, 1997), p. 24.

77   One of the few other contemporary instances of duelling in a Huguenot community occurred in Russia in 1689, where F.H. du Rouillé, from Brabant, was killed in an affair of honour. It is significant that there is considerable doubt regarding his religion: at least one historian of the Huguenots in Russia – J. Kämmerer – is convinced that Rouillé was a

It was not only their religion which restrained outrageous and scandalous activity among the refugees. All the Huguenot communities in Britain were sensitive to native opinion, which often regarded them with suspicion or disdain. A cult of respectability was, therefore, fostered among the refugees in order to survive in, and adjust to, their new home. They were particularly careful not to 'scandalise the English nation which it is so much in our interest not to offend, and cause our nation to be held in poor esteem by them, which could lessen their compassion towards our poor refugee brethren and stem the flow of their charity and alms'.[78] Similarly, when several Camisard rebels found their way into London in 1707, after the failure of the last great Huguenot insurrection in the Cévennes, some prophets among them were charged with 'fraud' and 'fanaticism'. They were thought to 'dishonour Religion and draw down censure upon our Refuge'.[79] In this context, Serment's behaviour can probably be taken as an all too human lapse in a concentrated ghetto of poor and sometimes ailing or frustrated Huguenot exiles, where tensions must inevitably have boiled over from time to time.

Bernard Cottret points out the rarity of actual manslaughter amongst the Huguenot communities in England. He adds, however, that wounds 'and swollen heads' were rife.[80] Cottret cites several examples of near duels between Huguenots in England from as early as 1571, but in each case it is clear that the *fracas* reflected general societal levels of violence and were in no way culturally determined by the Huguenots' 'Frenchness'. The high level of personal restraint which Huguenots practised is clear from the statistics from their magistrates' registers.[81] Robin Gwynn says restraint and respectability were common features of the Huguenot congregations in England throughout the seventeenth century.[82] Janine Garrisson's figures, relating to pre-Revocation south-west France, where so many Huguenots lived, are a reasonable

---

Catholic French adventurer and not therefore a member of the Huguenot refuge at all: Jürgen Kämmerer, *Rußland und die Hugenotten im 18. Jahrhundert (1685–1789)* (Wiesbaden, 1978), p. 33; Andreas W. Fechner, *Chronik der Evangelischen-Gemeinden in Moskau. Zum dreihundertjähren jubiläum der Evangelisch-Lutherischen St. Michaelis-Gemeinde zusammengestellt* (2 vols, Moscow, 1876), vol. 1, p. 388; Pierre Avril, *Voyage en divers etats d'Europe et d'Asie, entrepris pour decouvrir un nouveau chemin à la Chine* (Paris, 1692), p. 251.

78 18 February 1690, Cottret, *Huguenots in England*, p. 242; Eileen Barrett, 'Regulating Moral and Social Behaviour in the French Church of London, 1680–1689', *PHS*, 27/2 (1999): 232–45.

79 Hillel Schwartz, *Knaves, Fools, Madmen and that Subtle Effuvium: A Study of the Opposition to the French Prophets in England, 1706–1708* (Gainesville, 1978) and *The French Prophets: The History of a Millenarian Group in Eighteenth-Century England* (Berkeley, 1980). A full condemnation of the prophets from Languedoc is contained in the Threadneedle Street Consistory, 23 July 1707, cited in Cottret, *Huguenots in England*, pp. 283–4.

80 Ibid., p. 243.

81 Robin D. Gwynn, 'Disciplines of Huguenot Churches in England: The Need for Further Research', *PHS*, 22/6 (1976): 590–8.

82 Robin D. Gwynn, 'The French Churches in England in the 1640s and 1650s', *PHS*, 23/4 (1980): 256–61.

indication of Huguenot criminal activity. Violent misdemeanours only accounted for 7 per cent of crimes, whereas insults, at 33 per cent, represented by far the greatest breaches of good behaviour. Significantly, the second highest breach was sexual misconduct, demonstrating that the magistrates of the Huguenot communities in France were as interested in sins of the flesh as were their contemporaries in Scotland.[83]

One of the many problems that faced the Huguenot settlers at Portarlington in Dublin and, indeed, throughout Britain, was the practice of their faith. The non-conformist nature of the Huguenots' Calvinist principles sat awkwardly with England's and Ireland's Anglican élite. Many Huguenots totally rejected High Anglicanism as 'une espèce de romanisme' ['a species of romanism'] which was essentially 'demi-Papiste' ['semi-Papist'].[84] Central to this view, was the understanding that an ordained minister in the Church of England was 'a priest, who takes his place in the long line of apostolic succession' rather than a minister elected from among his peers.[85] Rejection of the Anglican form of worship was further aggravated by the knowledge of the persecution of Presbyterians in Scotland and, to a lesser extent, in Ireland during the 'killing times' in the reign of Charles II. Jacques Fontaine said that many of his fellow Huguenots saw the persecution of the Presbyterians in Scotland as a 'unique crime de ces pauvres malheureux ... presbytériens' ['singular crime against these poor unhappy ... Presbyterians'].[86] For this reason and others many Huguenots viewed the Anglican form of worship with suspicion. Anglican Tories had, after all, supported James II's short reign and had continued to promote anti-Williamite action after James's flight.

One of the most immediate debates which presented itself before William of Orange, after he and Mary secured the English throne in 1688, was that of comprehension within the Church of England. Even before his arrival in Britain, the Prince of Orange was of the opinion that the Anglican establishment could well do with a broadening of the base of its liturgy.[87] This desire was clearly designed with the aim of encompassing the non-conformist Huguenot, Presbyterian and dissenting communities which William patronised abroad. It also had the aim of maintaining England's membership of the international Protestant community, of which William was one of the principal figures.[88]

---

83   Janine Garrisson, *Les protestants au XVIe siècle* (Paris, 1988), p. 72; For Scottish Calvinists see, A.B. Calderwood (ed.), *The Buik of the Kirk of the Cannongate, 1564–1567* (Edinburgh, 1961) and *Acts and Proceedings of the General Assembly of the Kirk of Scotland, 1560–1618*, ed. T. Thomson (Edinburgh, 1839–45).

84   Fontaine, *Memoirs*, p. 70.

85   Elizabeth Labrousse, 'Great Britain as Envisaged by the Huguenots of the Seventeenth Century', in Scouloudi, *Huguenots in Britain*, p. 147.

86   Ibid., p. 147; Gwynn, *Heritage*, p. 94.

87   Charles Rose, *England in the 1690s: Revolution, Religion, and War* (Oxford, 1999), pp. 110–12.

88   Ibid., p. 109.

William's regime was hampered in its pursuit of the policy of wider comprehension, by the intransigence of the Tory interest. The opinions of this group, regarding non-conformist Protestants in England, were well represented in a London play by Thomas Shadwell. This play, entitled *The Scowrers*, appeared in 1690 and presented the character of a corrupt Jacobite who, upon hearing of the suppression of the Protestants of the Vaudois, exclaimed 'they are damned Presbyterian fellows, and hate the Church, for my part, had I my will, I would put all the Phanaticks in Christendom in pitch'd shirts, light them and let them blaze like City Funerals'.[89] The debate regarding comprehension reflected William III's lack of interest in religious dogma in general in Britain for the new king did not desire the creation of an anti-Catholic cartel of Protestant nations and his war against Louis XIV was not a war of religion.

William III had far too many and too prominent Catholic allies – among them Pope Innocent XI and the Emperor Leopold I – to be prey to religious fanaticism. Only in Ireland, where Huguenot refugees and Ulster Protestants played such a prominent part in the struggle against a largely Irish Catholic and Catholic French force, did the saga of William's struggle against Catholic France take on the dimensions of a war of religion. Even in this theatre it could still be argued that the war was more one of personal vengeance against the person of Louis XIV than one caused by religion. This was certainly the view taken of William's wider struggle against the man whose designs were feared by all Europe, regardless of religion. Hostile contemporaries said Louis XIV 'aimed at the destruction and enslaving [of] all the kingdoms and States of Europe: No distinction of Protestant or Papist, Enemy or Ally'.[90] The French king's willingness to league with the Ottoman Turks against the Holy Roman Empire confirmed such fears and earned for him the title of 'Most Christian Turk' as a replacement for the tradition form of address for French monarchs as 'Most Christian King'.[91]

Religion was, however, at the heart of most of the Huguenots' problems. In England comprehension, or the inclusion of dissenting beliefs within the Anglican Church, remained a contentious issue. A disagreement over ceremonial practices in the church forced Jacques Fontaine to abandon his ministry at Cork 'pour la paix de l'église' ['for the peace of the Church'] after the Earl of Galway had complained of his poor observance of Anglican rites.[92] Cottret is just one historian of the Huguenots who has seen High Church Huguenots as natural Low Church Anglicans.[93] How

---

89   Thomas Shadwell, *The Scowrers: A Comedy, Acted by their Majesties Servants* (London, 1691), p. 7.

90   William King, *Europe's Deliverance from France and Slavery: A Sermon Preached at St. Patrick's Church, Dublin, On the 16th November 1690* (Dublin, 1691), pp. 8–9.

91   Charles Ingrao, *The Habsburg Monarchy, 1618–1815* (Cambridge, 1994), pp. 80–1; John C. Rule, 'France Caught Between Two Balances: the Dilemma of 1688', in L.G. Schwoerer (ed.), *The Revolution of 1688–1689: Changing Perspectives* (Cambridge, 1992), pp. 43–5; Rose, p. 115.

92   Fontaine, *Memoirs*, p. 75.

93   Cottret, *Huguenots in England*, p. 172.

many High Church Huguenots there may have been, especially among the soldiery, is probably impossible to calculate.

Huguenot soldiers shared the common plight of the entire refugee community in that they lacked an assured ongoing occupation or career. Jacques Fontaine says that more than one of his fellow Huguenots in Ireland became a 'chevalier d'industrie' or 'Jack of all trades' in order to make a living.[94] Fontaine also reported on the almost universal poverty of the Huguenot settlers, whether at Portarlington, or elsewhere in Ireland and mentioned two French families at Cork, for example, who were 'fort pauvres' ['very poor'] for want of work.[95] Herbert Lüthy has, however, highlighted the importance of Calvinist Huguenot morality in promoting the economic determinism and success of Huguenot communities. With this attitude they could 'tackle the paramount issue of pauperism not through plain charity, but through work discipline, social organisation, apprenticeship and education in general'.[96]

The financial assistance lent by Huguenots to the developing stock trade companies of the early eighteenth century was indeed large. Huguenot skill in silk weaving, precious metalworking and manufactures helped finance English shipping and colonisation, encouraged stability in foreign trade and helped provide much-needed credit assurance.[97] Huguenots provided 15 per cent of the proprietors and an equal amount of the first public stock issued in 1720 by the London Assurance Company.[98]

The Huguenots of the exodus were destined to remain an exiled people. The 1697 Treaty of Ryswick, which concluded the Nine Years' War or War of the Grand Alliance (1688–97), failed to secure their return to France. Secret meetings, regarding a return-clause in the treaty, had been held at the nonconformist temple at Leicesterfields, in London, in October 1696. As Bernard Cottret points out, however, we only know of these meetings because of a hostile pamphlet published at Cologne entitled *Mémoires envoyés de Londres à M * par M * au sujet de l'établissement d'un conseil pour veiller sur la conduite des protestants réfugiés en Angleterre*. The pamphlet's author maintained that a small clique of Huguenots so dominated the London refuge, and that their control of relief funds was 'so much to their advantage', that 'there is nothing which they would not gladly sacrifice to their determination to hold their position'.[99] To support his thesis, the anonymous author of the memoir maintained that the secret Huguenot council included the most important members of the refugee community. Cottret suggests that they may have enjoyed the support of the Marquis de Ruvigny, by that time created Earl of Galway, and Cottret provides

---

94   Fontaine, *Memoirs*, p. 58.

95   Ibid., p. 162.

96   Herbert Lüthy, *La Banque protestante en France, de la révocation de l'Edit de Nantes à la Révolution* (Paris, 1959), p. 7.

97   G.N. Clark, *The Seventeenth Century*, 2nd edition (Oxford, 1953), p. 35.

98   Gwynn, *Heritage*, p. 87.

99   Anon., *Mémoires envoyés de Londres à M * par M * au sujet de l'établissement d'un conseil pour veiller sur la conduite des protestants réfugiés en Angleterre* (Cologne, 1699), p. 10, cited in Cottret, *Huguenots in England*, pp. 22–56.

proof of the existence of a governing Huguenot clique by producing the *Memorandum in Defence of the French Committee*. This document not only proves that the clique existed, but that its premier concerns were with the maintenance of the respectability and orthodoxy of the Huguenot community in Britain:

> It was of the utmost importance that none but suitable persons should enter the French ministry. Some time afterwards, the existence of scandalous preachers among the French was an established fact, though there were no means of bringing them back to their duty, as they belonged to no Church in particular.[100]

Far from suggesting a Huguenot clique bent on restoring the Edict of Nantes through concessions which might have been forced upon the French at the time of the Treaty of Ryswick, this evidence points to a remarkably fixed, and increasingly established, English refugee governance. This was centred on London, but encompassed international Huguenot figures such as the Earl of Galway. Despite this, the anonymous author of the memoir claimed that the Huguenot clique's 'great purpose was to work for the recall of all Protestants to France, without concerning themselves over-scrupulously to ensure the restoration of the Edict of Nantes'.[101] The author's hostile intention seems to have been to suggest that the clique designed a return to France, without ratifying their community's rights of conscience, in order to secure their forfeited estates and possessions.

In defence of the committee's concerns, it should be mentioned that there was a long-standing precedent for the existence of non-clerical elders and directors of Huguenot communities. In June 1582, the creation of magistrates within Huguenot communities was recommended as a means by which 'those who cannot be governed by the ministry of the Church should be curbed by the authority of the said magistrate, whom God has ordained to this end'. At the turn of the seventeenth century, the Huguenot settlements at Canterbury and Norwich had *hommes politiques* who were responsible for the community's behaviour. These non-clerical directors of the community kept registers in which were recorded the settlement of grievances within the group.[102] There are, however, important factors which point to the existence of a novel and untraditional clique of refugees in the London of the late 1690s. Good evidence for this exists in the complaint, made to the Archbishop of Canterbury, by a group of conformist Huguenot ministers who purported to represent the pre-Revocation Huguenot settlement whose identity had been overrun by the legion of refugee arrivals after 1685:

---

100   Lambeth Palace Library, MSS Gibsoniani 941, f. 87, cited in Cottret, *Huguenots in England*, p. 226.

101   Anon., 'Mémoires envoyés de Londres', p. 30, cited in Cottret, *Huguenots in England*, p. 227.

102   Ibid., pp. 238–9; 'Register of Norwich, 1605–15', British Library, Additional MS 43862.

> The underwritten French Ministers actually officiating in four French churches united to one another and wholly conform to the Church of England are forced by their wants to represent to your Lordships and worships that though their churches be the first established here in London by public authority, since the last Persecution in France and by a Patent under the great seal of England, in which they are called by the name of the Refugees, yet they are ready to fall and their Ministers to starve for want of a competent subsistence.[103]

These internal conflicts within the Huguenot community helped bring about the failure of an effective Huguenot lobby group to argue in favour of the inclusion of a general relief for Huguenots in France in 1697. This effectively terminated the last chance for the refugees of the exodus generation to return to their native soil. Their descendants would henceforth only see France as conquerors in the armies of foreign nations like England and Prussia. William III was therefore left with an army of landless and dependent Huguenots.

The Peace of Ryswick of 1697 witnessed the failure of Huguenots across Europe to secure a return to France. From this point onwards, Huguenot soldiers suffered mass unemployment during a time of general (if temporary) peace. Both French and English observers understood that William would try to make use of the Huguenot soldiers wherever the energy of these itinerants could be diverted as he continued to enjoy the loyalty and dependence of hundreds of Huguenots.[104] After 1697, it was clear to many Huguenots that they had little option but to abide by William III.

Conclusion

Huguenot soldiers stood apart from the rest of the French refugee community. Having survived as proud professional soldiers, as opposed to penniless civilians, the Huguenot soldiery was automatically segregated from the alms-receiving settlers of Europe's Protestant capital cities. The segregation of the soldiers from civilian life was further enhanced by the fact that many of them belonged to the *petite noblesse*, a class which in southern France especially had maintained a strong separation from non-noble groups. This distinction might have been insignificant were it not for the fact that so many of the descendants of the original Huguenot soldiers who accompanied William of Orange to Britain in 1688 chose military and ecclesiastical careers. These occupations perpetuated their social position in the face of the poverty, obscurity and racial hostility which continued to afflict centres of Huguenot settlement at Portarlington, Dublin and London well into the next century. The continued presence of Huguenot gentlemen in both the army and the church, greatly aided their acceptance among the English and Anglo-Irish gentry and as a result many Huguenot officers married into British church and army families

---

103 Lambeth Palace Library, MSS Gibsoniani, 1, f. 929.
104 Gerald E. Aylmer, 'Unbelief in Seventeenth-Century England', in G.E. Aylmer (ed.), *Puritans and Revolutionaries* (Oxford, 1978); Théodore de Bèze, *Du Droit des Magistrats*, ed. Richard M. Kingdon (Geneva, 1971); Cottret, *Huguenots in England*, p. 239.

throughout the eighteenth century. By the turn of the nineteenth century, their manners, speech and appearance were indistinguishable from that of their brother officers. Only their names continued to remind them of their origins in France. The Huguenot soldiers who played such an important part in the events of the 'Glorious Revolution', and who were such a prominent factor in European politics at the close of the seventeenth century, simply melted into other cultures. Thus ended one of Europe's most energetic, devout, industrious and brave peoples.

Chapter 6

The Huguenot Soul

The Calvinism of Reverend Louis Rou

Paula Wheeler Carlo
Nassau Community College, State University of New York, USA[1]

Several hundred Huguenots arrived in the British colony of New York in the years immediately surrounding the Revocation of the Edict of Nantes. Along with Huguenots who had come to New York before the 1680s, these new arrivals founded L'Eglise Française du St Esprit in 1688. This church was one of only a few independent French Reformed congregations in North America that remained in existence beyond the colonial period.[2] Louis Rou was the pastor of St Esprit from 1710 until his death in 1750. During his long ministry he composed a rich collection of documents that illuminate eighteenth-century Huguenot beliefs and practices. They also shed light on contemporary controversies that plagued the French Church of New York. This paper explores Rou's background and theology as well as his occasionally contentious tenure at St Esprit.

Louis Rou was born around 1683 in Holland. He was the eldest son of Jean Rou, a one-time *conseiller* at the Parlement of Paris, who lost his position during Louis XIV's mounting persecution of the Huguenots. The Rou family fled to the Netherlands in the early 1680s, where Jean became an interpreter at the States-General. The Rous formed close ties to other refugees in the Netherlands, including the apocalyptical theologian, Pierre Jurieu. Louis eventually studied Latin, Greek and Hebrew, in addition to theology, at the University of Leyden. After completing a ministerial apprenticeship with the Huguenot refugee congregation in Copenhagen, he was ordained by the Walloon Synod at Tertholen on 31 August 1709. In July of the following year, he began his career at St Esprit, which was one of New York's oldest and largest congregations.

---

1   I am grateful to the Huguenot Society of America for a grant that helped to fund my travel and research expenses. I also want to thank my friend and colleague, Dr Patricia Caro, for her editorial suggestions.

2   St Esprit was closed during the American Revolution when it was used to store supplies for British troops. The church was reopened in the 1790s but fiscal problems prompted the congregation to join the Episcopalian fold in 1804.

It did not take long before Rou's personal life affected his professional one. Shortly before his arrival in New York, Rou was married to fellow-refugee Marie Le Bouteaux. Marie gave birth to a son, also named Louis, on 25 December 1712, but both she and the child died soon afterwards. Within a year the thirty-year-old Rou wanted to marry fourteen-year-old Renée Marie Gougeon of New Rochelle, a rural, predominantly-Huguenot settlement located slightly north of New York City. At this time, Huguenot women in New York typically were married in the early- or mid-twenties.[3] Because of Renée's tender age, the Reverend Daniel Bondet, the Huguenot minister in New Rochelle who had conformed and received Anglican ordination, refused to perform the marriage. The ceremony was eventually conducted by Gualtherus Du Bois, a Dutch Reformed minister in New York. Although Dutch women sometimes were married when they were eighteen or nineteen, a fourteen-year-old bride was a rarity. Indeed, Du Bois must have had some qualms about the marriage since he referred to Renée as a 'young maid' in the church records.[4]

Rou's hasty remarriage to someone so young angered and embarrassed his congregation. Apparently Rou's 1711 sermons on the evils of gossip were disregarded, as his personal life became a popular topic of discussion.[5] Elias Neau, a well-known Huguenot who had conformed to Anglicanism, observed that Rou's actions created an uproar in the French Church and that nobody knew his reasons for the marriage, 'for the young Creature has not much'.[6] Renée eventually produced 14 children, five of whom died in childhood. Such a large number of offspring was far above the norm for Huguenots in New York. Thus, the couple's fecundity further alienated the congregation, especially when Louis asked for increases in salary.

Undoubtedly motivated by their disapproval of Rou's personal life, the church elders hired an assistant minister, Jean Joseph Brumeau de Moulinars, who assumed many of Rou's duties beginning in 1718. One of these obligations was to visit the independent Huguenot congregation in New Rochelle four times a year to perform baptisms and communion. Rou resented this task for he believed that the

---

3   Paula Wheeler Carlo, *Huguenot Refugees in Colonial New York: Becoming American in the Hudson Valley* (Brighton and Portland, 2005), pp. 119, 127–9, for New Paltz and New Rochelle. There are no marriage age composites for Huguenot women in New York City (Manhattan), however, figures for all New York City women in the late-seventeenth to early-eighteenth centuries support a similar pattern. See Joyce Goodfriend, *Before the Melting Pot: Society and Culture in Colonial New York City, 1664–1730* (Princeton, 1992), p. 33.

4   Samuel S. Purple, *Records of the Reformed Dutch Church in New Amsterdam and New York: Marriages from 1639 to 1801* (New York Genealogical and Biographical Society, 1890), p. 120. The marriage ceremony was held in the New Rochelle home of Renée's father, Grégoire Gougeon, implying parental consent to the marriage. Rou's background, education, and profession must have seemed very attractive to the family.

5   Louis Rou, 'Sermons and Other Writings', vol. 1, Manuscript collection, New York Public Library.

6   'Neau to Secretary of the Society for the Propagation of the Gospel' (hereafter SPG), as quoted in Jon Butler, *The Huguenots in America: A Refugee People in New World Society* (Cambridge, Mass., 1983), p. 192.

nonconforming congregation should attend the French-speaking Anglican church in New Rochelle, whose Huguenot ministers, including the aforementioned Daniel Bondet, had been ordained according to Anglican rite. In so doing, Rou felt the nonconformists would avoid fomenting and furthering a schism. Rou's attempt at ecumenicism was not very far removed from Calvin's conciliatory position towards the Church of England in the sixteenth century, but his attitude was not embraced by all eighteenth-century Huguenots.[7] Despite his trepidation, Rou made several visits to the nonconforming congregation in New Rochelle, as is indicated in the records of St Esprit. Moulinars, however, eagerly ministered to the nonconforming congregation, thereby deepening their breach with the conforming church.

An intense rivalry soon developed between the two men causing the New York congregation to drift into two opposing camps. Thus by 1724 Rou did not have the support of the newly-elected elders and, apparently, a significant minority of church members. Signatures in documents that were supplied as evidence in Rou's subsequent legal complaint indicated that 58 family heads were his supporters while 35 were detractors.[8] Regardless of Rou's relative support among church members, the elders flexed their authority. They declared Moulinars to be the only minister, locked Rou out of the church and refused to pay him.

In response, Rou asserted that the election had been rigged and initiated legal proceedings to reclaim his position. Meanwhile, his wife circulated a petition in his favor, securing signatures from many female congregants.[9] Additionally, Rou used his connections with prominent English officials to press his case. Among these politicians was his current chess partner, Governor William Burnet, son of the Anglican bishop Gilbert Burnet. In 1725 Rou turned the dispute into a public spectacle by publishing responses (in English) to his detractors in a brief book provocatively titled, *Collection of Papers Concerning Mr. Lewis Rou's Affair*. As a naturalised English citizen and an eloquent writer in that language, Rou cloaked himself in the protection of English law and the friendship of English politicians. He addressed Moulinars's accusation that he was an Anglican sympathiser by insisting that his 'esteem and respect' for the Church of England was not a crime. However, in the eyes of some Huguenots, including Moulinars, 'the Church of England and the Church of Rome were as like one another as two sisters can be'.[10] These, of

---

7   For further discussion see, W. Stanford Reid, 'The Ecumenicalism of John Calvin', in Richard C. Gamble (ed.), *Essays on Calvin and Calvinism*, vol. 10, *Calvin's Ecclesiology: Sacraments and Deacons* (14 vols, New York, 1992), pp. 105–6; John H. Kromminga, 'Calvin and Ecumenicity', ibid., pp. 37–53; John T. McNeill, 'Calvin and Episcopacy', ibid., pp. 54–6.

8   *Collection of Papers Concerning Mr. Lewis Rou's Affair* (New York: William Bradford, 1725), pp. 4, 7–8.

9   Butler, p. 193.

10 Pierre Stouppe, the Anglican conformist Huguenot minister in New Rochelle, reported on Moulinars's words and actions in that town in his letter to the Bishop of London. Apparently Moulinars was an incendiary figure there as well. Stouppe to SPG Secretary, in SPG, 'Records', Series A, 19: 363ff (Yorkshire, 1964).

course, were truly fighting words at the time. Rou further contended that the 20 or 30 people who had deposed him were 'depriving at least 80 families of his ministry and spiritual comforts' and that the elders had thrown the church into 'confusion and disorder'.[11] When the elders appealed to the consistory of the Huguenot Church on Threadneedle Street in London to intervene, Rou insisted that the New York Church's consistory had failed to prove that he was negligent in his duties. For good measure, he claimed that his predecessors, the Reverends Pierre Daillé and Pierre Peiret had 'lived in torment among them' and that the elders were using 'their liberty for a cloak of maliciousness'. He also noted that Moulinars and his followers had 'fomented for several years a scandalous schism at New Rochel' against the Church of England. Finally, in order to bypass the authority of the elders Rou insisted that only the 'Synod of the Walloon Churches of Holland ... can suspend or deprive me'.[12]

Rou's arguments proved to be highly effective. Governor Burnet and the New York Council ruled that traditional French Protestant discipline required that ministers be dismissed by colloquies, which did not exist in America.[13] They also decided that Rou's firing represented a breach of agreement on the part of the elders. Although it may appear that the Council was unduly influenced by Rou's friendships with persons in high places, this may not have been the case. The de Lancey family, who were among Rou's most vociferous opponents, also had highly-placed political and economic connections. Moreover, although Master of Chancery Cadwallader Colden's daughter had married into the de Lancey family, Colden went on the record stating that he found Moulinars's answers to Rou's complaints to be insufficient.[14] Thus, on 24 February 1725 the case was decided in Rou's favour and he was reinstated as pastor of the French Church in New York. Moulinars subsequently became the full-time minister to the nonconforming Huguenot congregation in New Rochelle, remaining there until his death in 1741. Ironically some of Rou's major opponents, including the prominent de Lanceys, left the French Church to attend Anglican Trinity Church. Their defection from St Esprit further substantiates the argument that distaste for Rou was driven by personal rather than theological reasons. On the other hand, not all of Rou's detractors left the church. Some of his opponents' names continued to surface in the church records, strongly suggesting that their sense of Huguenot identity took pre-eminence over personal animosity.

Having secured his ministry, Rou could concentrate his energies more fully on his theology. Ninety-six of his manuscript sermons, written between 1704 and 1750,

---

11   Rou was probably correct about confusion and disorder, which was a frequent problem for Huguenot Churches in the colonies as they lacked an outside governing body to supervise and intervene in disputes. On the other hand, the numbers of detractors are most likely understated, while the numbers of supporters may be overstated, based on the documents identified above in n. 7 and 8.

12   Louis [Lewis] Rou, 'Eighteen Pieces of Manuscript', 8 February 1725, New York Historical Society, Manuscript Collection, misc. MSS Louis Rou. Use of material courtesy of The New York Historical Society. The Walloon synod was the body that had ordained him.

13   Butler, p. 193.

14   Rou, 'Eighteen Pieces of Manuscript', 24 February 1725.

are still extant, undoubtedly a small portion of his total output. To the best of my knowledge, they are one of the few large collections of French Protestant sermons that have survived from colonial North America.[15] Rou's sermons are prepared in well-written French and they frequently showcase his erudition. Characterised by rigorous French logic, the sermons are organised into a series of points that emulate the Classical fashion.[16] Extensive marginalia in multiple languages refer to biblical passages, the early Church Fathers, French Reformed theologians, and diverse Classical sources, suggesting that Rou either had a prodigious memory or access to a well-stocked library as well as considerable linguistic abilities. If Rou owned all of these books it is very possible that he had one of the best, if not the best, private library in New York at that time. Occasionally he noted that it took between 40 and 50 minutes to deliver a particular sermon. Some were preached on multiple occasions, usually with amendments, while others may have been preached only once.

Rou's sermons sometimes reflect an interesting mix of the theological and political attitudes of two influential seventeenth-century Huguenot thinkers, Pierre Bayle and Pierre Jurieu, both refugees in Holland like the Rou family. Nevertheless, there is little in the content of Rou's sermons to suggest that the anti-monarchical politics of his father's friend, the theologian Jurieu, had any significant impact on Rou's political attitudes. Consider Rou's sermon 'On the Marvels of God's Law', which was first preached in Copenhagen in 1709 and subsequently on numerous occasions in New York, including once in the presence of the royal Governor. He stressed his firm support for the institution of monarchy and for the present king, urging his congregation to 'imitate the zeal and piety of the holy king' and to 'love, like him, the words of God'.[17] Although he differed with Jurieu on politics, Rou tended to be in complete accord with him on most theological issues. This is readily evident in Rou's hatred of Socinianism. Throughout his sermons Rou stressed Trinitarianism and the divinity of Christ and there are marginalia references to Jurieu's anti-Socinian treatises. Unlike Jurieu, however, Rou was able to inject a degree of toleration – at least for different branches of Protestantism – while maintaining Calvinist doctrines. Rou's political, as well as his ecumenical attitudes, are far more reminiscent of Jurieu's contemporary nemesis, Pierre Bayle. Even Rou's extensive sermon marginalia evoke images of Bayle's meaty footnotes in the *Dictionnaire*

---

15   Others collections are the manuscripts of Pierre Stouppe, 'Sermons, 1724–41' Library, Huguenot Society of America, New York, and Andrew Le Mercier, 'Sermons, 1710–20', Manuscripts, Massachusetts Historical Society. I have examined the Stouppe sermons, which are mentioned in this paper, but I have not perused the Le Mercier manuscripts. Stouppe was a Huguenot minister in New Rochelle who conformed to Anglicanism. Le Mercier was the minister of the independent French Reformed church in Boston in the early eighteenth century.

16   See Nigel Massey, 'The Sermons of Louis Rou, c.1680–1750, Rector of St Esprit in the City of New York', unpublished paper (Huguenot Historical Society Library and Archives), p. 6.

17   Rou, 'Sermons and Other Writings', vol. 3. All titles and quotations from sermons have been translated by the present writer.

Historique et Critique. Despite this, there were no marginalia references to Bayle in Rou's sermons. Moreover, Rou's tacit approval of Elijah's slaying of the prophets of Baal stands in stark contrast to Bayle's condemnation of this act in his article on Elijah in the *Dictionnaire*.[18]

Most of Rou's sermons focus on issues of central importance to Christian life and belief. All are rooted in a passage or verse from the Scriptures and biblical references predominate in both the sermons and the marginalia. Representative topics include: 'The Brevity and Uncertainty of Life'; 'The Necessity of Thinking about Death'; 'The Knowledge of God and Jesus Christ'; 'The Immensity of God'; 'The Immortality of the Soul'; 'The Character of the True Christian'; 'Discipleship'; 'The Nature and Conditions of Prayer'; 'The Resurrection'; 'Communion'; 'Charity' and 'Creation'. Sermon content demonstrates that Rou was a theological Calvinist who had not strayed from his seventeenth-century religious roots. He frequently mentions predestination, unconditional election, the perseverance of the elect, the total depravity of man, and refers to the Synod of Dordrecht in the marginalia. In short, there is nothing in these sermons to suggest that Rou promoted unorthodox doctrines that would have provoked his controversy with the elders. Thus his detractors' claims that Rou was an Anglican sympathiser must have referred to his political rather than his theological leanings and possibly his views about church governance. Indeed, I would theorise that if Rou were given the choice, he would have preferred a 'tyrant' 3,000 miles away in the form of the Bishop of London to the tyranny of the French Church of New York's consistory. Following his controversy with the church elders, Rou's sermons assumed an increasingly arrogant and sarcastic tone, which must have prompted even more church members to defect to Anglican or Dutch Reformed Churches as St Esprit's records indicate dwindling numbers of baptisms, especially after 1730.[19]

Some of Rou's sermons were devoted to topics that appear to be tangential to French Reformed beliefs and practices. For example, early in his tenure at St Esprit Rou preached at least six messages on the 'Vow of Jeptha'. He argued that Jeptha, whose story is found in *Judges* 11: 38–40, literally sacrificed his own daughter rather than sequestering her for life. Presumably, this was an attack on clerical celibacy and cloistering, a topic that seems to have limited value for Rou's congregation since there is no evidence that the New York Huguenots were tempted to convert to Roman Catholicism.[20] Nevertheless, Rou managed to give this dreadful tale a practical application, by including a cautionary note to 'consider the frightful danger of hasty and imprudent vows'. This topic also gave Rou an opportunity to demonstrate his command of the Classical and Judaeo-Christian traditions as well as his mastery

---

18   Rou, 'Fourth Sermon on the Vow of Jepthah', ibid., vol. 2.
19   Butler, p. 194.
20   These sermons reportedly originated when two unknown men declared in Rou's presence that Jepthah did not actually put his daughter to death to fulfil his vow. John A.F. Maynard, *The Huguenot Church of New York: A History of the French Church of St Esprit* (New York, 1938), p. 125.

of several ancient languages. He noted that similar stories could be found in Greek myths, such as the sacrifice of Agamemnon's daughter, Iphegenia. In addition, he carefully parsed words and meanings from the Hebrew texts, refuting a rabbinical tradition that denied a literal sacrifice took place. To further support his argument, he cited ancient sources, including Josephus, Augustine, Jerome, Ambrose, Athanasius and, not surprisingly, Calvin, all of whom believed that the immolation actually occurred.[21] Rou emphasised that God would not expect Christians to fulfil such a vow since it was an outrage to the laws of nature and of the Gospel. On the other hand, Rou felt that Jeptha's daughter was 'an admirable example of piety and virtue'. Her 'submission to her father and resignation to the orders of Providence' displayed heroic courage, thereby making her a prototype of the sacrifice of Jesus.[22] These comments shed some light on Rou's attitudes toward women's roles and place. Obviously he liked his women to be submissive to patriarchal authority, which may help to explain his attraction to the 'young maid' he had married.

While Rou apparently approved of frequent participation in certain carnal pleasures, he was adamantly opposed to wine bibbing. Taking this into consideration, he blamed the disastrous 1712 slave revolt in New York City on excess consumption of alcohol by the slaves![23] Rou seems to have imbibed contemporary attitudes about the inability of non-European persons to hold their liquor. This belief may have been rooted in the notion that non-European men, like all women, were not creatures of reason. Indeed, even when New York was New Netherland and under Dutch control, it had been illegal to sell or give alcohol to Indians.[24] This policy was likewise adopted in the British colonies in North America.

On the whole, Rou's sermons contain limited commentary about contemporary political or social issues. Nonetheless, one gets the sense that the Age of Reason had not completely bypassed Rou and that he viewed himself as an eminently rational and logical man, whose beliefs were shaped by the best and most enlightened wisdom of the Classical and Christian traditions. Despite these self-perceptions, a virulent anti-Catholicism permeates his sermons. Undoubtedly this was one of the more resonant themes for his Huguenot congregation. Certainly Rou was not alone in his contempt and hatred for the Roman Catholic Church: similar feelings were evinced by Anglicans, including Huguenots who had conformed to the Church of England, and were probably rife among other Protestants in the eighteenth century.[25]

Some of Rou's most scathing criticisms of the 'Church of Rome' were advanced in three sermons that critiqued the doctrine of transubstantiation. Describing

---

21   'Third Sermon on the Vow of Jeptha', in Rou, 'Sermons and Other Writings', vol. 2.

22   'Fifth and Sixth Sermons on the Vow of Jeptha', ibid.

23   'On Drunkenness', ibid.

24   Paul Otto, 'Common Practices and Mutual Misunderstandings: Henry Hudson, Native Americans, and the Birth of New Netherland', *de Halve Maen,* 72/4 (1999): 81.

25   Luc Racaut, 'Religious Polemic and Huguenot Identity', in Raymond Mentzer and Andrew Spicer (eds), *Society and Culture in the Huguenot World, 1559–1685* (Cambridge, 2002), pp. 42–3. Anti-Catholic rhetoric is also apparent in Stouppe, 'Sermons'.

transubstantiation as a repulsive absurdity and an indefensible dogma, Rou asserted that the Roman Church had corrupted and perverted the Lord's Supper. In one sermon he argued that to adore Jesus Christ in the sacrament is to be guilty of idolatry and, as St Paul noted, idolators will not inherit the kingdom of heaven. To put it bluntly, Roman Catholics and any other believers in transubstantiation are destined for hell. In another message Rou described transubstantiation as 'savage, barbarous, unnatural, and perverse' since it is 'repugnant to nature and to humanity to eat human flesh'. Placing his abhorrence into a New World context, Rou declared that defenders of transubstantiation were worse than the Iroquois Indians and the cannibals who ate their enemies rather than their gods. He contended that 'nothing provokes the jesting of the libertines and the scorn of the infidels more than this monstrous dogma that we attack'. He further noted that even the Arab philosopher, Averroës, who had seen and read about all kinds of religious sects, found nothing more ridiculous than the Christian belief that they eat the flesh of their God whom they adore. Rou concluded that transubstantiation conflicts with the senses of judgement and intelligence, is contrary to Scripture, and incompatible with nature and with the essence of the Lord's Supper, which is intended to be a commemoration of Christ's death.[26] Rou was not alone in his characterization of Roman Catholic beliefs and practices as worse than those of heathens, Jews and Muslims. The manuscript sermons of Reverend Pierre Stouppe, the Anglican-Huguenot minister in New Rochelle from 1725 to 1760, convey a similar perspective.[27] But unlike Rou, Stouppe was never arrogant, sarcastic or condescending in his sermons. Moreover, his church grew in size during his ministry and the sources indicate that he was well loved by his congregation.[28]

Rou also differed from Stouppe in references to a catechism. In nearly all of his manuscript sermons Pierre Stouppe mentioned a section of the French translation of the Anglican catechism as well as the biblical passage on which it was based. The only time that Rou referred to a catechism was in his four sermons on 'The Descent of Jesus Christ into Hell'. Rou insisted that this belief was not supported in the Scriptures and even contradicted them. To support his argument, Rou reminded his audience of Christ's words to the dying thief on the cross next to him: 'This day you will be with me in Paradise'. Assuming once again the mantle of reason and logic, Rou asked, 'How could Jesus greet the thief in Paradise if he had to visit hell first?' As further evidence he quoted the final words of Jesus, 'Father, into thy hands I commend my spirit', indicating that his soul immediately went to heaven upon the death of his body. He also asked why it was necessary to insist that Jesus descended into hell and suffered there with the demons and the damned when his body and soul had already suffered on the cross. Furthermore, he argued that this doctrine conflicted with Jesus' words: 'It is finished'. According to Rou this meant that Christ's victory

---

26   Rou, 'Sermons against Transubstantiation', in 'Sermons and Other Writings', vol. 2. Similar perspectives were advanced in the sermons of the Anglican-Huguenot minister in New Rochelle, Pierre Stouppe.
27   Stouppe, 'Sermons'.
28   For further discussion of Stouppe's ministry see Carlo, pp. 83–102.

over the power of evil and his redemption of mankind was complete once his blood had been shed. Thus the descent into hell was not literal but rather figurative and referred to Christ's intense suffering on the cross. Rou concluded that the alleged descent into hell was not congruent with Scripture, which must be the basis for all sound doctrines, but was instead a gross error created by the papists.[29] This topic was not addressed in any of Stouppe's extant sermons, so there is no basis for a comparison of the views of the two ministers. However, its absence suggests that it either had limited importance or was not a topic of controversy for the conforming Huguenots and their minister in New Rochelle.

Not surprisingly, Rou's sermon 'On the Necessity of Thinking about Death' struck a somber tone throughout. Rou noted that thoughts of death are the most useful reflections a man can occupy himself with since 'all of life is a road we follow towards death'. Once again demonstrating his knowledge of Classical sources, Rou quoted the Roman Stoic Seneca's position on the topic: 'it is necessary to think about death all of one's life'. Reverting to a Calvinistic and Augustinian context, Rou argued that divine predestination determines the duration of each man's life and that this information is completely unknown to us. Therefore, life's brevity and uncertainty justify the necessity of grace. Yet he more optimistically concluded that because of the shortness of life, 'if we suffer in this world it is not for long'.[30] Certainly Rou was no stranger to personal suffering as his first wife and son had died shortly after their arrival in New York and he later lost five of the 14 children he had with Renée. It is unclear whether or not these personal tragedies enabled Rou to deal more empathetically with members of his congregation who incurred similar losses because the extant records offer no insights into Rou's personal dealings with his flock.

In addition to impending death owing to natural causes, Rou sometimes reminded his congregation of an alternative end to this mortal life, namely the second coming of Christ and the ensuing Last Judgement. These ideas were most clearly explicated in a series of sermons on the 'Parallel between the Flood and the Last Judgement'. While Jesus' first sojourn on earth was characterised by humility and motivated by the need to redeem mankind, his second coming will be for a different purpose. Christ will be empowered to judge both the righteous and the wicked. Like the hour of our death, we cannot predict when Jesus will return since he will appear as a 'thief in the night'. In view of this we must practice virtue and live righteously in preparation for this 'fatal day'. Nevertheless, owing to our human frailty we need the grace of God to sustain us, otherwise we are damned.[31]

Rou's sermons as well as church records provide us with insights about the observance of communion at St Esprit. This sacrament was celebrated four times a year – in January, on Easter, in July, and in early fall. Quarterly observance was

---

29 Rou, 'The Descent of Jesus Christ into Hell', in 'Sermons and Other Writings', vol. 2.
30 Rou, in 'Sermons and Other Writings', vol. 1.
31 Ibid., vols 2 and 3.

in keeping with practices in the nonconforming as well as the conforming French congregations in New Rochelle. This was also the typical procedure for Dutch Reformed and Anglican churches in the colonies at the time. Louis Rou, like Pierre Stouppe in New Rochelle, preached a preparatory sermon on those Sundays when communion was celebrated. Infrequent observance of the Lord's Supper did not mean that it was unnecessary. While it did not bestow God's grace, as was the case with the Roman Catholic eucharist, the infrequency of the Calvinist celebration magnified the importance of communion since it served as a public confession of faith and thankfulness for Christ's one-time sacrifice. Nevertheless, at least one of Rou's sermons implied that many persons at St Esprit abstained from communion, prompting Rou to declare that those who neglected the Lord's Supper were disobedient to God's command.[32] It is unclear why so many church members did not partake of communion. A possible explanation is that they did not feel spiritually ready since Calvinists were cautioned not to eat or drink unworthily. Or, could it be that they were too consumed by salacious gossip about Rou's private life?

Rou preached at least five different sermons on prayer throughout his ministry. Regarding the 'Conditions of Prayer' he recommended that we 'should ask for piety, sanctity, and grace to resist temptation, to moderate our passions, to surmount our weaknesses, to have a well-ordered life, humility, a clean conscience, temperance, patience, and charity'. Yet the faithful 'should not ask for health, tranquility, or prosperity'. Furthermore, if we do not obtain what we ask for it is because we do not request what God wants us to and because we have not asked for it in the appropriate manner. To make our prayers agreeable to the Lord we must first develop the requisite interior conditions of piety, humility, faith, ardor, zeal, and perseverance. Then we must have appropriate exterior conditions, so we can avoid voluntary distractions and thereby focus our complete attention on God.[33] Although Rou encouraged his congregation to be humble, contemporary sources suggest that he did not practice what he preached. When Dr Alexander Hamilton visited St Esprit in 1744 he wrote that the minister was 'a man of good learning and sense; but being foolishly sarcasticall, he has an unlucky knack att dissobliging the best of his parishioners so that the congregation has now dwindled to nothing'.[34]

Despite the likelihood that Rou's arrogance and condescension increasingly alienated some members of his congregation, he was undeniably a man of diverse interests and talents. His 1725 responses to the charges by his opponents demonstrate a shrewd, legalistic mind, undoubtedly something he had inherited from his jurist father. Rou was also widely recognized as a chess devotee. In 1734 he wrote the no longer extant 'Critical Remarks upon the Letter to *The Craftsman* on the Game of Chess'. Summaries of this manuscript, which was dedicated to Rou's current chess partner, Governor William Cosby, attest to his mastery of the game and its history

---

32 Rou, 'Sermon on the Necessity and Excellence of Holy Communion', ibid., vol. 3.
33 Rou, ibid.
34 Hamilton as quoted in Butler, p. 197.

and vocabulary. Rou's chess manuscript was written in response to an anonymous letter on chess published in an English political journal, *The Craftsman*, in 1733. Although the original piece had Tory undertones, Rou's manuscript was devoid of politics and instead pointed out chess errors that appeared in the letter.[35] Numerous poems by Rou have survived, including one on chess written in Latin as well as French verses that he composed as a young man. Based on my cursory perusal of these verses, he was wise not to quit his ministerial position since his poetry was mediocre at best.[36] On the other hand, he may have been more inspired and in better form when he composed amorous verses. Unfortunately, Rou's romantic poems appear to have been lost since he felt it would be inappropriate to place them for safekeeping with his sermons.[37]

Rou persevered as minister of the French Church until he died in New York at the age of 67 following a lingering illness. His obituary, which was published in the *New-York Gazette, or Weekly Post Boy*, memorialised him as 'a gentleman of great learning and unaffected piety' who left 'a sorrowful widow with a numerous hopeful issue'. The obituary further noted that he was 'universally lamented' and that 'his character in the several capacities of Preacher, Husband, and Father was unexceptionable ... His remains were decently interred in the French Church, near the pulpit he had so long occupied'.[38] The French Church of New York provided his widow, who died six years later, with an annual pension of £12 because Rou left a very paltry inheritance.

All things considered, Rou's 40-year tenure, although at times contentious, secured greater stability for St Esprit than was typical of most independent Huguenot congregations in North America. Only the French Church in Charleston, South Carolina had a longer history. Moreover, Rou's erudition, his literary and linguistic abilities, as well as his friendships with prominent and powerful persons, made him a leading member of eighteenth-century New York society. In the final analysis, however, if Rou had been more humble and conciliatory and had spent more time trying to cultivate an amicable and respectful relationship with his congregation, the French Church of New York might have flourished for several more decades.

---

35 Daniel W. Fiske, 'The Lost Manuscript of the Rev. Lewis Rou's "Critical Remarks Upon the Letter to *The Craftsman* on the Game of Chess"' (Florence, 1902), p. 5. According to Fiske, Cosby apprised Rou of the letter.

36 Maynard's assessment of Rou's poetry is more positive. He wrote that they 'are not inferior to many of the printed works of the period [and] are typical of their day', Maynard, pp. 128–9.

37 Rou, in 'Sermons and Other Writings', vol. 2. The chess poem is not in this volume, but I have seen modern printed copies of it.

38 *New-York Gazette, or Weekly Post Boy*, 31 December 1750.

Chapter 7

The Influence of the Huguenots on Educated Ireland

Huguenot Books in Irish Church Libraries of the Eighteenth Century

Jane McKee
University of Ulster, Ireland

Huguenots came to Ireland in considerable numbers from the 1660s, and they and their descendants have made a very significant contribution to many aspects of Irish life. What concerns us here is not primarily the Irish Huguenots themselves, but the tradition from which they came. This study will seek to explore the continuing awareness in Ireland of the intellectual heritage of the Huguenots through an examination of the holdings of works by Huguenot authors of all periods in two Irish church libraries of the eighteenth century, the Bolton Library in Cashel in the prosperous south of the country and the Public Library in Armagh in the north. Before looking at authors and titles, however, we must first look at the libraries themselves, both eighteenth-century foundations belonging to the Anglican Church of Ireland, at the time the Established Church in Ireland.

Church libraries in eighteenth-century Ireland

These were by no means the first Church of Ireland libraries to be created in Ireland, nor were they the largest, but they were part of a significant development in the provision of libraries which took place in the dioceses of the Church of Ireland during the eighteenth century and which was part of an effort to provide better intellectual support for the clergy, particularly in the provinces where levels of absenteeism among senior clergy were causing considerable concern.[1] Several existing libraries were greatly enlarged at this time, among them those of Trinity College Dublin and of the diocese of Ossory, at Kilkenny. Trinity College Library had been founded at the end of the sixteenth century, but the eighteenth century saw the addition of a number of significant collections, among them that of Claudius Gilbert comprising some

---

1 Toby Barnard, 'Improving Clergymen', in A. Ford, J. McGuire and K. Milne (eds), *As by Law Established: The Church of Ireland since the Reformation* (Dublin, 1995), p. 138.

13,000 volumes purchased over many years and bequeathed to the College Library in 1735.[2] St Canice's Library in Kilkenny, although very much smaller than that of Trinity College, had a library which had been established in 1693 by a bequest from Bishop Otway, but this was greatly augmented by a bequest from Bishop Edward Maurice in 1756 which added several thousand volumes to the initial collection.[3]

The eighteenth century was to see the addition of many new Church of Ireland libraries to the existing number. These were usually intended to be used by the gentlemen of the diocese or town in which they stood as well as by local clergy. The first public library in Ireland was Marsh's in Dublin which was founded by Archbishop Narcissus Marsh in 1707, beside St Patrick's Cathedral, and which provided access to books for those who were not scholars or fellows of Trinity College Dublin and who therefore had no access to its library. There followed a number of other Church of Ireland libraries in Derry, Cashel and Armagh, as well as in Dromore and Clogher.[4] Those at Cashel and Armagh were part of larger schemes of urban redevelopment.[5] Indeed the library in Armagh was intended to serve as the foundation of a university, which was never built.[6]

These libraries all belonged to the Church of Ireland which served only a minority of the population, although it was the Established Church in Ireland. The activity of the majority Catholic Church in Ireland was much hampered by the Penal Laws during the eighteenth century. It was only permitted to found its National Seminary at Maynooth in 1795 and there were no Catholic libraries in Ireland during the century on the scale of those of the Church of Ireland.[7] The dissenting churches, for their part, were growing rapidly, particularly in the north of the country, but they too were not in a position to set up libraries to rival those of the Church of Ireland, and their presbytery libraries were generally much smaller.[8]

The table below lists the principal Church of Ireland and Presbyterian libraries in existence or founded in the eighteenth century, together with the dates when they were officially founded and their size, as noted in the earliest available records. It should be noted that many of these libraries had already been in operation on an ad hoc basis for some time before the date of their formal establishment. The Cashel

---

2   Peter Fox, 'They glory much in their library', in Peter Fox (ed.), *Treasures of the Library, Trinity College Dublin* (Dublin, 1986), p. 7.

3   Hugh Campbell, 'St Canice's Library: The Otway-Maurice Collection: Author List', Typescript (Kilkenny, 1994), n. pag.

4   Walter G. Wheeler, 'Libraries in Ireland before 1855: A Bibliographical essay', Ph.D. thesis (University of London, 1957, revised 1965), pp. 88–94.

5   R. Wyse Jackson, 'The Ancient Library of Cashel', *Cork Historical and Archaeological Society*, 52/1 (1947): 128.

6   Christopher Mohan, 'Bishop Richard Robinson, builder of Armagh', *Seanchas Ard Mhacha*, 6/1 (1971): 109–10.

7   Patrick J. Corish, *Maynooth College 1795–1995* (Dublin, 1995), pp. 9–13.

8   Wheeler, p. 105.

library, for example, was in existence from the early 1730s,[9] and building started on Marsh's in 1701.[10]

Table 7.1 Principal Church of Ireland and Presbyterian Libraries

Library	Date of establishment	Number of books
Trinity College, Dublin	1592–1601	30,000 (c.1735)
Kilkenny	1693	3,300 (c.1756)
Marsh's Library, Dublin	1707	18,000 (c.1849)
Derry	1729	1,550 (c.1848)
Bolton Library, Cashel	1744	12,000 (c.1757)
Antrim Presbytery Library, Belfast	c. 1765	2,700 (c.1849)
Public Library, Armagh	1771	8,000 (c.1797)

The founders of the Church of Ireland libraries were wealthy prelates who often used their own collections as the basis of the new libraries, adding to these by the purchase of other collections which had already been established by book lovers or scholars. Marsh's Library, for example contains the collection of Bishop Edward Stillingfleet and that of the Huguenot Elie Bouhéreau who was its first librarian, as well as part of the collection of Bishop John Stearne, acquired in 1745.[11] The much smaller diocesan library in Derry contains the books of two earlier bishops of the city, George Downame, bishop 1616–34, and Ezekiel Hopkins, bishop 1681–90. We do not yet know how Downame's books came to be in the library, but we know that Hopkins's library was purchased from his heirs by William King who succeeded him as Bishop of Derry and who created the Derry diocesan library through a bequest in his will.[12] King went on to become Archbishop of Dublin, and a large part of his personal collection was purchased in the 1730s by Archbishop Bolton of Cashel who merged it with his own library to form the basis of the Cashel diocesan library, now known as the Bolton Library, Cashel. It is also clear that this library was being enhanced and developed during the decades before Bolton's death, for it contains a considerable number of books dating from the 1730s. In the case of Armagh, we do not know how Archbishop Robinson gathered the books for his library. His desire for privacy led him to direct that his correspondence be destroyed after his death and

---

9   Ibid., pp. 100–101.
10   Newport J.D. White, *An Account of Archbishop Marsh's Library* (Dublin, 1926), p. 7.
11   Ibid., pp. 8–9.
12   Nicholas Pickwoad, 'Report on the Books in the Derry and Raphoe Diocesan Library', typescript (University of Ulster, 2003), pp. 1–32.

there is no trace of an earlier major collection in the library archives.[13] We know that his own collection formed the basis of the new library, and work on provenances, which has still to be done, may reveal information about the origin of the books of which we are currently not aware.

In general, once a Church of Ireland library was opened, there was little further regular purchasing and new acquisitions were acquired through bequests or gifts. Several of the founding bequests allowed for a small fixed income for library upkeep, but there is generally little evidence of regular additions to the book stock. In Armagh, however, funding arrangements were put in place to facilitate the future enlargement of the collection and books were regularly purchased. In contrast to the Church of Ireland libraries, the Presbyterian library which was started in Belfast by the Antrim Presbytery in around 1765 was a much less expensive affair, built up through regular purchasing of relatively small numbers of books, rather than the initial purchase of one or more large collections.[14]

Most of these libraries have modern catalogues, but it is much more difficult to know what these collections were like during the eighteenth century. We have no eighteenth-century catalogues for the largest libraries at Trinity College and Marsh's, although Trinity has a list of the books of Claudius Gilbert and, in both libraries, educated guesses can be made about the date of acquisition of books from their position on the shelves. The earliest catalogues to which we currently have access for the libraries in Derry, Kilkenny and Belfast, were compiled long after their foundation. The first available catalogue for Derry was printed in 1848, well over a 100 years after its establishment,[15] while that for Kilkenny is dated 1836, 80 years after the enlargement of the library by Edward Maurice in 1756.[16] A catalogue for the Antrim Presbytery Library in Belfast was printed in 1851, 86 years after the library opened.[17] Catalogues which are so far removed in time from the original library, or work based on shelf numbers where books may later have been added, cannot give us any very certain knowledge of the original collections. With the libraries of Cashel and Armagh, however, this problem does not arise, since we have early catalogues for both collections. William Cooper's manuscript catalogue for the Cashel library dates from 1757, only 13 years after it was officially established,[18] while the Armagh catalogue dates from around 1797, less than 30 years after its foundation, and was

---

13   George O. Simms, 'The Founder of Armagh's Public Library', *Irish Booklore*, 1/2 (1971): 140–41.

14   Wheeler, p. 105.

15   *A Catalogue of the Books in the Library of the Diocese of Derry* (Londonderry, 1848).

16   This catalogue, complied by the Reverend Francis Sandys, is very schematic. References to the collection in this chapter are based on Hugh Campbell's, 'The Otway-Maurice Collection: Author List', typescript (Kilkenny, 1995) which compiles the catalogues of 1836, 1851 and 1895 and identifies the catalogue(s) in which each title appears.

17   *A Catalogue of Books in the Library of the Presbytery of Antrim* (Belfast, 1851).

18   William Cooper, 'Catalogus Alphabeticus Bibliothecae Casiliensis', 1757.

written by its first keeper, William Lodge.[19] In the case of these libraries therefore, it is possible to know what was in the collections during the eighteenth century.

It should nevertheless be noted that these are eighteenth-century catalogues, and that it is not always easy to recognise authors or titles in them because titles are often abbreviated and names of authors sometimes omitted. In addition, many of the books have now vanished, so that modern catalogues are of limited assistance in identifying titles. However the early catalogues include the date and place of publication and often the format, so that it is possible to identify large numbers of the books with some certainty.

Huguenot authors in the libraries at Cashel and Armagh

Before dealing directly with the presence of Huguenot writers and books at Cashel and Armagh, a few general contextual points must be made. When the Huguenots came to Ireland, they were strongly encouraged to become integrated into the established Church of Ireland, using a French version of the Anglican liturgy in place of the traditional order of service of the Eglise Réformée de France. Acceptance of this state of affairs was by no means universal and a majority preferred to retain their own liturgy. The Church of Ireland was nevertheless the church to which many of them and their descendants belonged. The Church of Ireland libraries therefore belonged to a church which had a close involvement with the Huguenots and in which some Huguenot clergymen had achieved considerable success. Theologically and liturgically, however, the Eglise Réformée was closer to the fast-growing Presbyterian Church which also belonged to the Calvinist tradition.

Secondly, the task of deciding who is and who is not Huguenot is far from straightforward. Extensive use has been made here of *La France protestante* as a basis for selection of authors. However, some apostates and a few other figures not included in *La France protestante* have been included here, using Grente's *Dictionnaire des lettres françaises*[20] as the primary source of biographical and bibliographical information. Some gaps will inevitably remain. Finally, we have no current means of knowing how many of the books were read and how often. I have worked on the assumption that there is some significance in the fact that an author or a text appears in more than one collection.

A total of 106 Huguenot authors appear in the two catalogues, from the great sixteenth century founders, Calvin and Bèze, to the children of those who sought refuge in England, such as William Romaine, the famous mid-eighteenth century London preacher, whose father had left France to become a grain merchant in

---

19   William Lodge, 'Catalogue of Books in Armagh Public Library', Armagh, MS 1780 (n.dat.).

20   G. Grente (dir.), *Dictionnaire des lettres françaises. Le XVIIe siècle*, new edition, dir. Patrick Dandrey (Paris, 1996) and *Dictionnaire des lettres françaises. Le XVIIIe siècle*, new edition, dir. François Moureau (Paris, 1995).

Hartlepool.[21] The Cashel collection offers more variety than that in Armagh, with 101 different authors as opposed to only 62 in Armagh where the collection was considerably smaller, with approximately 8,000 titles, as opposed to the 12,000 in Cashel. There are 389 entries in the two catalogues for these authors, 244 in Cashel and 145 in Armagh. These books and authors, therefore, represent only a very small proportion of the total holdings of the two libraries. Indeed they do not represent the majority of French books in either library. In both collections, there are many other books by French authors of all periods, dealing with a wide variety of topics, from works of literature, science, travel and history, to the works of major Catholic theologians, historians and preachers.

Authors appearing in both Cashel and Armagh

If we look first at the 39 authors who appear in both libraries, they belong to all periods from the sixteenth to the eighteenth centuries and their works deal with a range of topics from theology, to law, history and literature. Table 7.2 provides a chronological list of these writers, of the numbers of titles and of books (in brackets) listed for each collection, and it also indicates where authors had links with England or Ireland. Asterisks are used to indicate that an author appears in the earliest available catalogue of one or more of the following Irish church libraries: Kilkenny, Derry and the Antrim Presbytery Library in Belfast.

Table 7.2 Huguenot authors occurring in the libraries of Cashel and Armagh

Name	Links with England or Ireland	Dates	Cashel	Armagh
Calvin***	-	1509–1564	7	3
Hotman*	-	1524–1590	5 (6)	1
Mornay***	England	1549–1623	4 (7)	1
du Moulin, P., père	England	1568–1658	7	1
Rivet, A.***	England	1573–1651	8 (9)	1
Rohan*	England	1579–1638	2	1 (2)
Saumaise**	-	1588–1653	9 (11)	3
Daillé***	England	1594–1670	11	2
Drelincourt, C.**	-	1595–1669	2	1
Bochart***	England	1599–1667	4	1
du Moulin, P., fils	England/Ireland	1600–1684	1 (2)	1

---

21   Haag, vol. 8, pp. 508–9.

Le Sueur*	-	c.1603–1681	1	1
Tavernier*	England	1605–1689	1 (2)	2
Duport*	England	1606–1679	1	3
Claude**	England	1619–1687	4	1
Jurieu, P.**	-	1637–1713	8	1 (2)
La Placette**	England	1639–1718	4	2
Allix*	England	1641–1717	2	1
Chardin	England	1643–1713	2	1
Lemery*	England	1645–1715	2 (3)	1
Poiret	-	1646–1719	1	4
Bayle***	-	1647–1706	7	7
Jaquelot*	-	1647–1708	1	1
Dacier, A**	-	1651–1722	1	1
Basnage*	-	1653–1723	3	1
Abbadie*	England/Ireland	1654–1727	2	1
Le Clerc, J.**	England	1657–1736	12	24 (28)
Rapin*	England/Ireland	1661–1725	2	2 (3)
Lenfant**	England	1661–1728	2	4
Boyer, A.*	England	1664–1729	1	1 (2)
Dumont	-	1666–1726/7	2	1
Moivre	England	1667–1754	2 (3)	2
Barbeyrac*	-	1674–1744	1	5
Cavalier	England	c.1680–1740	1	1
Desagulier*	England	1683–1744	2 (3)	1
Caillard*	Ireland	d. 1767[22]	1	1
Villette	Ireland	1688–1783[23]	1	1
Des Voeux	Ireland	d. 1792[24]	1	1

As far as earlier writers are concerned, their presence in these libraries is evidence of their continuing significance, and some of the most important figures of the Calvinist reformation are present, among them Jean Calvin, Théodore de Bèze and Philippe de Mornay. Calvin was the theologian at the origin not only of the Eglise Réformée de France but also of Irish Presbyterianism which was rapidly gaining ground in the eighteenth century. It would be astonishing if he were not present in both libraries. He is accompanied, however, by Bèze, and Mornay, both very important figures in French Calvinism but much less significant for Irish Presbyterians.

---

22 Grace Lee, The Huguenot Settlements in Ireland (London, 1936), p. 150.
23 Ibid., p. 130.
24 Ibid., p. 156.

The next generation of clergy is represented by Pierre du Moulin and his son-in-law, André Rivet. Then come Charles Drelincourt, Jean Daillé and Jean Claude, all ministers of the church of Charenton at a time when it was at the centre of the affairs of the Eglise Réformée, together with the church historian Jean Le Sueur. There are many serving clergymen from the period of the diaspora: Pierre Jurieu, Jacques Basnage and Pierre Poiret in Holland; the Arminians, Isaac Jaquelot and Jacques Lenfant in Germany; Jean La Placette in Denmark; Pierre Allix in England, and Jacques Abbadie, Gaspard Caillard, Antoine Vinchon des Voeux and Charles Louis de Villette in Ireland. There are also some members of the clergy who spent all of their working life or indeed their whole life in England, for example Pierre du Moulin, son of the celebrated clergyman of Paris and Sedan, and Jacques Duport whose father had been a clergyman in England before him.

These writers reflect the church of their own time, but they are not uniform and they are not all orthodox. Conservative and liberal strands of theological opinion are present with Rivet and Claude; pacifist and crusading attitudes to the Revocation are associated with Jurieu and Basnage, and unorthodox views are represented by the Arminians, Jaquelot, Lenfant and Le Clerc, and by the mystic Poiret who seems to have appealed greatly to some book purchaser, perhaps Robinson himself, judging by the cluster of four titles which appears in the Armagh catalogue.

The ecclesiastical authors appearing in the two collections stretch from the sixteenth to the eighteenth centuries, but there are also many other Huguenot writers. From the sixteenth century, we find François Hotman, the legal advisor to Henri IV. Writers of the seventeenth century include the scholars Claude Saumaise and Samuel Bochart; Henri de Rohan, the great military leader of the first half of the century; the businessmen and travellers Jean-Baptiste Tavernier and Jean Chardin, and the translator André Dacier. There are scientists too: Nicolas Lemery in the seventeenth century and Jean-Théophile Desaguliers in the eighteenth, along with the mathematician Abraham de Moivre, also a member of the Royal Society. That century's interest in travel literature is represented among the Huguenots by Jean Dumont's *Nouveau Voyage au Levant*, while history, law and grammar are represented by Paul Rapin, Jean Barbeyrac and Abel Boyer respectively, and the revolt of the Camisards is chronicled in Jean Cavalier's *Memoirs*. Pierre Bayle is very well represented with seven titles in each collection, but by far the most popular author is the scholar and populariser Jean Le Clerc with 12 titles in Cashel and a staggering 24 in Armagh.

These then are the writers whose works were bought, perhaps as part of an earlier collection or perhaps as an individual purchase, in the early 1730s and again around 1771. However there are considerable differences in the numbers of titles by each author in the two libraries. It is clear that interest in the earlier writers has diminished considerably between the 1730s and 1771. We must, of course, take account of the fact that the Cashel collection was half as large again as that in Armagh but, even if we take account of this factor, the difference is significant. Calvin and Bèze each have seven titles in Cashel, but only three in Armagh. Mornay, Hotman and du Moulin senior are all very well represented in Cashel but have only one title each in Armagh, while the number of works by the writers who were best represented in Cashel, Saumaise with nine titles, Daillé, with 11, Rivet with eight and Jurieu also with eight, has also been very much reduced in the Armagh collection where there are only three titles by Saumaise, two by Daillé, one by Rivet and two by Jurieu. Holdings of titles by Claude and La Placette have also reduced from four titles in Cashel to one and two respectively in Armagh. Indeed, it is only with writers born after 1645 that we see more titles in Armagh than in Cashel. There is therefore a tendency in the Armagh collection to include more contemporary authors, while maintaining a more limited interest in those of the earlier period.

Many of the authors listed above had significant links with England and Ireland. Some of the clergy, as we have already seen, exercised their ministry in one of the two countries. Allix and Pierre du Moulin the younger entered the Church of England, while Abbadie, Caillard, des Voeux and de Villette entered the Church of Ireland where Abbadie became Dean of Killaloe in 1699. The two scientists, Desaguliers and de Moivre were both members of the Royal Society and lived in London. Rapin de Thoyras had been a soldier in Ireland and had also lived in England, while Boyer, Cavalier and Chardin all settled in England.

Some had visited England, some of them attracting considerable publicity. These included Mornay, du Moulin, Daillé, Rivet, Tavernier and Lemery, while Lenfant, who preached in front of Queen Anne when he visited England in 1707, was later to develop links with the Society for Promoting Christian Knowledge, founded in 1699,[25] and Le Clerc had spent enough time in England as a young man to gain a reputation as the translator into Latin of Henry Hammond's *Paraphrase and Annotations upon all the Books of the New Testament*.[26]

Others had close family connections in England. The du Moulin family and their relatives are well represented on this list. Not only did Pierre du Moulin himself visit England at the invitation of James I, but two of his sons, Louis and Pierre, made their careers there.[27] Among other members of the family included on this list are André Rivet who married du Moulin's sister while on a visit to England, Samuel Bochart who was a nephew and Pierre Jurieu who was married to a grand daughter.[28] Charles Drelincourt also had a son who was the first Huguenot to become a Dean in the Church of Ireland. Pierre Drelincourt held the deanery of Armagh from 1691 to 1722 and commissioned the translation of his father's *Consolations de l'âme fidèle contre les frayeurs de la mort* by Marius d'Assigny in 1707.[29] He was a brother-in-law of the Bishop Edward Maurice of Ossory who so greatly enlarged the Kilkenny library in 1756, and his personal library forms part of the Kilkenny collection. Finally,

---

25   Sugiko Nishikawa, 'England as Protector of Protestant Minorities: The Early Eighteenth-Century Role of the SPCK', *PHS*, 27/5 (2002): 659.

26   Annie Barnes, *Jean Le Clerc (1657–1736) et la République des Lettres* (Paris, 1938), p. 70.

27   On Pierre [Peter] and Louis [Lewis] du Moulin, see above, chapter 3.

28   Haag, vol. 8, p. 445.

29   Charles Drelincourt, *The Christian's Defence against the Fears of Death*, trans. Marius d'Assigny (London, 1707), preface.

according to the Haag brothers, Jean La Placette, based in Copenhagen, was offered a post at a new university in Kilkenny, but declined. No university was established in Kilkenny, but St Canice's Library has 11 different titles by La Placette, whose work was clearly appreciated there.[30]

Many of the writers listed in Table 7.2, then, had links with the British Isles. These varied from visits in the relatively distant past, which were unlikely to be of major significance unless they were accompanied by major controversy or prolonged by settlement, to service in the army during the Williamite wars or domicile in England or Ireland after the Revocation of the Edict of Nantes. The intellectual contributions of those who came to live in England or Ireland or had close links with the British Isles are therefore particularly acknowledged in the two libraries.

Work on other libraries has not yet been completed. On current data, however, it is possible to make some assessment of the extent to which authors appearing in Cashel and Armagh are also to be found in other Irish Church libraries. The information which follows relates to the libraries of Kilkenny, Derry and the Antrim Presbytery in Belfast. It is complete in the cases of Kilkenny and Derry, but some work remains to be done in relation to the Presbyterian library in Belfast. The number of other libraries in which works by a particular author appear is indicated by the asterisks attached to the names listed in Table 7.2. Seven authors appear in all three collections. They are Jean Calvin, Théodore de Bèze and Philippe de Mornay, as well as the theologians André Rivet and Jean Daillé, the linguist and scholar Samuel Bochart and Pierre Bayle. Those who appear in two other libraries are also mostly men of the cloth and include Pierre du Moulin and his son, also Pierre, Charles Drelincourt, Jean Claude, Jean La Placette and Jacques Lenfant, as well as the scholar Claude Saumaise, the translator André Dacier and Jean Le Clerc. It should be noted that non-religious works are relatively well represented in the Kilkenny collection which, in addition to a large number of religious works, holds titles by Rohan, Tavernier, Lemery, Barbeyrac and Boyer. The Presbyterian library, on the other hand, is much more narrowly focused on religious writing, with works by a large number of clergy of the refuge as well as of the earlier period. Allix, Basnage, Abbadie, Caillard, Lenfant, La Placette and Le Clerc are accompanied in this library by Calvin, Bèze, Mornay, the du Moulins, father and son, Rivet, Bochart, Drelincourt, Le Sueur, Claude and Jurieu. Indeed the only laymen from Table 7.2 who appear in this collection are Saumaise and Bayle. The books in the Derry collection tend to be older than those in the other libraries and are mostly religious, but there are also titles by Bayle and Desaguliers.

Table 7.2 allows us to draw a number of interim conclusions about the importance of Huguenot writers in these libraries. Many of the writers found in both the Armagh and Cashel collections appear also in other church libraries. Those who appear most often tend to be mainly religious writers of the sixteenth and early to mid-seventeenth centuries. With the exception of Bayle, Lenfant and Le Clerc, the writers of the Refuge are less widely represented. Armagh is a much more secular library

---

30   Haag, vol. 6, p. 315.

The Influence of the Huguenots on Educated Ireland 131

than Cashel and is clearly open to Enlightenment ideas, judging by the number of works by writers such as Montesquieu, Voltaire and Rousseau on its shelves. Interest in Huguenot writers in this collection is clearly declining, if numbers of titles are compared with those in the collection in Cashel. The list of authors in Table 7.2 is dominated by clergymen, still the intellectual core of the Huguenots, but there are also writers in many fields other than religion, and there is considerable variety among the religious writers themselves. Finally, many of the writers on the list had moved to the British Isles or had reason to be well-known there.

Authors appearing in either Cashel or in Armagh

Space here does not permit detailed examination of the 66 authors who appear in one of the two libraries, but a few general points can be made about them. As we have seen, the Bolton Library in Cashel has a much larger number of authors than Armagh, even if we make allowance for the difference in size of the two collections. The Cashel collection contains many of the great names of the sixteenth and seventeenth centuries, from the scholar Pierre de la Ramée (Ramus), the theologian François du Jon (Junius) and the poet Guillaume de Salluste, sieur du Bartas, to the famous preachers Alexandre Morus and Jacques Saurin. Earlier periods are much better represented in Cashel than in Armagh where, however, we continue to find a small number of authors from the sixteenth and earlier seventeenth centuries, among them Robert and Henri Estienne and Henri IV's great minister, Maximilien de Béthune, duc de Sully. For the later period, authors born after 1645, the balance shifts once again, and it is in the Armagh collection that titles by writers of the refuge such as Isaac de Beausobre, Pierre Des Maizeaux and Elie Benoît are to be found. Some of these authors appear in the collections of Kilkenny, Derry and the Antrim Presbytery Library in Belfast. Table 7.3 below examines the distribution of authors who appear in Cashel or Armagh and in one or more other libraries.

Table 7.3 Huguenot authors in Cashel or Armagh who appear in other libraries

Author	Kilkenny 1693/1756	Derry c.1729	Cashel 1744	Belfast c.1765	Armagh 1771
du Moulin, C.	-	X	X	-	-
Ramus	-	X	X	-	-
Du Bartas	-	-	X	X	-
Du Jon	-	X	X	-	-
Chamier	-	X	X	X	-
Cameron, J.	X	X	X	-	-
Mestrezat	-	-	X	X	-

Amyraut	X	X	X	-	-
du Moulin, L.	-	-	X	X	-
Ablancourt, P. de	X	-	-	-	X
Le Blanc de Beaulieu	X	X	X	-	-
Morus	X	-	X	-	-
Drelincourt, C. fils	X	-	X	-	-
Martin, D.	X	-	X	-	-
Benoît	-	-	-	X	X
Madame Dacier	X	-	-	-	X
Beausobre	-	-	-	X	X
Saurin	X	-	X	X	-

Cameron, Amyraut and Le Blanc de Beaulieu appear in three libraries and all were associated with doctrinal controversy. Cameron's teaching on grace and freewill gave rise to controversy after his death.[31] His student Amyraut, together with Cappel and La Place who both appear in the Cashel collection, followed his teaching and was at the centre of the great dispute over universal grace which split the church in the 1630s and 1640s. Amyraut's most controversial work, *De la Prédestination*, is not found in any of the libraries, but the *Theses Salmurienses*, written by Amyraut, Cappel and La Place, appear in both Cashel and Derry. Le Blanc de Beaulieu, on the other hand, was controversial because he supported the idea of reuniting the Eglise Réformée with the Catholic Church, and it is the book in which this opinion was expressed, his *Theses theologicae*, which we find in Kilkenny, in Derry and in Cashel. The other authors who appear in three libraries are the minister Daniel Chamier, famously a victim in 1621 of the siege of Montauban, and the celebrated preacher, Jacques Saurin.

With Cameron, Amyraut and Le Blanc de Beaulieu, then, there is clear evidence that there was some interest, in late seventeenth and early eighteenth-century Ireland, in the major theological debates within the French Church in the seventeenth century, and it is perhaps worth mentioning here that a title by the Arminian clergyman Tilenus is also present in Cashel. Significantly, these figures of controversy do not appear either in the Presbyterian library in Belfast which did not rest on a pre-existing collection of books and was built up by regular small purchases, or in Armagh. Interest in these debates seems therefore to have waned by the end of the century, although it clearly informs the collections of which the Cashel library is composed.

---

31   Brian Armstrong, *Calvinism and the Amyraut Heresy: Protestant Scholasticism and Humanism in Seventeenth-Century France* (Madison, 1969), pp. 42–70.

Those who appear twice are a very varied group. Representing the sixteenth century are the legal expert Charles du Moulin and Pierre de la Ramée, who was a victim of the St Bartholomew's Day massacre, as well as du Bartas and the scholar and theologian François du Jon. From the seventeenth century come Jean Mestrezat, polemist and pastor of Charenton and the Arminian Alexandre Morus. Louis du Moulin, son of the celebrated professor of Sedan, who made his career in England like his brother Pierre, but who favoured the Cromwellian side in the English Civil War, is also present in both Cashel and Belfast. Books by Charles Drelincourt the younger, a professor of Medicine in Leyden are to be found in both Cashel and Kilkenny, while the translations of Nicolas Perrot d'Ablancourt and titles by Madame Dacier appear in both Kilkenny and Armagh. Finally the Biblical scholar David Martin, the historian Elie Benoît, the preacher Jacques Saurin and the pastor of the French Church in Berlin, Isaac de Beausobre all belong to the period of the Refuge.

As with the authors appearing in both Cashel and Armagh, the authors listed in Table 7.3 belong to all periods, from the Reformation to the Refuge. Once again, the clergy predominate, but there are also writers on legal, literary and historical subjects. Taken as a whole, our study of Huguenot authors in these Irish libraries shows a considerable and wide-ranging interest in the theological, polemical and spiritual writings of the French church. There is evidence of interest in some of the major disputes within the Eglise Réformée, but this has waned by the 1760s, for this material is not found in either the Antrim Presbytery library or in Armagh. In both Cashel and Armagh, and to a lesser extent in the other libraries, particularly in Belfast and Derry, there is considerable interest in the writers of the Refuge, many of them based in England or Ireland and writing in English.

Titles held in common by the libraries of Cashel and Armagh

Let us turn now to a brief examination of some of the titles held in common in Cashel and Armagh. There are 34 titles which appear in both collections. These are the work of 27 authors and in 16 cases the same edition of a work appears in both collections. In six of these cases, the title is in English and the book was published in England or in Ireland. However there are editions in both libraries in Latin, in English and in French and, for these titles, no clear pattern emerges of a greater preference for English editions in Armagh towards the end of the century than in the earlier Cashel collection.

The works held by both libraries are once again very varied, both in terms of the period to which the author belonged and in terms of their subject matter. The oldest edition, a first edition of Philippe de Mornay's *Traité de la vérité de la religion chrétienne*, published in Antwerp in 1581, appears, rather surprisingly, in Armagh, but this is the only sixteenth-century edition. There are 23 editions from the seventeenth century and 34 from the eighteenth. Most of the eighteenth-century editions, of course, belong to the early years of the century, before the establishment of the Cashel library, but there are only two editions later than the 1730s on this list.

One, a 1760 London edition of des Voeux's essay *On Ecclesiastes*, which appears in both collections, is likely to have been a donation, possibly by its author. The other is a 1756 edition of the *Memoirs* of the duc de Rohan, held in Armagh. The list of titles held in common is given below. Where different editions of the same title are held, the place and date of each edition is given and the library to which it belongs is identified. Asterisks identify titles held in other libraries.

Table 7.4 Titles appearing in both Cashel and Armagh

Author	Title	Location
Barbeyrac	*Traité du juge compétent des ambassadeurs*, trad. du latin de Bynckershoek, La Haye, 1723	C & A
Basnage	*History of the Jews*, London, 1708	C & A
Bayle	*Commentaire philosophique*, Rotterdam, 1703	Cashel
	Commentaire philosophique, London, 1708	Armagh
	**Dictionary Historical and Critical*, London, 1710	Cashel
	Dictionnaire historique et critique, Rotterdam, 1720	Armagh
	Lettres choisies, Rotterdam, 1714	C & A
Bèze	****Les Psaumes de David*, London, 1701	Cashel
	Psaumes de David, Paris, 1686	Cashel
	Les Pseaumes de David, Dublin, 1721	Armagh
	Les Pseaumes de David, Dublin, 1731	Armagh
Caillard	*Sermons sur divers textes de l'Ecriture Sainte*, Dublin, 1728	Cashel
	Sermons sur divers textes de l'Ecriture Sainte, Amsterdam, 1735	Armagh
Calvin	**Institutions*, Basle, 1607	Cashel
	Institutions, London, 1634	Armagh
	Institutions, Leyden, 1654	Armagh
Cavalier	*Memoirs*, Dublin, 1726	C & A
Chardin	*Travels*, London, 1686	Armagh
	Voyages, Amsterdam, 1711	Cashel
Claude	*Oeuvres posthumes*, Amsterdam, 1688	C & A
Daillé	***On right Use of ye Fathers*, London, 1651	Cashel
	On the Right Use of the Fathers, London, 1675	Armagh
Desaguliers	**A System of Experimental Philosophy . . .* , London, 1719	C & A
Des Voeux	*On Ecclesiastes*, London 1760	C & A
Dumont	*New Voyage to the Levant*, London, 1702	C & A
du Moulin, P. père	**Vates*, Leyden, 1640	C & A
du Moulin, P. fils	* a *Vindication of the Sincerity of the Protestant Religion*, London, 1664	C & A
	a *Vindication of the Sincerity of the Protestant Religion*, London, 1668	Cashel

Hotman	*Francogallia*, London, 1711	C & A
Jaquelot	*Conformité de la foy et de la raison*, Amsterdam, 1705	C & A
La Placette	*Traité de l'aumône*, Amsterdam, 1699	C & A
Le Clerc	*Traité de l'incrédulité*, Amsterdam, 1696	Armagh
	On Causes of Incredulity, London, 1697	C & A
	Ars critica, Amsterdam, 1697	Armagh
	Ars critica, London, 1698	Cashel
	Ars critica, Amsterdam, 1730	Armagh
	Parrhasiana, London, 1700	C & A
	Parrhasiana, Amsterdam, 1701	Armagh
	Historia ecclesiastica, Amsterdam, 1716	C & A
	Bibliothèque choisie, Amsterdam, 1703	Cashel
	Bibliothèque choisie, Amsterdam, 1712	Armagh
Lenfant	*Histoire du concile de Pise*, Amsterdam, 1724	C & A
	**Histoire du concile de Constance*, Amsterdam, 1714	Cashel
	Histoire du concile de Constance, Amsterdam, 1727	Armagh
Le Sueur	*Histoire de l'Eglise et de l'Empire*, Geneva, 1686	Cashel
	Histoire de l'Eglise et de l'Empire, Amsterdam, 1730–32	Armagh
Mornay	**Traité de la vérité de la religion chrétienne*, Antwerp, 1581	Armagh
	Of the Truth of the Christian Religion, London, 1617	Cashel
	Of the Truth of the Christian Religion, Herborn, 1632	Cashel
Poiret	*L'Oeconomie divine*, Amsterdam, 1687	Cashel
	Divine Oeconomy, London, 1713	Armagh
Rapin	*Histoire d'Angleterre*, La Haye, 1724	Armagh
	Histoire d'Angleterre, London, 1729	Armagh
	History of England, London, 1729	Cashel
Rohan	*Memoirs*, London, 1660	Cashel
	Memoirs, Amsterdam, 1756	Armagh
	Memoirs, MS	Armagh
Saumaise	*De re militari Romanorum liber*, Leyden, 1657	C & A
-	*Vie de Coligny*, Cologne, 1686	C & A

The authors with the largest number of titles here are Le Clerc with four titles, Bayle with three and the historian Lenfant with two. Of these, Bayle is the one who is still a major figure today, but Lenfant was much admired at the time for his lack of bias in dealing with church history and Le Clerc was very widely admired in his own time. Of the 27 authors represented, nine were born before 1600 and another eight before 1650, with ten born after that date. This would suggest that, by the second half of the eighteenth century, there were a number of writers of the earlier periods whose works were considered classics, and therefore desirable elements of a library collection. This becomes clearer if we look for these titles in collections other than those of Cashel and Armagh. Bèze's *Psaumes de David* are present in all the libraries examined here, while the titles by Mornay and Daillé, together with Lenfant's *Histoire du Concile de Constance* and Bayle's *Dictionary*, are found in four out of the five libraries, and the titles by Calvin, Desaguliers, the du Moulins, Hotman, La Placette, Le Sueur and the second titles by Mornay and Lenfant, together with Le Clerc's *Traité de l'incrédulité* all appear in one library other than Cashel and Armagh. Finally, there are a number of books here which reflect an interest in the history of the Huguenots, among them the *Life* of Coligny, killed during the St Bartholomew's Day Massacre and the *Memoirs* of Rohan, the opponent of Louis XIII and Richelieu as well as the *Memoirs* of the Camisard leader Jean Cavalier. The presence of these books would seem to suggest an interest in the story of the Huguenots as well as in their beliefs and this interest does not diminish toward the end of the century, for, if Cashel has the biography of Louis de Marolles, who was one of the most eminent victims of the Revocation, Elie Benoît's history of the Edict of Nantes is to be found in both Armagh and Belfast. By the mid-eighteenth century, the legend of the Huguenots had clearly begun to take root.

Conclusion

Some general conclusions can be drawn from this study. We do not know if, or how often, the books were read, but the fact that names and titles reappear in two collections and sometimes more would seem to indicate that there was some interest in them in eighteenth-century Protestant Ireland and that some of them at least were considered necessary elements of an ecclesiastical library at that time. There were close links, as we have seen, between the Church of Ireland and at least a section of the Huguenots in Ireland, those belonging to conforming churches. Huguenot clergy of the Irish churches and of the Refuge in general are well represented here alongside those from earlier periods. However, it is clear that interest in the internal affairs of the Church and in doctrinal differences of the seventeenth century is declining by the end of the eighteenth, and representation of theologians of the earlier period has also declined in the Armagh library, leaving a relatively small number of classic authors and texts. As far as writers of the refuge on non-religious subjects are concerned, there is no indication that they owe their place to their Huguenot roots, and the subjects about which they write: science, law, history and travel are generally well represented in these collections. What does seem to remain constant and perhaps to grow, is an interest in the history of the Huguenots.

Chapter 8

The Role of Huguenot Tutors in John Locke's Programme of Social Reform

S.J. Savonius
Clare Hall, Cambridge, UK[1]

The radicalism of Locke's programme of reform

In 1689 John Locke seized the opportunity provided by the English Revolution, which had overthrown James II, to publish the trilogy for which he is now famous – the trilogy of the *Two Treatises of Government*, the *Epistola de tolerantia* and the *Essay Concerning Human Understanding*. Within a few years, he published his *Some Thoughts Concerning Education* and *Reasonableness of Christianity*. The corpus of Locke's works published after the Revolution was a remarkable achievement. To a great extent, this corpus was the fruit of the massive intellectual labours of his exile – of the five and a half years he stayed in the Dutch Republic from September 1683 until February 1689. It was also a remarkably subversive corpus. In his works Locke called both for the overthrow of tyrants and for a transformation in the cultural milieu of politics. The fact that he published most of his works anonymously attests to the radicalism of his programme of reform. Even the *Essay*, published under his own name, proved extremely controversial, and was attacked for Socinianism in the 1690s.[2]

During the Allegiance Controversy, which followed the Revolution, whigs sympathetic towards Locke's politics considered the diffusion of his *Two Treatises*, Mark Goldie has recently observed, a part of 'a deliberate programme of political education'.[3] The few whig writers who paraphrased, or alluded to, Locke's articulation of anti-monarchic values in the early 1690s wanted to eliminate the 'ridiculous and

---

1 I am very grateful to Mark Goldie and Markku Peltonen for their help and for many discussions about Locke. It is a particular pleasure to thank Anne Dunan-Page for her assistance and hospitality at Cambridge and Montpellier.

2 See John Dunn, *Locke* (Oxford and New York, 1984), esp. pp. 12–15. On Locke's intellectual trajectory, see also Ian Harris, *The Mind of John Locke: A Study of Political Theory in its Intellectual Setting* (Cambridge, 1994).

3 Mark Goldie, 'Introduction', in Mark Goldie (ed.), *The Reception of Locke's Politics* (6 vols, London, 1999), vol. 1, p. xxxiii.

false' notions typical of the Stuart era.[4] In 1690 William Atwood recommended that the *Two Treatises* be read 'every morning' as a 'Catholicon' against tory absolutism.[5] He sought to educate Englishmen after the Revolution. This was also the rationale for the monumental undertaking of James Tyrrell, a close friend of Locke, to compose the *Bibliotheca Politica*, intended to discredit the doctrine of *jure divino* and Robert Filmer's version of England's history.[6]

Tyrrell's *Bibliotheca Politica* did not disclose Locke's authorship of the *Two Treatises*. The first English-language publication to name him as its author was *The Case of Ireland*, written by William Molyneux, another friend of Locke, which appeared in 1698.[7] Yet no secret was revealed by Molyneux. By 1698 it was a matter of common knowledge in England and among the men of letters who lived in the midst of the Refuge that Locke had written the anonymously published works.[8]

In 1698, there appeared a book in London which assaulted the views of both Locke and the Remonstrant Jean Leclerc, Locke's closest disciple and the principal early carrier of his ideas into continental discussion. It had been written by a Cambridge graduate who complained that recently Locke had begun 'to be very daring, and with disdain to trample upon Universities, publick Schools, Clergymen, &c.' Moreover, associating Leclerc with Locke, he claimed that they had turned their attention to the education of the youth because 'if they cannot sufficiently proselyte the men of this Age, they will make sure of those of the next; if they can't succeed at present, they will gain Posterity'.[9] A year earlier the same critic, John Edwards, had noted that Locke, in the footsteps of Thomas Hobbes, disparaged 'the Learning now in fashion in the Schools of Europe' and that Locke 'is a Catholic Hater' of all

---

4   Anon., *Political Aphorisms: Or, the True Maxims of Government* (1690), in Goldie, *The Reception of Locke's Politics*, vol. 1, p. 6; and Goldie, 'Introduction', ibid., p. xxxiii.

5   William Atwood, *The Fundamental Constitution of the English Government* (1690), in Goldie, *The Reception of Locke's Politics*, vol. 1, p. 38.

6   James Tyrrell, *Bibliotheca Politica: Or, an Enquiry into the Antient Constitution of the English Government*, 2nd collected edition (London, 1718). Tyrrell published the first collected edition in 1694. Goldie, 'Introduction', p. xxxiii; and J.W. Gough, 'James Tyrrell, Whig Historian and Friend of John Locke', in Richard Ashcraft (ed.), *John Locke: Critical Assessments* (4 vols, 1976; London and New York, 1991), vol. 1, pp. 120–50.

7   William Molyneux, *The Case of Ireland's Being Bound by Acts of Parliament in England Stated* (Dublin, 1698).

8   See, for example, Pierre Bayle, *Dictionnaire Historique et Critique* (originally 1697), art. 'Sainctes', remark F, in Pierre Bayle, *Political Writings*, ed. and trans. Sally L. Jenkinson (Cambridge, 2000), p. 236; Henri Basnage de Beauval to François Janiçon, 14 April 1695, and 20 June 1696, in Hans Bots and Lenie van Lieshout (eds), *Contribution à la connaissance des réseaux d'information au début du XVIIIe siècle: Henri Basnage de Beauval et sa correspondance à propos de l'Histoire des Ouvrages des Savans (1687–1709)* (Amsterdam and Maarssen, 1984), pp. 75, 112; and Mark Goldie, 'The Earliest Attack on Locke's *Two Treatises of Government*', *Locke Newsletter*, 30 (1999): 73–84.

9   John Edwards ['F.B.'], *A Free but Modest Censure on the late Controversial Writings and Debates of the Lord Bishop of Worcester and Mr. Locke* (London, 1698), pp. 15, 30.

universities, whether domestic or foreign.[10] Besides, it was easy to understand that Locke 'hath a fling at Latin (as well as Logick) ... for what need he be at the pains to learn this Tongue when Pedlars French best suits his way of living, and those he converses with?'[11]

The critical works by Edwards, who savaged Locke and Leclerc for their views on logic and Latin, universities and education, religion and politics, give us the clue to understanding their programme of social reform. In the 1690s education moved to centre-stage in their plans for reform. This emphasis on the significance of education for politics was immediately clear to Michel de Laroche, a young Huguenot admirer of Leclerc's work, after he had read the first volume of Leclerc's main work on civil philosophy, the *Parrhasiana* of 1699. Laroche hoped that by attacking the current educational system, as Leclerc had done, things could finally be set right. He wished the majority of the learned would follow Leclerc's example and 'expose the failings which prevail among men', for it was imperative 'to try to cure men'.[12] Much later, in 1727, Laroche could celebrate the appearance of the Swedish translation of Locke's 'Second Treatise', published after Sweden's estates had decided, in 1719, to 'dismantle, suffocate, dismiss, and destroy ... completely' Charles XII's absolutist regime. Laroche commented: 'Happy are those countries where such a Book can be printed ... The Swedes are a free people'.[13]

The clarity with which Edwards and Laroche identified Locke and Leclerc's anti-monarchic politics with their pedagogical aims provides a sharp contrast to the confusion that has characterised the modern scholars' interpretations of their ideas on education. In order to account for Locke's stance on education, several scholars have taken one of two approaches. On the one hand, when modern commentators have devoted some attention to Locke's rejection of the humanist curriculum, they have

---

10   Here Edwards quoted Locke's work on education: see John Locke, *Some Thoughts Concerning Education*, eds John W. and Jean S. Yolton (Oxford, 1989) [hereafter *Education*], § 94, p. 155 (added to the third edition).

11   John Edwards, *A Brief Vindication of the Fundamental Articles of the Christian Faith* (London, 1697), title-page, sig. A2, pp. 3, 5. This work was dedicated 'to both Universities' (ibid., sig. A2).

12   Michel de Laroche (or de La Roche) to Jean Leclerc (or Le Clerc), 10/20 December 1699, in Jean Leclerc, *Epistolario*, ed. Maria Grazia and Mario Sina (4 vols, Florence, 1987–97) [hereafter *Epistolario*], vol. 2, p. 328: 'Plût à Dieu que la plupart des bons Esprits travaillassent, à vôtre exemple, à étaler les defauts qui regnent parmi les hommes. C'est un champ bien vaste, et je ne vois rien de plus necessaire que de tâcher de corriger les hommes. Peut étre qu'à force d'écrire contre la pedanterie et la sotte maniere dont on instruit les jeunes gens, on pourroit enfin mettre les choses sur un bon pied'.

13   *New Memoirs of Literature*, ed. Michel de Laroche (London, 1725–27), vol. 6, September 1727, art. 26, p. 236. S.J. Savonius, 'The Swedish Translation of John Locke's "Second Treatise", 1726', *Locke Studies*, 1 (2001): 191–219. On Laroche, see Ross Hutchison, *Locke in France, 1688–1734* (Oxford, 1991), p. 34; and Margaret D. Thomas, 'Michel de La Roche: A Huguenot Critic of Calvin', in H.T. Mason (ed.), *Studies on Voltaire and the Eighteenth Century*, 238 (Oxford, 1985): 97–195.

either ignored or denied the political impetus for it.[14] They may have been guided by the explanation, commonplace in our present-day guidebooks to his thinking, that he assaulted the liberal arts because he was impervious to aesthetic values.[15]

On the other hand, it has not been uncommon for modern commentators to tone down the extremism of Locke's attack on the contemporary educational system. John and Jean Yolton, the editors of his *Some Thoughts Concerning Education*, have taken this approach to the puzzling length of asserting that 'he saw no need to break out of the social mould and rear children outside the traditional norms ... Locke's curriculum goes on to include rhetoric, logic, and natural science ... It was a typical gentleman's education'.[16] In Locke's *Education*, according to Philip Carter, 'education was intended to fashion a moral character well versed in Christian and humanist thought'.[17] If Carter's claim is accepted, it is difficult to understand Edwards's contemporary critique. According to Edwards, the *Education* attacked the humanist disciplines and manifested 'Mr. Lock's forgetfulness of Christianity ... Is not his young Master ... baptized? Doth he address himself to him as to a Pagan, Turk, or Jew?'[18]

The position of Carter and other Locke-tamers appears to tally with the tradition of interpretation which has hailed – or denounced – Locke as the founder of political liberalism.[19] It is notable that Edwards's and Laroche's understanding of his aims is incompatible with the modern view that he was a cautious and moderate theorist and, in the *Two Treatises*, 'close to being as conservative a revolutionary as a revolutionary could be'.[20] In this chapter I hope to stand back from, and perhaps even to question the validity of, the interpretative paradigm that has made him a forerunner of our modern liberalism. I seek to uncover aspects of what he was doing

---

14   Brian Vickers, *In Defence of Rhetoric* (Oxford, 1988), pp. 199–200. See also J.B. Schneewind, 'Locke's Moral Philosophy', in Vere Chappel (ed.), *The Cambridge Companion to Locke* (Cambridge, 1994), pp. 199–225, esp. p. 206.

15   See, for example, D.A. Lloyd Thomas, *Locke on Government* (London, 1995), p. 8; and John W. Yolton, *Locke: An Introduction* (Oxford, 1985), p. 14.

16   John W. and Jean S. Yolton, 'Introduction', in Locke, *Education*, pp. 1–75, at pp. 27, 33.

17   Philip Carter, *Men and the Emergence of Polite Society, Britain 1660–1800* (Harlow, 2001), p. 53.

18   Edwards, *A Free but Modest Censure*, p. 12.

19   Exponents of this prevalent tradition include both critics and defenders of liberal politics: see, for example, Lucio Colletti, *From Rousseau to Lenin: Studies in Ideology and Society*, trans. John Merrington and Judith White (1969; London, 1972); A. John Simmons, *The Lockean Theory of Rights* (Princeton, 1992); Jeremy Waldron, *Liberal Rights: Collected Papers 1981–1991* (Cambridge, 1993). See also the restatement of this interpretation in Jonathan I. Israel, *Radical Enlightenment: Philosophy and the Making of Modernity, 1650–1750* (Oxford, 2001), esp. p. 259.

20   John Marshall, *John Locke: Resistance, Religion and Responsibility* (Cambridge, 1994), p. 283.

both when he published his post-revolutionary works and when he encouraged the attempts of Huguenots driven from the Continent to secure tutorships in England.

Three assumptions embedded in Edwards's critique of Locke's and Leclerc's works seem to me very important. It is these assumptions that I wish to bring into focus, and I have therefore divided the rest of the chapter into three main sections. First, taking a lead from John Marshall's work on Locke's close ties with the Refuge, I situate Locke in the context of the cosmopolitan Protestantism which conditioned his post-revolutionary outlook.[21] It is worth mentioning at the outset that, as Goldie has shown, during the eighteenth century there emerged a cult in England which gave him iconic status as the English philosopher whose thought embodied the whiggish principles. Busts of Locke and of his friends Robert Boyle and Isaac Newton, England's cultural heroes, were placed in the grotto of the hermitage at Richmond which was built for Caroline of Ansbach, George II's consort, round 1730. The Temple of British Worthies at Stowe in Buckinghamshire, erected by Lord Cobham in the 1730s, was adorned with another bust of Locke. Cobham's estate soon became – and still remains – a tourist attraction.[22] Today, almost three centuries after the beginning of Locke's taming and anglicising, most scholars still tend to discuss his intellectual context in a largely Anglocentric way.[23] Strikingly, however, Edwards proffered the opinion that 'Pedlars French best suits his way of living, and those he converses with'. From this contemporary point of view, he belonged to an alien, allegedly French way of living and endorsed its foreign values in the 1690s.

Secondly, I wish to draw attention to the rationale behind the critic's claim that Locke had begun to concentrate on the process of education. One reason for my adopting this focus is that, as indicated above, little scholarly attention has so far been devoted to his antagonism towards the system of scholastic and rhetorical education. Yet my principal reason is that his attempt to reform this system appears to me to constitute the core of his post-revolutionary thought. What is distinctive about his attempt is the political impetus for it. Locke never saw the Revolution of 1688–89 as the consummation of his aspirations. In his view, the constitutional

---

21   John Marshall, 'Huguenot Thought after the Revocation of the Edict of Nantes: Toleration, "Socinianism", Integration and Locke', in Vigne and Littleton, *Strangers*, pp. 383–96.

22   Goldie, 'Introduction', pp. xvii–lxxi; and 'John Locke: Icon of Liberty', *History Today*, 54/10 (2004): 31–6.

23   Earlier it was commonplace to relate the *Two Treatises* to its English discursive contexts, without considering the European contexts: see, for example, C.B. Macpherson, *The Political Theory of Possessive Individualism: Hobbes to Locke* (Oxford, 1962), and Richard Ashcraft, *Revolutionary Politics and Locke's* Two Treatises of Government (Princeton, 1986). Whilst Peter Laslett argued that Locke invented the ideal of English gentility (Laslett, 'Introduction', in John Locke, *Two Treatises of Government*, ed. Peter Laslett (Cambridge, 1988), pp. 3–133, at p. 37), recent work has shown that 'Locke's definition of civility was entirely familiar' and articulated in a context defined by the Italian and French discourses of civility (Markku Peltonen, *The Duel in Early Modern England: Civility, Politeness and Honour* [Cambridge, 2003], p. 153).

changes of 1689 could not solve, on their own, the problems of royal and clerical hubris which had characterised the Stuart regime. Nor could William III's war effort against Louis XIV – the most prominent protagonist, or incarnation, of the doctrines of *jure divino* and universal monarchy – fulfil, on its own, his wish to cleanse the European societies of the superstitious reverence and courtly fawning encouraged by absolutist and clericalist royalism. The right solution was to educate citizens: to transmute the slavish subjects into free citizens. In other words, he aspired towards a rebirth of the civic ethos through education.

In the section on the critique of the contemporary curriculum, we encounter Locke the civic-minded philosopher, whose problem was the restoration of political life in corrupt monarchies and priest-ridden communities. The last main section of this chapter then focuses more closely on his efforts to draft in Huguenot tutors. We encounter Locke the citizen, whose concrete problem was to translate his ideals into reality. My key argument is that the Huguenot tutors were expected to help change the intellectual milieu of politics. For Locke, they were instruments of reform. The suggestion I want to end by exploring is that there were particular values embedded in the exiled Huguenots' religious culture that, from his vantage-point, made them suitable agents in England.

Locke's cosmopolitan associates

In the 1670s and 1680s much of Locke's philosophical development took place on foreign soil. It took place during his travels in France in 1675–79 and in the Dutch Republic in 1683–89. By the time he finally settled again in England, he struck his critics as a Frenchified thinker. More precisely, Locke was seen as intellectually kin to a particular group of Protestants. Its members belonged to a race of self-confident and bold men of letters. They included a couple of English merchants, namely William Popple (1638–1708), a wine merchant at Bordeaux and the Unitarian author of *A Rational Catechism*, who settled in London in 1688 and subsequently translated Locke's *Epistola de tolerantia* into English, and Popple's friend Benjamin Furly (1636–1714), who had moved to the Dutch Republic in the mid-1650s, probably settling permanently in Rotterdam, *c.*1660.[24] Prosperous, Furly was able to amass a substantial library, and keep an open house for such fugitives as Algernon Sidney and Locke.[25]

---

24 William Popple, *A Rational Catechism* (Amsterdam, 1712) [originally 1687], title-page, a quotation from 'Locke of *Education*, §. 136. Edit. 1695' concerning 'the Foundation of Vertue'. On Popple, see Peter Laslett, 'John Locke, the Great Recoinage, and the Origins of the Board of Trade: 1695–1698' (originally 1957), in Ashcraft, *John Locke*, vol. 1, pp. 181–209, at pp. 194–5; and Caroline Robbins, 'Absolute Liberty: The Life and Thought of William Popple, 1638–1708', *William and Mary Quarterly*, 24/2 (1967): 190–223.

25 Maurice Cranston, *John Locke: A Biography* (London, 1957), pp. 280–311; E.S. de Beer, 'Introduction', in John Locke, *The Correspondence of John Locke*, ed. E.S. de Beer (8 vols to date, Oxford, 1976–89) [hereafter *Correspondence*], vol. 1, pp. xv–lxxix, at p.

Most men in this group of Locke's associates were exiled francophone Protestants who had clerical backgrounds but also confidence in their ability to make their own way in the secular world of learning. They included Jean Leclerc (1657–1736), Jean Cornand de Lacrose (c.1660–94), Charles Lecène (c.1647–1703) and Jaques Bernard (1658–1718), all editors of the Amsterdam-based journal *Bibliothèque Universelle et Historique*.[26] The group's francophone members were knit together, most conspicuously, by the intellectual activities – especially by the activities stimulated by their interest in theological heresy – which had pushed them towards the margins of mainstream culture in their native communities and by their subsequent experience of decamping to the Dutch Republic. They arrived in the Dutch cities as outcasts, rejected by the establishment. In Amsterdam, Leyden or Rotterdam, they remained associated with displacement, never fully assimilating into the Dutch culture. A misleading impression of their identity is given by Samuel Golden's study, which is based on the suppositions that Leclerc was a Dutchman 'in all but name' and that the *Bibliothèque* was one of the 'basically Dutch enterprises'.[27] Golden's standpoint is implausible, for the exiles' Francophone communities coexisted with the Dutch-language world of native inhabitants. Although Furly frequented both worlds, and Locke visited them too, Leclerc lived in Amsterdam for 53 years without achieving a satisfactory command of the Dutch language. He lectured in Latin at the Remonstrant College from 1684 until 1728.[28]

The Dutchman closest to these expatriates was Philip van Limborch (1633–1712), who had been professor of divinity at the Remonstrant College since 1667.[29] He offered protection for the refugees. After the Revolution of 1688–89, when Lecène tried to secure employment in England, van Limborch wrote a letter of

---

xxvi; William I. Hull, *Benjamin Furly and Quakerism in Rotterdam* (Swarthmore, 1941), pp. 83–100; and Johan A. van Reijn, 'Benjamin Furly. Engels koopman (en meer) te Rotterdam, 1636–1714', *Rotterdams Jaarboekje* (1985): 219–46.

26   On their lives, see Annie Barnes, *Jean Le Clerc (1657–1736) et la République des Lettres* (Paris, 1938); and H. Bots, J. Janssen and L. van Lieshout, 'De Bibliothèque Universelle et Historique. De redactie en haar beleid', in H. Bots, H. Hillenaar, J. Janssen, J. van der Korst and L. van Lieshout, *De 'Bibliothèque Universelle et Historique' (1686–1693), een periodiek als trefpunt van geletterd Europa* (Amsterdam, 1981), pp. 1–146.

27   Samuel A. Golden, *Jean Le Clerc* (New York, 1972), esp. pp. 22, 25–6.

28   See Barnes, *Jean Le Clerc*, pp. 74–5; and Jonathan I. Israel, *The Dutch Republic: Its Rise, Greatness, and Fall, 1477–1806* (Oxford, 1995), pp. 1038–9. Locke's library included 18 works at least partly in Dutch (including dictionaries and other reference books), 669 works in French and 1,326 works in Latin (Peter Laslett, 'John Locke and His Books', in John Harrison and Peter Laslett, *The Library of John Locke*, 2nd edition (Oxford, 1971), pp. 1–61, at p. 19).

29   Jaques Bernard (ed.), *Supplement aux anciennes editions du Grand Dictionaire Historique de Mre. Louis Moreri. Ou le mélange curieux de l'histoire sacrée et profane* (2 vols, Amsterdam, The Hague and Utrecht, 1716), vol. 2, s.v. '(Philippe de) Limborch', p. 94. De Beer, editorial note, in *Correspondence*, vol. 2, pp. 648–52; and Mario Sina, editorial apparatus, in *Epistolario*, vol. 1, s.v. 'Philippus van Limborch', pp. 549–50.

recommendation to Bishop Kidder on his behalf.[30] Before the Revolution, when the position of exiled Englishmen in Dutch territory was in doubt because of James II's spies, van Limborch's circle of friends arranged places of safety for Locke.[31] After Leclerc's move to Amsterdam in 1683, van Limborch helped him to obtain, first, a modest salary for preaching weekly in the Remonstrant church and, subsequently in April 1684, his initial appointment as professor of philosophy, Hebrew and Greek at the Remonstrant College.[32]

It was from this continental milieu of expatriates that Locke's publications appeared to emanate. After his anonymous *Epistola* had been published in April 1689, the tolerationist Huguenot journalist Henri Basnage de Beauval assumed that it had been written by a French refugee, and attributed it to Bernard, Leclerc's cousin and Locke's friend, in the *Histoire des Ouvrages des Sçavans*.[33] In July 1689 van Limborch, who had arranged for the *Epistola* to be published, delighted in observing that it was believed in the Dutch Republic that Locke's work must have emanated from 'the Remonstrant workshop'. He was especially glad that the *Epistola* had been translated 'into French by Mr. de Cene [that is, Lecène]', for French was 'a tongue which is now generally familiar to all'.[34]

Locke had made his debut as a scholarly author in the July 1686 issue of the *Bibliothèque*, edited at the time by Leclerc and Lacrose.[35] He also contributed a handful of book reviews to the journal.[36] The most original of all his contributions was, however, the 'Extrait', his abridgement of the manuscript of the *Essay*, translated

---

30 Van Limborch to Locke, 12/22 January 1692, in *Correspondence*, vol. 4, p. 359. Richard Kidder had been appointed bishop of Bath and Wells in August 1691.

31 Compare Bernard (ed.), *Supplement aux anciennes editions du Grand Dictionaire Historique*, vol. 2, s.v. '(Jean) Locke', p. 101: 'Comme il [Locke] étoit en danger, Mr. Guenelon lui procura une retraite chez Mr. Veen, où il demeura caché deux ou trois mois.' See Luisa Simonutti, 'Religion, Philosophy, and Science: John Locke and Limborch's Circle in Amsterdam', in James E. Force and David S. Katz (eds), *Everything Connects: In Conference with Richard H. Popkin. Essays in His Honor* (Leyden, Boston and Cologne, 1999), pp. 295–324.

32 Leclerc to Antoine Vattemare [10 November 1684], in *Epistolario*, vol. 1, pp. 262–3. Bots, Janssen and van Lieshout, 'De Bibliothèque Universelle et Historique', p. 6.

33 Henry Basnage de Beauval (ed.), *Histoire des Ouvrages des Sçavans* (24 vols, Rotterdam, 1687–1709) [hereafter *Histoire*], September 1689, art. II, pp. 20–26. The attribution to Bernard was countermanded in *Histoire*, February 1690, p. 278, after Bernard had written to Beauval.

34 Van Limborch to Locke, 8/18 July 1689, in *Correspondence*, vol. 3, pp. 647–8 (trans. de Beer).

35 John Locke, 'Methode Nouvelle De dresser des recueils', in Jaques Bernard, Jean Cornand De Lacrose, Charles Lecène and Jean Leclerc (eds), *Bibliothèque Universelle et Historique* (25 vols, Amsterdam, 1686–93) [hereafter *Bibliothèque*], vol. 2, July 1686, pp. 315–40.

36 Jean S. Yolton, *John Locke: A Descriptive Bibliography* (Bristol, 1998), pp. 313–15. For the books reviewed in the *Bibliothèque*, see Lenie van Lieshout, 'Analytisch-thematische index op de *BUH*', in Bots *et al.*, *De 'Bibliothèque Universelle et Historique'*, pp. 147–283.

by Leclerc and published, under his own supervision,[37] in the January 1688 issue of the *Bibliothèque*.[38] Despite the fact that the 'Extrait' dismissed, with three sentences only, the assault on innatism with which Locke was to open the English *Essay*, his anti-innatism in the epitome still caught the attention of its early readership.[39]

Anti-innatism was unacceptable to Lacrose. His criticism of the *Essay* was a manifestation of the widening rift between the founding editors of the *Bibliothèque*.[40] Leclerc had ended his collaboration with Lacrose in January 1689. Dismissed from the co-editorship, Lacrose had moved from Amsterdam to London; in the summer of 1689 Leclerc had expected Locke to meet Lacrose in London, and asked him to procure Lacrose an inmate's place in Bedlam.[41] The personal animosity between Leclerc and Lacrose dovetailed with the intellectual antagonism between their post-revolutionary publications. Whilst Leclerc espoused anti-innatism and followed Locke's doctrines in his philosophical works,[42] Lacrose's journal articles made Leibniz, Locke's opponent, consider him the only writer in England who was cosmopolitan enough to edit good journals.[43]

---

37   Locke travelled from Rotterdam to Amsterdam in order to supervise the process of printing. See, for example, Locke to Furly, 9/19 January 1688, in *Correspondence*, vol. 3, pp. 330–31; and 16/26 January 1688, ibid., p. 337. De Beer, 'Introduction', pp. xxvi–xxvii; and Cranston, *John Locke*, pp. 289–93.

38   John Locke, 'Extrait d'un Livre Anglois qui n'est pas encore publié, intitulé *Essai Philosophique concernant L'entendement*, où l'on montre quelle est l'étenduë de nos connoissances certaines, & la maniere dont nous y parvenons', *Bibliothèque*, vol. 8, January 1688, art. II, pp. 49–142. There also appeared a separate printing, the *Abregé d'un ouvrage intitulé Essai philosophique touchant l'entendement*, trans. Jean Leclerc (Amsterdam, 1688).

39   Fredericus van Leenhof [to Guenellon?], 4/14 March 1688, in *Correspondence*, vol. 3, p. 397; Christian Knorr von Rosenroth, 'Observations' [May-June? 1688], ibid., pp. 400–404; Guenellon to Locke, 15/25 March 1688, ibid., p. 412; Lady Masham, formerly Damaris Cudworth, to Locke, 7 April [1688], ibid., p. 433; Joseph Bowles to Furly [May 1688], ibid., pp. 464–5; and John Locke, *An Essay Concerning Human Understanding*, ed. Peter H. Nidditch, revised edition (Oxford, 1979) [hereafter *Essay*], 'Epistle to the Reader', p. 10. *Bibliothèque*, vol. 17, May 1690, art. V, pp. 399–427, concerned book 1 of the *Essay*.

40   Jean Cornand de Lacrose (ed.), *Memoirs for the Ingenious, containing Observations in Philosophy, Physick, Philology, and Other Arts and Sciences* (London, 1693), January 1693, letter III, pp. 16–17; and February 1693, letter X, pp. 57–9. See also Jean Cornand de Lacrose (ed.), *The Works of the Learned, or, an Historical Account and Impartial Judgment of Books* (London, 1691–92), art. XXXVII, 'Explication of the Mystery of the Holy Trinity'.

41   Leclerc to Locke, 25 June/5 July 1689, in *Correspondence*, vol. 3, p. 642. See also Leclerc to Locke, 7/17 March 1690, ibid., vol. 4, p. 24.

42   Jean Leclerc, *Pneumatologia seu de spiritibus*, I.v.25, in Jean Leclerc, *Ontologia; sive de ente in genere* (London, 1692), pp. 102–3. This final paragraph of the anti-innatist chapter, 'De Idearum Natura, atque an sint innatæ?', referred the reader to book I of Locke's *Essay*. See also W. Molyneux to Locke, 22 December 1692, in *Correspondence*, vol. 4, p. 601.

43   G.W. Leibniz to Antonio Magliabechi, 7 December 1691, in Gottfried Wilhelm Leibniz, *Sämtliche Schriften und Briefe: Erste Reihe: Allgemeiner politischer und historischer*

Lacrose was concerned to reject Locke's anti-innatism, not because it struck at the epistemological foundation of Cartesianism, but because it seemed to imply a Socinian view of morality. Locke's arguments appeared to chime with Arminian and Socinian optimism about the power of reason in the lives of the majority, and to question the Calvinist understanding of the debilitating consequences of original sin upon man's moral faculties.[44] The *Essay*, in Lacrose's view, 'would induce any one, who were not thoroughly acquainted with the Author', to ascribe to Locke a Socinian stance. Knowing the author, however, he was 'perswaded that Mr. Locke is far from such thoughts, and that if there be any color for drawing such consequences out of his Book, it proceeds only from this, that he has applied himself more to pulling down than to building up'.[45]

It is necessary, in order to understand better Lacrose's criticism of the *Essay* for Socinianism, to discover why it was of particular importance for him to be seen to rebut Locke's theory. Lacrose made (to anticipate the conclusion somewhat) an attempt both to highlight his connection with Locke and Leclerc, whose reputations were soaring in the Republic of Letters, and to ward off any charge that, due to this connection, he must also sympathise with aspects of anti-Trinitarianism. The Refuge was divided into two camps: whilst the overwhelming majority supported Calvinist Trinitarianism, several francophone friends of Locke belonged to a camp which supported, or connived at, various anti-Trinitarian, Arminian or Pajonist tendencies. After 1689 it was important for Lacrose to distance himself from the heterodox minority because of the power relations in the Refuge.

The conflicts about dogma in the Refuge were rooted in the earlier dogmatic controversies, conducted at the academies of Geneva, Saumur and Sedan.[46] The men who transmitted Locke's doctrines to the Continent during his lifetime, translating his works into French and reviewing them in French – Bernard, Leclerc, Lecène and David Mazel as well as Pierre Coste – were all alumni of the academy of Geneva.[47]

Briefwechsel, eds Wolfgang Bungies, Georg Gerber, Albert Heinekamp, Kurt Müller, Günter Scheel, Franz Schupp, Sabine Sellschopp and Gerda Utermöhlen (vols 7–14, Berlin, 1964–93), vol. 7, p. 458; and Leibniz to Thomas Burnett of Kemney, 24 August/3 September 1697, ibid., vol. 14, p. 442.

44 Compare Mark Goldie, 'The Reception of Hobbes', in J.H. Burns and Mark Goldie (eds), *The Cambridge History of Political Thought, 1450–1700* (Cambridge, 1991), pp. 589–615, at pp. 608–9; and Knud Haakonssen, *Natural Law and Moral Philosophy: From Grotius to the Scottish Enlightenment* (Cambridge, 1996), pp. 54–8.

45 Lacrose (ed.), *Memoirs for the Ingenious*, February 1693, letter X, pp. 57–8. Compare Locke, *Essay*, 'Epistle to the Reader', p. 10.

46 Brian G. Armstrong, *Calvinism and the Amyraut Heresy: Protestant Scholasticism and Humanism in Seventeenth-Century France* (Madison, 1969); Walter Rex, *Essays on Pierre Bayle and Religious Controversy* (The Hague, 1965); and Frans Pieter van Stam, *The Controversy over the Theology of Saumur: Disrupting Debates among the Huguenots in Complicated Circumstances, 1635–1650* (Amsterdam and Maarssen, 1988).

47 On Mazel, see S.J. Savonius, 'Locke in French: The *Du Gouvernement Civil* of 1691 and Its Readers', *Historical Journal*, 47/1 (2004): 47–79. On Coste, see de Beer, editorial note,

At Geneva, a central controversy had raged over the nature of salvation, grace and predestination from 1669 when Lecène began his studies there, and at the time Bernard, Leclerc, Mazel and Coste were studying there, it had translated into an argument over the *Consensus Helveticus*, composed by strict Calvinists and finally adopted in Geneva in 1678–79. Those who championed the *Consensus* were led by François Turretin, the rigorist rector of the academy, whom Leclerc's friend Jacques Lenfant styled 'the patriarch of Geneva's inquisitors'.[48]

Later on, in exile, persecution was the corollary of the orthodox Calvinists' determination to uphold the purity of their faith. Leclerc and Locke knew several ministers suspected of heresy who finally turned Roman Catholic because of the intolerance they faced. For instance, Isaac Papin and Nöel Aubert de Versé were harried by Pierre Jurieu, a professor at the academy of Sedan before its closure in 1681. Abroad, Jurieu did his utmost to police the faith of expatriate Huguenot ministers.[49] He managed to prevent Papin and Versé from securing employment wherever they tried to settle – in Holland, Hamburg, Danzig, England. The lack of employment forced them to return to Paris and abjure Protestantism in 1689–90.[50] The Calvinists' attempts to impose doctrinal uniformity on the clergy were also the rationale behind Bernard's and Leclerc's interest in obtaining appointments in the Remonstrant Church. When they decamped to the Dutch Republic, they were fleeing, not primarily Louis XIV's Counter-Reformation, but the persecuting Protestants.[51]

Significantly, after Lacrose and Mazel had settled in London, each styled himself 'priest of the Church of England'.[52] Whilst the Toleration Act of 1689 had reaffirmed protection to the fundamental Trinitarianism of orthodox belief, it seemed to Locke's associates that the ejection of nonjurors and the new churchmanship of Archbishop

---

in Locke, *Correspondence*, vol. 5, p. 395; and Anne Goldgar, *Impolite Learning: Conduct and Community in the Republic of Letters, 1680–1750* (New Haven and London, 1995).

48   Jacques Lenfant to Leclerc [early December 1683?], in *Epistolario*, vol. 1, p. 110: 'le Patriarche des Inquisiteurs de Geneue'. See also Bernard to Leclerc, 9 November 1685, ibid., p. 408. On Turretin (1623–87), or Turrettini, see Eugène de Budé, *Vie de François Turrettini, théologien genevois, 1623–1687* (Lausanne, 1871), esp. p. 155 on the *Consensus*. On Lenfant (1661–1728), see Haag, vol. 6, pp. 547–52.

49   Robin D. Gwynn, 'Disorder and Innovation: The Reshaping of the French Churches of London after the Glorious Revolution', in Ole Peter Grell, Jonathan I. Israel, and Nicholas Tyacke (eds), *From Persecution to Toleration: The Glorious Revolution and Religion in England* (Oxford, 1991), pp. 251–73, esp. p. 259; Marshall, 'Huguenot Thought after the Revocation of the Edict of Nantes', esp. p. 384; and Savonius, 'Locke in French'.

50   Paul J. Morman, *Nöel Aubert de Versé: A Study in the Concept of Toleration* (Lewiston, and Queenston, [1987]), pp. 58–9, 65–6. On Papin (1657–1709), see below.

51   Leclerc to Vattemare [10 November 1684], in *Epistolario*, vol. 1, p. 263; and Bernard to Leclerc, 9 November 1685, ibid., p. 409.

52   John Tillotson, *Formulaire de prieres dont se servoit sa majesté Guillaume III*, preface by John Moore, bishop of Norwich, trans. David Mazel (London, 1704), title-page: Mazel, 'Prêtre de l'Eglise Anglicane'; Jean Cornand De Lacrose, *An Historical and Geographical Description of France* (London, 1694), title-page: 'J. De Lacrose, Eccl. Angl. Presb'.

Tillotson signalled a cleansing of the ethos of tyrannising clericalism in the Church of England. In 1692 van Limborch praised Tillotson for his defence of Protestant liberty against what was known as popery.[53] For everyone in Locke's circle, 'popery' meant, not simply adherence to Roman Catholicism, but imperious clericalism under any guise and any unwarranted attempt to persecute reasonable dissenters.[54] Locke's Francophone associates found Calvinist 'popery' in the establishment of the Refuge and preferred to try entering the Church of England.[55]

Locke's animosity towards rhetorical education

The Revolution of 1688–89 did not, in Locke's view, eradicate the authoritarianism which had characterised Restoration England. One manifestation of authoritarianism was the 'popery' which continued to cause his friends, such as Lecène, anguish. On account of his alleged 'Pelagianism', Lecène's temporary ministry at Charenton had ceased before the Revocation of the Edict of Nantes; subsequently he had conspicuous difficulty in securing a permanent position abroad. In 1694 Bishop Burnet wrote to Leclerc that Lecène, for whom Leclerc had hoped Burnet would secure some preferment, was 'under such suspitions of socinianisme that till he clears himselfe from these it will not be possible to doe any thing for him'. The efforts to silence and ostracise heterodox ministers had allied the Francophone Calvinists with the High-Church clerics at Oxford, who hoped 'to destroy the Tolleration that is setled by law among us which the farre greater part of the Clergy doe detest'.[56] Lecène, marked out by the High-Church party as a Socinian, began falling into poverty; Locke gave him financial assistance.[57]

Another manifestation of authoritarianism was the survival of absolutist doctrines. That they survived in their most virulent form, in the form of Filmer's patriarchalism, seemed confirmed by Furly's encounters with two Englishmen soon after the Revolution. Writing to Locke in June 1689, Furly, then in England, reported having had pleasant sport with a scrupulous Cambridge scholar upon Filmer's 'maggot'. It is emblematic that Furly had managed to reduce the Cantabrigian,

---

53   Philip van Limborch, *Historia inquisitionis. Cui subjungitur Liber sententiarum inquisitionis Tholosanæ ab anno Christi 1307 ad annum 1323* (Amsterdam, 1692), dedication to Tillotson, sig. 2–3. Luisa Simonutti, 'Limborch's *Historia inquisitionis* and the Pursuit of Toleration', in A.P. Coudert, S. Hutton, R.H. Popkin, and G.M. Weiner (eds), *Judaeo-Christian Intellectual Culture in the Seventeenth Century: A Celebration of the Library of Narcissus Marsh (1638–1713)* (Dordrecht and London, 1999), pp. 237–55.

54   See Mark Goldie, 'The Huguenot Experience and the Problem of Toleration in Restoration England', in Caldicott *et al.*, *Huguenots in Ireland*, pp. 175–203, at pp. 177–9.

55   See, for example, Leclerc to Locke, 10/20 January 1692, in *Correspondence*, vol. 4, pp. 354–5.

56   Gilbert Burnet to Leclerc, 17 November 1694, in *Epistolario*, vol. 2, pp. 136–7.

57   Van Limborch to Locke, 12/22 January 1692, in *Correspondence*, vol. 4, p. 359. Leclerc to Burnet, early January 1695, in *Epistolario*, vol. 2, p. 144. Marshall, 'Huguenot Thought after the Revocation of the Edict of Nantes', p. 390.

disposed to nonjuring, to silence at every turn of their argument – but that Furly's demolition of Filmerian premises did not prevent the scholar from 'holding fast the conclusion'.[58] After a brief respite, Furly had been faced with yet another debate about the legitimacy of the Revolution, and had again attempted to convert his opponent, this time apparently a Quaker. The second conversation had resulted in the same impasse: though Furly's antagonist had been reduced to being at a nonplus and Furly had imagined he 'had fully convinc'd him', the antagonist would not alter his principles. Furly concluded from the scholar's and the Quaker's inability to be satisfied with reasoning and to give up supporting James II that 'I see not, that university learneing, nor inspiration, does make all that pretend to it wise, or give them Common Sense'.[59]

The more closely Locke examined authoritarianism after the Revolution, the more clearly he saw that its roots ran into the cultural soil of rhetorical education. In general, after 1688–89 whigs were reluctant to send their sons to be educated at Oxford, which was seen to be a bastion of High-Church ideals.[60] They had to search for alternative educational arrangements that would reflect their distinctive political values. For instance, Richard Coote, Earl Bellomont, who was a staunch whig, chose to have his eldest son tutored by the Huguenot refugee Jacques-Louis Cappel at home and then wrote to Locke about his plan to send him to study philosophy with Leclerc at Amsterdam.[61]

Undoubtedly Locke shared Bellomont's concerns over the absolutist and High-Church doctrines espoused by the dons and over the subtle indoctrination in the universities. In 1689 Locke's *Essay* accused the scholastic 'Disputants, these all-knowing Doctors' of having justified 'strange and absurd' doctrines 'in these last Ages'.[62] Yet it is important to notice at this juncture that he was also concerned about the deeper problem that the system of education itself was corrupt, and became more and more convinced that the curriculum had to be recast. It was not enough, for example, to replace the reading of Virgil's imperial epic with Lucan's republican

---

58   Furly to Locke, 10 June 1689, in *Correspondence*, vol. 3, pp. 638–9. De Beer notes that a 'maggot is a whimsical or perverse fancy' (ibid., p. 639).

59   Furly to Locke, 10 June 1689, in *Correspondence*, vol. 3, p. 639. See also Locke, *Two Treatises of Government*, preface, lines 33–49; and *Education*, § 147, pp. 207–8: 'I think Learning ... helps them only to be the more foolish, or wicked Men' (the reading of Locke's manuscript).

60   G.V. Bennett, *The Tory Crisis in Church and State, 1688–1730: The Career of Francis Atterbury, Bishop of Rochester* (Oxford, 1975): the point is made in several places, but see esp. p. 5. Compare Robert Molesworth, *Etat present de Danemarc* (London, 1694), preface, sig. **7: 'Nos Universitez paroissent aussi mal reglées dans ce qui regarde le sçavoir, que dans ce qui concerne la politique.' Molesworth (1656–1725) was 'an Harty Admirer and Acquaintance' of Locke (W. Molyneux to Locke, 11 September 1697, in *Correspondence*, vol. 6, pp. 192–3).

61   Richard Coote, first earl of Bellomont, to Locke, [25?] May 1697, in *Correspondence*, vol. 6, p. 131. Bellomont's eldest son was Nanfan Coote (c.1681–1708).

62   Locke, *Essay*, III.x.9, p. 495.

poetry,[63] or John Dryden's with the whig poet Richard Blackmore's work.[64] Locke wished to dismiss poetry itself, as an integral part of rhetorical education, from the curriculum.

One reason for Locke's stance was the threat of moral relativism inherent in rhetorical education. Rhetoricians showed how there are always two sides to any question, and how both sides can be defended with equal rhetorical force in a dispute.[65] Their exercises in argument *in utramque partem* required that one pupil presented both sides of an argument, arguing first *pro* and then *contra*. Precisely this kind of exercising, which seemed to make pupils deny the truth, was condemned by Locke in the 1690s.[66] In his view, rhetorical education was likely 'to turn young Men's Minds from the sincere Search and Love of Truth ... and to make them doubt whether there is any such thing'. That the curriculum included training which contributed towards citizens' disingenuousness could scarcely be believed by 'the rational part of Mankind not corrupted by Education'.[67] What was going on in European societies was systematic education in what Locke termed bluntly 'the great Art of Deceit and Errour' and what Leclerc termed simulated rhetoric, 'which defends truth and falsehood alike'.[68]

Another reason for Locke's rejection of the Renaissance curriculum was his conviction that rhetorical studies compromised, not only the status of moral truth in civil society, but also the activity of frank truth-telling. This activity was captured

---

63   On Hugo Grotius's, Algernon Sidney's and Marchamont Nedham's interest in Lucan, see David Norbrook, 'Lucan, Thomas May, and the Creation of a Republican Literary Culture', in Kevin Sharpe and Peter Lake (eds), *Culture and Politics in Early Stuart England* (London, 1994), pp. 45–66, esp. pp. 54, 65. Note that 'Lucan's work ... is pervaded – one might almost say, poisoned – by the rhetoric of the schools': J.D. Duff, 'Introduction', in Lucan, *Lucan: The Civil War*, ed. and trans. J.D. Duff (London and Cambridge, Mass., 1928), pp. ix–xv, at p. x.

64   Locke knew Blackmore (*c*.1654–1729), whose *King Arthur* of 1697, an allegory of William III, was praised by Molyneux. See, for example, Paul D'Aranda to Locke, 15 July 1695, in *Correspondence*, vol. 5, p. 412; W. Molyneux to Locke, 27 May 1697, ibid., vol. 6, p. 134; and Locke to W. Molyneux, 15 June 1697, ibid., p. 144.

65   Quentin Skinner, 'Thomas Hobbes: Rhetoric and the Construction of Morality', *The Proceedings of the British Academy*, 76 (1990): 1–61; and *Reason and Rhetoric in the Philosophy of Hobbes* (Cambridge, 1996), pp. 8–10. Compare Cicero, *On Duties*, ed. and trans. E.M. Atkins and M.T. Griffin (Cambridge, 1991), II.8, p. 65; Locke, *Essay*, IV.xx.14–15, pp. 715–16; and Peter Burke, 'The Renaissance Dialogue', *Renaissance Studies*, 3 (1989): 1–12.

66   Locke, *Education*, § 171, p. 229; and 'Of the Conduct of the Understanding', ed. Paul Schuurman, Ph.D. thesis (University of Keele, 2000) [hereafter 'Conduct'], § 67, pp. 217–18 (cited by the new paragraph numbers and page numbers in Schuurman's edition).

67   Locke, *Essay*, IV.vii.11, p. 601 (added to the fourth edition).

68   Locke, *Essay*, 'Index', s.v. 'Rhetorick', p. 743; III.x.6–7, pp. 493–4; and III.x.34, p. 508 (the reading of the first edition). Jean Leclerc, *Ars critica, in qua ad studia linguarum Latinæ, Græcæ, et Hebraicæ via munitur*, 2nd edition (2 vols, London, 1698), vol. 1, 'Præfatio', iii.1, p. 4: 'veræ Rhetorices, non fucatæ illius, quæ mendacio æque ac veritati patrocinatur'.

in the Classical figure of free speech, παρρησία, linked in the Greek tradition with democratic boldness – with the freedom to speak truth boldly to power.[69] There were several characteristics of the Greek ethos of παρρησία that resembled, and influenced, the Roman ethos of *ingenuitas*. In Classical Rome, *ingenuitas* connoted both the condition of one freeborn and the uprightness and frankness characteristic of freemen.[70] It was in fact central to the Roman accounts of ingenuous behaviour that a free man can speak plainly without fear. Such behaviour was contrasted with that of the slavish flatterer, who tries to ingratiate himself with others.[71] This classical attitude was adopted by Locke, who noted that whilst the 'disingenuous' speak only what they expect their superiors want to hear, and 'dissemble their mistakes for fear of blemishing their reputation',[72] the ethos of free speech guides the conduct of the 'ingenuous'.[73] In 1689 he hoped that the future generations 'will abhor the Memory of such servile Flatterers, who whilst it seem'd to serve their turn, resolv'd all Government into absolute Tyranny'.[74]

Exhortations to *ingenuitas* and praise for παρρησία were commonplace in the writings of Locke's associates. After 1688–89, van Limborch believed that, unlike those who are 'dependent on the will of others, and ... compelled to further ... measures of which they themselves disapprove', Locke should offer frank counsel on Europe's politics.[75] Earlier van Limborch had claimed that the 'ingenuous παρρησια as well as liberty' are protected by the law of nature, in his preface to the

---

69   Locke, *Essay*, II.xxii.10, p. 293: 'Boldness is the Power to speak or do what we intend, before others, without fear or disorder; and the Greeks call the confidence of speaking by a peculiar name παρρησια'. David Colclough, '*Parrhesia*: The Rhetoric of Free Speech in Early Modern England', *Rhetorica*, 17 (1999): 177–212. Another important discussion is Martin Dzelzainis, 'Milton *Parrhesiastes*', an unpublished paper given at the tenth international conference of the Centre for Seventeenth-Century Studies, University of Durham (14–17 July 2003). See also J.A. Simpson and E.C.S. Weiner (eds), *The Oxford English Dictionary*, 2nd edition (Oxford, 1989), vol. 11, s.v. 'Parrhesia'.

70   Cicero, *Epistvlae: Vol. II Epistvlae ad Atticvm: Pars prior*, ed. L.C. Purser (Oxford, 1903), I.xvii.5; and *Orationes in C. Verrem*, ed. Albert Clark, I.xliv.113 and I.lviii.152, in Cicero, *Orationes: Divinatio in Q. Caecilium. In C. Verrem*, ed. William Peterson (Oxford, 1917). Tacitus on eloquence '*sine ingenuitate*' in *Dialogus de oratoribus*, chapter 32, sections 4–5, in Tacitus, *Opera minora*, ed. Henry Furneaux (Oxford, 1900). Suetonius and Tacitus on the distinction between a freedman (*libertus*) and one freeborn (*ingenuus*) in Suetonius, *Suetonius: Volume I*, intro. K.R. Bradley, trans. J.C. Rolfe, revised edition (London and Cambridge, Mass., 1998), II.lxxiv, pp. 262–3; and Tacitus, *Annales ab excessu divi Augusti*, ed. Charles Dennis Fisher (Oxford, 1906), book 13, chapter 27.

71   Compare Aristotle, *Nicomachean Ethics*, ed. and trans. Terence Irwin (Indianapolis, 1985), 1124b25–1125a5: 'all flatterers are servile and inferior people are flatterers'.

72   Adapted from Locke, *Essay*, II.xxi.72, p. 285 (added to the second edition).

73   Locke, *Education*, §§ 45–7, pp. 111–12; § 72, p. 134; and § 142, pp. 199–200 on 'what is to be aimed at in an ingenuous Education'.

74   Locke, *Two Treatises of Government*, II.239.49–56.

75   Van Limborch to Locke, [*c*.12/22 April and] 26 April/6 May 1689, in *Correspondence*, vol. 3, p. 610 (trans. de Beer).

reader in Etienne de Courcelles's *Opera theologica*.[76] In 1680 this edition had been sifted by Leclerc, Courcelles's descendant,[77] who cited the preface in his first letter to van Limborch.[78] Impressed by Leclerc's candour and παρρησία, van Limborch had promised to answer Leclerc's with 'the same παρρησία'.[79]

Much later the motif of truthful outspokenness became central to Leclerc's vision of politics in his *Parrhasiana*. Both Leclerc and Locke expected the *parrhesiastes*' outspokenness from the people's elected representatives, who must 'freely act and advise, as the necessity of the Commonwealth, and the publick Good should, upon examination, and mature debate, be judged to require'.[80] This they should do impartially, yielding to reasons unlike the pupils engaged in argument *in utramque partem*. However, whilst the system of rhetorical education prevailed, it seemed impossible to reach the ideal of political activity as public debate in assemblies which safeguard παρρησια and weigh 'the Reasons on all sides' before reaching any decision.[81] Rhetorical exercising made youngsters intent on winning debates – hence often domineering and irascible, always eager to follow their self-interest, never willing to devote their energy to the pursuance of the common good. As Bernard noted, ideally education should produce, not 'contradicting Spirits', but 'persons who follow the road prepared for them'.[82]

The curriculum of rhetorical education, which the Renaissance humanists understood as training for civic life, usually covered grammar (or Latin), rhetoric, ethics, poetry and history.[83] Each subject of this curriculum came under attack in Locke's *Education*. His manuscript advised parents to select a tutor who considers

---

76 Philip van Limborch, 'Praefatio ad Lectorem', in Etienne de Courcelles [Stephanus Curcellaeus], *Opera theologica*, ed. Philip van Limborch (Amsterdam, 1675), sig. *3: 'Hisce accedit ingenua παρρησια ac libertas, qua veritatem candide, sine cujusquam gratia aut odio indagat, inventamque ingenue amplectitur, et ad nominis divini gloriam sincere profitetur ... Libertatem enim hanc natura dictat, ratio suadet, utilitas veritatisque studium commendat ... Hic naturæ lex dictat, unicuique in argumentorum robur inquirendi libertatem permittendam, ut nulli dogmati, nisi de cujus veritate est persuasus, assensum præbeat'.

77 Jean Leclerc, *Joannis Clerici Philosophiæ et S. Linguæ, apud Remonstrantes, Amstelodami Professoris Vita et opera ad annum MDCCXI* (Amsterdam, 1711), pp. 22–3.

78 Leclerc to van Limborch, 10 August 1681, in *Epistolario*, vol. 1, p. 14.

79 Van Limborch to Leclerc, 30 August 1681, in *Epistolario*, vol. 1, p. 17.

80 Locke, *Two Treatises of Government*, II.222.44–6.

81 Jean Leclerc, *Parrhasiana ou pensées diverses sur des matiéres de critique, d'histoire, de morale et de politique* (2 vols, Amsterdam, 1699 and 1701), vol. 1, pp. 88–9; and vol. 2, p. 146. Locke, *Education*, § 189, p. 241. Locke, *Essay*, IV.xv.5, p. 656; and IV.xvi.9, p. 663. Compare Clarke to Locke, 23 January 1692, in *Correspondence*, vol. 4, p. 373, on the Commons' debates.

82 Jaques Bernard, *De l'excellence de la religion* (Amsterdam, 1714), II.i, pp. 75–6: 'des Esprits contredisans ... des personnes, qui suivent le chemin qu'on veut leur marquer'.

83 Paul Oskar Kristeller, 'Humanism', in Eckhard Kessler, Jill Kraye, Charles B. Schmitt, and Quentin Skinner (eds), *The Cambridge History of Renaissance Philosophy* (Cambridge, 1988), pp. 113–37; Skinner, *Reason and Rhetoric in the Philosophy of Hobbes*, pp. 19–26; and Vickers, pp. 7–8.

'Latin and language the least part' of the pupil's education and takes 'the greatest care of formeing his minde and disposeing of that aright'.[84] Still in 1686 Locke asserted that when Edward Clarke's son 'can read English perfectly, the next thing, of course, to be learnt is Latin'; but in the *Education*, published in 1693, he declared that nobody doubts French must follow English 'because People are accustomed to the right way of teaching that Language, which is ... not by Grammatical Rules'.[85]

Tracing the progression of humanist education, the *Education* then turned to rhetoric and logic. Locke noted that they are 'the Arts, that in the ordinary method usually follow immediately after Grammar'; he considered them useless. The third edition of 1695 expanded his treatment in the *Education* of the contemporary curriculum. It broadened the discussion of logic to highlight his view that the skills learnt through disputation are, not only useless, but also destructive in the debates gentlemen have. Nothing was more 'disingenuous' and 'mis-becoming a Gentleman' than that disputants never 'yield to plain Reason, and the Conviction of clear Arguments'. Rhetorical situations led pupils 'into a captious and fallacious use of doubtful Words, which ... least suits a Gentleman or a lover of Truth'. Locke claimed that the English landed gentry did not possess 'the Qualities of Gentlemen'. This was not their fault but the fault of the educational system prevalent, not merely in England, but also in the neighbouring countries.[86]

In this system of *studia humanitatis* there was a close connection between poetry and music. The ancient Greek lyric, much imitated by early-modern poets, had originally been sung to a lyre. Dryden's ode of 1697 on how Timotheus, playing the lyre, could move Emperor Alexander to any emotion at will, drew on a Classical and Renaissance understanding of the power of music to achieve the rhetorical aim, *movere*.[87] Quintilian's Classical work on rhetoric – the central authority in the seventeenth-century English and French curricula – associated music with rhetoric primarily because both arts turned on variations of expression that stirred emotions appositely.[88] A distinctive Renaissance innovation was to subsume music under the purview of rhetorical theorising, inducing the birth of opera.[89]

Leclerc's *Parrhasiana* castigated the mental world of opera and poetry – the world 'of a false rhetoric' – where one forgives oneself for errors in reasoning and

---

84 Locke, *Education*, § 164, p. 217. See also ibid., § 93, p. 150 (added to the third edition), and § 147, p. 207, on the study of Latin and Greek as a waste of time.

85 Locke to Clarke, 29 January/8 February [1686], in *Correspondence*, vol. 2, p. 774. Locke, *Education*, § 162, p. 216.

86 Locke, *Education*, §§ 188–9, pp. 240–43 (partly added to the third edition).

87 John Dryden, 'Alexander's Feast; or, the Power of Musique' [originally 1697], in John Dryden, *The Works of John Dryden*, intro. David Marriott (Ware, 1995).

88 Quintilian, *The Orator's Education*, ed. and trans. Donald A. Russell (5 vols, London and Cambridge, Mass., 2001), I.x.22–7 and 31, vol. 1, pp. 224–7 and 228–9. Compare Beauval (ed.), *Histoire*, August 1697, art. VII, pp. 532–45, on Cardinal Sfondrato's view that 'la Musique & la Rhetorique ... font le même effet sur l'ame: elles changent la volonté'.

89 Vickers, pp. 360–72.

is in no 'condition to judge correctly of things', being in the grip of passions.⁹⁰ Locke remarked in the *Education* that should the son 'have a Poetick Vein ... the Parents should labour to have it stifled, and suppressed', and warned youngsters against wasting their time on music. Locke gave musicality 'the last place' in his all-inclusive 'List of Accomplishments'. He also noticed that the study of music often engages youngsters 'in such odd Company, that many think it much better spared'.⁹¹ How poor the actual prospects for its elimination were was shown by the anger Bernard's colleagues and congregation expressed in Lausanne in 1685. They were scandalised by his attack, in his sermon, upon such useless pursuits as music. Ministers – who, Bernard jeered, wanted to pay God by singing – wrote to Bern in order to have him deposed, but he was only banned from preaching.⁹²

It remains to consider, in this discussion of Locke's anti-humanism, the disciplines which he substituted for rhetorical education. His pupil, 'whilst others of his Age are wholly taken up with Latin and Languages', would follow a curriculum dominated by geography, arithmetic, astronomy, chronology, anatomy and geometry.⁹³ Yet it was not important for pupils to study this precise selection of subjects. In January 1687 Locke wrote that children 'might practise drawing, a great deal of anatomy, botany, geography and astronomy'; in April that Clarke's son can be taught these subjects 'or the knowledg of any other sensible parts of nature'.⁹⁴ A decade later he recommended chronology, geography, anatomy and chemistry; but 'not the Ethicks of the Schools ... not how to difine distinguish and dispute about the names of virtues and vices', nor any other liberal arts.⁹⁵ The controlling tendency of his advice was that studying anti-rhetorical subjects would help form a 'Mind free, and Master of it self and all its actions'⁹⁶ insofar as they deflected the pupil's love away from himself

---

90   Leclerc, *Parrhasiana ou pensées diverses*, vol. 1, pp. 8–9 and 12: 'On n'est plus en état de bien juger des choses, dès que l'on est passionné. On pardonne tout, & l'on trouve tout beau, dans un Poëte qui a sû nous ébra[n]ler'.

91   Locke, *Education*, § 174, p. 230; and § 197, pp. 252–3.

92   Bernard to Leclerc, 9 November 1685, in *Epistolario*, vol. 1, pp. 407–8: 'qu'en parlant des Sciences, apres avoir dit qu'il falloit les raporter toutes à la conduite de la vie, ie dis que de la il suivoit qu'il y en avoit plus[ieu]rs d'assez inutiles parmi lesquelles ie mis la musique. Cet article scandalisa particulierement un ministre Musicien et quelques autres qui veulent paier Dieu en Chansons ...'.

93   Locke, *Education*, § 166, p. 219, and §§ 178–83, pp. 234–8.

94   Locke to Clarke, [11/21?] and 18/28 January 1687, in *Correspondence*, vol. 3, pp. 108–9; and 19/29 April [1687], ibid., p. 183.

95   Locke to Cary Mordaunt, Countess Peterborough [September/October 1697?], in *Correspondence*, vol. 6, pp. 213–15.

96   Locke, *Education*, § 66, p. 123. Ibid., § 75, p. 136: 'If by this Means the Mind can get an habitual Dominion over it self ... it will be an Advantage of more Consequence than Latin or Logick'.

towards truth and taught him to order his ideas.⁹⁷ In short, the pupil was to learn to live by reason alone and overcome the power of emotions.⁹⁸

This was also the rationale behind the focus in Locke's *Education* on harsh, character-building methods. The Lockean tutor's primary task was to instil the habit of disregarding selfish desires into his pupil. Locke conceded that most people considered 'Learning' the end of education, but insisted that learning is 'the least part' of virtuous gentlemen's education.⁹⁹ Their training in how 'to submit their Desires' begins, 'contrary to the ordinary way ... from their very Cradles' and continues at table where whatever they crave, they are denied. Locke noted that children crying for sweet things, such as sugar candy, should never be indulged.¹⁰⁰

The recruitment of Huguenot tutors

From 1687 onwards, in order to help translate the ideal of *ingenuitas* and παρρησία into reality, Locke was involved with his English friends' efforts to draft in Huguenot tutors. His preference for home education stood in sharp contrast to the Quintilianic advice that children should attend school to become accustomed to the kind of public competition that faces orators.¹⁰¹ But if children stayed at home, prospective tutors needed to be carefully vetted before appointed. The Huguenots employed were expected, as he first stressed in 1687 to Clarke, to follow 'our method of education', that is, the rules Locke the selector prescribed.¹⁰²

A decade later, in 1697, Locke met the Huguenot refugee de La Treille, Popple's friend, in order to engage him to tutor Francis Cudworth Masham.¹⁰³ However, La Treille decided to enter the household of Bellomont, who had asked Locke 'to recommend me a good sort of French man to be Governour to my sons'.¹⁰⁴ Locke then offered Leclerc's friend Coste a chance to join the Masham household in Essex.

---

97   Locke, *Education*, § 94, pp. 156–7; and § 195, p. 249 (added to the third edition).
98   See Locke to Clarke, 31 December 1686/10 January 1687, in *Correspondence*, vol. 3, pp. 93–4.
99   Locke, *Education*, § 38, p. 107; § 94, p. 156 (added to the third edition); and § 147, pp. 207–8. Compare John Dunn, *The Political Thought of John Locke: An Historical Account of the Argument of the* Two Treatises of Government (Cambridge, 1969), p. 114.
100   Locke, *Education*, §§ 38–9, pp. 107–9; and Locke to Clarke, 29 January/8 February [1686], in *Correspondence*, vol. 2, p. 771.
101   Quintilian, *The Orator's Education*, I.ii, vol. 1, pp. 82–97. See, for example, Locke to Clarke, 29 January/8 February [1686], in *Correspondence*, vol. 2, p. 776.
102   Locke to Clarke, [11/21?] and 18/28 January 1687, in *Correspondence*, vol. 3, p. 109; and 27 Dec. [1691], ibid., vol. 4, p. 347. Compare W. Molyneux to Locke, 2 June 1694, ibid., vol. 5, p. 70: Molyneux's son was 'bred exactly ... to the Rules you prescribe, I mean as to forming his Mind and Mastering his Passions'.
103   Locke to Lady Masham, 3 July 1697, in *Correspondence*, vol. 6, pp. 147–8; F.C. Masham to Locke, 5 July 1697, ibid., pp. 150–51; and R. De La Treille to Locke, [c.8? July 1697] and [c.17 July 1697], ibid., pp. 153–4 and 157–8.
104   Earl Bellomont to Locke, [25?] May 1697, in *Correspondence*, vol. 6, p. 131.

Although Locke thought that he knew little about mathematics and natural history, Coste, 'an ingenious man', was liked 'very well for our purpose'.[105] After Locke's death, he was offered a place at the Clarkes', who lived at Chipley near Taunton, Somerset. Edward Clarke had been Locke's close friend from the early 1680s, managed his affairs in England during his exile, and acted as his spokesman in the House of Commons in the 1690s. It had been as a response to Clarke's request for advice on the upbringing of his son that Locke had begun articulating his theory of education.

Before Coste's coming to live at Chipley, the Clarkes had already employed a series of Huguenots. Between 1687 and 1710 their house was the home of six Huguenot tutors altogether.[106] Here I want to focus, not merely on these six refugees, but also on those whom the Clarkes failed to engage. The first Huguenot with whom they contracted was Monsieur Fouquet, recommended by Henri Justel. At the time, in 1687, Leclerc and Locke had recommended that the Clarkes employ Papin, Claude Pajon's nephew and a *proposant* too heterodox to be ordained at Saumur in 1683. Unable to gain a ministerial post, having refused to condemn Pajonism, Papin had secured employment as tutor in Popple's home at Bordeaux. Following the Revocation of 1685 Papin sought refuge in England where he took Anglican orders, before crossing the Channel back to the Dutch Republic in 1687.[107]

After Papin's *Essais de theologie* had appeared in 1687, Lacrose's review in the *Bibliothèque* drew out the differences between his rational Pajonism and Jurieu's Calvinist emphasis on the workings of the internal divine grace, which 'must move the will' when one converts to Christian faith, by placing their tenets in juxtaposition with one another.[108] Since the mid-1680s Papin's opposition to orthodox Calvinism had been a matter of common knowledge among Locke's associates. In 1684 Papin had praised Leclerc for his rare characteristics of 'impartiality, humility, freedom of reasoning, renunciation of prejudices' and castigated the majority of 'our savants', who were 'rather slaves than disciples of their teachers', unable to prefer the truth and liberty to everything else.[109]

---

105 Locke to W. Molyneux, 10 January 1698, in *Correspondence*, vol. 6, p. 294.

106 Listed in chronological order, they were D'eully (or Duelly), Passebon, de Grassemare (or Grasemar), de La Rocque (or de Laroque), Dubois and Coste. On their daily grind of work in deepest Somerset, see Bridget Clarke, 'Huguenot Tutors and the Family of Edward and Mary Clarke of Chipley, 1687–1710', *PHS*, 27 (2001): 527–42.

107 Barnes, *Jean Le Clerc*, pp. 104–5 and 108; R.W.J. Michaelis, 'Isaac Papin', *Oxford DNB*; and Sina, editorial apparatus, in *Epistolario*, vol. 1, s.v. 'Isaac Papin', p. 553.

108 *Bibliothèque*, vol. 7, December 1687, art. XVII-2-3, pp. 528–45. Pierre Jurieu, *Traitté de la nature et de la grace* (Amsterdam, 1715) [originally 1687], pp. 230-32: 'la grace interne doit toucher la volonté devant que de pénetrer absolument l'entendement pratique, qui dans le fond n'est rien que l'acte de la volonté même'.

109 Papin to Leclerc, 19 February 1684, in *Epistolario*, vol. 1, p. 124: 'le désinterressement, l'humilité, la liberté du raisonnement, le renoncement aux préjugez ... capables de préférer la Vérité et la Liberté à toutes choses. Presque tous nos savans sont plustôt les Esclaves, que les disciples, de leurs maistres.'

It is unsurprising – given this praise, Papin's experience for the task, gained at the Popples', and the animosity between him and Jurieu – that Leclerc believed Papin to be a suitable tutor. When he was recommended as tutor to the Clarkes, Leclerc stated that he is 'well skilled in the politer parts of learning, without being infected with the pedantry of scholarship'. Clarke delighted in the *ingenuitas* of Papin, 'soe ingeniouse a Gentleman'. Significantly, he agreed to follow Locke's method of education so that, Locke told Clarke, 'we shall be able to manage him exactly to our design'. This design was, Locke went on to explain, 'to have the mind of your son formed to virtue ... and that languages and letters are valued ... no otherwise than as they may be subservient to make your son ... fitter for ... the employments of a gentleman', and 'to teach him the mastery of his passions'. Subsequently these basic principles as well as the resultant rejection of rhetorical education constituted, as noticed above, the core of Locke's theory in the *Education*.[110]

However, despite Leclerc and Locke's efforts to gain the post for him, Papin rejected Clarke's offer.[111] After this setback for his plans, Clarke received 'severall Offers from amongst the French-Protestants' but found it difficult to 'gett another that may Answere our Designe'. Without a tutor, he could not 'prevaile with' his son 'by Reasoning and the other mild wayes that were formerly made use of'; he began fearing that 'I shall never bee able to Govern Him intirely by our Method'.[112] Such fears were fuelled by Locke's view that 'corporal Punishments, are not the Discipline fit to be used in the Education of those we would have ... ingenuous Men': 'slavish Discipline makes a slavish Temper'.[113]

Fortunately, Clarke was able to enter into an agreement with Fouquet, who promised to follow Locke's educational method.[114] This method was, nevertheless, 'soe much out of the road, and thoughts' of most men of letters that Fouquet was expected to have as much to learn as his pupil.[115] Unfortunately, he could not take up his job due to illness. Instead, Clarke appointed Monsieur D'eully, who was eager to

---

110 Locke to Clarke, 31 December 1686/10 January 1687, in *Correspondence*, vol. 3, pp. 93–4; and Clarke to Locke, 21 and 25 January 1687, ibid., p. 117.

111 Locke to Clarke, 7/17 January 1687, and [11/21?] and 18/28 January 1687, in *Correspondence*, vol. 3, p. 101 and 107–10. Clarke to Locke, 21 and 25 January 1687, and 8 February 1687, ibid., pp. 116–17 and 132. Mrs Mary Clarke to Locke, 8 February 1687, ibid., p. 134.

112 Clarke to Locke, 28 January 1687, in *Correspondence*, vol. 3, pp. 119–20. Compare Sir Walter Yonge to Locke, 28 January 1687, ibid., p. 122.

113 Locke, *Education*, § 50 and 52, p. 113.

114 Clarke to Locke, 8 February 1687, in *Correspondence*, vol. 3, pp. 132–3; Mrs Clarke to Locke, 16 February 1688, ibid., p. 373; and Locke to Mrs Clarke, 28 February/9 March 1688, ibid., p. 386.

115 Locke to Clarke, 19/29 April [1687], in *Correspondence*, vol. 3, p. 173.

comply with Locke's rules.[116] He was later replaced with Monsieur Passebon, who had been engaged by Furly and Locke.[117]

Locke praised Passebon's *ingenuitas*, his 'fairnesse and ingenuity'.[118] Presumably Locke regarded Passebon as 'one to our purpose' when they met in London in 1689, but he was nevertheless required to follow Locke's detailed advice and report to him on the pupil's progress.[119] Had Locke been satisfied with progress reports on the studies, Passebon's burden would have been lighter. But Locke showed indifference to such reports, insisting that Passebon continue struggling to mould his pupil into an ingenuous gentleman.[120] In 1691 Passebon and his pupil had to undergo Locke's tests in Essex.[121] Passebon failed this trial: afterwards Clarke started to consider replacing him with Matthieu Souverain.[122]

A couple of years before the Revocation of 1685 Souverain had been deprived of his ministry in France because of his 'Arminianism'. He had moved to the Dutch Republic, but could not secure employment there because of his refusal to endorse the rigorous Dordrecht canons of 1619. Subsequently he moved to England.[123] In London he was persecuted by the orthodox ministers of the Threadneedle Street French church.[124] His notorious *Le Platonisme devoilé* was published posthumously in Amsterdam with the assistance of the Unitarians Samuel Crell and Sebastian Petzold.[125]

---

116   Clarke to Locke, 24 October 1688, in *Correspondence*, vol. 3, p. 513; Locke to Clarke, 18/28 January [1689], ibid., p. 536; and Clarke to Locke, 20 April 1689, ibid., p. 605. Clarke, 'Huguenot Tutors and the Family of Edward and Mary Clarke of Chipley', p. 529.

117   Clarke to Locke, 20 April 1689, in *Correspondence*, vol. 3, pp. 605–6. See also Locke to Clarke, [13] April [1689], ibid., p. 602, on Furly's role in the joint effort to secure Huguenot tutors.

118   Locke to Clarke, 7 December 1691, in *Correspondence*, vol. 4, p. 338.

119   Locke to Clarke, 18/28 January [1689], in *Correspondence*, vol. 3, p. 513; Passebon to Locke, 22 October 1689, and 7 January 1690, ibid., pp. 711–12 and 775–6; and Passebon to Locke, 14 March 1690, ibid., vol. 4, pp. 34–5.

120   Passebon to Locke, 14 March 1690, in *Correspondence*, vol. 4, p. 34. Compare Locke to Clarke, 19/29 April [1687], ibid., vol. 3, p. 183.

121   Clarke to Lady Masham, 15 September 1691, in *Correspondence*, vol. 4, p. 310. Compare Locke to Clarke, 7 December 1691, ibid., pp. 338–9.

122   Locke to Clarke, 27 December 1691, in *Correspondence*, vol. 4, pp. 346–7; and Passebon to Locke, 21 April 1692, ibid., pp. 448–9.

123   Haag, vol. 9, pp. 294–5; and Erich Haase, *Einführung in die Literatur des Refuge. Der Beitrag der französischen Protestanten zur Entwicklung analytischer Denkformen am Ende des 17. Jahrhunderts* (Berlin, 1959), pp. 237–8.

124   Yet the consistory of the Threadneedle-Street church refused to give its official sanction to Charles Piozet and Testas's anti-Socinian schemes against him: see Gwynn, *Minutes*, the entries under 25 March 1691 and 30 October 1692, pp. 332–3 and 355. Gwynn, 'Disorder and Innovation', pp. 256–7; and Marshall, 'Huguenot Thought after the Revocation of the Edict of Nantes', pp. 383–4 and 390–91.

125   Matthieu Souverain, *Le Platonisme devoilé. Ou essai touchant le Verbe Platonicien* ('Cologne' [Amsterdam], 1700). See Coste to Locke, 29 June 1699, in *Correspondence*, vol.

In 1691, when Clarke was planning to employ Souverain, Locke stressed the need, whoever would teach Clarke's son, to 'preserve as much of our method of education as could be, and at least not perplex him with grammar, much less with themes, declamations, and making verses, but only reading and translating prose authors'. Moreover, given the hold of the entrenched curriculum over candidates, Locke advised Clarke to test whether Souverain 'be not superstitiously wedded to the methods he himself was educated in, for from such a man I should not expect much'.[126] Presumably he satisfied Locke's requirements, given his commitment to the ethos of frankness and fearless speech, and contempt for disputation in his *Platonisme devoilé*.[127] However, instead of travelling down to Chipley, Souverain became tutor in the household of Paul D'Aranda, the second-generation Huguenot immigrant accused of Socinianism, who knew Locke well and helped Lecène.[128]

At Chipley, the successor to Passebon was Monsieur de Grassemare, whom Locke probably recruited in London in the summer of 1693.[129] In November 1693 he completed a report on his pupil's progress that must have disappointed Locke, for his pupil had spent his time on the Latin declinations and conjugations, despite Grassemare's apparent familiarity with Locke's *Education*.[130] In his replies, which are not extant, Locke seems, as he indicated to Clarke, to 'have a litle corrected Monsr Grasemar'.[131]

Why, then, did Locke assume, from about 1687 onwards, the role of a promoter of refugees who sought tutorships in English households? Why did he not recommend a single Englishman to the Clarkes? Here it is important to recognise that, after the Revocation of 1685, his preference for Huguenot tutors probably chimed with a desire to help refugees whose economic desperation was unquestionable. Another practical reason for his preference was the growing popularity and importance of the French language. Owing to the Revocation, there existed a pool of educated native speakers of French who sought employment in England. Yet these were not, in my view, the principal reasons. Locke was far from indiscriminate in his encouragement of Huguenots, recruiting only those who could serve his educational plan to revive England. He was groping towards a new spirit of citizenship, and wanted therefore the citizenry's character to be moulded by tutors who rejected rhetorical education and endorsed the ethos of ingenuousness and fearless speech.

6, pp. 650–51; and van Limborch to Locke, 30 April/11 May 1700, ibid., vol. 7, pp. 76–7.
  126 Locke to Clarke, 27 Dec. [1691], in *Correspondence*, vol. 4, p. 347.
  127 See Souverain, *Le Platonisme devoilé*, sig. *2 ('Avertissement') and pp. 79–80.
  128 Marshall, 'Huguenot Thought after the Revocation of the Edict of Nantes', p. 390.
  129 Locke to Clarke, 15 May [1693], in *Correspondence*, vol. 4, pp. 678–9.
  130 De Grassemare to Locke, 21 November [1693], in *Correspondence*, vol. 4, pp. 748–9.
  131 Locke to Clarke, 23 November 1694, in John Locke, *The Correspondence of John Locke*, 'Vol. 9: Index and Addenda', ed. E.S. de Beer, Mark Goldie *et al.* (Oxford, forthcoming), letter no. 1818A. I am grateful to Mark Goldie for sending me a copy of this letter in advance of publication. See also Locke to Clarke, [12?] January 1694, in *Correspondence*, vol. 4, p. 774.

Whilst in exile in the Dutch Republic, Locke became associated with a particular group of Protestants whose anti-authoritarianism and commitment to the ideal of truthful outspokenness mark them out as the protagonists of a specific ideology. Since they diluted the rulers' and clergy's authority, they were able to assume the right to speak truth to power, and they also spoke truth to power in practice. Lecène stressed that one must have the courage to speak the truth in order to liberate those in error, as well as the daring to challenge the erroneous views upheld by the establishment, even if at considerable personal cost.[132] In Geneva in 1683, Lenfant infuriated Turretin by his commitment to the liberty to say what Scripture and reason dictate. According to Turretin, this liberty had its limits; Lenfant retorted that no-one could limit it without claiming infallibility and compromising his Protestantism.[133] In Switzerland in 1685, Mazel, who was to translate Locke's 'Second Treatise' into French, and Bernard, who was to publicise the appearance of Mazel's translation in the *Bibliothèque*, refused to sign the *Consensus Helveticus* despite the pressure exerted by the authorities. Bernard wrote to Leclerc that many ministers will sign it because they believe in it, 'others in fear of losing a certain pension ... and there will be only five who will have enough courage not to sign it'.[134] In the Dutch Republic in 1688, Furly helped Foecke Floris, a Mennonite minister suspected of Socinianism and persecuted by the Calvinists. Though Furly was not acquainted with Floris, he waited on William of Orange and implored him to shelter Floris from his persecutors. According to Locke, Furly, 'considering that the liberty of Floris was a matter of common concern to all Christians, took up his cause with enthusiasm and pursued it energetically; without his παρρησία there would have been no progress'.[135]

---

132 Charles Lecène, *Projet d'une nouvelle version françoise de la Bible*, ed. Michel-Charles Lecène (2 vols, Amsterdam, 1741), vol. 1, p. 1 (third pagination): 'Audendum est, ut illustrata Veritas pateat, multique ab errore liberentur.' The motto is from Lactantius: see *The Works of Lactantius: In Two Volumes.* Vol. I, ed. and trans. William Fletcher (Edinburgh, 1871), book IV, chapter v, p. 219: 'wisdom and religion cannot be separated ... the attempt must be ventured, that the truth may be made clear and brought to light, and that many may be freed from error and death, who despise and refuse the truth, while it is concealed under a covering of folly'.

133 Lenfant to Leclerc [early December 1683?], in *Epistolario*, vol. 1, p. 110: 'Je lui dis que si mes sentimens étoient bons ie ne pouuois les dire auec trop de liberté et que s'ils étoient mauvais il [Turretin] m'obligeroit de me le faire voir ... Je lui dis que c'etoit un des privileges de nôtre reformation de choisir le tour le plus conforme a l'Ecriture et a la raison sans s'attacher a celui de personne, et que ceux qui vouloient obliger les autres a parler ainsi ou ainsi étoient de mauuais reformez'.

134 Bernard to Leclerc, 9 November 1685, in *Epistolario*, vol. 1, pp. 408–9: 'plus[ieu]rs signeront par ce qu'ils croyent les choses, les autres par ce qu'ils auront peur de perdre une certaine pension que leur font leurs Excellences, et il ne s'en trouvera que cinq qui auront assez de courage pour ne signer point'. The five clergymen were Bernard, Mazel, Gonnon, Joseph Saurin and Daniel Rally. Savonius, 'Locke in French'.

135 Locke to van Limborch, 14/24 November 1688, in *Correspondence*, vol. 3, p. 521: 'Sed communem Christianorum rem in ejus libertate agi ratus Causam illius prono animo

When Locke interviewed prospective tutors on his friends' behalf, he could expect that heterodox Huguenot refugees would be likely to share his ideal of *ingenuitas* and παρρησία, and to sympathize with his method of education. This heterodox minority seemed particularly suitable for his purposes because of their courage to defend 'the Naked Gospel' and their anti-rhetorical attempt 'to discover the Naked Truth'.[136] The anti-Trinitarian or Pajonist refugees were bold enough to defy the Calvinist establishment of the Refuge.[137] In practice, however, some of Locke's Huguenot recruits appear to have failed to fulfil his expectations.

Conclusion

Locke was, I have suggested, engaged in an ambitious project of shaking up his contemporaries' understanding of their own civic identity. The Huguenot tutors he recruited were meant to serve his project by training frank and energetic citizens capable of standing eye to eye with their rulers, buoyed up by their character-building education. In Edwards's view, Locke belonged to the circles of these Huguenots, the heterodox 'Pedlars French', and his project made him, not the great English philosopher, but a dangerous Francophile.

Subsequently the nature of Locke's programme has been obscured, not only by the belief that there must be something peculiarly English about his philosophy, but also by his status as a forerunner of our modern liberalism. Whilst his *Two Treatises* undoubtedly served as a canonical work in the making of pluralist liberalism, his doctrines were twisted in unexpected ways conditioned by the readers' horizons. Let the ideal of 'freedom of speech' not mislead: the gulf, the ocean, between Locke's παρρησία and the sceptical liberals' subjective freedom of speech could not be wider. He never defended the view that the individual's intellectual and communicative freedom is a general entitlement to think as one happens to think and to express one's subjective beliefs as one feels inclined. The *parrhesiastes'* challenge to the authorities relied on the anti-rhetorical assumption that there is always one true way of describing the moral character of any action or situation.[138] It was the firm conviction they were speaking the objective truth that made Locke's

---

suscepit et strenue egit, si enim abfuisset παρρησια nihil promovisset.' See also Locke to van Limborch, 15/25 November [1688], ibid., p. 524.

136 Jean Leclerc, *An Historical Vindication of the Naked Gospel, Recommended to the University of Oxford* (London, 1691), preface to the reader, sig. A2. Leclerc defended Arthur Bury's *The Naked Gospel* of 1690, reviewed in *Bibliothèque*, vol. 19, October 1690, pp. 391–435. See also Furly to Locke, 16/26 October 1690, in *Correspondence*, vol. 4, p. 147; and Leclerc to Locke, 22 October/1 November 1690, ibid., p. 150.

137 On the anti-Trinitarians' deliberate Nicodemite prevarication, see Edwards, *A Brief Vindication of the Fundamental Articles of the Christian Faith*, p. 20; Goldie, 'The reception of Hobbes', p. 613; and Stephen D. Snobelen, 'Isaac Newton, Heretic: The Strategies of a Nicodemite', *British Journal for the History of Science*, 32 (1999): 381–419.

138 See Locke, *Essay*, III.x.22, p. 504; and 'Conduct', § 49, p. 194.

Francophone associates adopt the ethos of fearless speech when they opposed the orthodox Calvinists, running the risk of losing their ministerial posts and falling into disrepute and poverty.

Chapter 9

The Rainbow Coffee House and the Exchange of Ideas in Early Eighteenth-century England

Simon Harvey and Elizabeth Grist
Queen Mary, University of London, UK

Introduction

In a recent critical edition of Diderot's *Lettre sur les aveugles*, the question arose as to how this *philosophe* came to have such a detailed knowledge of unorthodoxy among English thinkers of the first half of the eighteenth century.[1] Was his imputation of atheistic tendencies to the Cambridge mathematician Nicholas Saunderson just an inspired guess, or did it derive from what one might call insider information? Whatever the answer to that might be, his depiction of Saunderson as a serious unbeliever was almost certainly responsible for the rejection of Diderot's application to join the Royal Society. It simply would not do for that body to have had as one of its members an infidel Lucasian professor.

Setting aside the notion that Diderot produced these remarks off the top of his his head, we wanted to test the hypothesis that news of what was really going on in England filtered through to France via a network of radical French intellectuals mainly based in London. Where else to look other than amongst the group of Huguenot immigrants who had settled there in ever-increasing numbers after Louis XIV's Revocation of the Edict of Nantes? Did they actually constitute a 'circle' in the socio-intellectual sense of that term, and what was the extent of their contacts with English writers and scientists of the period? Furthermore, what were the means of disseminating the new ideas that were surfacing in the wake of the discoveries of Newton and Locke?

We decided in the first instance to concentrate our attention on the large manuscript collection of the Des Maizeaux correspondence housed in the British Library. This is where we fell upon what could be loosely described as the Rainbow group. Pierre Des Maizeaux came to London at the turn of the century with letters of recommendation from Pierre Bayle and from the Socinian Jean Leclerc. Over

---

1   Denis Diderot, *Lettre sur les aveugles*, ed. Marian Hobson and Simon Harvey (Paris, 2000).

the next 30 years he made himself into the leading French journalist of the capital, regularly contributing reports on English publications to the main Huguenot journals being printed in Holland by Jacques Bernard, Henri Basnage de Beauval, Samuel Masson, and Henri Du Sauzet. He also became closely involved in the so-called priority dispute between Newton and Leibniz, and, together with Michel de Laroche (who was said to frequent society 'unfriendly to Bible religion'), he published in French a collection of pieces relating to this quarrel.

Reading through the correspondence one is staggered by the sheer range of Des Maizeaux's contacts – booksellers, printers, publishers, Latitudinarian Churchmen, freethinking philosophers, scientists and academicians all figure in it. What is also striking are the very numerous letters addressed to him c/o the Rainbow Coffee House in Lancaster Court off St Martins Lane. There may have been several reasons for this, which will be discussed later. What Des Maizeaux and his fellow Huguenots had done in the early 1700s was to found a sort of informal talking-shop which met regularly at the Rainbow and in which he in particular seems to have played a leading role for at least a couple of decades (in 1729 one of the correspondents refers to him as 'le très révérend père' ['the Most Reverend Father'] of the group). Its membership is hard to pin down with absolute accuracy, but, from references in the correspondence and elsewhere, we do know that, at one time or another, it contained some important members of the Huguenot community in London – Pierre Coste (the translator of Locke and Newton), Abraham de Moivre (mathematician, close associate of Newton and according to Mathieu Maty very 'incrédule' ['unbelieving']), Pierre Daval (another mathematician and Fellow of the Royal Society), Pierre Daudé (unorthodox minister and theologian who also held a post in the Exchequer), Abel Boyer (the historian recommended by Pierre Bayle to Gilbert Burnet the Latitudinarian Bishop of Salisbury), David Durand (another highly unorthodox minister who wrote a life of the atheist Vanini), Pierre Silvestre (a medical man and fellow of the Royal Society), Pierre-Antoine Motteux (the translator of Rabelais), Paul Colomiès (who, despite his appointment as a Reader in one of the French churches, was described by Saint-Evremond as an unbeliever), Jean-Théophile Desaguliers (Newton's demonstrator at the Royal Society and a noted freemason), César de Missy (yet another dissenting minister who refused to sign the Calvinist act of orthodoxy).

But it is not just the non-conforming members of the Huguenot intelligentsia who are connected with the Rainbow: there is plenty of evidence that key English figures from various quarters contributed to the discussions, and equally a number of German thinkers such as Zollman (Leibniz's intermediary in the dispute with Newton) and also Daniel Maichel who speaks of 'cette savante Société qui se rassemble chaque soir dans le Caffé de Rainbow' ['that learned Society which meets every evening in the Rainbow']. And when Voltaire comes to London in 1727 it is at the Rainbow that he meets Des Maizeaux to sort out a dispute with Prévost. On the English side the names of several *habitués* stand out amongst others, coming as they do from very different backgrounds: Anthony Collins the deist and freethinker who is in constant touch with Des Maizeaux at the coffee-house; Richard Mead, Newton's doctor and fellow of the Royal Society of whom it was said that his only belief lay in his own remedies; and even a Church representative in the figure of Bishop Sprat who was attacked at the time for being 'destructive to Established Religion'. Less frequent callers include men like the free-thinking John Toland.

There can be no doubt that the Rainbow provided one forum for the debate of issues which have to do with the growth of scepticism in early eighteenth-century Europe. We say one forum because it certainly was not the only meeting-place of its kind. At his house in Rotterdam Benjamin Furly – friend of Locke, Bayle, Leclerc, and Collins, occasional host to John Toland and whose library of anti-clerical books contained a rare manuscript copy of the atheistic treatise *Les Trois Imposteurs* – this Quaker-in-exile gathered together from the late 1680s onwards an assembly of freethinking philosophers: 'Hereticks of the Lanterne' (the name of the club) was what John Locke jokingly called them. After Furly's death another society took on the mantle of unorthodoxy, the so-called 'Chevaliers de la Jubilation'. In France, in the early years of the Regency, the Club de l'Entresol was founded, which had amongst its clientele the grammarian Du Marsais whose *Examen de la Religion* (thought to be composed around 1705) is another major atheistic text. And in England William Stukeley, Newton's biographer, tells us of an Infidel Club set up in the 1720s at a house in Ormond Street by Martin Folkes, who was later to become President of the Royal Society: it was intended, we are told, for 'those of a heathen stamp'. We might even speculate as to the topics of conversation in Princess Caroline's circle which met at her new residence in Leicester Fields and where she entertained amongst others Samuel Clarke who was living on the very knife-edge of respectability – Rector of St James, Piccadilly but very much a closet Socinian.

Such clubs or assemblies were, of course, very private affairs compared to meetings held in coffee-houses. But the coffee-house offered considerable advantages. As a public space it offered much freer access to those who were inclined to join in the discussions (meetings in private homes are restricted to a privileged few who presumably are admitted by invitation only). Many other activities going on there could provide a sort of cover for 'audacious' talk: one of the later advertisements for the Rainbow refers to Dr Misaubin's presence there (he was a leading Huguenot physician) to give advice for the relief of 'sorebuttock disorders'. As far as the Rainbow is concerned, another advantage was its very location in the capital: close to the Huguenot community in the Strand area, a mere stone's throw away from their chapels at the Savoy and in Leicester Fields, not excessively distant from the Royal Society – in other words at the heart of thinking London. Newton lived nearby, De Moivre almost next door to him. As with its Parisian equivalent, the Caffé Procope (where Du Marsais was one of the regulars), there was no fixed agenda – conversation could range boldly and freely over a wide range of topics, reflecting the broad spectrum of participants.

Disadvantages certainly existed. Spies, for example, might be able to eavesdrop on such conversations, rather in the manner imagined by Voltaire in his short story *L'Ingénu*. Yet the fear of this happening was in fact very real. There exists a report by English undercover agents in the late 1680s who are suspicious of 'dangerous Frenchies' and listen in to their coffee-house chat. Once again the Des Maizeaux correspondence gives us a clue to the sensitive nature of the exchanges between minds of an unorthodox stamp. Letter-writers had to be cautious if they were to put enemies off the scent: intermediaries were used in the sending of letters, aliases were employed to avoid any suspect signature, parcels were hidden in bales of respectable books. One of the Rainbow regulars was Daniel Preverau, a personal friend of Des Maizeaux. As head clerk to ministers like Townshend and the Duke of Newcastle he was a means of free and safe communication with the Continent via diplomatic channels. Sometimes abbreviations were used to guard against unwelcome readers. A letter to Benjamin Furly starts off with the word 'Beware' and urges him to destroy the piece of paper once he has read it. Just as it was safer to use a trusted messenger in the transmission of dangerous material, so too the coffee-house itself offered a degree of security: it was being used for the receipt of mail much in the way that the system of newspaper boxes today ensures a certain amount of anonymity. The Rainbow undoubtedly played a key role in all this semi-clandestine activity. The group that met there saw itself as a 'coterie' to use the expression of one of the regulars and the discussions they had were noted for the freedom of their ideas ('des conversations dégagées de tous préjugés' ['conversations devoid of all prejudice']). It was most certainly one important network in that tight but complex web of relationships embracing Huguenots in England and Holland and linking them with unorthodox thinkers amongst the London intelligentsia.

Two French journalists in London

In the early years of the eighteenth century, two members of the Rainbow Coffee House circle in London made a particular contribution to the spread of unorthodox ideas from England to continental Europe: the Huguenot journalists Pierre Des Maizeaux (1673–1745) and Michel de Laroche (d. 1742). Both had met Pierre Bayle in Holland and had been influenced by his ideas; both had some theological expertise, and in the articles and reviews they wrote for French-language journals published in Holland they both consistently focused on the need for religious toleration.

This is hardly surprising, as they had themselves suffered the consequences of religious intolerance, but their sympathies developed well beyond the Latitudinarian toleration they found within the Anglican Church. Even the Act of Toleration of 1689 gave no protection to those who publicly denied the doctrine of the Trinity.[2] But some of the writers whose work Des Maizeaux and de Laroche introduced to a European public – Anthony Collins, John Toland, Bernard de Mandeville – went so far as to challenge the whole notion of organised religion and a clerical hierarchy. Their sources of inspiration were Spinoza, reviled as an atheist (his *Tractatus* had circulated widely though clandestinely in England from 1675), and Locke, himself

---

2   John Marshall, 'Huguenot thought after the Revocation of the Edict of Nantes', in Vigne and Littleton, *Strangers*, p. 385.

suspected of 'spinozisme', whose application of reason to religion paved the way for a broad deism in place of scriptural authority.³

How far these two journalists actually sympathised with the most radical ideas is uncertain, but they both demonstrated a personal commitment to the growing campaign against dogmatism and intolerance, directed particularly at the French Catholic Church for its savage persecution of Protestants. Although their reviews aimed at impartiality, they alerted French readers to the existence of books that would have been impossible to obtain through official sources in France. England might be geographically isolated from the rest of Europe, and knowledge of the English language limited, but these two Huguenot writers assisted the circulation of ideas between scholars at an international level. 'La République des Lettres' wrote Pierre Des Maizeaux in 1713, 'est un Pays libre, où chacun a droit de juger des choses selon qu'elles lui paroissent' ['The Republic of Letters is a free country, where every man has the right to judge things as they appear to him'].⁴

Des Maizeaux had studied theology in Geneva for four years before he travelled to England, via Holland, in 1699. Soon after his arrival he was recruited by Jacques Bernard as a regular correspondent for his *Nouvelles de la République des Lettres*. This was one of the earliest periodicals, originally founded by Bayle in 1684, and published in Amsterdam but widely circulated in France. Des Maizeaux began by using the *Philosophical Transactions* of the Royal Society as his source material for a monthly newsletter to Bernard, sent via Benjamin Furly in Rotterdam, and he was soon contributing articles to other journals as they became established in Holland.⁵

Although the international scholarly community was known as 'la République des Lettres', these French-language journals published in Holland actually showed a bias towards scientific and philosophical topics, and from the start of his collaboration with Bernard we find evidence of Des Maizeaux's interest in controversial philosophical and theological issues. The first article he sent, early in 1700, mentioned a new edition of Locke's *Essay on Human Understanding*, and included an extract from Burnet's *Exposition on the thirty-nine Articles*, which Bernard felt unable to print in full because, as he wrote to his English correspondent, 'nous vivons dans un pays où nous ne sommes pas si libertins que vous l'êtes en Angleterre' ['we live in a country where we are not as free-thinking as you are in England'].⁶ It was not the last time he had to warn Des Maizeaux of the need for circumspection on theological topics; he eventually made alterations himself before publishing the extract.⁷

---

3   British Library, Additional MSS 4281/20 from Jean Barbeyrac to Des Maizeaux, Berlin, 22 December 1706: 'Ce que vous dites du spinozisme de feu Mr Locke, me surprend beaucoup' ['What you say about the Spinozism of the late Mr Locke surprises me very much'].

4   British Library, Additional MSS 4289/134.

5   See J.H. Broome, *An Agent in Anglo-French Relationships: Pierre Des Maizeaux*, Ph.D. thesis (University of London, 1949).

6   Letters to Pierre Des Maizeaux, British Library, Additional MSS 4281/86.

7   British Library, Additional MSS 4281/90–91, Bernard to Des Maizeaux, 5 August 1700.

The following year Des Maizeaux entered into a theological dispute in the pages of the *Nouvelles de la République des Lettres* with Isaac Jaquelot, on the subject of Descartes' proof of the existence of God, and this debate established Des Maizeaux's reputation as a serious journalist.[8] During the ten years he contributed to the *Nouvelles* he promoted the ideas of Locke and reviewed the work of unorthodox writers including Whiston, Toland, Collins, Shaftesbury and Tindal, with translated extracts from their books; in many cases the extracts published in journals were the first French translations of the authors concerned. It has been estimated that about 40 per cent of his articles covered religious and philosophical topics.[9]

But Des Maizeaux was not only a journalist, and his activities as an editor and biographer equally demonstrate a particular interest in unorthodox ideas. He wrote the first biography of Saint-Evremond, published both in French and in English, and with Dr Silvestre he edited a selection of Saint-Evremond's writings; he produced a biography of Bayle and an edition of his letters; he published a volume on the life and work of Toland in 1726 and he wrote biographies of the Latitudinarians John Hales and William Chillingworth. Another significant aspect of his work was his collaboration with the deist Anthony Collins. He became a personal friend and frequent visitor to Collins's country house: there are 66 letters from Collins in the British Library collection, most of them addressed to Des Maizeaux at the Rainbow Coffee House. In return for Collins's patronage and financial assistance, he evidently contributed his theological expertise and knowledge of French to assist Collins's research and the development of his anti-clerical and freethinking views.[10] And Des Maizeaux published the first French translation of Collins's *Philosophical Enquiry* in his *Recueil de diverses pièces sur la philosophie, la religion naturelle, l'histoire, les mathématiques &c* of 1720.[11]

The publication of this collection made a major contribution to the spread of English scientific and philosophical ideas in continental Europe. Des Maizeaux's long preface indicates the questions to be discussed – problems of perception, time, space, the nature of God and of man's free will – and also gives a detailed account of the priority dispute between Leibniz and Newton, as to which of them had first invented the differential calculus.[12] (Some of the correspondence about this dispute, first published by the Royal Society, had already circulated in Europe in a French translation by Abraham De Moivre.) Letters from the publisher Du Sauzet to Des Maizeaux reveal that Newton himself was consulted in the early stages of preparation of the *Recueil*, and that some pages were reprinted at his request and his

---

8   Joseph Almagor, *Pierre des Maizeaux (1673–1745): Journalist and English Correspondent for Franco-Dutch Periodicals, 1700–1720* (Amsterdam and Maarsen, 1989), Introduction, pp. 28–35.

9   Ibid., p. 46.

10   See J.H. Broome, 'Une Collaboration: Anthony Collins et Desmaizeaux', *Revue de Littérature Comparée*, 30 (1956): 161–79.

11   Henri Du Sauzet (2 vols, Amsterdam, 1720).

12   See A.R. Hall, *Philosophers at War* (Cambridge, 1980).

own expense.[13] In addition to Collins's *Philosophical Enquiry* and a commentary by Samuel Clarke, volume 1 included letters between Leibniz and Clarke, translated by Michel de Laroche; volume 2 contained letters between Leibniz and Newton, other letters of Leibniz and his *Reflections* on Locke's *Essay on Human Understanding*. Also in 1720 Des Maizeaux edited and published in London a collection of hitherto unpublished pieces by Locke. A second edition of the *Recueil* appeared in Amsterdam in 1740, indicating the success of the first.

Apart from his own writing and editing, Des Maizeaux played a key role in circulating books and manuscripts between writers and publishers all over Europe, and he came to be regarded as an expert on English freethinkers. We know from his letters that he supplied French books to Collins and other English friends, and English books to correspondents in Europe. In 1705, for example, he sent Tillotson's sermons to Jean Barbeyrac in Berlin for translation into French. In 1722 he sent a copy of Toland's *Pantheisticon* to the historian Denis-François Camusat, librarian to the Maréchal d'Estrées in Paris; Camusat responded with great interest, asking for more information about Toland and other English freethinkers, and one can readily imagine the book being passed around intellectual circles in Paris and eagerly discussed.[14] Another correspondent in Paris was the writer and editor Thémiseul de Saint-Hyacinthe, who asked Des Maizeaux to send him books by Collins, Whiston, Mandeville, Tindal and Woolston, and commented on the problems of censorship in Paris.[15] Most daringly, Des Maizeaux assisted the publication in 1719 of the openly atheist *Traité des Trois Imposteurs*, otherwise known as *L'Esprit de Spinoza*, by sending a copy of the manuscript to Holland via the translator Pierre Coste, another member of the Rainbow group.[16] In 1731 the German writer Friedrich Hagedorn asked him to supply information on Collins, Toland, Woolston and Mandeville 'que je souhaiterois de faire connoitre à mes compatriotes' ['which I would like to introduce to my fellow-countrymen'] but he prudently added: 'Je vous promets de ne découvrir à personne d'où j'ai ces anecdotes, que j'ose vous demander' ['I promise not to reveal to anyone the source of the information I dare to ask of you'].[17] Letters to Des Maizeaux from publishers in Holland are concerned above all with exchanges of books and manuscripts, sent whenever possible by a trusted messenger, as the postal service was expensive and unreliable and parcels containing books were liable to be confiscated.[18]

---

13   British Library, Additional MSS 4288, nos 15, 36, 42.

14   British Library, Additional MSS 4282 nos 23–31.

15   British Library, Additional MSS 4284/161 and 163.

16   Rienk H. Vermij, 'The English Deists and the Traité', in Silvia Berti, Françoise Charles-Daubert and Richard H. Popkin (eds), *Heterodoxy, Spinozism and Free Thought in Early Eighteenth-Century Europe: Studies on the* Traité des Trois Imposteurs (Dordrecht, 1996), pp. 241–54.

17   British Library, Additional MSS 4284/61.

18   See for example letters from Camusat, British Library, Additional MSS 4282/33, and from Collins, British Library, Additional MSS 4282/218.

Information about Pierre Des Maizeaux comes from a number of sources, chiefly from his correspondence; by contrast what we know of Michel de Laroche is drawn almost entirely from his own journalistic writings. He came to England at an early age, having personally experienced Catholic persecution in France, and he was naturalised in 1701.[19] At some point after his arrival in England he studied mathematics with De Moivre, and he knew Des Maizeaux by 1705, probably earlier. It is clear from references in Des Maizeaux's correspondence that the two journalists were close friends; they would certainly have exchanged books and ideas, and they may have collaborated in writing articles. Like Des Maizeaux, de Laroche had met Pierre Bayle in Holland, and he was one of the translators of Bayle's *Dictionnaire historique et critique* into English. In London in 1710 de Laroche founded his first journal, *Memoirs of Literature*, published in English but intended as 'a correspondence with the Commonwealth of Learning abroad'. De Laroche evidently produced the journal single-handed from 1710 to 1714, writing some articles, translating others from the *Journal des Sçavants* and *Mémoires de Trévoux*, and reporting the work of the Académie des Sciences in Paris. In 1713 he wrote a sympathetic article on William Whiston, defending him against attack for his anti-Trinitarian views. Two years later he translated Cerri's *Account of the Roman Catholic Religion* from Italian, and it was published in London with a dedication by Bishop Benjamin Hoadly deploring both Catholic and Protestant intolerance. Hoadly was probably a personal friend, as was Samuel Clarke, and it was de Laroche who translated Clarke's letters to Leibniz defending Newton, which Des Maizeaux included in his *Recueil*.

In 1717 Michel de Laroche became the first editor of the *Bibliothèque Angloise*, published in Amsterdam, the first French-language periodical dedicated to reporting news from England, 'pour donner une juste idée de l'état où les Sciences s'y trouvent aujourd'hui' ['to give an accurate idea of the state of scientific knowledge today']. He printed long extracts from *Philosophical Transactions*, with descriptions of scientific studies and experiments in clear, non-technical language, and enthusiastically reviewed the work of Newton and his close associates. There were also numerous articles on contentious theological topics – the work of Collins, Clarke and Whiston, disputed passages of scripture, the history of 'Michel Servet' or Servetus, burned as an heretic by Calvin in Geneva in 1553 – and the personal comments de Laroche added to extracts and reviews make clear his own support for the principle of toleration.

In 1718 de Laroche reported on dissent among the French churches in London, when 'several worthy ministers', including his friends Jacques Cappel and André L'Ortie, were involved in a dispute with Armand de La Chapelle, minister of the Artillery Lane Church. The following year de Laroche was replaced as editor of the *Bibliothèque Angloise* by the same La Chapelle, a more orthodox figure later dismissed by Anthony Collins in a letter to Des Maizeaux as an 'incorrigible malicious priest', and it was apparently de Laroche's promotion of religious toleration that cost him

---

19 See Margaret D. Thomas, *The Life and Works of Michel de Laroche*, Ph.D. thesis (University of London, 1978).

the job. According to his own account of the episode, some Dutch theologians had accused him of hostility to Calvinism and excessive indulgence towards the Roman Catholic Church, but he insists: 'Je n'attaque aucune Religion ... je me contente de blâmer l'Intolerance, partout où je la trouve ... je ne crois pas qu'il y ait de vrai Christianisme sans Modération' ['I do not attack any religion ... I merely condemn intolerance wherever I find it ... I do not believe there can be true Christianity without moderation'].[20] His aim was to encourage toleration by acquainting his readers with unorthodox ideas.

After this setback, de Laroche founded another journal of his own to compete with La Chapelle. *Memoires literaires de la Grande Bretagne* was published in The Hague and lasted for four years (1720–24). In addition to reporting on scientific developments, with summarised proceedings of the Royal Society, de Laroche continued to cover theological topics and ecclesiastical history, especially as it related to contemporary controversy. He reviewed the work of deist writers Thomas Woolston and Bernard de Mandeville, both of whom advocated complete religious freedom. He continued a series of articles begun in the *Bibliothèque Angloise* on Joseph Bingham's *Antiquities of the Christian Church* – a work not in itself controversial, but de Laroche's articles underlined the fallibility of Church teaching and its history of persecution.[21] He published more extracts from Whiston, Woolston and the deist Thomas Morgan; he reviewed the latest work of Toland. He printed extracts from Gerard Brandt's *History of the Reformation* in the *Bibliothèque Angloise* and *Memoires literaires*, and his abridgment of the work was published in book form both in French and in English, with de Laroche adding his own comments to Brandt's condemnation of both Catholic and Calvinist inflexibility and persecution, and consistently arguing the need for religious toleration.

Despite their efforts in promoting English scientific and philosophical thought, there were limits to the acceptance of refugees in England. Pierre Des Maizeaux's letters reveal his hopes of an official appointment through one of his influential friends, in particular Lord Halifax, but all he obtained was a pension of three shillings and sixpence per day. Much of his work as an English correspondent may have been unpaid.[22] Des Maizeaux was eventually elected to the Royal Society in 1720, after publication of his *Recueil*, but Michel de Laroche was never granted membership, despite his reputation as a translator of scientific and philosophical writing. Huguenot writers in London did provide mutual support by reviewing each other's work; so for example Des Maizeaux's newsletters in the *NRL* mentioned de Laroche's *Memoirs of Literature*, and he in turn reviewed Des Maizeaux's collection of pieces by Locke and his biographies of Hales and Chillingworth. Des Maizeaux also praised the work of Pierre Coste and Abel Boyer, fellow members of the Rainbow circle.

---

20   *Memoires literaires de la Grande Bretagne* (16 vols, The Hague, 1720–24), vol. 1, 'préface'.

21   *Bibliothèque Angloise*, 2–5 and *Memoires literaires de la Grande Bretagne* 1–15 (18 articles); see Thomas, p. 601.

22   Almagor, p. 13.

In France, these two Huguenot journalists played a significant role in disseminating the ideas and discoveries of English scientists and philosophers. Copies of de Laroche's *Memoires literaires de la Grande Bretagne* were found in 40 private libraries, and the French-language periodicals to which Des Maizeaux contributed were also widely read.[23] Des Maizeaux's *Recueil* was well known – Voltaire owned a copy, perhaps presented to him when they met in London at the Rainbow.[24] Through their work in reviewing, editing, translating, and maintaining contact between scholars throughout Europe, they facilitated the circulation of ideas in the 'commonwealth of learning'; and their support for religious toleration helped to create the climate in which the radical thought of the Enlightenment could develop later in the eighteenth century. Which was not quite what Louis XIV had in mind in 1685.

---

23   Daniel Mornet, 'Les Enseignements des Bibliothèques Privées (1750–1780)', *Revue d'Histoire Littéraire de la France*, 17 (1910): 449–96.
24   Broome, p. 345.

Chapter 10

Huguenot Traces and Reminiscences in John Toland's Conception of Tolerance

Myriam Yardeni
University of Haifa, Israel

Translated by Matt Legg
Sidney Sussex College, Cambridge, UK

It has often been said that the Irish philosopher John Toland found new ways to perceive the problems that he pondered in the world around him. So it is perhaps surprising that he did not actually invent anything new. Toland gathered ideas from many different sources, digested them and appropriated them for himself, and like many of his contemporaries, he often advocated contradictory positions or concealed his true opinion.[1] 'When did he mean what he wrote? When did he write what he meant?'[2] This diversity and instability together explain why it is so difficult to place Toland as a thinker or to classify his writings. He was certainly an 'Irish philosopher', born in Ireland and raised as a Catholic, but at the age of 16 he converted to Protestantism and studied Anglican theology at Glasgow University.[3] He considered himself an *Englishman,* or better still, a *Commonwealthman*.[4] His work does little to clarify his complex affiliations in later life, and leaves many

---

1   See Leo Strauss, *Persecution and the Art of Writing* (Glencoe, 1952); Gavina Cherchi, *Pantheisticon, eterodossia e dissimulazione nella filosofia di John Toland* (Pisa, 1990); Silvia Berti, 'At the Roots of Unbelief', *Journal of the History of Ideas*, 56 (1995), p. 555.

2   Robert Sullivan, *John Toland and the Deist Controversy. A Study in Adaptations* (Cambridge, Mass. and London, 1982), p. 46.

3   See *John Toland's Christianity not Mysterious, Text, Associated Works and Critical Essays*, ed. Philip McGuiness, Alan Harrison and Richard Kearney (Dublin, 1997), and also Pierre Lurbe, 'En relisant *Christianity not Mysterious*', in *Foi et raison dans l'Europe des Lumières: Le Spectateur Européen*, 3 (Montpellier, 2001): 47–66.

4   'This is the Sense in which I own my self a Common-wealth-man and in which I take *England* to be now a *Common-wealth*. This is what I mean by being a Whig ...', John Toland, *Vindicius Liberius, or Mr Toland's Defence of himself. Against the late Lower House of Convocation and Others* (London, 1702) as quoted in *Christianity not Mysterious*, p. 158. More specifically, see Luc Borot (ed.), *James Harrington and the Notion of Commonwealth* (Montpellier, 1998).

questions unanswered in the reader's mind. Was he a deist, a pantheist, an atheist, a freethinker, a freemason or a materialist?[5] Do his writings present us with a profound and innate inconstancy? If so, we are not exactly dealing with a *philosopher* and we cannot look to his works for either a system of thought or a pervasive method.

And there is another difficulty: despite the monumental work by Giancarlo Carabelli,[6] the authenticity of many works attributed to Toland remains questionable, while a considerable number of anonymous pamphlets, not to mention some very widely dispersed manuscripts, have a Tolandian character which suggests that they may be from his pen.[7] These problems help to explain why only a small number of books, in English and Italian, are dedicated exclusively to Toland.[8] But the material which does exist leaves no doubt that he is widely regarded today as a major thinker. To the modern studies we may add the special editions of the *Revue de Synthèse* under the direction of Geneviève Brykman and dedicated entirely to Toland.[9] Looking more broadly, it is difficult to find a book or an article dealing with the pivotal period of 1680 to 1720 which does not mention Toland's name or cite one of his works. It suffices to glance at their indexes to sense the importance that modern researchers accord to Toland in the genesis of the European Enlightenment.[10]

Taking all these circumstances together, any attempt to consider Huguenot traces and reminiscences in a relatively confined area of Toland's work might seem to be doomed to failure. And yet, if there is one idea – one value – which Toland addresses throughout the course of his life and work, it is tolerance.

---

5   Pierre Lurbe, one of the finest contemporary Toland specialists, vigorously rejects the deist attribution and considers Toland as belonging to 'a lineage which runs from the radical Reform all the way to Protestantism, via enlightened orthodoxy', in Lurbe, 'En relisant Christianity not Mysterious'.

6   *Tolandiana. Materiali bibliografica per lo studio dell'opera e della fortuna di John Toland (1670–1722)* (Florence, 1975).

7   See for example S. Brown, 'Toland's clandestine pantheism as partly revealed in his neglected *Remarques critiques sur le système de M. Leibniz* ... and partly concealed in the last of his *Letters to Serena*', in Gianni Paganini, Miguel Benitez and James Dybikowski (eds), *Scepticisme, clandestinité et libre pensée* (Paris, 2002), p. 346.

8   Other than Carabelli's *Tolandiana*, which somewhat rekindled 'Tolandian' studies, Clara Giuntini, *Toland e i liberi pensatori del 1700* (Florence, 1974), *Panteismo e ideologia republicana. John Toland (1670–1722)* (Bologna, 1979); Robert Sullivan, *John Toland and the Deist Controversy. A Study in Adaptations* (Cambridge Mass. and London, 1982); Stephan H. Daniel, *John Toland: His Methods, Manners and Mind* (Kingston and Montreal, 1984); Gavina Cherchi, *Pantheisticon, eterodossia e dissimulazione nella filosofia di John Toland* (Pisa, 1990); Robert Rees Evans, *Pantheisticon: The Career of John Toland* (Bern, 1991); Justin Champion, *Republican Learning: John Toland and the Crisis of Christian Culture, 1696–1722* (Manchester, 2003).

9   *Revue de Synthèse*, 2 and 3 (1995).

10   On this problem, see especially F.H. Heinemann, 'John Toland and the Age of Enlightenment', *Review of English Studies*, 20 (1944): 125–46.

Hence the relevance of Toland to the concerns of this volume, for in Toland's treatment of this theme, indeed in every phase of his reading, his journeys and his travels, there is always a Huguenot element. It is no coincidence that Stephen M. Daniel, referring to the epitaph which Toland devised for himself, thought that the date of his death was later added by 'Pierre Desmaizeaux or another of Toland's French Refugee friends'.[11] Toland had such associates, acquaintances and contacts throughout the countries of the Refuge. It is enough to follow the different stages of his scholarly travels and his sojourns 'on assignment' for the Whigs to sense how extensive these networks were. After Glasgow and Edinburgh, Toland pursued his studies at Leyden where he met some leading figures of the Huguenot emigration who frequented the home of the rich Quaker merchant Benjamin Furly, as did Toland. In Dublin, where he returned shortly after the publication of his book *Christianity not mysterious*, he may well also have met Huguenot refugees, but that cannot be proven.

We possess far more detailed information about his travels 'on assignment', especially his journey to the Prussian Court in Berlin where he promoted the cause of the Hanoverian succession to the English throne.[12] His *Letters to Serena* were conceived at the court of Queen Sophie Charlotte,[13] a 'philosopher-Queen' with a passion for learning, whose circle included certain Huguenot refugee *Hofprediger* (court chaplains), among them David Ancillon the younger, Jacques Lenfant and Isaac de Beausobre, who were joined in January 1702 by Isaac Jaquelot and François Martel.[14] One of these men, Isaac de Beausobre, gives a lengthy account of a rather ill-tempered encounter with John Toland in the newspaper that he edited entitled *La Bibliothèque Germanique*. There Beausobre vehemently attacks his interlocutor's 'pantheism'[15] in a scene which Jean-Paul Erman incorporated into his *Mémoires pour servir à l'Histoire de Sophie-Charlotte*.[16] An acquaintance probably no less important was Jacques Lenfant, who contributed greatly to a change in the image of Jews and Judaism, a subject to which we shall return.

From his early years in London onwards, Toland frequented the haunts of Huguenot refugees. He formed a friendship with Pierre Des Maizeaux, a close friend

---

11   Daniel, *John Toland*, p. 13.

12   See *An Account of the Courts of Prussia and Hanover: Sent to a Minister of State in Holland* (London, 1705) and *The Declaration Lately Publish'd, In Favour of His Protestant Subjects by the Elector Palatine* (London, 1707).

13   John Toland, *Letters to Serena* (London 1704).

14   Rudolf Von Thadden, *Die Brandenburgisch-Preussischen Hofprediger im 17. und 18. Jahrhundert* (Berlin, 1959), pp. 194–9.

15   *Bibliothèque Germanique* 6 (1723): 39–50

16   Jean-Paul Erman, *Mémoires pour servir à l'histoire de Sophie Charlotte, Reine de Prusse* (Berlin, 1801).

of Pierre Bayle,[17] who would later become Toland's first biographer.[18] He was fond of the coffee houses of the English capital. In those days, London had no fewer than 500 of these establishments[19] where visitors could socialise, exchange information and read the latest London or Dutch newspapers.[20] Toland assiduously frequented two of these coffee houses, the Grecian and the Rainbow, the latter being the meeting place of preference for Huguenot refugee scholars, journalists and intellectuals when visiting London.[21]

At that time, England was also the home of clubs and secret societies.[22] Toland himself was the founder of a secret and 'Socratic' society,[23] but of more consequence were his links, in The Hague, with the Dutch *Chevaliers de la Jubilation*, the first Masonic Lodge in Europe, according to Margaret Jacob.[24] The 'knights', including Toland, would meet regularly at a coffee house called the *Gaillardin,* during the years 1708–10 when Toland was resident in the city. The protocols of these meetings were set out by the famous Huguenot refugee editor Prosper Marchand.[25] All of the signatories to the meeting of 24 November were Protestants, or more precisely, as Jacob specifies, 'most were French refugees from religious persecutions'.[26]

Toland knew several victims of religious persecution and intolerance closely and personally. To what he learned by acquaintance with them we should add the fruits of

---

17 Joseph Almagor, *Pierre Des Maizeaux (1673–1745), Journalist and English Correspondent for Franco-Dutch Periodicals, 1700–1720* (Amsterdam and Maarssen, 1989); J.H. Broome, 'Bayle's biographer: Pierre Des Maizeaux', *French Studies*, 9 (1955): 1–17; Elisabeth Labrousse, 'Bayle et l'établissement de Desmaizeaux en Angleterre', *Revue de Littérature Comparée*, 30 (1956): 251–7; 'Introduction', in *Inventaire critique de la correspondance de Pierre Bayle* (Paris, 1961) pp. 13–62 and *Pierre Bayle* (2 vols, The Hague, 1963–64).

18 Published amongst Toland's works in Pierre Des Maizeaux, *A Collection of several pieces of Mr. John Toland, Now first published from his original manuscripts, with some memoirs of his life and writings* (2 vols, London, 1726).

19 Bryant Lillywhite, *London Coffee Houses* (London, 1950), p. 23.

20 Amongst which we also find, one might suppose, Jean de Fonvive's *Post-Man*. See I. Raban, 'The Newspaper *The Post-Man* and its editor, Jean Lespinasse de Fonvive' in Vigne and Littleton, *Strangers*, pp. 396–403.

21 Daniel, *John Toland*, p. 147. See also chapter 9 above.

22 Peter Clark, *British Clubs and Societies. The Origins of an Associational World* (Oxford, 2000).

23 *Pantheisticon, sive Formula celebrandae sodalitatis socraticae* (Cosmopoli, 1720), 'faithfully rendered into English' as *Pantheisticon, or the form of celebrating the Socratic Society* (London, 1751).

24 Margaret C. Jacob, *The Radical Enlightenment, Pantheists, Freemasons and Republicans* (London, 1981), p. 247.

25 Christiane Berkvens-Stevelinck, *Prosper Marchand. La Vie et l'œuvre (1678–1756)* (Leyden, 1987).

26 Jacob, *The Radical Enlightenment*, p. 268, and again in Jacob, *Living the Enlightenment. Freemasonry and Politics in Eighteenth-Century Europe* (Oxford, 1991), p. 91.

his remarkable reading, erudition and study. Indeed, Toland is now widely regarded as one of the most scholarly personalities of his generation. As Max Wiener has said: 'All of Toland's writings reveal that, more than most deistic thinkers, he fathomed the depth of oriental and biblical scholarship ... and is sufficiently at home in Old Testament exegesis to cope with certain special problems in that field'.[27] Toland had mastered the writings of Spinoza, Richard Simon, Locke and Bayle. He criticises them, refutes them, quotes them, or quite simply integrates them into his own works. We may add many other famous names to the list, such as Leibniz, Jean Le Clerc, Swift and Defoe, who had little esteem for Toland. He was also a formidable and sought-after polemicist who worked for the Tory Harley, with whom he quarrelled on several occasions.[28] In short, he plunged deeply into English political life at a time when discussions about the problem of tolerance occupied a prominent position in the country's intellectual and scholarly life.[29] Toland was well equipped to participate in these debates.

The problem of tolerance, in all its aspects, is a major issue in much of what Toland contributed. In his theological, or rather, anti-theological writings, he is preoccupied with religious tolerance and in his political writings with civil tolerance. To this we may add a novel dimension, which we may term anthropological and cultural tolerance.

Although Toland's concept of tolerance may be the most generous, indeed the most original, of his day, it is not a tolerance that extends to Catholics. In the first instance, this is for political reasons:

> The King of these Nations ... as a mere Politician he ought to discountenance and root out Popery with all imaginable diligence. Nor can the Divine, and truly Protestant principle of Toleration be pleaded in their behalf; first because the Papists own a forreign Power, incompatible with the allegiance due to their natural Soveraign: secondly, because they allow the Pope's dispensing with oaths and keeping no faith with those he declares to be hereticks; which subverts all honour and government at once, this being as bad, if not worse than Atheism: and thirdly, because the Papists never grant a Toleration to *others*; whereas all others, even *Turks* and *Heathens* tolerate every Religion not inconsistent with common Justice and Morality.[30]

---

27   Max Wiener, 'John Toland and Judaism', *Hebrew Union College Annual*, 16 (1942): 216; Francis Schmidt, 'John Toland, critique déiste de la littérature apocryphe', in P. Geoltrain, J-C. Picard and A. Desreumaux (eds), *La Fable apocryphe* (Turnhout, 1990) pp. 118–51.

28   James Alan Downie, *Robert Harley and the Press. Propaganda and Public Opinion in the Age of Swift and Defoe* (Cambridge, 1979), p. 36.

29   Such debates raged at the heart of the Huguenot refugee community. See John Marshall, 'Huguenot thought after the Revocation of the Edict of Nantes', in Vigne and Littleton, *Strangers*, pp. 389–95. See also Hubert Bost, 'Le Refuge huguenot, un laboratoire de la tolérance ?', in N. Piqué and G. Waterlot (eds), *Tolérance et Réforme. Eléments pour une généalogie du concept de tolérance* (Paris, 1999), pp. 169–94.

30   *The State-anatomy of Great Britain, containing a particular account of its several interests* (London, 1716–17), p. 21. There is a French manuscript version of the work under

To be sure, Toland did not need Huguenot sources to find arguments against the Catholics. England was already the inheritor of a longstanding anti-Catholic tradition, culminating in the Glorious Revolution and the overthrow of the Stuart dynasty. However, some of his arguments are also drawn from the Huguenot arsenal, and some from the period of the Wars of Religion. Thus the Pope is depicted as a foreign political potentate in competition with the legitimate king. The second argument, which claims that the Pope releases the king's subjects from their oath of loyalty to the monarch under the pretext that he is a heretic, was a major argument in the days of the League when Sixtus V excommunicated the King of Navarra in 1585 and signed a monitory in 1589 threatening Henri III with excommunication.[31] The third argument sounds echoes of the Wars of Religion, namely with the claim that the Turks are more tolerant than Catholics.

Even though Catholicism may be judged the most odious of all religions, it is not because of religious considerations that it does not deserve to be tolerated:

> As for the Papists, I have shown you before, that it is not on account of any speculative or Scholastick points, or any merely religious Doctrines tho ever so false, or religious Ceremonies tho ever so superstitious, that we exclude them from Offices and Employments. Tis *se defendendo* that we did do it.[32]

It is for the same reason, legitimate self-defence, that Toland also excludes from his total tolerance perjurers and nonjurors, the adversaries of King George I who are but 'Papist Protestants'.[33] Papist Protestants, like almost all of those who profess the religious and political doctrines of the High Church, were the adversaries of the Whigs.

And yet this 'pamphlet' intolerance, created by the contemporary political situation – indeed by the party system in England – should not overshadow the more theoretical and more generous aspects of Toland's concept of tolerance. Like his intolerance of Catholics – and of political adversaries – Toland's tolerance of all other religions is founded upon the omnipresent and omnipotent principle of Reason: reasons of state, and theological and philosophical considerations.

---

the title of *L'Anatomie de la Grande Bretagne Contenant un compte particulier de ses différens intérêts et partis, ses inclinations et son génie* which is found in the Royal Library of Copenhagen (Kongelike Bibliotek Copenhagen, Thott 1352, [4to]). It is, doubtless, a French version set out by Toland himself, who sometimes prepared French versions of his works for special audiences. See John Toland, *Nazarenus*, ed. Justin Champion (Oxford, 1999), p. 70.

31 Two famous Huguenot pamphlets came into the world upon this occasion, François Hotman's *Brutum fulmen papae Sixti V* and Pierre de Belloy's *Moyens d'abus, entreprises et nullitez du rescrit et bulle du Pape Sixte du nom ...*

32 Toland, *State-anatomy*, p. 32.

33 Furthermore, he unleashes a broadside at the excessive tolerance which they are accorded in England: 'The doctrine and practice of these Nonswearers, render them absolutely incapble of being tolerated, or as much as conniv'd at in this kingdom; which is the only kingdom in the world, that ever extended the protection of the Laws, to such as publickly disown'd the authority of the Legislative and Supreme Powers ... ' (ibid., p. 83).

After the great scandal caused by his *Christianity not mysterious* Toland, for reasons of decorum and personal safety, declared himself loyal to the Anglican Church, the incarnation of the best of religions because of its Protestantism which is 'preferable to all others in spiritual as well as temporal regards, the most conformable to Scripture, and the most agreeable to Reason ...'.[34] And at the heart of the Anglican Church, Toland considered himself a loyal member of the Low Church.

This should not obscure the fact that, for Toland, all religions contain a large measure of superstition, and that every established Church exploits its status cynically in order to profit from it.[35] But Toland's religious positions may also be defined from another perspective: namely, that in all religions there is a common core of truth based on man's natural illuminations.[36] Upon these truths, a common fabric of justice, of morality, indeed of charity, the basis of every civil society, is draped. Within these two facets of Toland's view of religion, we may discover Huguenot traces and reminiscences, which lead inevitably to the concept of tolerance which characterizes his work.

In the matter of superstition, Toland was part of a large European movement comprising Catholics, Protestants and Jews. The trickery at the heart of all religion is constantly evoked in the writings of the freethinkers – to such an extent indeed that it is even found in the work of the famous atheist cleric Meslier, who lived, meditated and wrote virtually isolated from the world around him.[37] Even before its publication, clandestine manuscripts of the *Trois Imposteurs* enjoyed an immense popularity.[38] And the choir of denouncers was bolstered by the loud and clear voice of the Protestant refugee.

This voice is first heard, among others, in the works of certain marginal and utopian Huguenot refugees. Denis Veiras, for example, preceded Toland by several

---

34   Ibid., p. 20.

35   For the English context, see Justin Champion, *The Pillars of Priestcraft Shaken: The Church of England and Its Enemies (1660–1730)* (Cambridge, 1992).

36   'Locke and Toland suggest that we distinguish between the theological content of a religious belief, and a meta-theory about religious belief which is established by 'reason'. So long as we stay within the perspective of faith, there is no hope of resolving the competing claims of different churches. One can tolerate the most extravagant claims of different religious traditions, however, if religious believers adopted a philosophical account of faith which limited its claims on the belief and actions of others', in D.M. Clarke, 'Locke and Toland on toleration', *Studies on Voltaire and the Eighteenth Century*, 335 (1995): 261–71.

37   See Roland Desné, 'L'Homme et son œuvre', in 'Prefaces' to the *Œuvres complètes of Jean Meslier* (3 vols, Paris, 1970–1972), vol. 1, pp. xx–xxi.

38   The three impostors are Moses, Jesus and Mohamed. See Silvia Berti, 'Jan Vroesen, autore del "Traité des trois imposteurs"?', *Rivista Storica Italiana*, 103 (1991): 528–43, which deals with the problem of the attribution of its authorship to Jan Vroesen. See also Berti's 'Scepticism and the "Traité des trois imposteurs"', in Richard H. Popkin and Arno Vanderjagt (eds), *Skepticism and Irreligion in the Seventeenth and Eighteenth Centuries* (Leyden, 1993), pp. 216–29.

decades[39] with the publication, in English and in London, of his book *The History of the Sevarites or Sevarambi*.[40] Repeatedly translated and often reprinted,[41] the book presents a hero, Severias, who establishes a Utopia for the Severambi which combines religious trickery with a just and impartial regime whose goal is to secure the happiness of all inhabitants.

We find ideas equally subversive in Gabriel Foigny's *La Terre Australe connue*, published in 1676 and once again in a reworked edition of 1692 under the title of *Les Aventures de Jacques Sadeur*.[42] It is no coincidence that Pierre Bayle dedicated a long article to Jacques Sadeur in his *Dictionnaire historique et critique*. We can also add to this list the professor of mathematics Simon Tyssot de Patot, with his *Voyages et Aventures de Jacques Massé*, published in 1710,[43] and the defrocked Benedictine Nicolas Gueudeville, who converted to Protestantism during his long stay in Holland where he published for twelve years one of the most widely-read and discussed of all contemporary newspapers, *L'Esprit des Cours de l'Europe*, from 1699 to 1710.[44] The goal of Gueudeville's newspaper was to unmask the means by which Louis XIV won the admiration of his subjects, despite the fact that he exploited them with utter cynicism. One of these means, if not the main one, was the manipulation of the common people with the aid of religion.[45] Toland dedicates the first of his *Letters to Serena* to 'The Origin and Force of Prejudices such as are widespread and accepted in all human societies. Gueudeville also reprinted the *Dialogues* of the Baron de Lahontan in 1710. We may also add Lahontan himself.[46]

---

39   See Ernest Van der Mühll, *Denis Veiras et son histoire des Sévarambes* (Paris, 1938).

40   Denis Veiras, *The History of the Sevarites or Sevarambi* (London, 1675).

41   See the list in the excellent critical edition of Aubrey Rosenberg, *L'Histoire des Sévarambes*, pp. 18–30 (Paris, 2001).

42   For a critical bibliography of Foigny's works, see Pierre Ronzaud, *L'Utopie hermaphrodite. La Terre australe connue de Gabriel Foigny (1676)* (Marseille, 1982), pp. 321–7.

43   Aubrey Rosenberg, *Tyssot de Patot and his Work (1655–1738)* (The Hague, 1972). On the community of ideas between Tyssot de Patot and Toland, see Wijnand W. Mijnhart, 'The Dutch Enlightenment: Humanism, Nationalism and Decline', in Margaret C. Jacob and W.W. Mijnhart (eds), *The Dutch Republic in the Eighteenth Century* (Ithaca and London, 1992) p. 204, and Rosenberg, *Simon Tyssot de Patot, Lettres choisies et discours sur la chronologie* (Paris, 2002).

44   See *Dictionnaire des Journaux, 1600–1789* (Paris and Oxford, 1991), article by François Moureau, vol. 1, pp. 379–81, and especially Aubrey Rosenberg, *Nicholas Gueudeville and His Work* (The Hague, 1981).

45   M. Yardeni, 'Gueudeville et Louis XIV. Un précurseur de socialisme, critique des structures sociales louisquatorziennes', *Revue d'Histoire Moderne et Contemporaine*, 19 (1972): 598–620.

46   Baron de Lahontan, *Dialogues ou entretiens entre un Sauvage et le Baron de Lahontan*, in *Œuvres complètes*, ed. R. Quellet and A. Beaulieu (2 vols, Montreal, 1990), vol. 2, pp. 801–28.

And finally, there is Pierre Bayle, whose influence upon Toland is very marked. In the received ideas and public opinion of the day, the two men were so closely associated with each other that when Elie Benoît attacked Toland he was in fact simply wishing to denounce Bayle, as Pierre Rétat has shown.[47] Several researchers have amused themselves by seeking out the 'word for word' borrowings which Toland takes from Bayle.[48] And it is Pierre Bayle who, in his famous thesis on the rights of the erring conscience unites the two aspects of religion found in Toland's work.[49] On the one hand, there is the individual's right to err, even in the matter of superstitions and false religion, while on the other there is deism. These two aspects of religion lead to a conception of tolerance.

For Toland, as we have seen, there were the tolerables and the intolerables. Amongst the intolerables were the Catholics and the nonjurors, the groups of most danger to the security of the state and the good of civil society. And yet, Toland does not wish that they should be actively persecuted. The ideal outcome would be for them to leave the country, but not in the spirit of *cuius regio, eius religio* (he is too Whig, and indeed too republican, for that) but of their own free will. This solution is similar to the one advocated by Calvin in order that the believer should lapse neither into the sin of revolt, nor into the sin of nicodemism.

As regards England, Toland recommended before all else the immediate tolerance of dissenters and of foreign Lutheran and Calvinist Protestants. In truth, the dissenters were native Britons, but they did not enjoy the same rights as members of the Anglican Church. Toland sees more natural links between the dissenters and the Low Church than between the Low Church and the High Church.[50] Amongst the foreigners, Toland's preferred group was the Huguenot refugees, to be naturalised without delay in the interests of the state and of civil society. For Toland, civil society and the state are almost synonymous. Together, they give birth to what Toland calls a 'national religion'. In every state there should be a national religion that may work in perfect harmony with what Herder and German Romanticism will call the *Volksgeist*. For England, such a religion would obviously be Protestantism, indeed, Anglicanism, in spite of its High-Church component.

---

47   Pierre Rétat, *Le Dictionnaire de Bayle et la lutte philosophique au XVIIIe siècle* (Paris 1971), p. 35.

48   See Sullivan, *John Toland and the Deist Controversy*, p. 47 and Geneviève Byrkman, 'Pour en savoir plus, cherchez dans mes écrits', *Revue de Synthèse*, 116 (1995): 222.

49   The bibliography on the subject of 'Bayle and tolerance' continues to be enriched. For an excellent and recent update, see Gianluca Mori, *Introduzione a Bayle* (Rome and Bari, 1996), pp. 41–77, and the bibliography, pp. 205–8 and Justin Champion, '"Most truly ... a protestant": Reading Bayle in England', in Antony McKenna and Gianni Paganini (eds), *Pierre Bayle dans la Republique des Lettres. Philosophie, religion, critique*, 'La vie des Huguenots' 36 (Paris, 2004) pp. 503–26.

50   Not only on a religious level, but also on a political level. 'The Dissenters have highly merited of the Protestant Interest and of our Protestant King', Toland, *State-anatomy*, p. 26.

Toland's great innovation was to argue that that the national religion must tolerate all particular religions as the expressions of a distinct consciousness because the national religion is in perfect harmony with the freedom of conscience. Freedom of conscience, he argues, does not mean moral dissoluteness or indifference to religion. It is a free tolerance of the doctrines and opinions that do not harm human society and religion and which consists

> in bare speculation, and solely regarding the conscience or persuasion of men. The equity of this Liberty is grounded upon the use of Reason which is equally the right of all men, upon the nature of things, and upon the difference of Education as well as of Capacities. But, as comeing under a political regulation, it is either entire or partial. Entire Liberty of Conscience, is, where a man according to the dictates of his own Conscience, may have the free exercice of his Religion, without any impediment to his Preferment or Imployment in the State. Partial Liberty of Conscience is, where a man according to the dictates of his own Conscience, may have the free exercice of his Religion; but if it be not National Religion, he is thereby render'd incapable of Perferment or Imployment in the State.[51]

Consequently, tolerance and freedom of conscience do not mean equality of rights. Freedom of conscience is the choice made by the individual: a choice determined by his capacities, his education and the fruits of his reason. It is out of free choice that he may also adhere to the national religion and enjoy equality of rights. Such a conception of tolerance is profitable to the state and civil society because it allows foreigners to be welcomed and then naturalised. Here lies the key difference between Whigs and Tories:

> A material difference between the Tories and the Whigs, is the latter's being civil and friendly to Foreigners ... whereas the former are their declar'd enemies, treating all nations ... with the utmost inhumanity, scurrility and contempt. This makes all Foreigners, excepting the same French [Papists], against them in their turn.[52]

Tolerance, strangers, wealth and commerce form a chain of inseparable entities for Toland. 'Trade is the soul of our *British* world', as he says, and he knows that 'generally speaking, the Whigs are the trading people of this country'.[53] Interest and patriotism complement one another. 'In the multitude of inhabitants consists the riches, and consequently the power of a nation'.[54] Nations which have persecuted and driven away foreigners have paid dear for their intolerance: 'Incontestable examples were laid before those Bigots, of nations that perish'd by keeping out strangers, and of others that flourish'd by admitting them, without any one instance brought by them to the contrary'.[55] Tolerance means wealth, power and prosperity,

---

51 Ibid., p. 27.
52 Ibid., p. 15.
53 Ibid., pp. 43, 45.
54 Ibid., p. 56.
55 Ibid., p. 56.

while intolerance means loss and decline.⁵⁶ Before the Edict of Nantes was revoked, the Huguenot campaign of propaganda and persuasion, seeking to stave off the inevitable, used the same arguments in dozens of pamphlets and scholarly treatises. What is more, the economic and demographic decline of France after the Revocation gave irrefutable proof of the soundness of such arguments, much discussed and analysed in the important newspapers of the Refuge in Holland.⁵⁷ Doubtless Toland read these newspapers and he may perhaps even have known some of the journalists who wrote for them, such as Henri Basnage de Beauval and Jacques Bernard, who wrote upon such subjects.

Amongst the strangers useful and beneficial to England, Toland puts the Huguenots before all others:

> To name no others, I appeal to the whole kingdom in general, whether there be any subjects more peaceable than the *French* refugees? whether they are not so far from being a burthen to any, that they maintain their own poor, and yet contribute to ours? whether any be more industrious, and whether the fruits of that Industry do not entirely redound to our benefit? for I suppose no body will doubt that they live in *English* houses, that they eat *English* beef and pudding, that they drink *English* strong beer, that they pay *English* taxes. I appeal in particular to our Merchants, whether any have more improv'd our encourag'd our Manufactures, whether any have come more readily into our publick stocks and fonds? I appeal to our Generals, whether any have serv'd with greater fidelity or bravery? I appeal to our Bishops, whether any have given less disturbance to the Church? and lastly I appeal to his Majesty and his Ministers, whether any were more firm to his Interest, and suffer'd more for being so?⁵⁸

The great success of the French refugees, once they had been naturalized and once they had become loyal subjects, was to serve as an example: 'How much more reason have we to expect the same, from nations more resembling us in language and manners, and especially from those of his Majesties country, which is the hear of the ancient *Saxony*, from whence the *English* originally came'.⁵⁹

---

56   A paragraph of *Reasons for Naturalising the Jews* is particularly eloquent on this subject: 'We all know that numbers of people are the true riches and power of any country, and we have often been told, that this is the reason why *Spain* (since the expulsion of the *Jews* and *Moors*) being continually drain'd of her inhabitants ... is grown so prodigiously weak and poor: whereas, tho *Holland* has comparatively but few native inhabitants ... allowing an unlimited liberty of conscience, and receiving all nations to the right of citizens, the country is ever well so stockt with people, and consequently both rich and powerful to any eminent degree ...' (p. 6). Lurbe in his French translation, *Raisons de naturaliser les Juifs en Grande Bretagne et en Irlande* (Paris 1998), gives us Toland's English sources regarding this point.

57   Myriam Yardeni, 'Naissance et essor d'un mythe: la Révocation de l'Edit de Nantes et le déclin économique de la France', *BSHPF*, 142 (1993): 76–94, taken up again in Yardeni, *Repenser l'histoire: Aspects de l'historiographie huguenote des guerres de religion à la Révolution française* (Paris, 2000) pp. 191–206.

58   Toland, *State-anatomy*, p. 56.

59   Ibid., p. 57.

In effect, we may distinguish two phases in Toland's conception of tolerance. One can and one ought to tolerate everyone whose religion does not menace civil society and who is useful to the national community. But this kind of tolerance is also a process in proportion to the rights to be conferred upon those who are tolerated. The equality of rights, which is the apex of tolerance, remains the goal when the tolerated are integrated and they are accommodated to what Toland calls the national religion. The second phase of tolerance for Toland is integration, understood to be the minimisation of religious differences but not their total disappearance (for, in spite of everything, Toland appreciates the benefits that diversity brings). We have seen that he regards the Huguenot refugees in England as especially well suited to a project of integration conceived in this way.

But from the outset, there is one sole people, one sole nation and one sole religion that corresponds to the preconditions for this second phase of tolerance: the Jews. In his *Reasons for Naturalising the Jews*, Toland speaks of integration, and not of tolerance.[60] All those who have dealt with the conception of Jews and Judaism in Toland's work have underlined his truly exceptional attitude in this matter, especially his call for the total and immediate integration of the Jews into different national communities, and above all into the communities of England and Ireland.[61] Curiously, it is here that the Huguenot traces and reminiscences, although they are still present, are at their least dominant in Toland's work. For in Toland's thinking the immediate and unconditional integration of the Jews into the country, the state and civil society are required by what we might call the 'English Utopian Tradition' and by his own conception of the Christian religion and its origins.

With regards to the utopian tradition, the names of Francis Bacon and James Harrington loom large.[62] In Bacon's *New Atlantis*, the Jews enjoy perfect tolerance and love the country – Bensalem – sincerely.[63] Of all the utopians, Toland is the closest to Harrington.[64] In *The Commonwealth of Oceana*, Harrington proposes the colonisation of Panopea – Ireland, in his allegory – and the settlement there of the Jews. They are a people, in his view, whom it is impossible to assimilate, but none the less a people whose talents, above all in agriculture (well-known from the Bible) could be employed to much profit.[65] To these traditions, inherited from English utopianism, we should add the 'baroque' philosemitic trends of the mid-

---

60   A fact made evident by Pierre Lurbe in his work.

61   Cecil Roth, *A History of the Jews in England* (1941; Oxford, 1964); Léon Poliakov, *Histoire de l'antisémitisme*, volume 1: *Du Christ aux Juifs de Cour* (Paris, 1955); Jacob Katz, *Out of the Ghetto: The Social Background of Jewish Emancipation, 1770–1870* (Syracuse, 1998) and David S. Katz, *The Jews in the History of England, 1485–1850* (Oxford, 1994).

62   Myriam Yardeni, 'The Solution of the Jewish Problem in the Utopianism of the Seventeenth and Eighteenth Centuries', in Myriam Yardeni, *Anti-Jewish Mentalities in Early-Modern Europe* (Lanham, 1990) pp. 225–39.

63   Francis Bacon, *New Atlantis* (London, 1627).

64   In 1700, he edits Harrington's works, including his biography.

65   Yardeni, 'The Solution of the Jewish Problem'.

seventeenth century[66] that culminated in Menasse Ben Israel's intercession with Cromwell, and the tacit tolerance of Jews in England.[67] But it is probably Toland's *Nazarenus* which reveals the surest route towards an understanding of the *Reasons for Naturalising the Jews*.[68]

For Toland, there is no antagonism between Judaism and true Christianity; the two religions complement each other. Jesus did not seek to abolish Judaic law, which is rational and moral. All this has nothing to do with the reception or rejection of Jesus by the Jews. Moreover, there is an equality between the three monotheistic religions. Toland founds his argument here upon an Italian manuscript which he had seen, the *Gospel according to Barnabas*, which presented a version of the life and death of Jesus quite unlike the versions in the four canonical gospels. In the *Gospel according to Barnabas*, the man who betrayed the true intentions of Jesus, a human being, was Paul. The true disciples of Jesus were the Ebionites, or the Nazarenes, whereas Paul, who did not know Jesus personally, supplanted Jesus' teachings with his own. Just as for Selden, for Toland too Christianity is but a reformed Judaism. Jesus never spoke against Judaic law, only against the excesses of the Pharisees in their application of it. Jesus wanted to expand, not to abolish, Judaic law. The Fathers of the Church had also wrongly interpreted Jesus and had thereby distorted true Judaism.

The *Nazarenus* at once clears the name of the Nazarenes in the distant past and the Jews in the present. The Nazarenes' Christianity was a Christianity without mysteries and without miracles, a rational and moral religion, whilst Judaism was the specific, local, and indeed national and political version of that same religion. Placing himself within the republican tradition of Milton and Harrington, Toland also sings the praises of the republican values of the Jewish state.

It is Toland's anti-apostolic, anti-Pauline and above all anti-patristic polemic that leads us, in this context, to the Huguenots. Justin Champion, in his introduction to the reprinting of *Nazarenus*, draws our attention to the role that Jean Daillé may have played in the elaboration of Toland's anti-patristic theme.[69] Daillé was one of the great Calvinist theologians of Charenton and an author of the *Traicté de l'employ des saincts Pères pour le jugement des différends qui sont aujourd'hui en la religion* (Geneva, 1632), translated into English in 1651 and reprinted in 1675.[70] Daillé's work may be placed within the tradition of polemic between Catholics and Protestants, concerned to establish the true faith to be followed. 'The design of Daillé's work

---

66   Hans Joachim Schoeps, *Philo-Semitismus im Barock* (Tübingen, 1952), David S. Katz, *Philo-Semitism and the Readmission of the Jews to England, 1603–1655* (Oxford, 1982).

67   Menasseh Ben Israël, *Espérance d'Israël*, ed. and trans. H. Méchoulan and G. Nahon (Paris, 1979).

68   Pierre Lurbe, 'John Toland et l'utilisation de l'histoire juive: entre l'histoire et le mythe' in *La République des Lettres et l'histoire du judaisme antique: XVIe–XVIIIe siècles* (Paris, 1992), pp. 149–62.

69   Champion, 'Introduction' to *Nazarenus*, p. 48.

70   Under the title *A treatise concerning the right use of the Fathers*.

was to negate the authority of the fathers as a determinant of theological dispute: the church fathers were contradictory, textually corrupt and theologically untrustworthy, neither accurate, nor infallible'.[71]

According to Daillé, the errors, although pious, began directly after the death of the Apostles and not in the following centuries. This brings us to the soundness of the Nazarenes' and Ebionites' interpretations. For, as Max Wiener states in his crucial article 'John Toland and Judaism', Toland seeks the retrospective tolerance of the Nazarenes and desires the immediate toleration of the Jews. 'Within the framework of this treatise about the history of religion, he is chiefly interested in establishing their theological rights. For this reason, he combats tirelessly and repeatedly the anti-Semitism of the church'.[72] We have seen that, for Toland, Christianity becomes a natural and rational religion, devoid of mysteries and miracles. Christianity and Judaism are nothing more than the different faces of the same natural religion. Consequently, the persecution of the Jews is as absurd as it is unjust. Hence the immanent conclusion that they should be naturalised without delay.

In the *Nazarenus*, Toland sets out the theological bases for the tolerance of the Jews. In *Reasons for Naturalising the Jews* he extends this tolerance to an immediate integration without restriction by adding two major arguments: one of them utilitarian, the other moral. The utilitarian argument is the one that Toland develops to plead for the naturalisation of foreigners in general, with the Huguenots heading the queue. The only, rather sizeable, difference is that the Jews will prove to be even more useful and loyal than the French:

> Their having no [Country] to which they are ty'd by inclination or interest as their own, will never likewise enter into any political engagements, which might be prejudicial to ours, as we have known (for Example) certain *French* Refugees to have done, notwithstanding their protection; nay, and to be ever pleas'd with any successes against us ... as making for the greatness of their nation, wherein they still took a sort of pride, and to which, some of 'em are gone back again, after failing of their expectations here.[73]

And further:

> It is evident, that by receiving of the *Jews*, no body needs be afraid that any religious Party in the Nation will thereby be weakn'd or enforc'd ... they'll never join with any Party in civil Affairs, but that which patronizes liberty of conscience and the naturalization, which will ever be the side of Liberty and the Constitution.[74]

Not only were they to become Whigs, but they were also to contribute to the beautification of London and Bristol, as they had done in Amsterdam and The

---

71 Champion, 'Introduction' to *Nazarenus*.
72 Wiener, *John Toland and Judaism*, p. 230.
73 Toland, *Reasons*, p. 13.
74 Ibid., pp. 11–12

Hague.⁷⁵ The moral argument which Toland proffers in favour of the tolerance of the Jews is part of the fight he leads against prejudice and the injustice it causes: injustices which have hit the Jews harder than others:

> But no people or sect in the world, has had sadder experience of these truths in all times, than the *Jews*; for their religious customs differing in the whole from all other nations, and being in the parts directly contrary to those of several, they had all nations therefore for their enemies.⁷⁶

False accusations that triggered persecutions created a vicious circle that affected Jews everywhere, and had done so for many centuries. 'But the *Annals* of *European* nations are fouly besmear'd with their blood', he writes, 'since *Christianity* got the mastery'.⁷⁷ When he recounts these persecutions we sometimes encounter Huguenot sources, above all Jacques Basnage and his *Histoire des Juifs*.⁷⁸ We should also add other works by Basnage,⁷⁹ as well as the *Histoires* by Larrey and Lenfant.⁸⁰

The information that Toland draws from his Huguenot sources is important because it strengthens his argument for the naturalisation of the Jews. He also uncovers the links between barbarity, prejudice and religious fanaticism: 'Zeal for the glory of God was alleg'd; which is the most terrible and bloody expression in any language, when a bigot speaks it'.⁸¹ In this context, Toland does not fail to cite the role that the hated Priests had played in the persecution of the Jews: 'But their most inveterate Enemies were the *Priests*, who devoutly offer'd up those human Sacrifices, not only to share their Goods with the rapacious *Prince*, but also to acquire the reputation of zeal and sanctity among the credulous vulgar'.⁸²

---

75   'I envy not those whole streets of magnificent buildings that the *Jews* have erected at *Amsterdam* and the *Hague*: but there are other *Jews* enow in the World to adorn *London* or *Bristol* with the like', Ibid., p. 17.

76   Ibid., p. 22.

77   Ibid., p. 22.

78   Basnage de Beauval, Jacques, *L'Histoire et la Religion des Juifs depuis Jésus-Christ jusqu'à présent. Pour servir de supplément et de continuation à l'Histoire de Joseph* (6 vols, Rotterdam, 1707), and the later edition, *Histoire des Juifs depuis Jésus-Christ jusqu'à présent* (15 vols, The Hague, 1716). Pierre Lurbe underlines, in his translation, many of the borrowings and pieces of information that Toland gleaned from Basnage.

79   Above all, his *Histoire de l'Eglise, depuis Jésus Christ jusqu'à présent* (Rotterdam, 1699), and the *Histoire du Vieux et Nouveau Testament* (Amsterdam, 1705).

80   Isaac de Larrey, *L'Héritière de Guyenne ou l'histoire de l'Eleonore* (Rotterdam, 1691), *Histoire d'Angleterre, d'Ecosse, d'Irlande avec un abrégé des évenemens les plus remarquables arrivez dans les autres états* (4 vols, Rotterdam, 1697–1713); Jacques Lenfant, *Histoire du Concile de Constance* (2 vols, 1727).

81   Toland, *Reasons*, p. 23.

82   Ibid., p. 25.

We do well to recall that the Huguenots also held the Catholic clergy responsible for the persecutions that they had undergone.[83] Toland acknowledges his debt to 'the reverend Mons[ieur] Banage, with some other learned and moderate *Protestant Divines*' who had helped him to uncover the mechanisms of the persecution of the Jews and who had 'likewise undeniably prov'd this murder of Children to be a gross fable invented out of perfect malice and calumny'.[84] Serving as far more than a historical source – and Toland has many other sources at his disposal[85] – Basnage and (above all) Bayle proved to Toland the soundness of his conviction that 'the *Jews* therefore are both in their origine and progress, not otherwise to be regarded, than under the common circumstances of human nature'.[86] Bayle and Basnage also show that Jewish history can be explained and understood just like any other normal human history.[87] Bayle also puts forward that it is neither their corruption nor their wickedness which hinder the Jews from opening up to the world but the influence of their Rabbis and the education that they receive.[88] Hence the importance of education in the battle against prejudices is omnipresent in Toland's work.

The Huguenot traces and reminiscences in Toland's conception of tolerance bear witness to a common mental universe, indeed, to a single mentality which abhors fanaticism, prejudice and persecution. But it is a unity without uniformity: one where the tolerated and the degrees of tolerance are not always the same. Toland and the Huguenot refugees experienced the crisis of European thought in different fashions. Their existential, psychological and intellectual conditions were not the same. Toland was part of a *Commonwealth* and is conscious of this fact whereas the Huguenots were searching, after the revocation of the Edict of Nantes, for an identity. But it is precisely this existential difference which leaves the path open to differentiation and which allows the cultural enrichment of the concept of tolerance.

---

83   For an example, see Jean Claude, *Plaintes des protestants cruellement opprimés dans le Roïaume de France* (Cologne, 1713).

84   Toland, *Reasons*, p. 27.

85   Lurbe, in his French translation, mentions all of Toland's English historical and theological sources.

86   Toland, *Reasons*, p. 20.

87   Myriam Yardeni, 'Une nouvelle conception de l'histoire juive après la destruction du Temple: Bayle et Basnage' in *Repenser l'histoire*, pp. 93–107.

88   See Myriam Yardeni, 'La vision des Juifs et du judaïsme dans l'œuvre de Pierre Bayle' in *Les Juifs dans l'histoire de France* (Leyden, 1980) pp. 86–95, and also *Huguenots and Jews* in Hebrew (Jerusalem, 1998). A French edition of the latter is forthcoming.

Bibliography

Manuscript sources

Armagh, Public Library, MS 1780, William Lodge, 'Catalogue of Books in Armagh Public Library' (n. dat.).
Copenhagen, Kongelike Bibliotek Copenhagen, Thott 1352, 'L'Anatomie de la Grande Bretagne Contenant un compte particulier de ses différens intérêts et partis, ses inclinations et son génie'.
London, British Library, Additional MSS 4281–89, 'Letters to Pierre Des Maizeaux'.
London, British Library, Additional MS 8880.
London, British Library, Additional MS 21132.
London, Public Record Office SP/44/337.
London, Public Record Office SP/31/3.
London, University of London, University College, Huguenot Library, Bounty MS 6.
London, University of London, University College, Huguenot Library, Burn Donation MS 28.
London, University of London, University College, Wagner Wills: De Gastigny, Dutry.
New York, Huguenot Society of America, Pierre Stouppe, 'Sermons, 1724–1741'.
New York, New York Historical Society, Manuscript Collection, BV New York City Churches: French Church of St Esprit, 'Consistory Minutes, 1723–1766' [copy].
New York, New York Historical Society, Manuscript Collection, Louis Rou, 'Eighteen Pieces of Manuscript'.
New York, New York Public Library, Manuscript and Archives Section, Theodorus Bailey Myers Collection, Louis Rou, 'Sermons and Other Writings, 1704–50', 3 vols. Originals and microfilm.
Oxford, Bodleian Library, MS Tanner 92.
Oxford, Bodleian Library, MS Tanner 124.
Oxford, Bodleian Library, MS Rawlinson A478.
Oxford, Bodleian Library, MS Rawlinson C984.
Oxford, Bodleian Library, MS Rawlinson D641.
Paris, Archives du Ministère des affaires Etrangères, *Cahiers Politiques Hollande* 1656, September–December 1688, *despatches D'Avaux*.

Primary sources

Abbadie, Jacques, *Défense de la nation Britannique ou les droits de Dieu, de la Nature and de la Societé clairement établis au sujet de la revolution d'Angleterre, contre l'auteur de L'Avis important aux Refugiés* (London, 1692).

An Account of the Courts of Prussia and Hanover: Sent to a Minister of State in Holland (London, 1705).

Ailesbury, Thomas Bruce, Earl of, *Memoirs*, ed. W. E. Buckley, 2 vols (Edinburgh, 1890).

Avril, Pierre, *Voyage en divers etats d'Europe et d'Asie, entrepris pour decouvrir un nouveau chemin à la Chine* (Paris, 1693).

Bacon, Francis, *New Atlantis* (London, 1627).

Basnage, Jacques, *Histoire de l'Eglise, depuis Jésus Christ jusqu'à présent* (Rotterdam, 1699).

—, *Histoire du Vieux et Nouveau Testament* (Amsterdam, 1705).

—, *L'Histoire et la Religion des Juifs depuis Jésus-Christ jusqu'à présent. Pour servir de supplément et de continuation à l'Histoire de Joseph*, 6 vols (Rotterdam, 1707).

—, *Histoire des Juifs depuis Jésus-Christ jusqu'à présent*, 15 vols (The Hague, 1716).

Basnage de Beauval, Henri (ed.), *Histoire des Ouvrages des Sçavans* (24 vols, Rotterdam, 1687–1709).

—, *Contribution à la connaissance des réseaux d'information au début du XVIIIe siècle: Henri Basnage de Beauval et sa correspondance à propos de 'l'Histoire des Ouvrages des Savans' (1687–1709)*, ed. Hans Bots and Lenie van Lieshout (Amsterdam and Maarssen: APA-Holland University Press, 1984).

Baxter, Richard, *Calendar of the Correspondence of Richard Baxter*, ed. Neil H. Keeble and Geoffrey F. Nuttall, 2 vols (Oxford: Clarendon Press, 1991).

Bayle, Pierre, *Political Writings*, ed. and trans. Sally L. Jenkinson (Cambridge: Cambridge University Press, 2000).

Benoît, Elie, *Histoire de l'Edit de Nantes*, 5 vols (Delft, 1693–95).

Bernard, Jaques, *De l'excellence de la religion* (Amsterdam, 1714).

—, (ed.), *Supplement aux anciennes editions du Grand Dictionaire Historique de Mre. Louis Moreri. Ou le mélange curieux de l'histoire sacrée et profane*, 2 vols (Amsterdam, The Hague and Utrecht, 1716).

—, Jean Cornand de Lacrose, Charles Lecène, and Jean Leclerc (eds), *Bibliothèque Universelle et Historique*, 25 vols (Amsterdam, 1686–93).

Bèze, Théodore de, *Du Droit des Magistrats*, ed. Richard M. Kingdon (Geneva: Droz, 1971).

Bold, Samuel, *A Sermon Against Persecution* (London, 1683).

A Calendar of the Letter Books of the French Church of London from the Civil War to the Restoration, 1643–1659, ed. Robin D. Gwynn, HSQS, 54 (London, 1979).

Calvin, Jean, *Institutions of the Christian Religion*, ed. John T. McNeill (2 vols, Philadelphia: Westminster Press, 1960).

Chamberlen, Peter, *The Poore Man's Advocate, or, England's Samaritans* (London, 1649).
Chenu de Chalezac, Guillaume, *Guillaume Chenu de Chalezac: The 'French Boy'*, ed. Randolph Vigne (Cape Town: Van Riebeeck Society, 1993).
Claude, Jean, *An Account of the Persecution and Oppression of the Protestants of France* (London, 1707).
——, *Plaintes des protestants cruellement opprimés dans le Roïaume de France* (Cologne, 1713).
Cooper, William, *Catalogus Alphabeticus Bibliothecae Casiliensis* (Bolton Library, Cashel, 1757).
Correspondentie van Willem III en van Hand Willem Bentinck, eersteen Graaf van Portland: Het archief van Welbeck Abbey, 2 dln. Tweede gedeelte: Uit Nederlandsche en Engelsche archieven en bibliotheken, ed. N. Japikse, 5 vols (The Hague: R.G.P. kleine serie, 1927–33).
Courcelles, Etienne de [Stephanus Curcellaeus], *Opera theologica*, ed. Philip van Limborch (Amsterdam, 1675).
Daillé, Jean, *Traicté de l'employ des Saincts Pères pour le jugement des différends qui sont aujourd'hui en la religion* (Geneva, 1632).
Dangeau, Philippe de Courcillon, Marquis de, *Journal du Marquis de Dangeau*, ed. Soulie, Dussieux, de Channevières, Mantz, de Maintaiglou, with additions by the Duc de Saint-Simon (Paris, 1854–60).
Des Maizeaux, Pierre (ed.), *Recueil de diverses pièces sur la philosophie, la religion naturelle, l'histoire, les mathématiques andc*, 2 vols (Amsterdam, 1720).
——, *A Collection of several pieces of Mr. John Toland, Now first published from his original manuscripts, with some memoirs of his life and writings*, 2 vols (London 1726).
Despagne, Jean, *Abrege du sermon funebre sur la mort du tres-honorable Phillipe comte de Pembroke and Montgomery, advenue le 23 de Janvier l'an 1650* (London, [1651]).
——, *An Essay of the Wonders of God* (London, 1662).
Diary of the Times of Charles the Second by the Honourable Henry Sidney, afterwards Earl of Romney; including his correspondence with the Countess of Sunderland and other distinguished persons at the English Court; to which are added letters illustrative of the times of James II and William III, ed. R. W. Blencowe, 2 vols (London, 1843).
Diderot, Denis, *Lettre sur les aveugles*, ed. Marian Hobson and Simon Harvey (Paris: Garnier Flammarion, 2000).
Drelincourt, Charles, *The Christian's Defence against the Fears of Death*, trans. Marius d'Assigny (London, 1707).
Dubourdieu, John-Armand, *An Appeal to the English Nation: or, the body of the French Protestants, and the honest proselytes, vindicated from the calumnies cast on them by one Malard and his associates ...* (London, 1718).
Dumont de Bostaquet, Isaac, *Mémoires Inédites de Dumont de Bostaquet, Gentilhomme, Normand*, ed. F. Read and R. Waddington (Paris, 1864).

Durel, Jean, *Sermon prononcé en l'eglise francoise* (London, 1661).
——, *A View of the Government and Publick Worship of God in the Reformed Churches beyond the Seas* (London, 1662).
Edwards, John, *A Brief Vindication of the Fundamental Articles of the Christian Faith* (London, 1697).
——, *A Free but Modest Censure on the late Controversial Writings and Debates of the Lord Bishop of Worcester and Mr. Locke* (London, 1698).
Erman, Jean-Paul, *Mémoires pour servir à l'histoire des réfugiés français dans les états du roi*, 9 vols (Berlin, 1782–99).
——, *Mémoires pour servir à l'histoire de Sophie Charlotte, Reine de Prusse* (Berlin, 1801).
Firmin, Thomas, *Proposals for the Imployment of the Poor and for the Prevention of Idleness* (London, 1681).
Fontaine, Jacques, *Les Mémoires d'une famille huguenote victime de la révocation de l'Edit de Nantes*, ed. Bernard Cottret, (Montpellier: Presses du Languedoc, Max Chaleil, 1992).
——, *Memoirs of the Reverend Jaques Fontaine, 1658–1728*, ed. Dianne W. Ressinger, Publications of the Huguenot Society of Great Britain and Ireland, New Series 2 (London, 1992).
French Protestant Refugees Relieved through the French Protestant Church of London, 1681–1687, ed. A.P. Hands and Irene Scouloudi, HSQS, 49 (London, 1971).
Gerbier, Balthazar, *A New-Years Result in Favour of the Poore* (London, 1654).
——, *Some Consideration of the two Great Single Commodities of England* (London, 1654).
Israël, Menasseh ben, *Espérance d'Israël*, ed. and trans. H. Méchoulan and G. Nahon (Paris: Vrin, 1979).
Jurieu, Pierre, *Traitté de la nature et de la grace* (Amsterdam, 1715).
Kazner, Johann F. A., *Leben Friedrichs von Schomberg, oder Schönburg*, 2 vols (Mannheim, 1789).
[Kennett, White], *A Register and Chronicle, Ecclesiastical and Civil: containing matters of fact delivered in the words of the most authentick books, papers, and records, ... towards discovering and connecting the true history of England, from the Restauration of King Charles II ... taken from the manuscript collections of the Lord Bishop of Peterborough* (London, 1728).
King, William, *Europe's Deliverance from France and Slavery: A Sermon Preached at St Patrick's Church, Dublin, On the 16th November 1690* (Dublin, 1691).
Lacrose, Jean Cornand de, *An Historical and Geographical Description of France* (London, 1694).
—— (ed.), *The Works of the Learned, or, an Historical Account and Impartial Judgment of Books* (London, 1691–92).
—— (ed.), *Memoirs for the Ingenious, containing Observations in Philosophy, Physick, Philology, and Other Arts and Sciences* (London, 1693).

Lahontan, Baron de, *Dialogues ou entretiens entre un Sauvage et le Baron de Lahontan*, in *Œuvres complètes*, ed. R. Quellet and A. Beaulieu, 2 vols (Montreal: Presses de l'Université de Montréal, 1990), vol. 2, pp. 801–28.
La Roche, Michel de (ed.), *Bibliothèque angloise* (Amsterdam, 1717–19).
——, (ed.), *Memoires Literaires de la Grande-Bretagne* (The Hague, 1720–24).
Larrey, Isaac de, *L'Héritière de Guyenne ou l'histoire de l'Eleonore* (Rotterdam, 1691).
——, *Histoire d'Angleterre, d'Ecosse, d'Irlande avec un abrégé des évenemens les plus remarquables arrivez dans les autres états*, 4 vols (Rotterdam, 1697–1713).
The Last Words of Lewis du Moulin (London, 1680).
Lecène, Charles, *Projet d'une nouvelle version françoise de la Bible*, 2 vols (Amsterdam, 1741).
Leclerc, Jean, *An Historical Vindication of the Naked Gospel, Recommended to the University of Oxford* (London, 1691).
——, *Ontologia; sive de ente in genere* (London, 1692).
——, *Ars critica, in qua ad studia linguarum Latinæ, Græcæ, et Hebraicæ via munitur*, second edn, 2 vols (London, 1698).
——, *Parrhasiana ou pensées diverses sur des matières de critique, d'histoire, de morale et de politique*, 2 vols (Amsterdam, 1699–1701).
——, *Joannis Clerici Philosophiæ et S. Linguæ, apud Remonstrantes, Amstelodami Professoris Vita et opera ad annum MDCCXI* (Amsterdam, 1711).
——, *Epistolario*, ed. Maria Grazia and Mario Sina, 4 vols (Florence: Olschki, 1987–97).
Leibniz, Gottfried Wilhelm, *Sämtliche Schriften und Briefe: Erste Reihe: Allgemeiner politischer und historischer Briefwechsel*, ed. Wolfgang Bungies, Georg Gerber, Albert Heinekamp *et al.*, vols 7–14 (Berlin: Akademie-Verlag, 1964–93).
Lenfant, Jacques, *Histoire du Concile de Constance*, 2 vols (1727).
Letters of Denization and Acts of Naturalization for Aliens in England and Ireland, 1603–1701, ed. W.A. Shaw, HSQS, 11 (London, 1911).
Limborch, Philip van, *Historia inquisitionis. Cui subjungitur Liber sententiarum inquisitionis Tholosanæ ab anno Christi 1307 ad annum 1323* (Amsterdam, 1692).
Livre des Tesmoignages de l'Eglise de Threadneedle Street 1669–1689, William Minet and Susan Minet (eds), HSQS, 21 (London, 1909).
Locke, John, *Abregé d'un ouvrage intitulé Essai philosophique touchant l'entendement*, trans. Jean Leclerc (Amsterdam, 1688).
——, *An Essay Concerning Human Understanding*, ed. Peter H. Nidditch, rev. edn, (Oxford: Oxford University Press, 1979).
——, *Two Treatises of Government*, ed. Peter Laslett (Student edn, Cambridge: Cambridge University Press, 1988).
——, *Some Thoughts Concerning Education*, eds John W. and Jean S. Yolton (Oxford: Oxford University Press, 1989).
——, 'Of the Conduct of the Understanding', ed. Paul Schuurman, Ph.D.. thesis (University of Keele, 2000).

——, *The Correspondence of John Locke*, ed. E.S. de Beer, 8 vols (Oxford: Oxford University Press, 1976–89).

Maitland, William, *History of London* (London, 1739).

Martheile, Jean, *Mémoires d'un Protestant condamné aux Galéres de France pour cause de Religion, écrits par lui-même* (Rotterdam, 1755).

*Mémoires envoyés de Londres à M * par M * au sujet de l'établissement d'un conseil pour veiller sur la conduite des protestants réfugiés en Angleterre* (Cologne, 1699).

Migault, Jean, *Journal de Jean Migault ou malheurs d'une famille protestante du Poitou victime de la Révocation de l'Edit de Nantes (1682–89)*, ed. Yves Krumenacker (Paris: Editions de Paris, 1995).

Minutes of the Consistory of the French Church of London, Threadneedle Street, 1679–1692, ed. Robin D. Gwynn, HSQS, 58 (London, 1994).

Molesworth, Robert, *Etat present du Danemarc* (London, 1694).

Molyneux, William, *The Case of Ireland's Being Bound by Acts of Parliament in England Stated* (Dublin, 1698).

Moulin, Lewis [Louis] du, *Petri Molinaei SS. Theol. Doct and Profess.* Anatome missae (London, 1637).

——, [Irenaus Philadelphus], *Vox populi, expressed in xxxv motions to this present parliament* (London, 1641).

——, [Irenaeus Philanax], *Aytomaxia: or, the Selfe-Contradiction of some that contend about Church-Government* (London, 1643).

——, *Of the Right of Churches and of the Magistrates Power over them* (London, 1658).

——, *Proposals and Reasons ... Humbly presented to the parliament* (London, 1659).

——, *La tyrannie des prejugez, ou reflexions sur le fragment d'une lettre de Mademoiselle Marie du Moulin ... en forme d'Epitres sur la puissance ecclesiastique et l'excommunication, pour servir de response a Monsieur Jurieu* (London, 1678).

——, *A Short and True Account of the Several Advances the Church of England hath made towards Rome* (London, 1680).

Moulin, Peter [Pierre] du, *Petri Molinaei filii carmen heroicum ad regem* (London, 1625).

——, *A Letter of a French Protestant to a Scotishman of the Covenant* (London, 1640).

——, *Ecclesia gemitus sub anabaptistica tyrannide* (n. pl., 1649).

——, *Regii sanguinis clamor ad coelum adversus paricidas Anglicanos* ([London], 1652).

——, *The Novelty of Popery* (London, 1662).

——, *A Week of Soliloquies and Prayers* (London, 1677).

——, *A Sermon Preach'd at St Martin's Church ... Canterbury, Sept 14 1669* (London, 1709).

Nicolai, C. Friedrich, *Beschreibung der Königlichen Residenzstädte Berlin und Potsdam*, 3 vols (Berlin, 1779).
Pantheisticon, sive Formula celebrandae sodalitatis socraticae (Cosmopoli, 1720).
Popple, William, *A Rational Catechism* (Amsterdam, 1712).
Pufendorf, Samuel von, *De rebus gestis Friderici Wilhelmi Magni, Electoris Brandenburgici* (Berlin, 1695).
——, *Friederich Wilhelm der Grosse Churfürsten zu Brandenburg, Leben und Thaten* (Berlin, 1710).
Records of the Reformed Dutch Church in New Amsterdam and New York: Marriages from 1639 to 1801, ed. Samuel S. Purple (New York, 1890).
Registers of the Births, Marriages, and Deaths of the 'Eglise Française à la Nouvelle York', from 1688 to 1804, ed. Alfred V. Wittmeyer (Baltimore: Genealogical Publishing, 1968).
Rou, Louis, *Collection of Papers Concerning Mr. Lewis Rou's Affair* (New York, 1725).
Shadwell, Thomas, *The Scowrers: A Comedy, Acted by their Majesties Servants* (London, 1691).
Souverain, Matthieu, *Le Platonisme devoilé. Ou essai touchant le Verbe Platonicien* ('Cologne' [Amsterdam], 1700).
Soyres, John de, *The Huguenots and the Church of England* (London, 1885).
Spanheim, Ezechiel, *Relation de la cour de France, 1690*, ed. E. Bourgeois and M. Richard (Paris: Mercure de France, 1973).
Statuts et Règlements [of the French Hospital for Poor French Protestants Residing in Great Britain] (London, 1810).
Thiers, Jean-Baptiste, *Traité des superstitions* (Paris, 1679).
Tillotson, John, *Formulaire de prieres dont se servoit sa majesté Guillaume III*, preface by John Moore, bishop of Norwich, trans. David Mazel (London, 1704).
Toland, John, *Vindicius Liberius, or Mr Toland's Defence of himself. Against the late Lower House of Convocation and Others* (London, 1702).
——, *Letters to Serena* (London, 1704).
——, *Reasons for Naturalising the Jews* (London, 1714).
——, *The State-anatomy of Great Britain, containing a particular account of its several interests* (London, 1716–17).
——, *Christianity not Mysterious, Text, Associated Works and Critical Essays*, ed. P. McGuiness, A. Harrison and R. Kearney (Dublin: The Lilliput Press, 1997).
——, Toland, John, *Nazarenus*, ed. Justin Champion, (Oxford: Voltaire Foundation, 1999).
Trosse, George, *The Life of the Reverend Mr. George Trosse. Written by Himself, and Published Posthumously According to his Order in 1714*, ed. A.W. Brink (Montreal and London: McGill-Queen's University Press, 1974).
Tyrrell, James, *Bibliotheca Politica: Or, an Enquiry into the Antient Constitution of the English Government*, second collected edn (London, 1718).
Veiras, Denis, *The History of the Sevarites or Severambi* (London, 1675).
——, *L'Histoire des Sévarambes*, ed. Aubrey Rosenberg (Paris, 2001).

Secondary sources

Adams, Geoffrey, *The Huguenots and French Opinion, 1685–1787: The Enlightenment Debate on Toleration* (Waterloo: Wilfried Laurier University Press, 1991).

Agnew, David C.A., *Protestant Exiles from France in the Reign of Louis XIV; or, The Huguenot Refugees and their Descendants in Great Britain and Ireland*, second rev. edn, 3 vols (London, 1871).

Almagor, Joseph, *Pierre des Maizeaux (1673–1745): Journalist and English Correspondent for Franco-Dutch Periodicals, 1700–1720*, Studies of the Pierre Bayle Institute 20 (Amsterdam and Maarsen: APA-Holland University Press, 1989).

Armstrong, Brian G., *Calvinism and the Amyraut Heresy: Protestant Scholasticism and Humanism in Seventeenth-Century France* (Madison: University of Wisconsin Press, 1969).

—, *Bibliographia Molinaei: an Alphabetical, Chronological and Descriptive Bibliography of the Works of Pierre du Moulin (1568–1658)* (Geneva: Droz, 1997).

Ascoli, George, *La Grande-Bretagne devant l'opinion française au XVIIe siècle* (Paris: Gamber, 1930).

Ashcraft, Richard, *Revolutionary Politics and Locke's* Two Treatises of Government (Princeton: Princeton University Press, 1986).

Aylmer, Gerald E., 'Unbelief in Seventeenth-Century England', in Donald Pennington and Keith Thomas (eds), *Puritans and Revolutionaries. Essays in Seventeeth-Century History Presented to Christopher Hill* (Oxford: Clarendon Press, 1978), pp. 22–46.

Barnard, Toby, 'Improving Clergymen', in Alan Ford, James McGuire and Kenneth Milne (eds), *As by Law Established: The Church of Ireland since the Reformation* (Dublin: Lilliput Press, 1995), pp. 136–51.

Barnes, Annie, *Jean Le Clerc (1657–1736) et la République des Lettres* (Paris: Droz, 1938).

Barrett, Eileen, 'Regulating Moral and Social Behaviour in the French Church of London, 1680–1689', *PHS*, 27 (2) (1999): 232–45.

Beeman, George B., 'Notes on the City of London Records Dealing with the French Protestant Refugees, Especially with Reference to the Collections Made under Various Briefs', *PHS*, 7 (1901–04): 108–192.

Benedict, Philip, *The Faith and Fortunes of France's Huguenots, 1600–1685* (Aldershot: Ashgate, 2001).

Bennett, Gareth Vaughan, *The Tory Crisis in Church and State, 1688–1730: The Career of Francis Atterbury, Bishop of Rochester* (Oxford: Clarendon Press, 1975).

Berkvens-Stevelinck, Christiane, *Prosper Marchand. La vie et l'œuvre (1678–1756)* (Leyden and New York: Brill, 1987).

—, Hans Bots *et al.* (eds), *Le Magasin de l'Univers. The Dutch Republic as the Centre of European Book Trade*, papers presented at the international colloquium held at Wassenaar, 5–7 July 1990, Brill's Studies in Intellectual History 31 (Leyden and New York: Brill, 1992).

Berti, Silvia, 'Jan Vroesen, autore del "Traité des trois imposteurs"?', *Rivista storica italiana*, 103 (1991): 528–43.

—, 'Scepticism and the "Traité des trois imposteurs"', in R.H. Popkin and A. Vanderjagt (eds), *Skepticism and Irreligion in the Seventeenth and Eighteenth Centuries* (Leyden and New York: Brill 1993), pp. 216–29.

—, 'At the Roots of Unbelief', *Journal of the History of Ideas*, 56 (1995): 555–75.

Birnstiel, Eckart and Chrystel Bernat (eds), *La Diaspora des Huguenots. Les réfugiés protestants de France et leur dispersion dans le monde (XVIe–XVIIIe siècles)*, 'La vie des Huguenots' 17 (Paris: Honoré Champion, 2001).

Bosher, Robert S., *The Making of the Restoration Settlement: The Influence of the Laudians, 1649–1662*, rev. edn (London: Dacre Press, 1957).

Borot, Luc (ed.), *James Harrington and the Notion of Commonwealth* (Montpellier: Presses Universitaires de Montpellier, 1998).

Bost, Hubert, 'Le Refuge huguenot, un laboratoire de la tolérance ?', in N. Piqué and G. Waterlot (eds), *Tolérance et Réforme. Eléments pour une généalogie du concept de tolérance* (Paris: L'Harmattan, 1999), pp. 169–94.

—, *Ces Messieurs de la R.P.R. Histoires et écritures de Huguenots, XVIIe–XVIIIe siècles* , 'La vie des Huguenots' 18 (Paris: Honoré Champion, 2001).

Bots, Hans, 'La Migration Huguenote dans les Provinces-Unies, 1680–1715. Un nouveau bilan', in Philippe Henry and Maurice de Tribolet (eds), *In Dubiis Libertas. Mélanges d'Histoire offerts au Professeur Rémy Scheurer*, (Hauterive: Gilles Attinger, 1999), pp. 271–81.

—, H. Hillenaar, J. Janssen *et al.*, *De 'Bibliothèque Universelle et Historique' (1686–1693), een periodiek als trefpunt van geletterd Europa* (Amsterdam: Holland Universiteits Press, 1981).

—, and G.H.M. Posthumus Meyjes (eds), *The Revocation of the Edict of Nantes and the Dutch Republic*, International Congress of the Tricentennial, Leyden, 1–3 April 1985 (Amsterdam and Maarsen: APA-Holland University Press, 1986).

Broome, J.H., *An Agent in Anglo-French Relationships: Pierre Des Maizeaux*, Ph.D. thesis (University of London, 1949).

—, 'Bayle's biographer: Pierre Des Maizeaux', *French Studies*, 9 (1955): 1–17.

Browning, A.G., 'On the Early History of the French Hospital (La Providence)', *PHS*, 6 (1898): 39–80.

—, 'The Influence Asserted by the Huguenot Refugees of the Seventeenth and Eighteenth Centuries upon the Social and Professional Life of England', *PHS*, 7 (1901–04): 304–23.

Budé, Eugène de, *Vie de François Turrettini, théologien Genevois 1623–1687* (Lausanne, 1871).

Burke, Peter, 'The Renaissance Dialogue', *Renaissance Studies*, 3 (1989): 1–12.

Burn, John S., *The History of the French, Walloon, Dutch, and other Foreign Protestant Refugees Settled in England, from the Reign of Henry VIII to the Revocation of the Edict of Nantes* (London, 1846).

Butler, Jon, *The Huguenots in America: A Refugee People in New World Society*, Harvard Historical Monograph 72 (Cambridge, Mass: Harvard University Press, 1983).

Byrkman, Geneviève, 'Pour en savoir plus, cherchez dans mes écrits', *Revue de Synthèse*, 116 (1995): 221–9.

Caldicott, C.E.J., H. Gough and Jean-Paul Pittion (eds), *The Huguenots in Ireland: Anatomy of an Emigration*, Dublin Colloquium of the Huguenot Refuge in Ireland, 1685–1985, 9–12 April 1985, Trinity College, Dublin (Dun Laoghaire: Glendale Press, 1987).

Carabelli, Giancarlo, *Tolandiana. Materiali biografica per lo studio dell'opera e della fortuna di John Toland (1670–1722)* (Florence: La Nueva Italia, 1975).

Carlo, Paula Wheeler, *Huguenot Refugees in Colonial New York: Becoming American in the Hudson Valley* (Brighton and Portland: Sussex Academic Press, 2005).

Carter, Alice C., 'The Huguenot Contribution to the Early Years of the Funded Debt, 1694–1714', *PHS*, 19 (3) (1955): 21–41.

Carter, Philip, *Men and the Emergence of Polite Society: Britain 1660–1800* (Harlow: Longman, 2001).

Champion, Justin, *The Pillars of Priestcraft Shaken: The Church of England and Its Enemies (1660–1730)* (Cambridge: Cambridge University Press, 1992).

——, *Republican Learning: John Toland and the Crisis of Christian Culture, 1696–1722* (Manchester: Manchester University Press, 2003).

Cherchi, Gavina, *Pantheisticon, eterodossia e dissimulazione nella filosofia di John Toland* (Pisa: ETS editrice, 1990).

Churchill, Winston S., *Marlborough his Life and Times*, 2 vols (1933; London: Harrap, 1963).

Clark, Peter, *British Clubs and Societies. The Origins of an Associational World* (Oxford: Clarendon Press, 2000).

Clarke, Bridget, 'Huguenot Tutors and the Family of Edward and Mary Clarke of Chipley, 1687–1710', *PHS*, 27 (4) (2001): 527–42.

Clarke, D.M., 'Locke and Toland on toleration', *Studies on Voltaire and the Eighteenth Century*, 335 (1995): 261–71.

Colclough, David, '*Parrhesia*: The Rhetoric of Free Speech in Early-Modern England', *Rhetorica*, 17 (1999): 177–212.

Colletti, Lucio, *From Rousseau to Lenin: Studies in Ideology and Society*, trans. John Merrington and Judith White (London: NLB, 1972).

Corish, Patrick, *Maynooth College 1795–1995* (Dublin: Gill and Macmillan, 1995).

Cottret, Bernard. *Terre d'exil. L'Angleterre et ses réfugiés français et wallons, de la Réforme à la Révocation de l'Édit de Nantes, 1550–1700* (Paris: Aubier, 1985).

——, *The Huguenots in England: Immigration and Settlement c.1550–1700*, trans. Peregrine and Adriana Stevenson (Cambridge: Cambridge University Press, 1991).

Cranston, Maurice, *John Locke: A Biography* (London: Longmans, 1957).
Cross, Francis W., *History of the Walloon and Huguenot Church at Canterbury* (London, 1898).
Daniel, Stephan H., *John Toland: His Methods, Manners and Mind* (Montreal and London: McGill-Queen's University Press, 1984).
De Beer, E.S., 'Introduction', in John Locke, *The Correspondence of John Locke*, ed. E.S. de Beer, 8 vols (Oxford: Oxford University Press, 1976–89), vol. 1, pp. xv–lxxix.
——, 'The Huguenots and the Enlightenment', *PHS*, 21 (3) (1968): 179–95.
Desné, Roland, 'L'Homme et son œuvre', in 'Prefaces', *Œuvres complètes of Jean Meslier*, 3 vols (Paris: Anthropos, 1970–72), vol. 1, pp. xvii–lxxix.
Dodge, Guy H., *The Political Theory of the Huguenot of the Dispersion, with Special Reference to the Thought and Influence of Pierre Jurieu* (New York: University of Columbia Press, 1947).
Downie, James Alan, *Robert Harley and the Press. Propaganda and public opinion in the Age of Swift and Defoe* (Cambridge: Cambridge University Press, 1979).
Doyle, S., 'La messe trouvée dans l'Escriture: a New Attribution', *PHS*, 24 (5) (1987): 457–8.
Duff, J.D., 'Introduction', in Lucan, *Lucan: The Civil War*, ed. and trans. J.D. Duff (London and Cambridge, Mass.: Heinemann and Harvard University Press, 1928), pp. ix–xv.
Dunn, John, *The Political Thought of John Locke: An Historical Account of the Argument of the* Two Treatises of Government (Cambridge: Cambridge University Press, 1969).
——, *Locke* (Oxford and New York: Oxford University Press, 1984).
Eisenstein, Elizabeth L., *Grub Street Abroad: Aspects of the French Cosmopolitan Press from the Age of Louis XIV to the French Revolution*, Lyell Lectures, 1989–90 (Oxford: Clarendon Press, 1992).
Elliott, John H., *Europe Divided: 1559–1598* (London: Fontana, 1968).
Evans, Robert Rees, *Pantheisticon: The Career of John Toland* (Bern: Peter Lang, 1991).
Faber, Robert and Brian Harrison, 'The *Dictionary of National Biography*: a Publishing History', in Robin Myers, Michael Harris and Giles Mandelbrote (eds), *Lives in Print: Biography and the Book Trade from the Middle Ages to the Twenty-First Century* (London: Oak Knoll Press and the British Library, 2002), pp. 171–92.
Fechner, A.W., *Chronik der Evangelischen-Gemeinden in Moskau. Zum dreihundertjähren jubiläum der Evangelisch-Lutherischen St. Michaelis-Gemeinde zusammengestellt*, 2 vols (Moscow, 1876).
Feingold, Mordechai, 'The Humanities', in Nicholas Tyacke (ed.), *The History of the University of Oxford*, vol 4, *Seventeenth Century Oxford* (Oxford: Clarendon Press, 1996), pp. 211–358.
Fiske, Daniel W., 'The Lost Manuscript of the Reverend Lewis Rou's "Critical Remarks upon the Letter to the *Craftsman* on the Game of Chess," written in

1734 and dedicated to His Excellency William Cosby, Governor of New York' (Florence: Landi Press, 1902).

——, 'The Reverend Lewis Rou, Pastor of the French Protestant Church, New York City, and the Missing Manuscript of his Tract Relating to Chess, entitled "Critical Remarks upon the Letter to the *Craftsman* on the Game of Chess"' (Florence: Landi Press, 1902).

Flick, A., 'Huguenot Research in the Hanover Area', *Huguenot Families*, 3 (2000): 9–14.

Forrest, G.A., 'Schism and reconciliation: the 'Nouvelle Eglise' de Ste Marie, Dublin 1705–1716', *PHS*, 26 (2) (1995): 199–213.

Fox, Peter (ed.), *Treasures of the Library, Trinity College Dublin* (Dublin: Royal Irish Academy, 1986).

Gamble, Richard C. (ed.), *Articles on Calvin and Calvinism* (New York: Garland, 1992).

Garrisson, Janine, *L'Edit de Nantes et sa Révocation. Histoire d'une intolérance* (Paris, 1985).

——, *Les protestants au XVIe siècle* (Paris: Fayard, 1988).

Geisendorf, Paul F., *Théodore de Bèze* (Geneva: Labor et Fides, 1949).

Gibbs, Graham C., 'The Role of the Dutch Republic as the Intellectual Entrepôt of Europe in the Seventeenth and Eighteenth Centuries', *Bijdragen en mededelingen betreffende de geschiedenis der Nederlanden*, 86 (3) (1971): 323–49.

——, 'Some Intellectual and Political Influences of the Huguenot Emigrés in the United Provinces, c.1680–1730', *Bijdragen en mededelingen betreffende de geschiedenis der Nederlanden*, 90 (2) (1975): 255–87.

Giuntini, Chiara, *Toland e i liberi pensatori del 1700* (Florence: Sansoni, 1974).

——, *Panteismo e ideologia republicana. John Toland (1670–1722)* (Bologna: La Mulina, 1979).

Glozier, Matthew R., *The Huguenot Soldiers of William of Orange and the Glorious Revolution of 1688: The Lions of Judah* (Brighton and Portland: Sussex Academic Press, 2002).

——, *Marshal Schomberg, 1615–1690: 'The Ablest Soldier of his Age': International Soldiering and the Formation of State Armies in Seventeenth-Century Europe* (Brighton and Portland: Sussex Academic Press, 2005).

Golden, Samuel A., *Jean LeClerc* (New York: Twayne Publishers, 1972).

Goldgar, Anne, *Impolite Learning: Conduct and Community in the Republic of Letters, 1680–1750* (New Haven and London: Yale University Press, 1995).

Goldie, Mark, 'The Reception of Hobbes', in J.H. Burns and Mark Goldie (eds), *The Cambridge History of Political Thought, 1450–1700* (Cambridge: Cambridge University Press, 1991), pp. 589–615.

——, 'John Locke's Circle and James II', *Historical Journal*, 35 (3) (1992): 557–86.

——, 'The Earliest Attack on Locke's *Two Treatises of Government*', *Locke Newsletter*, 30 (1999): 73–84.

——, 'John Locke: Icon of Liberty', *History Today*, 54 (10) (2004): 31–6.

——, Tim Harris and Paul Seaward (eds), *The Politics of Religion in Restoration England* (Oxford: Blackwell, 1990).
——, (ed.), *The Reception of Locke's Politics*, 6 vols (London: Pickering and Chatto, 1999).
Gonin, François and Frank Delteil (eds), 'La Révocation de l'Edit de Nantes vue par les informateurs du Grand Condé', *BSHPF*, 118 (1972): 115–72.
Goodfriend, Joyce, *Before the Melting Pot: Society and Culture, 1664–1730* (Princeton: Princeton University Press, 1992).
Gough, J.W., 'James Tyrrell, Whig Historian and Friend of John Locke', in Richard Ashcraft (ed.), *John Locke: Critical Assessments*, 4 vols (London and New York: Routledge, 1991), vol. 1, pp. 120–50.
Grant, Alison and Robin Gwynn, 'The Huguenots of Devon', *Report and Transactions of the Devonshire Association for the Advancement of Science, Literature and the Arts*, 117 (1985): 161–94.
Gray, Irvine E. (comp.), *Huguenot Manuscripts: A Descriptive Catalogue of the Remaining Manuscripts in the Huguenot Library*, HSQS, 56 (London, 1982).
Greaves, Richard L., *Deliver Us from Evil: The Radical Underground in Britain, 1660–1663* (Oxford: Oxford University Press, 1986).
——, *Enemies under his Feet: Radicals and Nonconformists in Britain, 1664–1677* (Stanford: Stanford University Press, 1990).
——, *Secrets of the Kingdom: British Radicals from the Popish Plot to the Revolution of 1688–1689* (Stanford: Stanford University Press, 1992).
Greengrass, Mark, 'Protestant Exiles and their Assimilation in Early-Modern Europe', *Immigrants and Minorities*, 4 (3) (1985): 68–81.
——, Michael Leslie and Timothy Raylor (eds), *Samuel Hartlib and Universal Reformation. Studies in Intellectual Communication* (Cambridge: Cambridge University Press, 1994).
Grell, Ole Peter, *Calvinist Exiles in Tudor and Stuart England* (Aldershot: Ashgate, 1996).
——, Jonathan Israel and Nicholas Tyacke (eds), *From Persecution to Toleration: The Glorious Revolution and Religion in England* (Oxford: Clarendon Press, 1991).
——, and Bob Scribner (eds), *Tolerance and Intolerance in the European Reformation* (Cambridge: Cambridge University Press, 1996).
——, and Roy Porter (eds), *Toleration in Enlightenment Europe* (Cambridge: Cambridge University Press, 2000).
Grente, Cardinal Georges (dir.), *Dictionnaire des lettres françaises. Le XVIIIe siècle*, new edn, dir. François Moureau (Paris: Fayard, 1995).
Grente, Cardinal Georges (dir.), *Dictionnaire des lettres françaises. Le XVIIe siècle*, new edn, dir. Patrick Dandrey (Paris: Fayard, 1996).
Griffiths, D.N., 'The French Translation of the English Book of the Common Prayer', *PHS*, 22 (2) (1972): 90–114.
——, 'The Early Translations of the Book of the Common Prayer', *The Library*, sixth series, 3 (1) (1981): 1–16.

Groenveld, S., 'The Mecca of Authors? State Assemblies and Censorship in the Seventeenth-Century Dutch Republic', in A.C. Duke and C.A. Tamse (eds), *Too Mighty to be Free: Censorship and the Press in Britain and the Netherlands*, Britain and the Netherlands 9 (Zutphen: De Walburg Press, 1987), pp. 63–86.

——, 'The Dutch Republic, an Island of Liberty in the Press in Seventeenth-Century Europe?', in Hans Bots and Françoise Waquet (eds), *Commercium Litterarium: Forms of Communication in the Republic of Letters, 1600–1750*, Lectures held at the Colloquia of Paris (1992) and Nijmegen (1993), Studies of the Pierre Bayle Institute 25 (Amsterdam and Maarssen: APA–Holland University Press, 1994), pp. 218–300.

Gusdorf, George, 'L'Europe protestante au siècle des Lumières', *Dix-Huitième Siècle*, 17 (1985): 13–40.

Gwynn, Robin D., *The Huguenots of London* (Brighton: Alpha Press, 1998).

——, *Huguenot Heritage: The History and Contribution of the Huguenots in Britain*, second rev. edn (Brighton and Portland: Sussex Academic Press, 2001).

——, 'The Arrival of Huguenot Refugees in England, 1680–1705', *PHS*, 21 (4) (1969): 366–73.

——, 'The Distribution of Huguenot Refugees in England', *PHS*, 21 (5) (1970): 404–36.

——, 'The Distribution of Huguenot Refugees in England, II: London and Its Environs', *PHS*, 22 (6) (1976): 509–68.

——, 'The Ecclesiastical Organization of French Protestants in England in the Later Seventeenth Century, with special reference to London', Ph.D. thesis (University of London, 1976).

——, 'James II in the Light of his Treatment of Huguenot Refugees in England, 1685–1686', *English Historical Review*, 92 (1977): 820–33.

——, 'The Number of Huguenot Immigrants in England in the Late Seventeenth Century', *Journal of Historical Geography*, 9 (1983): 384–95.

Haag, Eugène and Emile, *La France protestante, ou vies des protestants français qui se sont fait un nom dans l'histoire* (9 vols, Paris: Joël Cherbuliez, 1846–59; rpt Geneva: Slatkine Reprints, 1966).

Haakonssen, Knud, *Natural Law and Moral Philosophy: From Grotius to the Scottish Enlightenment* (Cambridge: Cambridge University Press, 1996).

Haase, Erich, *Einführung in die Literatur des Refuge. Der Beitrag der französischen Protestanten zur Entwicklung analytischer Denkformen am Ende des 17. Jahrhunderts* (Berlin: Duncker and Humblot, 1959).

Hall, A.R., *Philosophers at War* (Cambridge: Cambridge University Press, 1980).

Hamilton, C.L., 'Jean d'Espagne and the Earl of Bridgewater (1622–86)', *PHS*, 24 (1983–88): 232–9.

Harris, Ian, *The Mind of John Locke: A Study of Political Theory in Its Intellectual Setting* (Cambridge: Cambridge University Press, 1994).

Harrison, Brian, 'National Biography for a Computer Age', *History Today*, 51 (8) (August 2001): 16–18.

Häseler, Jens and Antony McKenna (eds), *La Vie intellectuelle aux Refuges protestants*, 'La vie des Huguenots' 5, 2 vols (Paris: Honoré Champion 1999).
Hazard, Paul, *La crise de la conscience européenne, 1680–1715*, 2 vols (Paris: Boivin, 1935).
Heinemann, F.H., 'John Toland and the Age of Enlightenment', *Review of English Studies*, 20 (78) (1944): 125–46.
Herlihy, Kevin (ed.), *The Religion of Irish Dissent, 1650–1800* (Dublin: Four Courts Press, 1996).
Herlihy, Kevin (ed.), *Propagating the Word of Irish Dissent, 1650–1800* (Dublin, Four Courts Press, 1998).
The Huguenots and Ulster, 1685–1985: Historical Introduction and Exhibition Catalogue, 1 October 1985–30 April 1986 (Lisburn: Lisburn Museum, 1985).
Holt, Mack P., *The French Wars of Religion, 1562–1629* (Cambridge: Cambridge University Press, 1995).
Hull, William I., *Benjamin Furly and Quakerism in Rotterdam* (Swarthmore, Penn.: Swarthmore College, 1941).
Hutchison, Ross, *Locke in France, 1688–1734* (Oxford: Voltaire Foundation at the Taylor Institution, 1991).
Ingrao, Charles, *The Habsburg Monarchy, 1618–1815* (Cambridge: Cambridge University Press, 1994).
Israel, Jonathan I., *The Dutch Republic: Its Rise, Greatness, and Fall, 1477–1806* (Oxford: Oxford University Press, 1995).
——, *Radical Enlightenment: Philosophy and the Making of Modernity, 1650–1750* (Oxford: Oxford University Press, 2001).
Jacob, Margaret C., *The Radical Enlightenment, Pantheists, Freemasons and Republicans* (London: Allen & Unwin, 1981).
——, *Living the Enlightenment. Freemasonry and Politics in Eighteenth Century Europe* (Oxford, 1991).
Janssens, Uta, 'Jean Deschamps (1709–1767) and the French Colony in Brandenburg', *PHS*, 23 (4) (1980): 227–39.
Jones, James R., *The Revolution of 1688 in England* (London: Weidenfeld and Nicolson, 1972).
Kadane, Matthew, 'Les bibliothèques de deux théologiens réformés du XVIIe siècle, l'un puritain anglais, l'autre pasteur huguenot', *BSHPF*, 147 (2001): 67–100.
Kämmerer, Jürgen, *Rußland und die Hugenotten im 18. Jahrhundert (1685–1789)* (Wiesbaden: Steiner, 1978).
Katz, David S., *Philo-Semitism and the Readmission of the Jews to England, 1603–1655* (Oxford: Clarendon Press, 1982).
——, *The Jews in the History of England, 1485–1850* (Oxford: Clarendon Press, 1994).
Katz, Jacob, *Out of the Ghetto: The Social Background of Jewish Emancipation, 1770–1870* (Syracuse: Syracuse University Press, 1998).
Keeble, Neil H., *The Literary Culture of Nonconformity in Later Seventeenth-Century England* (Leicester: Leicester University Press, 1987).

——, *The Restoration: England in the 1660s* (Oxford and Malden: Blackwell, 2002).
Kershaw, Samuel, *Refugee Inscriptions in the Cathedral of Canterbury* (London, 1886).
King, Henry L., *Brandenburg and the English Revolution of 1688* (London: Oberlin, 1914).
Kingdon, Robert M., 'Pourquoi les réfugiés huguenots aux colonies américaines sont-ils devenus épiscopaliens?', *BSHPF*, 115 (1969): 487–509.
Kohnke, M., 'Das Edikt von Potsdam zu seiner Entetehung Verbreitung und Überlieferung', *Jahrbuch für Geschichte des Feudalismus*, 9 (1985): 241–75.
Kristeller, Paul Oskar, 'Humanism', in Eckhard Kessler, Jill Kraye, Charles B. Schmitt, and Quentin Skinner (eds), *The Cambridge History of Renaissance Philosophy* (Cambridge: Cambridge University Press, 1988), pp. 113–37.
Labrousse, E., 'Bayle et l'établissement de Desmaizeaux en Angleterre', *Revue de Littérature Comparée*, 30 (1956): 251–7.
Labrousse, E., 'Introduction', in *Inventaire critique de la correspondance de Pierre Bayle* (Paris: Vrin, 1961), pp. 13–62.
——, *Pierre Bayle*, 2 vols (The Hague: Martinus Nijhoff, 1963–64).
——, *'Une foi, une loi, un roi?' Essai sur la Révocation de l'Edit de Nantes* (Geneva: Labor et Fides; Paris: Payot, 1985).
——, *Conscience et Conviction. Etudes sur le XVIIe siècle* (Paris: Universitas; Oxford: Voltaire Foundation, 1996).
Lacey, Douglas R., *Dissent and Parliamentary Politics in England, 1661–1689* (New Brunswick: Rutgers University Press, 1969).
Laslett, Peter, 'John Locke and His Books', in John Harrison and Peter Laslett, *The Library of John Locke*, second edn (Oxford: Oxford University Press, 1971), pp. 1–61.
——, 'Introduction', in John Locke, *Two Treatises of Government*, ed. Peter Laslett (Cambridge: Cambridge University Press, 1988), pp. 3–133.
——, 'John Locke, the Great Recoinage, and the Origins of the Board of Trade: 1695–98', in Richard Ashcraft (ed.), *John Locke: Critical Assessments*, 4 vols (London and New York: Routledge, 1991), pp. 181–209.
Laursen, John Christian (ed.), *New Essays on the Political Thought of the Huguenots of the Refuge*, Brill's Studies in Intellectual History 60 (Leyden and New York: Brill, 1995).
Lee, Grace. *The Huguenot Settlements in Ireland* (London: Longmans, Green and Co., 1936).
Le Fanu, Thomas P., 'Mémoires Inédits d'Abraham Tessereau', *PHS*, 15 (4) (1937): 566–85.
Lillywhite, Bryant, *London Coffee Houses* (London: Allen & Unwin, 1950).
Lloyd Thomas, D.A., *Locke on Government* (London: Routledge, 1995).
Lougee Chappell, Carolyn, '"The Pains I took to Save My/His Family": Escape Accounts by a Huguenot Mother and Daughter after the Revocation of the Edict of Nantes', *French Historical Studies*, 22 (1999): 1–64.

Lurbe, Pierre, 'John Toland et l'utilisation de l'histoire juive: entre l'histoire et le mythe', in *La République des Lettres et l'histoire du judaisme antique: XVIe– XVIIIe siècles* (Paris: Presses de l'Université de Paris-Sorbonne, 1992), pp. 149– 62.

——, 'En relisant Christianity not Mysterious', in Clotilde Prunier (ed.), *Foi et raison dans l'Europe des Lumières* (*Le Spectateur Européen* 3) (Montpellier: Presses Universitaires de Montpellier, 2002): 47–66.

Lüthy, Herbert, *La Banque protestante en France, de la révocation de l'Edit de Nantes à la Révolution*, 2 vols (Paris: Touzot, 1959–61).

Macpherson, Crawford Brough, *The Political Theory of Possessive Individualism: Hobbes to Locke* (Oxford: Clarendon Press, 1962).

Magdelaine, Michelle and Rudolf von Thadden (eds), *Le Refuge Huguenot* (Paris: Armand Colin, 1985).

——, Maria-Christina Pitassi, Ruth Whelan and Antony McKenna (eds), *De l'Humanisme aux Lumières. Bayle et le protestantisme*, Mélanges en l'honneur d'Elisabeth Labrousse (Paris: Universitas; Oxford: Voltaire Foundation, 1996).

Manchee, W.H., 'Some Huguenot Smugglers: The Impeachment of London Silk Merchants, 1698', *PHS*, 15 (1933–37): 406–27.

——, 'The First and Last Chapters of the Church of "Les Grecs", Charing Cross Road', *PHS*, 16 (1937–41): 140–58.

Marmoy, Charles F.A., 'The Chelsea Pensioner and the Chaplain: The two Jacques du Plessis', *PHS*, 23 (1) (1977): 36–48.

——, 'More Pages from the History of the French Hospital', *PHS*, 22 (3) (1973): 235–47.

——, *The French Protestant Hospital ... Inmates and Applicants, 1718–1957*, 2 vols, HSQS 52 and 53 (London, 1977).

——, '"La Soupe", La Maison de Charité de Spittlefields', *PHS*, 23 (3) (1979): 134– 47.

——, *The Case Book of La Maison de Charité de Spittlefields*, HSQS, 54, (London, 1981).

——,'The "Pest House", 1681–1717, Predecessor of the French Hospital', *PHS*, 25 (4) (1992): 385–99.

Marshall, John, *John Locke: Resistance, Religion and Responsibility* (Cambridge: Cambridge University Press, 1994).

Martin, Joseph, August, *Christian Firmness of the Huguenots and a Sketch of the History of the French Church at Canterbury* (London, 1881).

Matthew, H.C.G. and Brian Harrison (eds), *Oxford Dictionary of National Biography*, 60 + 1 vols and online (Oxford: Oxford University Press, 2004).

Matthews, Arnold G. (ed.), *Calamy Revised: Being a Revision of Edmund Calamy's* Account of the Ministers and Others Ejected and Silenced, 1660–1662 (1934; Oxford: Clarendon Press, 1988).

——, *Walker Revised, being a revision of John Walker's* Sufferings of the Clergy during the Grand Rebellion 1642–1660 (1948; Oxford: Clarendon Press, 1988).

Maynard, John A.F., *The Huguenot Church of New York: A History of the French Church of Saint Esprit* (New York: French Church of St Esprit, 1938).
Mayo, Ronald, *The Huguenots in Bristol* (Bristol: Bristol Historical Association, 1985).
McCarthy, Muriel, 'Elie Bouhéreau, first public librarian in Ireland', *PHS*, 27 (4) (2001): 543–60.
McKenna, Antony and Gianni Paganini (eds), *Pierre Bayle dans la République des Lettres. Philosophie, religion, critique*, 'La vie des Huguenots' 36 (Paris: Honoré Champion, 2004).
Mentzer, Raymond A., and Andrew Spicer, *Society and Culture in the Huguenot World, 1559–1685* (Cambridge: Cambridge University Press, 2002).
Mijnhart, W.W., 'The Dutch Enlightenment: Humanism, Nationalism and Decline', in *The Dutch Republic in the Eighteenth Century*, ed. Margaret C. Jacob and Wijnand W. Mijnhart (Ithaca and London: Cornell University Press, 1992).
Miller, John, *Popery and Politics in England, 1660–1688* (Cambridge: Cambridge University Press, 1973).
——, 'Town Government and Protestant Strangers, 1560–1690', *PHS*, 26 (5) (1997): 577–89.
Milton, Anthony, *Catholic and Reformed: The Roman and Protestant Churches in English Protestant Thought, 1600–1640* (Cambridge: Cambridge University Press, 1995).
Mohan, Christopher, 'Bishop Richard Robinson, builder of Armagh', *Seanchas Ardmhacha* 6 (1) (1971): 94–130.
Mori, Gianluca, *Introduzione a Bayle* (Rome and Bari: Editori Laterza, 1996).
Morman, Paul J., *Nöel Aubert de Versé: A Study in the Concept of Toleration* (Lewiston, New York, and Queenston: E. Mellen Press, n. dat.).
Mours, Samuel, 'Les Pasteurs à la Révocation de l'Edit de Nantes', *BSHPF*, 114 (1968): 47–105; 291–316.
Mühll, Ernest, van der, *Denis Veiras et son histoire des Sévarambes* (Paris, 1938).
Muller, Franz, *De Nederlandsche Geschiedenis in platen. Beredeneerde beschrijving van Nederlandsche historieplaten, zinneprenten en historische kaarten*, 4 vols (Amsterdam, 1863–82).
Murdoch, Tessa (comp.), *The Quiet Conquest: The Huguenots, 1685 to 1985*, Catalogue of the Museum of London Exhibition, in association with the Huguenot Society of London, 15 May–21 October 1985 (London, 1985).
Nishikawa, Sugiko, 'England as Protector of Protestant Minorities: The Early Eighteenth-Century Role of the SPCK', *PHS* 27 (5) (2002): 659–70.
Nobbs, Douglas, 'New Light on Louis du Moulin', *PHS*, 15 (1933–37): 489–509.
Norbrook, David, 'Lucan, Thomas May, and the Creation of a Republican Literary Culture', in Kevin Sharpe and Peter Lake (eds), *Culture and Politics in Early Stuart England* (Basingstoke: Macmillan, 1994), pp. 45–66.
Ormrod, David, 'Puritanism and Patriarchy: The Career and Spiritual Writings of Thomas Papillon, 1623–1702' in Alec Detsicas and Nigel Yates (eds), *Studies in Modern Kentish History. Presented to Felix Hull and Elizabeth Melling on the*

Occasion of the Fiftieth Anniversary of the Kent Archives Office (Maidstone: Kent Archaeological Society, 1983).

Otto, Paul, 'Common Practices and Mutual Misunderstandings: Henry Hudson, Native Americans, and the Birth of New Netherland', *de Halve Maen*, 72 (1999): 75–83.

Paganini, Gianni, Miguel Benitez and James Dybikowski (eds), *Scepticisme, clandestinité et libre pensée* (Paris: Honoré Champion, 2002).

Papillon, A.W.F., *Memoirs of Thomas Papillon* (London, 1887).

Peltonen, Markku, *The Duel in Early Modern England: Civility, Politeness and Honour* (Cambridge: Cambridge University Press, 2003).

Pettegree, Andrew, *Foreign Protestant Communities in Sixteenth-Century London* (Oxford: Clarendon Press 1986).

Pickwoad, Nicholas, 'Report on the Books in the Derry and Raphoe Diocesan Library', unpublished report (University of Ulster, 2003).

Pinkham, Lucille, *William III and the Respectable Revolution: The Part Played by William of Orange in the Revolution of 1688* (Hamden, Conn.: Archon Books, 1969).

Poliakov, Léon, *Histoire de l'antisémitisme*, vol. 1, *Du Christ aux Juifs de Cour*, 3 vols (Paris: Calmann-Lévy, 1955).

Poole, Reginald L., *A History of the Huguenots of the Dispersion at the Recall of the Edict of Nantes* (London, 1880).

Poynter, F.N.L. and William R. le Fanu, 'A Seventeenth Century London Plague Document in the Wellcome Historical Medical Library: Dr du Moulin's Proposals to Parliament for a Corps of Salaried Plague Doctors', *Bulletin of the History of Medicine*, 34 (1960): 365–72.

Prestwich, Mena (ed.), *International Calvinism, 1541–1715* (1985; Oxford: Clarendon Press, 1986).

Rébelliau, Alfred, *Bossuet historien du protestantisme* (Paris, 1899).

Redstone, Vincent B., 'The Dutch and Huguenot Settlements of Ipswich' *PHS*, 12 (1919–1924): 183–204.

Reijn, Johan A. van, 'Benjamin Furly. Engels koopman (en meer) te Rotterdam, 1636–1714', *Rotterdams Jaarboekje* (1985): 219–46.

Rétat, Pierre, *Le Dictionnaire de Bayle et la lutte philosophique au XVIIIe siècle*, (Paris: Les Belles Lettres, 1971).

Rex, Walter, *Essays on Pierre Bayle and Religious Controversy* (The Hague: Martinus Nijhoff, 1965).

Robbins, Caroline, 'Absolute Liberty: The Life and Thought of William Popple, 1638–1708', *William and Mary Quarterly*, 24 (2) (1967): 190–223.

Ronzaud, Pierre, *L'Utopie hermaphrodite. La Terre australe connue de Gabriel Foigny (1676)* (Marseille: Publication du C.M.R., 1982), pp. 321–7.

Rose, Charles, *England in the 1690s: Revolution, Religion, and War* (Oxford: Oxford University Press, 1999).

Rosenberg, Aubrey, *Tyssot de Patot and his Work (1655–1738)* (The Hague: Martinus Nijhoff, 1972).

—, *Nicholas Gueudeville and his work* (The Hague: Martinus Nijhoff, 1981).

—, *Simon Tyssot de Patot, Lettres choisies et discours sur la chronologie* (Paris: Honoré Champion, 2002).

Roth, Cecil, *A History of the Jews in England* (1941; Oxford: Clarendon Press, 1964).

Rousset, Camille, *Histoire de Louvois et de son administration politique et militaire jusqu'à la Paix de Nimègue*, 4 vols (1862; Paris: Didier, 1879).

Rule, John C., 'France Caught Between Two Balances: the Dilemma of 1688', in Lois G. Schwoerer (ed.), *The Revolution of 1688–1689: Changing Perspectives* (Cambridge: Cambridge University Press, 1992), pp. 35–51.

Ruymbeke, Bertrand, van, *From New Babylon to Eden. The Huguenots in Colonial South Carolina* (Columbia: University of South Carolina Press, 2005).

—, and Randy J. Sparks (eds), *Memory and Identity: The Huguenots in France and the Atlantic Diaspora* (Columbia: University of South Carolina Press, 2003).

Savonius, S.J., 'The Swedish Translation of John Locke's "Second Treatise", 1726', *Locke Studies*, 1 (2001): 191–219.

—, 'Locke in French: The *Du Gouvernement Civil* of 1691 and Its Readers', *Historical Journal*, 47 (1) (2004): 47–79.

Schickler, Fernand de, *Les Eglises du Refuge en Angleterre*, 3 vols (Paris, 1892).

—, 'Les Eglises Françaises de Londres après la Révocation', *PHS*, 1 (1885–86): 95–115.

—, '"Reconnoissances" et Abjurations dans les Eglises de la Savoie et de Hungerford à Londres (1684–1733)', *BSHPF*, 39 (1890): 86–97.

—, 'Un Chapitre de l'Histoire des Eglises du Refuge de Langue Française en Angleterre après la Révocation de l'Edit de Nantes: les Deux Patentes', *PHS*, 6 (1898–1901): 268–94.

Schmidt, Francis, 'John Toland, critique déiste de la littérature apocryphe', in P. Geoltrain, J-C. Picard and A. Desreumaux (eds), *La Fable Apocryphe* (Turnhout: Brepols, 1990), pp. 118–51.

Schneewind, J.B., 'Locke's Moral Philosophy', in Vere Chappel (ed.), *The Cambridge Companion to Locke* (Cambridge: Cambridge University Press, 1994), pp. 199–225.

Schoeps, Hans Joachim, *Philo-Semitismus im Barock* (Tübingen: J.C.B. Mohr, 1952).

Schwartz, Hillel, *Knaves, Fools, Madmen and that Subtle Effuvium: A Study of the Opposition to the French Prophets in England, 1706–1708* (Gainesville: University of Florida Press, 1978).

—, *The French Prophets: The History of a Millenarian Group in Eighteenth-Century England* (Berkeley: University of California Press, 1980).

Scouloudi, Irene (ed.), *Huguenots in Britain and their French Background, 1550–1800*, Contributions to the Historical Conference of the Huguenot Society of London, 24–25 September 1985 (Basingstoke, Macmillan, 1987).

—, 'Thomas Papillon, Merchant and Whig', *PHS*, 18 (1) (1947): 49–72.

Simmons, A. John, *The Lockean Theory of Rights* (Princeton: Princeton University Press, 1992).

Simms, George Otto, 'The Founder of Armagh's Public Library', *Irish Booklore*, 1 (2) (1971): 140–48.

Simonutti, Luisa, 'Limborch's *Historia inquisitionis* and the Pursuit of Toleration', in A.P. Coudert, S. Hutton, *et al.* (eds), *Judaeo-Christian Intellectual Culture in the Seventeenth Century: A Celebration of the Library of Narcissus Marsh (1638–1713)* (Dordrecht and London: Kluwer Academic Publishers, 1999), pp. 237–55.

——, 'Religion, Philosophy, and Science: John Locke and Limborch's Circle in Amsterdam', in James E. Force and David S. Katz (eds), *Everything Connects: In Conference with Richard H. Popkin. Essays in His Honor* (Leyden: Brill, 1999), pp. 295–324.

Skinner, Quentin, 'Thomas Hobbes: Rhetoric and the Construction of Morality', *Proceedings of the British Academy*, 76 (1990): 1–61.

——, *Reason and Rhetoric in the Philosophy of Hobbes* (Cambridge: Cambridge University Press, 1996).

Slack, Paul, *From Reformation to Improvement: Public Welfare in Early Modern England* (Oxford: Clarendon Press, 1999).

Smiles, Samuel, *The Huguenots, their Settlements, Churches and Industries in England and Ireland* (London, 1867).

Smith, R., 'Financial Aid to the French Protestant Refugees, 1681–1727: Briefs and the Royal Bounty', *PHS*, 22 (3) (1973): 248–56.

——, *Records of the Royal Bounty and Connected Funds ... in the Huguenot Library*, HSQS, 51 (London, 1974).

Smith, R.W. Innes, *English-speaking Students of Medicine at the University of Leyden* (Edinburgh: Oliver and Boyd, 1932).

Snobelen, Stephen D., 'Isaac Newton, Heretic: The Strategies of a Nicodemite', *British Journal for the History of Science*, 32 (1999): 381–419.

Speck, W.A., 'The Orangist Conspiracy against James II', *Historical Journal*, 30 (2) (1987): 453–62.

Spurr, John, *The Restoration Church of England, 1646–89* (New Haven and London: Yale University Press, 1991).

Stam, Frans P., van, *The Controversy over the Theology of Saumur: Disrupting Debates among the Huguenots in Complicated Circumstances, 1635–1650* (Amsterdam and Maarssen: APA-Holland University Press, 1988).

Stoye, John, *Europe Unfolding* (London: Collins, 1969).

Strauss, Leo, *Persecution and the Art of Writing* (Glencoe: The Free Press, 1952).

Sundstrom, R.A., *Aid and Assimilation: A Study of the Economic Support given French Protestants in England, 1680–1727*, Ph.D. thesis (Kent State University Graduate School, 1972).

Swift, Catherine, 'The French Booksellers in the Strand: Huguenots in the London Book-Trade, 1685–1730', *PHS*, 25 (2) (1990): 123–39.

Ternois, René, 'Les Français, en Angleterre au temps de Charles II, 1660–1676', *Revue de littérature comparée*, 34 (1960): 196–211.

Thadden, Rudolf, von, *Die Brandenburgisch-Preussischen Hofprediger im 17. und 18. Jahrhundert* (Berlin: Walter de Gruyter, 1959).

Thomas, Margaret D., *The Life and Works of Michel de La Roche*, Ph.D. thesis (University of London, 1978).

——, 'Michel de La Roche: A Huguenot Critic of Calvin', in H.T. Mason (ed.), *Studies on Voltaire and the Eighteenth Century*, 238 (1985): 97–195.

Thorp, Malcolm R., 'The Anti-Huguenot Undercurrent in Late Seventeenth-Century England', *PHS*, 22 (6) (1976): 569–80.

Tsushima, Jean, 'The Founding Fathers', *PHS*, 24 (3) (1985): 177–88.

Turnbull, George Henry, *Hartlib, Dury and Comenius: Gleanings from Hartlib's Papers* (Liverpool: University Press of Liverpool; London: Hodder and Stoughton, 1947).

Vickers, Brian, *In Defence of Rhetoric* (Oxford: Clarendon Press, 1988).

Vigne, Randolph, 'The Killing of Jean Calas: Voltaire's First Huguenot Cause', *PHS*, 23 (5) (1981): 280–94.

——,' In the Purlieus of St Alfege's: Huguenot Families in 17th- and 18th-century Greenwich' *PHS*, 27 (2) (1999): 257–73.

——, 'René Baudouin: A Memorial Inscription', *Huguenot Families*, 3 (2000): 8.

——, '"A monument of the Piety of their Ancestors": Origin and Early History of the French Hospital, London, 1708–1740', *Bulletin*, 39 (2002): 196–207.

——, and Graham C. Gibbs (eds), *The Strangers' Progress: Integration and Disintegration of the Huguenot and Walloon Refugee Community, 1567–1889*, *PHS*, 26 (2) (1995): 135–314.

——, and Charles Littleton (eds), *From Strangers to Citizens. The Integration of Immigrant Communities in Britain, Ireland and Colonial America, 1550–1750* (Brighton and Portland: Sussex Academic Press, 2001).

Waldron, Jeremy, *Liberal Rights: Collected Papers 1981–1991* (Cambridge: Cambridge University Press, 1993).

Watts, Michael R., *The Dissenters*, vol. 1, *From the Reformation to the French Revolution* (1978; Oxford, Clarendon Press, 1985).

Webster, Charles, *The Great Instauration. Science, Medicine and Reform, 1642–1660* (London: Duckworth, 1975).

Weiss, Charles, *Histoire des Réfugiés Protestants de France depuis la Révocation de l'Edit de Nantes jusqu'à nos jours*, 2 vols (Paris, 1853).

Whelan, Ruth, 'The Huguenots, the Crown and the Clergy, Ireland, 1704', *PHS*, 26 (5) (1997): 601–10.

——, 'Persecution and Toleration: Changing Identities of Ireland's Huguenot Refugees', *PHS*, 27 (1) (1998): 20–35.

——, and C. Baxter (eds), *Toleration and Religious Identity: The Edict of Nantes and Its Implication in France, Britain and Ireland* (Dublin: Four Courts Press, 2003).

Wheeler, Walter G., 'Libraries in Ireland before 1855: A bibliographical essay' Ph.D. thesis (University of London, 1957).

White, Newport J.D., *Elias Bouhéreau of La Rochelle, First Public Librarian in Ireland* (Dublin: Royal Irish Academy, 1908).

——, *An Account of Archbishop Marsh's Library, Dublin* (Dublin: Hodges Figgis and Co., 1926).

Whiteman, Anne, 'The Restoration Church of England', in Geoffrey Nuttall and Owen Chadwick (eds), *From Uniformity to Unity, 1662–1962* (London: SPCK, 1962), pp. 19–88.

Wiener, M., 'John Toland and Judaism', *Hebrew Union College Annual* 16 (1942).

Wittmeyer, Alfred V., *An Historical Sketch of the 'Eglise Française à la Nouvelle York', from 1688 to 1804* (New York, 1886).

Wood, Peter, *Poverty and the Workhouse in Victorian Britain* (Stoud: Sutton, 1991).

Woodward, John, *To do the Sick no Harm: A Study of the British Voluntary System to 1875* (London and Boston: Routledge and Kegan Paul, 1974).

Worden, Blair 'Cromwellian Oxford' in Nicholas Tyacke (ed.), *The History of the University of Oxford*, vol. 4, *Seventeenth Century Oxford* (Oxford: Clarendon Press, 1996), pp. 733–72.

Wyse Jackson, Robert, 'The Ancient Library of Cashel', *Cork Historical and Archaeological Society*, 52 (1–2) (1947): 128–34.

Yardeni, Myriam, *Le Refuge protestant* (Paris: PUF, 1985).

——, *Anti-Jewish Mentalities in Early Modern Europe* (Lanham: University Press of America, 1990).

——, *Huguenots and Jews* (Jerusalem: Zalman Shazar Center, 1998).

——, *Repenser l'histoire: Aspects de l'historiographie huguenote des guerres de religion à la Révolution française*, 'La vie des Huguenots' 11 (Paris: Honoré Champion, 2000).

——, *Le Refuge huguenot. Assimilation et Culture*, 'La vie des Huguenots' 22 (Paris: Honoré Champion, 2002).

——, 'Gueudeville et Louis XIV. Un précurseur de socialisme, critique des structures sociales louisquatorziennes', *Revue d'Histoire Moderne et Contemporaine*, 19 (1972): 598–620.

——, 'La vision des Juifs et du judaïsme dans l'œuvre de Pierre Bayle', in *Les Juifs dans l'histoire de France* (Leiden and New York: Brill, 1980).

——, 'Naissance et essor d'un mythe: le Révocation de l'Edit de Nantes et le déclin économique de la France', *BSHPF*, 142 (1993): 76–94.

Yolton, Jean S., *John Locke: A Descriptive Bibliography* (Bristol: Thoemmes Press, 1998).

Yolton, John W., *Locke: An Introduction* (Oxford: Basil Blackwell, 1985).

Yolton, John W. and Jean S., 'Introduction', in John Locke, *Some Thoughts concerning Education*, eds John W. and Jean S. Yolton (Oxford: Oxford University Press, 1989), pp. 1–75.

Zuber, Roger and Laurent Theis (eds), *La Révocation de l'Edit de Nantes et le protestantisme français en 1685* (Paris: Société de l'Histoire du Protestantisme Français, 1986).

Index

Abbadie, Jacques 47, 50, 128, 129
Allegiance Controversy 137-8
Allix, Pierre 37, 128, 129, 130
almshouses 70, 74, 85
Amboise plot 87-8
Amsterdam *see* Netherlands
Anglicanism
   and Presbyterianism 13-15
   see also Church of England; conformity; episcopalianism
anti-innatism 145-6
Armagh library, Ireland 123-5
   Huguenot authors and titles 125-36
authors and titles, church libraries, Ireland 125-36

Bank of England 76-7
baptism records 40
Barnstable, Devon 28
Bartholomew's Day Massacre 15, 133, 136
Basnage, Jacques 187-8
Bayle, Pierre 113-14
   church libraries collection, Ireland 128, 130, 135, 136
   Rainbow coffee house circle 163-4, 166, 168, 170
   and John Toland 175-6, 180-1, 187-8
Benoît, Elie 180-1
Bèze, Théodore de 87, 88, 125, 127, 128, 130, 136
Bideford, Devon 28
Book of Common Prayer 59, 62
   French translation 45, 50
Boughton Malherbe, Kent 33, 36
Brandenburg, Germany
   army 95-6
   Huguenot communities in 92-3, 94
Bristol 27, 28, 78

Calvin, Jean 61, 87, 88, 100, 115
   church libraries collection, Ireland 125, 127, 128, 130

Calvinism/Calvinists
   British colony of New York 109-19
   England 35-6, 38, 46, 48
   Ireland 43, 45, 49-50, 52
   see also Presbyterianism
Cambridgeshire 28
Canterbury Cathedral (crypt) 1, 2-4, 29, 33
   poor relief 75, 77, 78
Cashel library, Ireland 122-3, 124-5
   Huguenot authors and titles 125-36
Castle Street, London 34
catechism 116-17
Catholicism/Catholics
   allies of William III 103
   anti-Catholicism 63-4, 114-16, 117, 138-9, 178, 181
   and Church of England 111-12
   conversion from 173
   conversion to 38, 89, 90, 91, 147
   dual allegiance to Protestantism and 10
   Ireland 43-4, 97
   Jews and Judaism 187-8
   monarchs *see* James II; Louis XIV
   persecution of Protestants 15-16, 38-9, 167, 170
      dragonnades 24, 30, 31, 32, 46-7, 49, 50, 77
   soldiers 97, 99
   tolerance of 177-8
   see also popery
Chamayou, Fabienne 27, 28-9, 32, 38-9
Chamberlen family 72-3
Chamberlen, Hugh 75
Charles I
   execution 32, 63
   Huguenot associates 71, 73, 74
Charles II 27, 30, 38, 46-7, 52
   accession 32, 45
   death 35
   poor relief 77
Church of England
   'dualism' of 2

and French Hospital 84
and Huguenot refugees 1-5, 45-9, 57-67 *passim*, 106
liturgy 3-4
    French translations 27, 31, 32, 45, 48
Reformed 2-3
and Roman Catholicism 111-12
and William III 102
see also Anglicanism; conformity; episcopalianism
Church of Ireland and Huguenot refugees 43-5, 47, 49-52
church libraries (18th c), Ireland 121-36
Clark, Edward 156, 157-8, 159
Clarke, Samuel 165, 169, 170
clericism 147-8
coffee houses, London 176
    Rainbow coffee house circle 163-72
Colchester, Essex 28
Collins, Anthony 164-5, 168
communion observance and abstention 117-18
Compton, Henry (Bishop of London) 45, 46-7, 79, 81
conformity
    boundaries of 32-3
    Huguenot acceptance of 27-8
    Huguenot refugee congregations in England 26-30
    Huguenot resistance to 33-9
    and non-conformity 13-15, 28-30, 35-7
    see also Anglicanism; Church of England; Church of Ireland; episcopalianism
Consistories 32, 33-4
Cornwall 28
Coste, Pierre 146-7, 155-6, 164, 169, 171
Cottret, Bernard 13, 23-4, 26, 38, 57, 98, 101, 103, 104-5
criminal activities 77, 101-2
Crispin Street, London 33-4

Daillé, Jean 185-6
Dartmouth, Devon 28, 36
De l'Angle, Jean-Maximilien de Baux 60, 66
death, attitude to 117

Declaration of Indulgence (1687) 25, 41, 46, 47
Des Maizeaux, Pierre 163-71, 172, 175-6
Devon 28, 36, 78
Dickens, Charles 86
Diderot, Denis 163
Dover, Kent 28
dragonnades 24, 30, 31, 32, 46-7, 49, 50, 77
Du Moulin family 74, 128-9
Du Moulin, Lewis 57-8, 59, 64-7
Du Moulin, Pierre 57, 59, 61-5
Durel, Jean 47-8, 50, 59-60, 61, 66

Edict of Nantes, revocation of *see* Revocation (of Edict of Nantes) (1685)
educated elite
    Ireland 121-36
    Rainbow coffee house circle, London 163-72
education
    recruitment of Huguenot tutors 155-61
    rhetorical 148-55
Edwards, John 138-9, 140, 141
Elector of Brandenburg 92-4, 95
Elliott, J.H. 87-8
England
    Calvinism/Calvinists in 35-6, 38, 46, 48
    early 18th century 163-72
    Huguenot refugee congregations in 26-30
    late 17th century 23-41, 55-67
    poor relief in 69-86
    re-introduction of popery 47, 48
    significance as refugee centre 39-41
    timing of migration to 24-6, 34
English Committee 77-8, 79
English Dissenters 32
English and French Protestant churches 1-5, 32-3
English monarchy, loyalty to (royal policy) 27, 28, 32, 34, 38-9
English spies, Rainbow coffee house 165-6
English translations, Rainbow coffee house circle 170
episcopalianism 58-9, 61-3, 64-5
Essex 28
Evelyn, John 78, 95
Exclusion Crisis 32
Exeter, Devon 27, 28

Faversham, Kent 28
financial elite 76-7
financial incentives
    popularity of London 31
    to accept conformity 36-7
financial support
    for industry 104
    poor relief 69-86
    Royal Bounty 46, 77-9, 86
Firmin, Thomas 75-6, 77-8, 79, 84
Foigny, Gabriel 180
Fontaine, Jacques 48, 49, 51, 79, 97-8, 99, 102, 103, 104
freedom of speech/*ingenuitas* 150-2, 155-61 *passim*
'French Anglicanism' 13
French Committee 77-80, 82, 83-4
French and English Protestant churches 1-5, 32-3
French Hospital, London 82-6
French translations
    Anglican liturgy 27, 31, 32, 45, 48
    Book of Common Prayer 45, 50
    catechism 116
    Locke 144-5, 146, 160, 168
    Rainbow coffee house circle 168-9
Furly, Benjamin 165, 166, 167, 175
    and John Locke 142, 143, 148-9, 158, 160

Gardiner, Samuel Rawson 58
Gastigny, Jacques de 80-1, 82, 83
Gerbier, Sir Balthazar 71-2
Germany *see* Brandenburg, Germany
Government policy 45-9
Greenwich 27, 28, 36
Greenwich Hospital 77, 78
Gwynn, Robin 5, 13, 14, 49, 98, 101

Hammersmith, London 34, 36
Hartlib, Samuel 71-2
    circle 73-5, 84
Holland *see* Netherlands
hospitals 70, 77, 78, 80, 82-6
Huguenot arrivals 24-6, 34
'Huguenot Heritage' commemorations (1985) 26
Huguenot Society 3, 40, 59

ingenuitas/freedom of speech 150-2, 155-61 *passim*
Interregnum 38, 45, 48
Ipswich, Suffolk 28, 31, 32, 76
Ireland
    Calvinism/Calvinists in 43, 45, 49-50, 52
    church, government and Huguenot refugees 43-5, 47, 49-52
    church libraries (18th c) 121-36
    educated elite, Huguenot influence on 121-36
    military campaigns (William of Orange) 44, 45, 97, 98, 99, 103
    Oaths of Allegiance and Supremacy 43, 44
    Sacramental Test 44, 47
    John Toland, early life in 173

James I 71, 73
James II
    appoints Catholic Viceroy in Ireland 43-4
    Declaration of Indulgence (1687) 25, 34, 41, 46, 47
    and Huguenot conformity 27, 30, 35, 37
    and Huguenot support for William of Orange 39, 93-4
Jesuit plot 63-4
Jewin Street, Aldersgate, London 37
Jews and Judaism 184-8

Kent 28, 31, 33, 36
King, William (Archbishop of Dublin) 44-5

'La Soupe' (Maison de Charité), Spitalfields 80-2, 86
Lacrose, Jean, Cornand de 143, 144, 145-6
Laroche, Michel de 139, 141, 166, 169, 170-1, 172
Latin 64, 66, 105, 119
    church libraries, Ireland 129, 133
    and Huguenot tutors 139, 143, 152-3
Le Carré, London 34
Leclerc, Jean 163
    and John Locke 138-60 *passim*
L'Estrange, Roger 18-19
Locke, John

animosity towards rhetorical education 148-55
cosmopolitan associates 142-8
French translations 144-5, 146-7, 160, 168
radicalism 137-42
recruitment of Huguenot tutors 155-61
'spinozisme' 166-7
London
   French Hospital 82-6
   Huguenot communities in 26-7, 28, 33-4, 36, 41
   Jewin Street, Aldersgate 37
   'La Soupe' (Maison de Charité), Spitalfields 80-2, 86
   Pest House 79-80, 82-3, 85
   popularity as destination 24-5, 30-1
   St Bartholomew's and St Thomas's Hospitals 70, 80
   silk weavers 76
   see also coffee houses; Savoy Church, London; Threadneedle Street, London; Westminster
Louis XIV 88-9, 90-1, 93, 94, 95-6, 98
lustrings see silk (lustrings and alamodes)

Maison de Charité ('La Soupe'), Spitalfields 80-2, 86
Mayerne, Sir Théodore Turquet de 71
medical care 70
   see also hospitals; Pest House; physicians
'merchant adventurers' 76
military campaigns
   Brandenburg army 95-6
   Louis XIV 88
   William of Orange 44, 45, 95-6, 97, 98-9, 103, 106
   see also soldiers
moral relativism of rhetorical education 150-1
More, Thomas 70, 71
Moulinars, Jean Joseph Brumeau de 110-11

naturalisation acts 46, 47, 50-1
Netherlands 18, 19-20
   migration to 24-5, 26, 143-4
   Rou family 109
   significance as refugee centre 39-41

New Rochelle, Huguenot congregation in 110-11, 112
New York, Huguenot community in 109-19 *passim*
non-conformity
   and conformity 13-15, 28-30, 35-7
   see also Calvinism/Calvinists; Presbyterianism; Quakers; Socinianism/Socinians
Norwich 29, 75, 78
Nusteling, Hubert P.H. 39-40

Oaths of Allegiance and Supremacy, Ireland 43, 44
obstetric forceps, invention of 72-3
Oxford Dictionary of National Biography (ODNB) 55-9

Papin 156-7
persecution *see dragonnades*; Protestants, Catholic persecution of
Pest House, London 79-80, 82-3, 85
Petticum, Simon von 94, 95
physicians 64, 71, 72-3
Plessis-Mornay, Philippe du 127, 128-9, 130, 133, 135-6
Plymouth, Devon 28, 36, 78
Poor Law 69-71
poor relief, Huguenot projects 71-86
popery
   anti-popery 44, 61, 63, 66-7, 147-8, 177
   re-introduction, England 47, 48
   see also Catholicism/Catholics
prayer
   conditions of 118
   see also Book of Common Prayer
Presbyterianism
   and Anglicanism 13-15
   libraries, Ireland 122-3, 130, 131
   Scotland 58-9, 61-2, 63, 102
   see also Calvinism/Calvinists; non-conformity
Preston, Kent 28
Protestantism/Protestants
   Catholic persecution of 15-16, 38-9, 167, 170
      dragonnades 24, 30, 31, 32, 46-7, 49, 50, 77
   dual allegiance to Catholicism and 10

French and English churches 1-5, 32-3
John Toland 173, 178-9
'public good' 71-2, 75
public health 71-2

Quakers 14, 74, 84
  see also Furly, Benjamin
Queen Anne 44
Quick, John 14

radicalism, Locke's programme of social reform 137-42
Rainbow coffee house circle 163-72
Reformation 69-70
Reneus family 76-7, 77-8, 82
Reneus, Hilaire 76-7, 78, 79, 80-1
Reneus, Pierre 76-7, 83, 84
Restoration 13, 32, 45, 46-7
Revocation (of Edict of Nantes) (1685) 88-96, 105-6, 182-3
rhetorical education 148-55
Rivet, André 128-9, 130
Romaignac, Colonel Pierre Chalant de 99-100
Rondeau, Jacques 33
Rou, Reverend Louis
  birth 109
  death and obituary 119
  and Moulinars 110-12
  personal life 110-12, 117
  sermons 112-18
  writings 118-19
Royal Bounty 46, 77-9, 86
Royal Lustring Company 75-6
royal policy (loyalty to English monarchy) 27, 28, 32, 34, 38-9
Ruvigny, Marquis de 89, 91, 104-5
Rye, Sussex 28, 31, 32, 33

Sacramental Test, Ireland 44, 47
St Bartholomew's Day Massacre 15, 133, 136
St Bartholomew's Hospital, London 70, 80
St Martin Orgars 34
St Thomas's Hospital, London 70, 80
Savoy Church, London 29, 31, 32, 33, 38, 45-6, 48-9
  Consistory 33-4
  inauguration 59-60
  poor relief 75, 77, 78
  Spring Gardens 34
Schickler, Fernand de 23-4
Schomberg, Marshal Frederick Herman von 88, 89-96 *passim*, 99
Scots Presbyterians 63, 102
  and episcopalianism 58-9, 61-2
silk (lustrings and alamodes) 75-6, 77, 82
social reform, Locke's programme of 137-42
social welfare see Poor Law; poor relief, Huguenot projects
Socinianism/Socinians 113, 137, 146, 148, 159, 160
  Rainbow coffee house circle 163, 165
soldiers 87-96 *passim*, 97-106, 106-7
  see also military campaigns
Somerset 28
Southampton 29, 75, 78
Souverain, Matthieu 158-9
Soyres, Rev. John de 1, 2-4, 5, 22
Spitalfields, 'La Soupe' (Maison de Charité) 80-2, 86
Stonehouse 27, 28
Suffolk 28, 31, 32, 76
Swallow Street, London 34

Thorpe-le-Soken, Essex 28
Threadneedle Street, London 24-5, 29, 31, 49
  Consistory 32
  poor relief 75, 77, 78
Toland, John
  anti-Catholicism of 178, 181
  concept of tolerance 177-88 *passim*
  and Huguenot associates 175-6, 179-81, 182-3, 187-8
  Jews and Judaism 184-8
  Protestantism of 173, 178-9
  writing and scholarship 173, 176-7
tolerance, concept of 177-88 *passim*
Toleration Act (1689) 44, 46, 47
transubstantiation 115-16
Treaty of Ryswick (1697) 105, 106
Trosse, George 14-15
tutors, recruitment of 155-61

Van Limborch, Philip 143-4, 147-8, 151-2
Veiras, Denis 179-80

Walloon migration 23-4
Wandsworth 28, 32-3
Wapping 36-7
West Street, London 33-4
Westminster 34, 35, 41, 78
    poor relief 78, 81, 86
Westminster Society 80
Whelan, Ruth 13, 14
Wiener, Max 177, 186
William of Orange (William III) 25, 39, 41, 49, 102-3
    and Elector of Brandenburg 92-4
    and Marshall Schomburg 88, 95-6, 97
    and Mary II 46, 49, 78
    military campaigns 44, 45, 95-6, 97, 98-9, 103, 106
    Toleration Act (1689) 44, 46, 47
Wiltshire 28
workhouses 70, 75, 86
writers and titles, church libraries, Ireland 125-36

Yardeni, Myriam 9, 18, 19, 188

For Product Safety Concerns and Information please contact our EU representative GPSR@taylorandfrancis.com
Taylor & Francis Verlag GmbH, Kaufingerstraße 24, 80331 München, Germany